THE CITIZEN FACTORY

SUNY series, Power, Social Identity, and Education

Lois Weis, editor

The Citizen Factory

Schooling and Cultural Production in Bolivia

AUROLYN LUYKX

Foreword by Douglas Foley

STATE UNIVERSITY OF NEW YORK PRESS

Published by
State University of New York Press, Albany

© 1999 State University of New York

For information, address State University of New York Press,
State University Plaza, Albany, N.Y. 12246

Production by Marilyn P. Semerad
Marketing by Nancy Farrell

Library of Congress Cataloging-in-Publication Data

Luykx, Aurolyn, 1963–
    The citizen factory : schooling and cultural production in Bolivia
 / Aurolyn Luykx : foreword by Douglas Foley.
        p. cm. — (SUNY series, power, social identity, and
education)
    Includes bibliographical references (p.) and index.
    ISBN 0-7914-4037-0 (hardcover : alk. paper). — ISBN 0-7914-4038-9
(pbk. : alk. paper)
    1. Aymara youth—Education (Higher). 2. Aymara youth—Ethnic
identity. 3. Aymara youth—Social conditions. 4. Indian students-
-Bolivia. 5. Teachers—Training of—Bolivia. 6. Nationalism-
-Bolivia. 7. Bolivia—Ethnic relations. I. Title. II. Series.
F2230.2.A9L89   1999
305.23′0984—dc21   98-13843
                                                                         CIP

10 9 8 7 6 5 4 3 2 1

This book is dedicated to the struggle and memory of
Avelino Siñani and Elizardo Pérez,
founders of the *escuela–ayllu* of Warisata,
and to all of Bolivia's rural schoolteachers.
Above all, it is dedicated to

Dora

Juan

Marga

Martina

Eusebio

David

Emma

Felix

Goni

Bethi

Nely

Fico

Mery

Paula

Inés

Yola

Max

Edwin

Daniel

CONTENTS

Contents   ix

FOREWORD

Douglas Foley

The Citizen Factory is a testimony to the organic character
of all ethnographic interpretation. Having completed an earlier
version in 1993, Aurolyn Luykx returned to Bolivia where she
is now involved in indigenous education and teacher training at
the university level. In the interim, her grasp of Bolivian popular political and ethnic sensibilities and of social theory has
continued to grow and evolve. The result is a study of one
Bolivian Normal School that will challenge comparative politics
and comparative education scholars to rethink their studies of
political socialization. Moreover, fellow anthropologists will be
drawn to her theoretical model for studying ideological hegemony and identity construction. Finally, educators will find it
full of policy implications for the teaching profession. In short,
Luykx has produced an "educational ethnography" that extends the genre itself.

Having worked in the same theoretical terrain, I am particularly drawn to her skillfull blending of Marx's classical theory
of value with contemporary postmarxist perspectives. Luykx
demonstrates the continuing utility of the theory of value through
contemporary discourse and state theory. To begin, she asks
the same simple but penetrating question of schools that Marx
asks of industrial labor and production: What are students
(workers) asked to produce, and for whom does it have value?
She proceeds by showing that one way to make sense out of
academic work, i.e., the endless and mindless lecture notes,
homework, tests, and student recitations, is to see curricular/
pedagogical practices as a complex linguistic exchange. She
chronicles in detail how students are routinely asked to learn
to speak in an alienating "academic register" and consume
prodigious quantities of useless, fragmented bits of "school

knowledge." In exchange for their labor, they receive grades and an economic future as "proletarian professionals." In the end, the significance of academic labor for the students themselves lies more in its exchange value (i.e., as a passport to social mobility) than in its use value (i.e., its applicability to real life situations). Even though their labor is primarily linguistic, it is as objectifying and alienating as industrial labor.

But if academic mental labor and industrial manual labor are both producing some kind of "surplus value," who is accumulating the surplus? And what commodity form does it take? Luykx answers these questions in a very interesting way, conceptualizing the relationship between schools and the state in a postmarxist framework. She contends that if one peers through the lens of Antonio Gramsci and Stuart Hall, one will see the Bolivian ruling bloc and state using the Normal School to build its political hegemony, and, simultaneously, an imagined community called "Bolivia." Working through various cultural institutions, the Bolivian ruling bloc is busy building a state-civil society complex that reproduces, in a broad cultural sense, the "social relations of production" that are needed to sustain the capitalist "forces of production." Initially, it is the state that accumulates the surplus value of student labor, and the form it takes is a particular kind of objectified, consenting citizen. Ultimately, of course, the government also benefits from the political order and stability produced through the state-civil society complex.

In this particular instance, the Normal school's mode of academic production "interpellates" Aymara youth to accept objectifying, stigmatizing ethnic, class, and gendered "subject positions." Open, critical debate about a host of burning questions on identity is simply not possible for two basic, related reasons. First, the curricular and pedagogical practices are so tightly structured to present reified, fragmented, meaningless official facts that they are little more than simulations of debate. Classroom discussions are so instrumental and undialogic that they rarely allow the experience of the students any legitimacy or forum.

Second, the more "subjective" hidden curriculum of class, ethnic, and gender bias works hand in hand with the formal, "objective" academic production process to incorporate these prospective teachers into an urban, Hispanicized, patriarchal bourgeois state formation. A well-intentioned but fundamentally authoritarian Normal school faculty works hard to get Aymara students to consent to the ruling hegemony of class, race, and gender ideas in Bolivian society. Various contradictory ideological discourses alternately glorify and denigrate peasants, Indians, and the "weaker sex," interpellating the students in contradictory ways and assigning them subordinate positions in Bolivian national culture. A rich vein of student narratives illustrate the alchemy of these ideological contradictions.

Theoretically, the array of state-sponsored and regulated cultural institutions that mark late twentieth-century capitalist civil societies have enormous potential to produce civil consent. But as Gramsci and many subsequent ethnographers have shown, ordinary people do not subordinate their ethnic, class and gendered selves to a mythical image of citizenship and state so easily. In this particular case, despite its well-oiled linguistic exchange process, the Normal school is unable to completely discipline its labor force. Students often acquiesce to the alienating labor process, but they also react to heavy-handed denigrations of their language and culture and to relentless gender surveillance. Thinly veiled rebellion—expressed through humor, stealth, and evasion—bubbles up through the conformity and quiescence. The carrot of individual upward mobility is dangled before students, but Aymaras who put on urban airs are still ridiculed mercilessly. Young women who acquiesce to tightly controlled campus life also question these rules and stereotypes.

Ultimately, Luykx leaves us with a complex portrait of the fragile, shifting, contradictory ideological space of these Aymara students. On one hand, many of these youth are beginning to distance themselves from their class and ethnic origins. On the other hand, hegemonic forces have rekindled a degree of ethnic, class, and gender consciousness. The bottom line seems to be that such fundamental notions of self as ethnicity, gender, and class are not easily remade. Whether these future teachers' contradictory view of themselves will lead to progressive, collective political action is anyone's guess, but Luykx ends on a hopeful Gramscian note.

In her search for a transformative Bolivian pedagogy, she takes dogmatic Bolivian leftists and the teachers' union to task for failing to understand Bolivian popular culture and the importance of ethnic and gender issues. Luykx finds Paulo Friere's more dialogic, popular-based pedagogy and notion of teachers as transformative intellectuals essential for deconstructing authoritarian Bolivian culture. The book ends with an expression of "strategic optimism" built upon Giroux's notion of a hopeful, practical critical consciousness and Gramsci's notion of ordinary people's good "common sense." Jim McGuigan would undoubtedly label Luykx's final comments "cultural populism," a malady from which many leftists allegedly suffer, but her extended theoretical discussion on what counts as "resistance" is far more thoughtful than romantic.

Liberal educators will find much to agree with in this fascinating study, but ultimately they will be unsettled by the sweeping argument that "schooling," as opposed to "education," has little or no use value to students. Liberal sociologists will surely point out that the credentials that Aymara students receive to become proletarian professionals empowers them with considerable symbolic and economic capital. They will also be quick to reaffirm how essential mass public schooling is for building a democratic, egalitarian society and for promoting social mobility. Luykx's way of theorizing the general connection between academic labor and production of hegemony and subordinated subject positions is generally persuasive, but she will need to address the liberal critique that schooling and credentials have a use value beyond the construction of hegemony. Such future discussions notwithstanding, *The Citizen Factory* is a fine study that scholars from a variety of disciplines will surely embrace with considerable enthusiasm.

PREFACE

Thoughts on Doing and Writing Ethnography

Arrival, and Some Points of Departure

This book is an attempt to engage theoretical questions of ethnicity, ideology, and identity as they are lived out in a specific setting: a small teachers' college in rural Bolivia. As most of the arguments presented here turn on the question of language, a word about the language of ethnography itself seems appropriate. Many have criticized social theory's tendency to become an elite discourse, isolated from popular expressions of discontent and "practical" political action. Yet doing ethnography in a foreign culture has an inherent peculiarity that, if cultivated, may counter this tendency: it brings home with inescapable force the organic unity between theory and practice, the political and the personal. In a setting where all things are new and strange, and familiar patterns of interpretation are suspended, the most casual daily interactions may appear as deeply significant expressions of identity, solidarity, alienation, or resistance, with transcendent (and often deceptive) clarity. The fieldworker's own personal and professional relationships are unavoidably infused with political overtones and cultural conflicts. While this can be an obstacle to research, it also forces us toward a more critical analysis, confronting us constantly with that which we wish to understand. And if researchers can avoid writing themselves out of their own texts, these lived instances of culture conflict may even survive the translation from doing ethnography to writing it.

The field dialectic between theory and practice is also one reason why so many ethnographies end up being about something quite different than what the fieldworker originally had in mind. One's theoretical framework cannot (or at least should not) gel completely until it has been carried into the field, to be measured against, and informed by, the data of everyday practice. This inconvenient fact of academic life tends to be collectively (though to some degree necessarily) disregarded during that ritual process of suspended disbelief known as grant writing.

When I arrived at the gates of the *Escuela Normal Rural "Kollasuyo"* in July 1991, I planned to observe the pedagogical techniques and discourse styles characteristic of Bolivian teacher training, compare these with the discourse styles and learning patterns of Aymara children at home, and extract from this comparison a sociolinguistic recipe for school reform. It seemed a sufficiently ambitious yet comfortingly straightforward task, of reasonable scope for a doctoral project. Its practical applicability allowed me to distance myself from those imagined ivory tower academics for whom Third World subjects were primarily stepping-stones to tenure; I was secure in the belief that my work would "give something back" to the people I studied. Still, as I set down my baggage on the edge of the basketball court, surrounded by curious students—country kids, most of them fresh out of high school and on the verge of adulthood, whispering to each other in Aymara and Spanish—I wondered, Will they ever talk to me, much less offer me their friendship? Will they think I'm here to get something from them? What can I offer them in return, without echoing the promises made by dozens of government officials, bureaucrats, and foreign aid workers before me?

I had plenty of time to ponder these questions during my first long, sleepless night in the school's unheated guest room, shivering in the grip of the frigid Andean winter under two thin blankets, too timid to ask for more. The next morning the rector asked if I had brought a sleeping bag with me; I confessed I had not. Within the hour, several young women from the dorm were at my door, arms piled high with blankets stripped from their own beds. With this simple gesture began the year-long process of coming to know one another—a process which, for me, continued long after my departure, as I reviewed the experiences and insights of that year.

Within a few months, I saw that my research project as originally conceived was hopelessly inadequate. The pedagogical and linguistic issues I had hoped to explore could not be disentangled from "the contradictions and ambivalences that constitute the very structure of human subjectivity" (Bhabha 1994:19). Portraying the situation in purely academic terms— that is, excluding questions of power and identity and their manifestations both in national discourses and in students' day-to-day lives—would distort the scene beyond recognition, producing an analysis that would be incomplete, even intellectually dishonest. The growing realization that a strictly sociolinguistic analysis would not provide solutions, even within the pragmatic discourse of "do-what-works" reform, eventually led me to view this discourse itself as part of the problem.

Reflexivity and Responsibility

The literature of "reflexive" anthropology (especially Marcus and Fischer 1986 and Clifford and Marcus [eds.] 1986) has been an invaluable step forward in a discipline that for too long left unproblematized the relationships between investigator and investigated, author and text. Recent deconstructions of the problems and politics of ethnography (both the doing and the writing) have left the theoretical foundations of anthropology poised for new growth—and vulnerable to attack. When one's objects of study are other human beings, the ethos and ethics of the relations among researcher, subject, and text are more complex and subtle, more piercing and personal, more gratifying, and more potentially damaging than in perhaps any other field of study. The fieldwork situation is tightly wound with imbalances of power and loaded with possibilities both for serendipitous revelation and for tangled conflict—indeed, the absence of either may signify lack of engagement. And yet a certain degree of disengagement is necessary; being a social scientist means learning to balance the "social" and the "scientific."

Efforts to adopt a critical perspective on ethnographic representations and to integrate analyses of the power/knowledge/ authorship complex into ethnographic writing at times seem to weave yet another veil of elitist discourse between author and reader. Certainly we must try to demystify and deconstruct our representational practices. Yet in doing this, we may perversely make those practices more opaque, limiting our audience to those willing to follow our meanderings through the epistemological maze of subject- and objectification. As both critics and inheritors of a colonial tradition, we have a moral and political responsibility to persevere through that maze. But if ours is in some real sense a political project, we must find a thread to lead our wanderings back to the outside world. If the ideas with which we work are important beyond the inner circle of academia, we should strive to communicate them to as large an audience as possible, and (more difficult) to do so without sacrificing theoretical complexity. This means balancing the interests of readers and ethnographic subjects and doing what we can to encourage overlap between those two categories.

The accessibility of ideas is important. If this book is not written in a way that can help educators and students examine their own ideology and practice, then it has failed in one sense. However, at the same time that one strives for one's work to be "popular,"[1] this shouldn't mean aiming at some imagined lowest common denominator, in terms either of narrative style or of theoretical sophistication. For this and other reasons, I have chosen to present most of the abstract theoretical discussions in distilled form in chapters 5 and 7.[2] The intention is not that readers unfamiliar with recent debates in social theory should skip the theoretical sections, but rather that the ideas presented therein, and their connections to daily practice, will reveal themselves more clearly after being presented in a less abstract, more grounded form throughout the ethnography. I hope in this way to demystify (at least partially) a discourse which, despite a literary tendency toward elitism, must become more accessible if it is to fulfill its political objectives.

Another way to demystify anthropological practice is to be explicit about procedures and methods, as well as about the limitations, silences, frustrations, and ethical dilemmas of ethnographic research. The temptation to present an ethnography as a personally unproblematic work, with the rough edges filed and the conflicts smoothed over, is great. Understandably, we as anthropologists wish to present ourselves as competent professionals, not as sowers of discord among the people we study. Accounts of "participant observation" have often privileged the latter half of that concept, relegating to the margins the investigator's participation in the ethnographic scene, under suspicion of violating the "prime directive" of cultural noninterference. But frequently the problems involved in setting up and carrying out anthropological fieldwork tell us as much about cultural difference and hegemonic structures as does that material more traditionally represented as "data."

As anthropologists, we inevitably become part of the social scenes we explore. In order to confront the ways we interact with the communities we study, we must integrate the experiences that frame our fieldwork—from the gatekeeping encounters of setting up the research, to the conflicts that our presence engenders—into our texts. In other words, we must "go public" with what all practicing anthropologists already know: that our role as intrusive knowledge seekers *is* problematic, that our presence entails risk for our subjects as well as ourselves, and that ambivalent soul-searching over issues of exploitation, manipulation, and professional honesty in delicate situations is part of our job.

Few authors have done this in as forthright a manner as Douglas Foley (1990), whose ethnography of a south Texas high school I take as something of a model in this regard. Foley also demonstrates rare authorial fortitude in his attempt to make ethnography a dialogic project between researcher and subjects (cf. also Feld 1987 and Limón 1989). Many ethnographers would no doubt wince at the prospect of their manuscript being read by the people analyzed within its pages; in our efforts to provide as incisive an interpretation as possible, we may paint portraits that are less than flattering, especially when tackling topics such as racism or oppressive school practices. The fact that most "traditional" ethnographic subjects do not speak or read the language in which the final text is presented has served as a guilty blessing for many ethnographers. However, giving subjects the chance to read and respond to what we say about them, and incorporating their criticisms into our work, is perhaps the most important step we can take toward making ethnography more dialogic.

Despite my attempts to make this work available to those presented in its pages and solicit their reactions to it, the degree to which I was able to do so in the field was very limited, for a number of reasons. Working largely from interviews about students' perceptions of their educational experience, I was mindful of two considerations. One was that, if made aware of the theoretical framework in which I was working, students might shape their comments to fit my concerns. I tried to conduct open-ended interviews that permitted subjects to range freely over any and all aspects of their institutional life, rather than only those they might perceive as examples of exploitation, identity conflicts, and so on. I also avoided using the kind of "social science language" that I am used to using with my academic peers and that students learned to manipulate to some degree in class. I wanted to collect their impressions and analyses in the kind of language that they used among themselves, rather than offering them analytic categories in which to present their experiences.

Explanations of what my research entailed thus were not always as explicit as they could have been. I did have more analytic discussions with a few subjects, after initial interviews had been gathered, both to share in a more detailed manner what I was doing and to seek feedback as to whether I was on the right track. I also showed to a few an article I wrote in the field (Luykx 1992) on the more pedagogical/linguistic aspects of the research. On such occasions, the responses I got were encouraging, leading me to believe I had succeeded in understanding students' perspectives on the problems they experienced and their relationships with the institution and with each other.

Initially, I presented my proposal to the rector and it was discussed among the faculty in order to decide whether I would be allowed to carry out research at the school. Upon arriving, I posted the proposal in the display case and encouraged faculty and students to read it (a very few actually did). When asked, I usually said I was studying Bolivian education and the linguistic and pedagogical problems faced by Aymara students, which was true enough at the time. Over the course of the fieldwork, however, my research plan changed to one more concerned with issues of institutional control, ethnic identity, and social reproduction than with strictly sociolinguistic issues.

I did not go out of my way to correct the earlier vague notions of my research aims that had circulated throughout the school, partly because the new framework took shape slowly in my own mind. More important, I felt that teachers (and perhaps some students) might be less willing to talk to me or to allow me to observe their interactions if they knew I was shifting toward a more critical analysis of their practices. When talking to teachers, I emphasized my interest in "students' learning problems" rather than "teachers' teaching practices." Those of them who eventually read this work[3] may be surprised or offended by my critiques of their actions and attitudes toward students. They may feel that I acted as a spy by attending to students' unflattering portrayals of them. I did try to sift out idle gossip from students' actual critiques of teachers' practices and the conditions in which they lived and studied. Nevertheless, some will no doubt feel that, by allowing me to observe them in and out of the classroom, they revealed more than they had intended.

Though the school administration granted me permission to carry out the research, and I only observed in classes where I had explicit permission from the teacher, students were never polled as to whether or not they wished to become research subjects. As is so often the case with subaltern groups, the subjects I hoped to observe most intimately were the ones with the least say about whether I should have been there at all. In general, my relations with students were much less problematic than those with teachers; most were as eager to interact with me as I was with them. The difficulty of obtaining consent from every member of a community is obvious, and in any case students seemed to have few objections to my presence; but the fact that there was no easy avenue for them to express their objections, should they have had any, is an uneasy one.[4] The degree to which students allowed me into their lives and the enthusiasm with which they took on the role of anthropological subjects remain a source of amazement and gratification to me.

Public Image, Personal Solidarities, and Social Access

While the image that I presented to the school community came naturally to me, it was also deliberately crafted to fit my research aims. I enjoyed certain ambiguities of status that often worked to my advantage. At twenty-eight, I was older than most students but younger than the professors. Many students took me for younger than I was, viewing me more or less as their peer in this regard. This was fortuitous, since I wanted to avoid having my position construed as one of authority. I hoped that aligning myself more closely with students than with teachers would lead the former to speak with me more freely, and this indeed turned out to be the case.

There was also some doubt, initially at the school and persisting in the surrounding community, over whether I was a student or a teacher. Originally, some students and villagers thought that I had come to teach English or some other subject at the school. I emphasized to students that I was a student also, though studying at a different level (and with considerably less supervision) than they were. I commiserated with them over the stress of exams, the drudgery of homework, and the tedium of class lectures. In class, I sat among them and took notes as they did. At times, even our differences were constructed in terms of similarity; we joked that, of all the students, I was the only one who could choose which classes I felt like attending.[5]

My social status was ambiguous among faculty as well; on the one hand, being younger, female, and a "student" of sorts, I was definitely lower in the school hierarchy than they. On the other hand, my First World origins and many years of education were at odds with their status as "teachers" and mine as "student." This caused a certain amount of tension with a few individuals.

Mealtimes were important for marking group boundaries. For the first few months I ate in the cafeteria with the majority of students and teachers. My first week there, a professor came over to where I was waiting to be served with the students, and led me to the teachers' table, telling me jovially "Your place is here." I stayed and ate with the faculty, but the next day went back to the students' table. Within a few days, the teachers realized I didn't want to be treated like a visiting authority, and I regularly made my way to the students' section without comment. Since all the teachers who ate in the cafeteria were men, and students tended to segregate themselves by sex, an available interpretation was that I chose my seat according to sex rather than by my place in the school hierarchy, and this seemed acceptable to all concerned.

Although I had access to the social scenes of both teachers and students, I was much more closely identified with the latter. One might say I enjoyed the best of both worlds; I played volleyball and basketball with students and danced with them (and with teachers) at school dances, but was also allowed to drink with teachers at those same dances, whereas students were not. I attended classes with students, but was an invited guest at the meals they served to faculty on special occasions. I enjoyed a degree of privacy and freedom much more typical of teachers than of students, and yet students teased, joked, and shared confidences with me in ways they did not with their teachers.

While I made it clear that I wished to take part in all aspects of school life, most students and teachers were only vaguely aware that such participation was part of my work. Indeed, had they been more conscious of the fact that any interaction I had with them might count as "data," they might well have been much more reticent in my presence. I suspect that many saw me almost as a tourist, there to pass the time in their midst, with no serious purpose in mind. The idea that just "hanging out" with them could be my actual "work"—taking part in their conversations, attending their civic presentations, and cheering school athletic contests—did not seem to make sense to them (as indeed it does not to many North Americans unfamiliar with the ethnographic method).

With few exceptions, neither students nor faculty pressed me for details on what my work actually involved, and despite the copy of my proposal posted in the display case and circulated among the interested few, they seemed not to have a clear idea of how my presence among them related to what I would eventually write. In class, students who looked at my notes sometimes expressed surprise that they were different from their own. People often remarked, "You're really working hard today!" when they saw me typing up my notes or transcribing interviews, tasks I considered more the tedious by-product of my "real" work of observing and trying to make sense of what I observed. The general perception that my days were spent in idle conversation and aimless wandering around the grounds was one I did not work very hard to discourage, since it helped maintain a casual "business as usual" air that was conducive to my observations. When, late in the research period, I discussed some of my conclusions with José, a student, he had this reaction: "It's incredible, I don't know how you were able to observe so much; it seemed to me that you didn't realize, that you weren't seeing anything, you didn't give any importance to some things, I thought. But on the contrary, you were seeing all those things! That's what really surprised me. And it's good to do it that way, no? Just go around normally, but nevertheless checking things out. On the sly, no?"

This characterization of my activity left me somewhat uneasy, but was probably quite in line with a couple of teachers' suspicions that I had hidden motives, probably political. The trope of "anthropologist as spy" was even more serious in the context of my observations in the city (at educational congresses, teachers' protest marches, etc.). The research took place during a period of conflict between the government and the teachers' union, and my contacts with teachers made me a frequent visitor to the union hall in La Paz. Though I was generally well received there, my teacher friends would joke with me about the standoffishness of those of their colleagues who suspected I was with the CIA. Considering that the union was firmly dominated by a Trotskyite faction and reportedly suffered from government infiltration, such suspicions were perhaps not unreasonable.

The political climate made for paranoia on both sides; while some teachers probably were not pleased to see me at their union events, I worried that the less anthropologically minded members of the U.S. embassy staff might misconstrue my presence there (or my disregard for their memos advising U.S. citizens to avoid street demonstrations). During one demonstration, while I diligently snapped photos of striking university students marching toward the U.S. embassy, someone suddenly clutched at my elbow and hissed angrily into my ear (in Spanish), "Why are you taking pictures?!" I jumped and spun around guiltily, only to face a journalist friend of mine, himself taking pictures and laughing at my high-strung reaction to his prank.

In many Bolivian circles, where the reputation of anthropologists does not far surpass that of government spies, defending oneself against suspicion by claiming to be "only an anthropologist" is not much of a defense. More than once, upon being asked what I did, I answered that I was a linguist, instead of a (linguistic) anthropologist. While such discretion perhaps fell outside the bounds of strict honesty, I feared that the charged term *anthropologist* would associate me with a tradition that many perceived as dishonorable. Though I felt it was my subjects' right to engage me in discussions of anthropologists' roles in imperialist exploitation, etc., such opportunities were more often presented by inebriated strangers than by the research subjects themselves, and I did not choose to take the bait in such circumstances.

As an outsider, I accepted that I would be barred from certain scenes that I would have liked to observe, such as inner-circle union meetings in the city and faculty conferences at the school itself. Another factor that restricted my access to some settings, and also shaped my social role within the institution, was gender. Since most of the faculty were men, my participation in their very male-oriented social scene was limited, though not nonexistent. If this book had been written by an older male ethnographer, it might well have reflected more of the teachers' point of view than it does. Being a young female researcher in a male-dominated setting has other risks as well. While the few sexual advances I received from students were nonthreatening and easily deflected, a few of my interactions with faculty could be labeled "sexual harassment." These incidents involved a very few individuals; in general, faculty and staff received me with much graciousness and hospitality. I was able to observe, take notes and photos, videotape, and ask annoying questions with almost total freedom. Furthermore, teachers never (to my knowledge) attempted to use my intermediary position to manipulate students or each other, which no doubt made my work much easier.

As far as student life was concerned, the only place that was off limits to me was the boys' dormitory, and in some sense the story of their lives there is one I cannot tell. I did, however, have access to the girls' dorm; I lived there for a few weeks, and after I had my own room, I still went frequently to visit and occasionally spend the night. It was perhaps this, more than anything else, that established among students the feeling that I was "on their side." The only faculty members who entered the dorms were the hygiene professor and the two inspectors (male and female) responsible for supervising students' conduct, who seldom stayed longer than the few minutes required to discharge their duties; they never went to the dorms just to visit with students.

As one with no official function within the institution, I eventually came to fulfill a role that had previously been empty: that of a (relatively) neutral party to whom students could air their grievances. As their confidence in me grew, students sometimes came to me for sympathy and advice on problems they had with faculty members or other students. It was in part this process that forced me to change my research plan. As the sounding board for students' concerns, I gradually realized that their strategies for getting through school went far beyond the academic, as did their frustrations with the training they received. The more I realized that sticking to my original proposal would be theoretically and pedagogically unsound, the more I felt that it would also be a betrayal of the very real concerns that my subjects had imparted to me.

Narrative Style and Ideological Stance

Aside from those "reflexive" issues already mentioned, there are others that directly concern the authorship of ethnographic texts. The current trend, which I applaud, is to experiment with genres and styles that open up new conceptual spaces and dedicate more text to the voices of the subjects themselves. Given that ethnography entails building relationships between researcher and subjects, I believe the researcher should be present, not only as author, but also as a "character" in ethnographic texts; the traditional erasure of the researcher from the narrative is a form of mystification. I have tried to portray the people with whom I worked as individuals with a past and a future, rather than mere objects of study, to avoid both their dehumanization as subjects and their exoticization as human beings. For this reason, and to grant their own analyses the legitimacy they deserve, I have tried to let their voices come through as much as possible. Ethnographers have a responsiblity to interpret; but at times subjects' voices escape easy interpretation along the lines that the ethnographer might wish, and that incongruity is part of our enterprise too.

I also believe that ethnography can be evocative in a literary sense without sacrificing representational realism. Anthropology's developing critique of traditionally conceived "science" has been accompanied by the realization that ethnography, both as investigative practice and as textual genre, has less to do with the scientific method than with the weaving of narratives about human behavior. Such accounts are rarely amenable to the scientific litmus test of "disprovability"; rather, the ethnographer's interpretation "draws its appeal from the power of its language, the depth of its explanations, the relevance of its examples, and the credibility of its theme" (Postman 1988: 12–13). Nevertheless, while much of our work involves the interpretation of socially constructed meanings, and the effort to situate, historically and politically, our own perspectives as authors, what we describe are real structures and processes with real effects on subjects' lives. Ethnography uses narrative to untangle the overdetermined and unpredictable expressions of everyday practice, revealing the underlying processes that give rise to such practice.

Clearly, our interpretations are not neutral. But, to quote Michael Apple, "the critical power of any social analysis does not arise from some alleged disinterestedness" (1986:180). Renato Rosaldo notes that the dominance of criteria such as "objectivity" and "neutrality" derives more from institutional authority than from any exclusive power to explain the human condition. This is especially true when the objects of analysis "are also analyzing subjects who critically interrogate their ethnographers—their writings, their ethics and their politics" (1989:21).

By engaging the processes of representation at all, we implicate ourselves in ideologies of power/knowledge (cf. Foucault 1980). Any authorial position implies an ideological stance; the ethnographer's responsibility is to make that stance explicit rather than covert. Furthermore, authorial power has a positive as well as a negative side (Giroux 1988). The task of radical scholars is to reveal the dynamics of ideology (in their own as well as others' practice), trace the vectors of that power which oppresses, and counter it with reclaimed power which liberates. As Postman affirms, "the purpose of social research is to rediscover the truths of social life; to comment on [. . . the . . .] behavior of people; and finally, to put forth metaphors, images and ideas that can help people live with some measure of understanding and dignity" (1988:18).

Correspondingly, we must shape our language to fit our aims. As discussed above, one way of confronting our own intimacy with power is to demystify our procedures and presence within the social scenes we study. Another way is to demystify our own academic discourse. I am not arguing that the majority of social theorists purposely adopt elitist language; the ideas we work with are complex, and a certain level of theoretical sophistication is necessary. But for large sectors of potential readers, the question of whether we are *intentionally* obfuscatory is moot.

In order to avoid the marginalization of our scholarship, and match the success with which the discourses of the right have taken root in popular opinion, we must take the question of audience much more seriously (Apple 1986:200). Is it possible to write critical ethnographies that people without several years of graduate study can understand, even enjoy? Perhaps, but it is not easy; anthropologists have spent decades devising discursive shorthands to express ideas that often have no simple analogue in everyday language. Additionally, many of the ideas with which we work have been systematically excluded from popular discourse; until recently, Marxist theory constituted one of the "structured silences" in mainstream North American thought. Having found a language to express our interpretations of social processes, and having made such language a key part of our academic practice, it requires effort to discuss such ideas without slipping into a jargon that seals itself off from popular discourse. To translate these ideas into a more widely familiar idiom, we must build discursive bridges between the new language and the old, the elite and the popular; this is vital to our work as transformative intellectuals and as concerned human beings.

Finally, the professional distance of the social critic must be complemented by an engaged solidarity with one's subjects. This does not mean uncritically celebrating any and all subaltern cultural practices, whether out of relativist or revolutionary sentiment. Rather, it means trying to understand such practices from the perspective of one's subjects, and seeking in them the potential for social transformation in line with subjects' collective interests and the interest of social justice.[6] While the notion of "interests" and how they are constructed is itself problematic (cf. Habermas 1968), its resolution lies neither in the indiscriminate acceptance of all popular practices and desires as "authentic," nor in the cavalier dismissal of those not corresponding to our own aims as "false consciousness." Rather, we must trace the strands of popular ideologies back to their multiple sources, analyzing both the repressive forces that give rise to resistant practices and the potential of such practices for meaningful social transformation.

At certain moments during the researching and writing of this book, I found myself having to balance the interests of teachers and administrators against those of students. All gave generously of themselves and through their sharing made this work possible. But in instances of conflict, solidarity with my subjects and with their struggle to form and transform meanings in a very restrictive environment led me to give the benefit of the doubt to students rather than to teachers. It is students—many acutely aware and apprehensive of the fact—who stand on the threshhold of a hegemony into which their teachers have, for the most part, already been absorbed. If at times I seem overly critical of teachers, it is because students' empowerment must occur at the expense of teachers' power over them. It is my hope that these critiques be received in the understanding that they are intended to foster more liberating forms of power for both parties.

For those living, studying, and working within the system here analyzed, the underlying question must be: "What is it [and *how* is it, I would add] that this society has made of me that I no longer want to be?" (Giroux 1988:8). Exploring these issues is one step on the long road toward transformation, a road too often obscured by the underbrush of despair. More experienced educators no doubt will encounter in these pages an attitude toward the possibility of change that seems naively optimistic at times. Nevertheless, this stance is intentional; one might even say strategic. As Giroux, Freire, Apple, and others have pointed out, many educators and theorists provide a language of critique without a language of possibility; too often, our work takes the form of theorizing *about* schools, rather than *for* schools. The possibilities for transformation may seem utopian to anyone intimately familiar with public schooling in Bolivia (or in the United States, for that matter), but the envisioning of utopian possibilities is a necessary element in any struggle. If the oppressive conditions found in most schools are not intrinsic to the practicalities of formal education, they must be viewed as a restricted set of forms and practices among a wide range of possible alternatives; and to conceive of those alternatives, one requires what Laclau and Mouffe (1985) term "the constitution of a radical imaginary."

There is yet another reason for my purposeful adoption of this idealistic stance. Throughout my year with the students of the *Escuela Normal Rural "Kollasuyo,"* I repeatedly heard their expressions of longing for a different way of doing things, and their attempts to envision what such a way might be. The formulation and sharing of this wistful discourse is, in a sense, counterhegemonic practice in action. Embattled by the deadening forces of disillusionment and alienation, students nevertheless were still engaged in the practice of radical imagining; and that deserves to be encouraged, for the wellspring of future possibility lies precisely there.

ACKNOWLEDGMENTS

Many people assisted in the research and in the production of the manuscript itself. First and foremost, my most heartfelt thanks go to the faculty and students of the Escuela Normal Rural "Kollasuyo," whose insight, candor, and enthusiasm made fieldwork not only a possibility, but a joy. In La Paz, my thanks to Tomás Huanca and the staff of the Taller de Historia Oral Andina (THOA), to Hugo Daniel Ruíz and the staff of the Museo de Etnología y Folklore (MUSEF), and to those members of the Federación de Trabajadores de la Educación Urbana de La Paz (FTEULP) who shared ideas and arguments with me during the course of the fieldwork.

Thanks also to the following individuals, who read various parts of the manuscript and provided many helpful suggestions: Robin Moore, Andrew Causey, Marlys West, Nancy Palmer, Glenn Parrice, Peter García, Daniel Mato, Richard Schaedel, and especially Dean Birkencamp, and to my doctoral committee members—Doug Foley, Joel Sherzer, Ted Gordon, James Brow, Greg Urban, and Keith Walters—for their constant willingness to strive for new heights in noninstrumental communication. Final preparation of the manuscript would not have been possible but for the invaluable support of Juan José Alba, director of the Instituto de Investigaciones en Humanidades y Ciencias de la Educación of the Universidad Mayor de San Simón in Cochabamba, Bolivia, my academic home of the past few years; such a harmonious combination of friendship and academic colleagueship is rarely found and is always an inspiration. I am also grateful to Luís Enrique López, for his valuable bibliographic and theoretical suggestions, and to Priscilla Ross and Marilyn Semerad of SUNY Press, for their help in preparing the manuscript for publication. Finally, a very special thanks to Patricia Oliart, for her assistance with the translations, her valuable insights, and her unflagging enthusiasm for tackling questions of Andean identity in the modern world.

Research for this book was carried out with support from the Fulbright Foundation, the National Science Foundation, and the Institute of Latin American Studies at the University of Texas at Austin.

INTRODUCTION

Educational Theory and School Ethnography

Culturally speaking, schooling has lost its innocence. While schools are still commonly conceived mainly as institutions of instruction, where objective knowledge is transmitted in a relatively straightforward manner to students who absorb it or not, educational theorists abandoned this view long ago. In recent decades, educational processes have been examined under the lens of ethnography, in the realization that they are, fundamentally, *cultural* processes. Many such analyses have been undertaken for pragmatic pedagogical reasons, since the most pressing educational problems often concern students who are culturally and linguistically different. Others have taken schools to task for reproducing the very social inequalities which they were supposed to alleviate. In either case, it has become virtually impossible to treat questions of academic success and failure in multicultural societies without also questioning the school's role in processes of identity formation and social stratification.

Central to recent critiques of schooling is the notion of a "hidden curriculum" that subtly and selectively guides educational practice, structuring classroom interactions in ways that seem natural but are in fact culturally determined, so that students from different cultural backgrounds experience frustration and failure at a disproportionate rate. The hidden curriculum also transmits to students an ideology about themselves and the world in which they live, an ideology that is all the more insidious because it is generally unacknowledged and thus unchallenged. Exposure of the hidden curriculum and inquiries into its functioning have revealed that schools do much more than simply transmit a set of academic skills and a body of academic knowledge.

Despite these insights, educational anthropology still has far to go in terms of understanding the myriad processes that interact with one another in schools. Culturally sensitive analyses of classroom interactions (e.g., Cazden and Hymes [eds.] 1972; Heath 1983; Philips 1983) have often limited their focus to micro-level processes, rather than interrogating such processes as social constructions arising out of specific historical conditions. Such studies have contributed much to our understanding of different groups' communicative and learning styles and the effects of cultural differences on academic outcomes. Still, their implicit aim seems to be to help teachers use anthropology's insights to guide their culturally different students more smoothly through the structures of standard educational practice, rather than to transform the structures themselves.

More radical approaches have often suffered from the opposite shortcoming. Early attempts to analyze schooling in the light of Marxist social theory tended to focus exclusively on macro-level processes and the school's general role in social reproduction, shedding little light on *how* specific kinds of knowledge, classroom social relationships, and pedagogical practices serve to maintain repressive ideologies and social structures. While exposing the school's tendency to reproduce social inequality rather than foster social mobility, reproduction theory's earlier proponents (Carnoy 1974; Bowles and Gintis 1976) paid scant attention to actual school practices or forms of student resistance. The powerful vision of factory-like schools mechanistically reproducing an oppressive division of labor tended to gloss over both the actual mechanisms involved and the frequent (and highly significant) failure of those mechanisms. Such theories were also insufficently cultural, tending to reduce all social inequality to the question of class.

Scholars from both ends of the theoretical spectrum drew attention to the fact that schools were not adequately serving students from subaltern groups. But in focusing exlusively on either micro- or macro-level processes, they ignored the middle-level circuits of social reproduction: the ways that specific practices, structures, and discourses interpellate culturally different students as certain kinds of subjects within a self-reproducing social order. Also missing was the students' side of the equation: a sense of students as agents and actors, who challenge old meanings and create new ones, rather than as docile products stamped out on the hegemonic assembly line. In contrast, the recent focus on "cultural production" in school settings has widened our conception of social reproduction to include questions of gender, race, and ethnicity, as well as providing theoretical space for student resistance to the reproductive process, via forms that are culturally derived as well as class-based.[1] Scholars such as Willis (1981a), Everhart (1983), MacLeod (1987) and Foley (1990) have forged new paths in school ethnography by linking the small daily dramas of classroom life to the reproduction of larger structures of inequality; that is, by making explicit the connections between micro- and macro-level processes. However, such an approach has rarely been applied to Third World societies, where postcolonial history, politics, demography, and efforts at "development" present educational theorists with a rather different set of questions.

Despite the scarcity of studies of the "hidden curriculum" in developing nations[2] (relative to the plethora of studies of North American schools), such study "is hardly any less relevant for an understanding of Third World education and its place in national cultures" (Hannerz 1987:554). With the increasing scholarly and political interest in issues of nationalism, ethnicity, and the conflicts that they generate, Third World schools would appear to be especially fruitful territory for investigating how nationalist and ethnic ideologies are both constructed and contested.

The Spanish conquest of Central and South America unleashed a torrent of ethnic and linguistic conflicts that continue to unfold today, in which schools have played a decisive role. Yet in much of Latin America, where underfunded school systems are often overwhelmed by linguistic and cultural diversity, there is a dangerous temptation to view this diversity as basically a technical or managerial problem, albeit a complex and challenging one. Stromquist (1992a:4) attributes this to the fact that recent advances in the study of education have yet to reach Latin America, where schooling is still seen as essentially pedagogical, its political, social, and cultural aspects seldom subject to examination and questioning.[3] As a result, proposed solutions to the numerous problems plaguing education have usually fallen within a relatively narrow range.

The most simplistic approach takes the form of calls for increased access to schooling. While a worthy goal in itself, this approach begs the question of what happens to students once they are in school. Another approach, prevalent in countries with large indigenous populations, places an almost messianic hope in bilingual education; the implicit assumption seems to be that if the linguistic barriers faced by indigenous students could only be eliminated, their schooling would automatically "take" and the system would begin to "work." Questions of just what is being taken, and precisely what the work of the system is, are raised with much less frequency.

> The rationality that dominates traditional views of schooling and curriculum is rooted in the narrow concerns for effectiveness, behavioral objectives, and principles of learning that treat knowledge as something to be consumed. . . . The issue of how teachers, students, and representatives from the wider society generate meaning tends to be obscured in favor of the issue of how people can master someone else's meaning, thus depoliticizing both the notion of school culture and the notion of classroom pedagogy. (Giroux 1988:6)

As will become clear in the following pages, rural education in Bolivia has as much (or more) to do with the generation of social meaning as it does with the transmission of academic skills. Bilingual education, while important, will not resolve those educational dilemmas that do *not* derive from students' lack of Spanish fluency; furthermore, the reliance on limited technical solutions to the "problem" of linguistically and culturally different students speaks volumes about the way that educators are taught to think about conflict. As Michael Apple (1990:8) observes, "the very fact that we tend to reduce our understanding of the social and economic forces underlying our unequal society to a set of skills, to 'how to's,' mirrors a much larger issue."

The larger issue is, of course, the mystification of the causes of social inequality and schools' role in maintaining it. For Bolivia's indigenous students, the issue is also largely one of identity. If "politics consists of the effort to domesticate the infinitude of identity" (Dirks, Eley, and Ortner 1994:32), the same might be said of traditional schooling. Schools fulfill a hegemonic function by intervening in the development of students' identities, creating the kinds of social subjects that are conducive to the maintenance of a certain social order. When the foundations of that order are shaken by other forces, the school system is apt to find itself in crisis. A brief look at the relationships among indigenous peoples, the nation-state, and the school as the prime mediator between the two will provide a framework for investigating these issues.

Indigenous Peoples, Schools, and the Nation-State

The relatively few ethnographic treatments of Third World schooling have mostly come out of anthropological linguistics and the "ethnography of speaking" tradition. But as Foley (1990:182) notes: "Anthropological studies of speech communities are rarely located in a larger class context. They are usually not conceptualized as studies of cultural assimilation and resistance to world capitalist development or 'modernity.' Anthropological linguistics, although rich in empirical studies of distinct cultural speech groups, has not generally studied speech communities as emerging class cultures."

Ethnographers such as Nash (1979), Taussig (1980), and Scott (1985, 1990) have combined class-based and cultural approaches to show how different groups use traditional cultural practices in their struggles against exploitation. Until recently, however, such approaches were rare, and ones focusing on language and/or schooling even more so. Anthropologists are now realizing that a reevaluation of the relationship between indigenous peoples and the nation-states in which they reside is necessary, if not long overdue. It is increasingly apparent that national and supra-national systems must be taken into account even when describing those "remotest people that anthropologists have made such a fetish of studying" (Gupta and Ferguson 1992:18). The hegemonic influence of international market capitalism has reached unprecedented levels, in terms of its penetration of formerly endogenous local economies. Third World cultures are involved in an ever-increasing "intercontinental traffic in meaning" (Hannerz 1987:552) around the political ideologies and cultural products of the "developed" nations. Pop culture commodities churned out in New York and Hong Kong regularly turn up in rural hamlets in Africa and Latin America, while the rhythms of those rural hamlets are heard on radio stations all over the United States and Europe. Many Third World cultures can indeed be described as "creolized," given that "people are formed from birth by these [syncretized] systems of meaning and largely live their lives in contexts shaped by them" (Hannerz 1987:552). Conversely, part of the heritage of colonialism is the fact that elites on different continents may have much more in common with each other than with the lower social strata of their own countries (Gupta and Ferguson 1992:20).

Given the reality of interpenetration on so many levels, those groups labeled "indigenous peoples" can no longer be treated as closed social systems. Indigenous groups' relationships with postcolonial elites, their corresponding nation-states, and global economic and cultural processes must be reformulated and translated into a "post-colonial ethnography of how Third World people see themselves and their society, its past, present, and future, and its place in the world; a cultural analysis of their fantasies and what they know for a fact" (Hannerz 1987:534). Though still in its beginning stages, such an approach is bearing fruit, particularly in the study of Latin America (Hill [ed.] 1988; García Canclini 1990; Urban and Sherzer [eds.] 1991; Rowe and Schelling 1991). Social scientists have begun to address cultural production and conflict from a variety of perspectives, but with the common recognition that "seemingly isolated communities of the world are no longer in fact isolated, that new webs are constantly being spun between such communities and broader national and international arenas, and that in many cases the assumption of community isolation seriously distorts research results" (Urban and Sherzer 1991:1).

Such distortions have repercussions not only for academia, but also for indigenous subjects themselves. For too long, rural societies have been treated as implicitly anachronistic, defined by their lack of contact with the urban center. Such characterizations often have resulted in the theoretical marginalization of such societies. Peasants have been portrayed as cut off from the dynamic exchanges of urban life, incorporating new elements only when the expansive tide of modernity overwhelms their traditional "resistance to change," or when modern pressures lead them to trade rural poverty for the urban squalor that surrounds every large Latin American city.

The degree to which such assumptions can distort the ethnographic picture is revealed in Orin Starn's (1991) blistering critique of how anthropologists "missed the war" in Peru by ignoring the presence, within the rural communities they were studying, of the urban political influences that later gave rise to the violent guerrilla movement Sendero Luminoso. Starn ascribes this blind spot to a view he labels "Andeanism" (in reference to Edward Said's "Orientalism"), within which peasant communities are imagined as frozen in time, living in a state of uncontaminated cultural purity and authenticity, unaffected by the flow of history, the grasping tendrils of the world economy, and the beat of urban popular culture. While "Andeanist" thinking may indeed distort research results, its persistence can be partly explained by the way it plays into the interests of both tourism and the academic commodification of cultural "others."

Starn's evidence of the degree to which urban-based ideologies can and do orient the world view and actions of rural communities should alert anthropologists in general. Too often, traditional ethnographies have provided a wealth of detail about the daily lives of indigenous peoples, while virtually ignoring the broader dynamics of the nation-states in which they live. More recently, social scientists are realizing that urbanites and peasants, though different, do not live "worlds apart," but rather occupy distinct yet interacting subsystems within a single overarching system, in which all parts are influenced by the global currents of the pop culture industry, international economic strategies, environmental concerns, and ideological debates.

This book is intended, on one level, to strike a blow against Andeanism, from which Bolivia has suffered perhaps more than any other nation. While half of all Bolivians live in small rural communities, and two-thirds speak Aymara or Quechua as their native language, urban culture is far from irrelevant to Bolivian rural life. Indeed, the study of rural-urban linkages becomes even *more* crucial when so much of national policy, resources, and debate is devoted to "integrating" the indigenous majority into the "national culture." The precise contents of this national culture are the subject of much debate, but one thing is clear: though many of its elements derive from the expressive practices of rural dwellers, it is urbanites who define its boundaries.

Teachers play a special role in the rural-urban interface, as the primary disseminators of the "national culture" throughout the rural population. Furthermore, they are often recruited from that population for intensive training in the national culture, leaving them stranded between the social categories of "peasant" and "professional." Isbell (1977), Primov (1980), and others have portrayed rural teachers as invasive bearers of contaminating, destructive urban influences to harmonious indigenous communities, but this interpretation (besides suffering from "Andeanist" romanticism and oversimplification), begins its analysis too late in the cycle. These days, rural teachers and rural students often are cut from the same social fabric, separated only by a generation. The story of their transformation from one category to the other is crucial to understanding the evolving relationship between urban center and rural periphery, as well as the points in between.

The subjects of this study are Aymara students in a rural teachers' college ("normal school") on the Bolivian *altiplano*, studying for jobs in small communities like the ones that many of them call home; still, their motivations, aspirations, antagonisms, and pleasures cannot be understood without reference to the urban culture radiating from La Paz, Bolivia's capital. This is not only because most students have some regular contact with the city, or because their own cultural practices draw upon transformed elements of urban life, or because as teachers they will become enmeshed in both the bureaucratic apparatus of the Ministry of Education and the urban street-level expressions of labor-government conflict. It is also due to their very status as Aymaras; for as indigenous people take part in debates over their own cultural identity and political future, that identity is increasingly defined against the collectively imagined leviathan of *lo urbano*. In an era when transnational capitalism and other belief systems penetrate daily practice in the remotest corners of the globe, and multiple oppressions are interlaced through conflated categories of race and class, Abercrombie's claim (1991:111) that indigenous peoples and cosmologies "are unintelligible apart from their struggle with the state" is one we cannot dismiss.

Furthermore, Bolivia's urban popular culture cannot be fully understood without examining the influence of the United States. While the popular North American conception of Bolivia is minimal at best, usually limited to media portrayals of the cocaine trade and a vague awareness of Indians and llamas, the United States is a constant presence in Bolivian politics and popular discourse. Both as an imagined cultural milieu against which their own is constantly compared, and as a political superpower whose foreign policy directly influences their lives, the United States is an important element in students' meaning-making about what it is to be Bolivian and Aymara.

The view of public meaning-making as a "war of position" between social groups diverges sharply from earlier views of "cultures" as coherent wholes. It sees culture as a set of "multiple discourses, occasionally coming together in large systemic configuration, but more often coexisting within dynamic fields of interaction and conflict" (Dirks, Eley, and Ortner 1994:4). One can still speak of cultural systems, but one is obliged to recognize that such systems leak; culture is patterned, but there are plenty of snags in the pattern. Moving down to the level of the individual subject, we can see that the notion of "identity" has evolved in similar directions (cf. Hall 1985).

Recent studies of nationalism and identity have been influenced by developments in ethnicity theory that move away from static classifications based on primordial characteristics. More recent perspectives conceive of ethnicity, not as an isolating category, but as a relational one; ethnic groups are defined primarily by their relation to other groups (Barth 1969; B. F. Williams 1989; Eriksen 1993). Furthermore, ethnicity is situational, not fixed; "it has no existence apart from interethnic relations" (Williams 1989:417). "Cultural groups in modern complex societies have no stable, essential cultural identities which are transmitted unproblematically from generation to generation. There are only 'discursive moments' or 'discursive skirmishes' between ethnic, gender, and class identity groups in the ceaseless production of shifting cultural images" (Foley 1996:87). The realization that ethnicity is not an inherent quality of individuals or groups, but rather is constructed in social intercourse and discourse—an achieved, rather than ascribed, characteristic—opens up questions of ethnic mobility, state/ethnic group relations, and engagement with theories of subjectivity, three areas central to the present work. The rapid social changes currently taking place in Bolivia have destabilized previously stable discourses about the meanings of Bolivianness, Indianness, integration, state responsibilities, and citizens' rights. In working to define themselves against the backdrop of school ideology, the subjects of this study engage questions that go far beyond their personal identities.

At the time of this writing, Bolivia is in the initial stages of a comprehensive, nationwide educational reform, which seeks to transform the relations between teachers, students, and the state, as well as the way that national, regional, and local cultures are treated and transmitted in schools. The reform, while inspiring hope among many that the school may emerge as the new champion of indigenous culture—after centuries of serving as an agent of cultural imperialism and homogenization—has also provoked a new crisis (or perhaps simply redrawn the battle lines of the existing crisis). The teachers' union has declared its firm opposition, fearing both the gradual privatization of schooling and the loss of its own political power. While many teachers privately dissent from the union's hardline position, any reform that is opposed by the most vocal and active wing of organized teachers will be difficult, if not impossible, to implement.

But like any crisis, this one indicates a widening both of the cracks in the national hegemony and of the possibilities for transformation. What remains clear is that neither privatization, decentralization, universal bilingual education, nor traditionally conceived socialist revolution will be sufficient to bring about "*la educación íntegra y liberadora*" espoused by Bolivian educators from all along the political spectrum. What is required is nothing less than a reconception and reapplication of the relationship between theory and practice in schooling.

> In order to decide on what to do, educators have got to figure out why things are the way they are, how they got that way, and what conditions are supporting them. . . . We are not interested here in chronology but rather in an understanding of how specific educational practices can be understood as historical constructions related to economic, social, and political events in a particular space and time. This is absolutely essential in order to be able to think about how specific instances of schooling and curriculum theory may represent one form among the many possible. (Giroux 1988:132)

Analyzing "the way things are" in Bolivian teacher education—how certain conceptions of teachers and teaching arise, what conditions maintain these concepts, how educational practices affect students, and how students resist these practices and their effects—is, on one level, what the present work is about. On another level, it is about questions of identity in modern nation-states, the school's role in the reproduction of the social order, subjects' resistance to that order, and the uses of language for both reproductive and resistant ends.

1

ETHNICITY AND THE CONSTRUCTION OF NATIONHOOD

To say "this combination of words makes no sense" excludes it from the sphere of language and thereby bounds the domain of language. But when one draws a boundary, it may be for various kinds of reasons. If I surround an area with a fence or a line or otherwise, the purpose may be to prevent someone from getting in or out; but it may also be part of a game and the players be supposed, say, to jump over the boundary; or it may show where the property of one man ends and that of another begins. So, if I draw a boundary line, that is not yet to say what I am drawing it for.

—Ludwig Wittgenstein

From Conquest to Crisis: An Overview of Bolivia's Political Development

Bolivia is the most "indigenous" country in South America. Though ethnic boundaries are increasingly fuzzy, the population remains, by most accounts, nearly two-thirds indigenous. Of a national population of 6.4 million, one-third are Quechua and one-fourth are Aymara (Diez Astete 1995:31), while the eastern lowlands contain some thirty other indigenous groups.[1] Spanish has been the official language since colonial times, but the majority of Bolivians did not speak it until the latter half of this century. The Aymara and Quechua communities of the western highlands (*altiplano*) and central valley regions have endured more successfully than the eastern tribal groups, whose numbers and cultural cohesiveness are much more precarious

1

(with the exception of the Guaraní, who number approximately 50,000 in Bolivia and are renowned for their level of political organization).

If we imagine New World indigenous populations along a continuum—from small, relatively isolated tribes to those constituting large, more or less integrated sectors of the nation-state—the highland Andean peoples fall nearer the latter end of this continuum than perhaps any other group (Urban and Sherzer 1991:5). Though far from being the "dominant group" politically, indigenous people dominate Bolivia's cultural landscape, urban as well as rural, by sheer force of numbers and the cohesion of a distinctive complex of cultural traits. Questions of indigenous identity and cultural legitimacy arise in debates over virtually every aspect of national policy. Furthermore, the discourse of indigenous rights is inevitably, if uneasily, yoked to the discourse of class conflict, which seethes constantly here in the poorest of all Latin American countries.

Bolivia's political history has always been complex, and at times chaotic. The Spanish Conquest was disastrous for the Andean civilizations, as it was throughout the Americas; highland populations fared somewhat better than others, by virtue of their numbers, inaccessibility, and level of organization. During the colonial period, the indigenous population was decimated by disease and slavery; tens of thousands died in the immense silver mine of Potosí alone. Indigenous social organization was severely disrupted, but not destroyed; in fact, it remained strong enough to stage a series of rebellions that at times seriously threatened Spanish rule. These reached their peak between 1778 and 1781, at which point 80,000 Indians were massacred in retaliation (Barton 1968:143); nevertheless, uprisings continued sporadically for decades thereafter.

In 1825, the revolution led by Simón Bolívar won independence from Spain but did little to improve the lot of the indigenous majority. Political life was characterized by a series of coups in the capital and continuing Indian rebellions in the countryside. Economically, the country depended on exports of metals, mainly silver and tin. By the early twentieth century, Bolivian mining was dominated by three families, collectively known as La Rosca, who effectively dominated political life as well. The majority continued to live in conditions of serfhood until the 1952 revolution led by the Movimiento Revolucionario Nacionalista (MNR). Though many argue that its true intent was simply another bourgeois takeover of the state apparatus, the coup catalyzed a groundswell of popular discontent and turned into a mass insurrection, with ramifications far beyond what its upper- and middle-class "leaders" probably had in mind.

One of the most significant changes was abolishing the literacy requirement for suffrage; "In one stroke, the Indian peasant masses were enfranchised, and the voting population jumped from some 200,000 to just under 1 million" (Klein 1982:232). The MNR also nationalized the mines, extended rural education, and introduced the country's first real land reform. This transferred land to the peasants, but also outlawed communal ownership, thus abetting in the disarticulation of indigenous land tenure systems and speeding the dissolution of many rural communities. Many Indians were granted small plots which, divided among subsequent generations, could not support an agricultural subsistence. The resulting land crisis has been a major cause of urban migration.

The shared excitement with which workers, peasants, and the middle class rushed to exercise their newfound political power temporarily concealed the deep social divisions in the revolutionary coalition. The limits of the MNR's revolutionary ideals soon became evident, as conservative party elements grew increasingly reluctant before the growing demands of the working class. No other mines were nationalized after those of La Rosca. By 1960, ten U.S. oil companies were operating in Bolivia and the government had resumed payments on defaulted loans from the 1920s, which the Roosevelt administration had itself declared fraudulent in 1943 (Klein 1982:240). The MNR, well aware of the U.S. response to Arbenz's radical reforms in Guatemala, was anxious to avoid the label of communist-inspired regime (Klein 1982:233). In return, the United States was mildly supportive, mistaking the MNR for a fascist Peronista-type party. But tepid U.S. support could not sustain the MNR against an impatient working class; the coalition's various factions grew increasingly hostile, until compromise was exhausted. The weakened government was ousted by a military coup in 1964, giving way to a series of military dictatorships characterized by frequent state violence and repression of dissent, lasting until 1982. Since then, Bolivia has enjoyed an unprecedented period of, if not democracy in the full sense of the word, at least the orderly transfer of power.[2]

During the research period, the country was governed by the "Acuerdo Patriótico" (AP), one of the more striking examples of "strange bedfellows" in recent Latin American politics. A principal member of this coalition was the Acción Democrática Nacionalista, the rightist political machine of General Hugo Banzer Suárez. Banzer previously ruled as dictator, seizing power via a military coup in 1971 and effectively suppressing dissent (with support from the United States) until ousted by another coup in 1978. The other major partner was the Movimiento Izquierdista Revolucionaria, led by Jaime Paz Zamora, who was president during the AP administration, despite having been imprisoned under Banzer's earlier regime. Founded in 1971 by a group of young Marxist intellectuals as an alternative to the hidebound syndicalism of the traditional leftist parties, the MIR later shiftly sharply to the right, eventually embracing the U.S.-blessed neoliberalism whose implementation has provoked heated debate at all levels of society.

The most prominent member of the opposition, and subsequent victor of the 1993 elections, was the MNR. Current president Gonzalo (Goni) Sánchez de Lozada[3] is a U.S.-educated millionaire whose formative years left him with such a marked English accent that he has acquired the nickname *el gringo.* Sánchez de Lozada's vice-president, apparently picked to offset the former's foreign image, is Aymara intellectual and former university professor Victor Hugo Cárdenas, heralded in the press as Bolivia's first indigenous vice-president (*NMH* November 25, 1992).[4]

While the election of an Aymara politician to such a prominent post is certainly a first, the 1993 election was notable for the strong presence of other candidates with indigenous ties. Among these were Max Fernández, a millionaire of humble Quechua origins, and Carlos Palenque, a charismatic musician and radio and television personality turned spokesman for La Paz's Aymara immigrant population.[5] Perhaps unsurprisingly, indigenous-identified politicians seem to enjoy their greatest popularity when not actually in power. In the wake of the MNR's unpopular policies, public opinion is as likely to paint vice-president Cárdenas as an ethnic token or political sell-out, as it is to laud him as a champion of the Aymara people. Nevertheless, the emergence of Aymara and Quechua leaders in the center of national politics suggests a trend that will not be turned back.

The programs and posturings of the major parties by no means exhaust the full range of Bolivian political life. Many smaller parties either form coalitions with the more powerful or eschew electoral politics altogether in favor of other types of action. Some have an explicitly pro-indigenous platform, though their success at mobilizing the indigenous masses has been limited. Much of Bolivia's urban working class and an even greater proportion of the peasantry have withdrawn from most political activity, disillusioned by continued poverty and corruption and skeptical of the ability or sincerity of elected officials; the ethnic solidarity inspired by indigenous politicians may abet that skepticism somewhat, but has by no means dissipated it entirely.

Yet while one source claims that 80 percent of the work force belong to no organized party,[6] it can be argued that, overall, Bolivians are politically involved to a degree rarely seen in North America. Voting (which is mandatory) may be one of the *least* important expressions of this involvement, which covers a wide range of activities (considerably restricted during past periods of government repression). Pressure tactics such as labor strikes, hunger strikes, and mass demonstrations are used frequently, though with less success under the current administration than previously. In turn, the MNR government hopes to incorporate popular political sentiment under an ambitious plan of "popular participation" that would organize citizen political activity at the community level.

The most significant entity representing "the masses" and providing structure to their discontent is the Central Obrera Boliviana, a nationwide coalition of labor unions, peasant federations, and other popular organizations. In terms of political power and institutional longevity, the COB is unequaled in Latin America (Dunkerly 1984:43). Born of the currents unleashed during the 1952 revolution, its strength has waxed and waned over the decades; at times it held virtual veto power over the government's actions, while during other periods its leaders were forced into exile as the political space for dissent clamped shut. Though traditionally nonpartisan (the leadership shifts among coalitions of militants from various parties), the COB maintains a generally socialist orientation, serving as the watchdog of proletarian interests. The various and often hostile factions of the left seem to agree that, while far from perfect, the COB is the highest and most durable achievement of Bolivian working-class power to date. Nevertheless, both its power and its credibility have been severely weakened by the economic and labor policies of the last decade (Davila 1991) and will likely decline even further if the privatization of state enterprises continues.

During the research period, Bolivia experienced a minor resurgence of armed revolutionary groups whose activities included sabotage and other acts usually characterized as "terrorism." The most active of these was the Ejército Guerrillero Tupac Katari,[7] whose political orientation was not so much communist as strictly *indigenista*, their fundamental demand being the return of the land to Bolivia's indigenous "nations." Though causing considerable alarm to Bolivian authorities, the EGTK was not nearly as large, well-organized, or single-mindedly violent as neighboring Peru's Sendero Luminoso; its members generally limited their attacks to infrastructure, rather than people, and in fact gained a reputation for being less than competent as terrorists (their first major action, against an electrical tower in Uyuni, cost the lives of two members through mishandling of explosives).[8]

No political overview of Bolivia would be complete without mention of coca and its derivative, cocaine. While cocaine use certainly exists in Bolivia, it is less common than in the United States (Bolivia's worst drug problem is unquestionably alcohol abuse). Furthermore, the city of La Paz is not a major drug trafficking center, certainly not in comparison to the burgeoning eastern city of Santa Cruz. However, La Paz is where political pressure from the United States is brought to bear upon the state decision-making apparatus, and this makes it an important battlefield in the cocaine wars.

Coca's role in Bolivian culture runs far deeper than the traffic of cocaine. Used by indigenous people for millenia, the leaf when chewed is a mild stimulant that provides temporary relief from hunger, cold, and fatigue. The benefits to a impoverished population that lives by arduous manual labor in a cold and rigorous environment are obvious. Beyond this, shared consumption of coca is an important element in many social and ritual gatherings and is central to Andean religion. Far from having been superseded by Christianity, this religion retains great significance for millions of Aymara and Quechua people, often existing in syncretized form along with Catholicism.

Coca is equally central to the Bolivian economy. The money it brings in (estimates range from $400 to 600 million a year) is close to that of all other exports combined (Andreas 1991). The coca industry employs 75,000 families and has led to the creation of another 175,000 jobs in other areas. Between 1980 and 1986, while the official unemployment rate rose to 25 percent, employment in the coca industry tripled. Clearly, coca is the buoy keeping a sinking economy afloat. The social upheaval that would be unleashed should its eradication become a reality (admittedly an unlikely prospect) can only be imagined. Yet, in an impressive display of political myopia, those touting the New Economic Plan (NEP) as the shock treatment for Bolivia's stagnation consistently leave coca out of their calculations; when asked how the International Monetary Fund was addressing the links between poverty and the drug trade, an IMF spokesman replied "We haven't looked at poverty in Latin America in this context" (Andreas 1991:15).

From another point of view, however, it would seem that this "quintessential expression of the market-driven enterprise" (Andreas 1991:15) does in fact play a role in economic policy. While a far cry from the "cocaine dictatorships" of the early eighties, when government involvement in the drug trade was pervasive and blatant, measures instituted by recent administrations—weaker disclosure requirements for the central bank, a tax amnesty for repatriated capital, and the prohibition of inquiries into the origins of all wealth entering Bolivia and of bank deposits made in dollars (this last was later rescinded)— indicate that government too knows on which side its bread is buttered.[9]

Nevertheless, the political exigencies of the Washington-imposed "war on drugs" generate a certain amount of aggressive and conspicuous action against the coca trade, including media campaigns of the "just say no" variety, half-hearted crop substitution programs, occasional military attacks on small-scale producers, and repression of the coca-growers' union. Law enforcement's abuses of peasants and other citizens, as well as Washington's demands for the extradition of drug traffickers, generate a good deal of resentment against the United States and have led virtually all parties of the left to adopt the free cultivation of coca ("for traditional uses") as a political plank, at the same time that they accuse their opponents of involvement in drug trafficking.

While the above sketch may suggest a nation barely held together at the seams, Bolivians have had plenty of practice in coping with such circumstances. In an urban atmosphere where marches, strikes, and tear gas are routine, even a national state of siege (such as the one that lasted through most of 1995) disrupts most people's lives only to a limited degree, though it may have extreme consequences for a small minority. Though wracked by severe difficulties and a disparity between rich and poor that would be shocking had such injustices not become commonplace, Bolivia is much less violently conflictive now than during the greater part of its history. Until the 1980s, coups were more common than elections and the country had had more governments than years of independence. The unprecedented decade of relative domestic peace (stressing the word *relative*) has permitted a new openness in political activity and broadened the spectrum of public debate. But while not in a period of such obviously convulsive change as a coup or a civil war, the economic, political, and social transformations being wrought in Bolivia are, arguably, just as revolutionary.

The central conflict that has divided Bolivia throughout most of its history derives from the schism between the poor indigenous majority and the elite *criollo* minority (with the small, mostly *mestizo* middle class aligning itself with one or the other as the situation warrants). Of course, this is a vastly simplified picture of a dynamic historical process involving shifting allegiances among the military, the peasantry, the urban proletariat, the business elite, and the burgeoning informal and service sectors. The most recent cluster of political crises springs from the government's shift toward neoliberalism and away from the country's long-term (though frequently interrupted) orientation toward more generally socialist goals. While many of the regimes of the last few decades were far from "socialist," they seldom threatened the economic changes implemented after 1952, such as the land reform and state control of the primary productive and service sectors.

In contrast, president Sánchez de Lozada has a technocratic approach to government (he is also credited with designing the plan that stemmed Bolivia's runaway inflation in the mid-1980s). Unsurprisingly, given his many years of study in the United States, he strongly supports the neoliberal model and bases his highly publicized "Plan de Todos" on a three-pronged approach: educational reform, "popular participation" (via government-organized citizens' groups), and "capitalization"—viewed by many as a euphemism for the surrender of Bolivia's economic base to foreign interests. While many Latin American nations are undergoing economic restructuring to meet foreign debt obligations, that restructuring has been even more profound in Bolivia. Sixty percent of Bolivia's dwindling exports go toward servicing the debt; with an annual per capita income of $288 (U.S.), Bolivia's debt amounts to $552 per capita.[10] The World Bank and the IMF have imposed stringent belt-tightening measures, pressuring Bolivia to streamline or sell off state-run enterprises, often at bargain-basement prices. The first sign of a major shift in direction came with the decision to privatize the mines—Bolivia's greatest source of legitimate revenue—after laying off close to 20,000 miners (this massive dismissal was officialy dubbed the *relocalización*, but in fact miners were not "relocalized" anywhere).[11] The miners' union, for decades the backbone of the Bolivian labor movement, today finds itself in severely weakened condition, with thousands of miners out of work, thousands more working in small cooperatives, and much of its political clout neutralized.

While many areas of the economy have suffered cutbacks (with the notable exception of the military), the mines provoke especially strong reactions. Aside from being the cornerstone of the legitimate economy, their nationalization was one of the centrally symbolic acts of the revolution; its reversal is practically unthinkable to many. Popular reaction to the continued privatization of other state enterprises has been intense and volatile. Not only is the working class alarmed at seeing the gains of the revolution melt away, there is also public outrage at what is seen as the surrender of national sovereignty to U.S. and multinational interests. Every step the government takes toward the neoliberal horizon provokes a new wave of public protest, but implementation of the NEP continues, albeit haltingly and with much resistance. The NEP's impact extends to the educational system as well; the direct effect this will have on the majority of the population, combined with the decline of the miners, has brought teachers to the fore as the most visible and combative sector confronting the government. Dominated by the Trotskyite Partido Obrero Revolucionario (POR), the teachers' union attempts to channel the tide of popular discontent toward the long-term goal of socialist revolution, with only limited success.

The global decline of socialism has provoked a crisis of another sort in some sectors of the working class. The traditional parties of the left find themselves swimming against the tide of world politics; even those who never supported a Soviet-style model have suffered the ideological fallout of events in eastern Europe, Nicaragua, and Cuba. The POR marches doggedly onward, attributing the Soviet collapse to the failure of Stalinism, not socialism, and characterizing the current era as "the crisis of capitalism." While such a claim may indicate more bravado than discernment, Bolivia's beleaguered and demoralized working class is clearly not ready to give up the ghost. On the contrary, as the crisis deepens, more fundamental questions of nationalism, ethnic identity, government responsibility, and class interests are drawn into the debate.

The Indigenous Metropolis: Urban Aymaras in La Paz

La Paz, Bolivia's capital, contains one-fifth of the country's population (INE 1992) and a similar fraction of the continent's Aymara speakers; one-half of its population is Aymara (Albó 1988:30). La Paz has a uniquely Indian-urban flavor, its meld of occidental and indigenous traits due to the thousands of rural immigrants from the surrounding *altiplano*. The "two faces of La Paz"—*criollo* and Aymara—are notable in the contrast between "inside" and "outside." Indigenous faces, dress, food, and language are ubiquitous on the street, but rarely pass the doors of expensive shops, restaurants, or hotels, where *de facto* segregation still reigns. Descending the steep cobblestone streets to the wider thoroughfare of the *prado*, one moves through a cultural scene busy with street vendors and the crush of passersby, as well as the numerous beggars and homeless, many of them immigrants who fled rural poverty only to confront an equally harsh reality in the city.

In La Paz, one seldom needs to enter a store; nearly everything one could want, from food and clothes to handicrafts and small appliances, is available from street vendors, many of them Aymara women wearing the characteristic multi-layered skirt (*pollera*) and bowler hat. Stooped *aparapitas* (porters) wearing the rural *lluch'u* (knitted cap) and *wisk"u* (sandals) maneuver impossibly bulky loads through the crowds; even on middle-class men, the *lluch'u* can often be glimpsed under the popular western fedora. Only upon entering an upper-class shopping mall or office building does one realize that Hispanic language and culture still hold exclusive sway in La Paz's formal sector. In the buildings where the city's business is done, the indigenous ambience gives way to a thoroughly hispanicized atmosphere. The powerful racism that still exists in Bolivia reveals itself when the two sectors are brought into contact; many establishments are off limits to women wearing the *pollera*, and one of the most difficult and humiliating experiences for a monolingual Aymara speaker is trying to get waited upon in one of the city's many government offices.[12]

Though most Aymaras are peasants (and in the *altiplano* virtually all peasants are indigenous), they are also an urban people and have been for generations (Albó 1990). In the familiar Third World pattern, urban migration increases with each passing year. In 1950, one-third of those living in the department of La Paz were urban dwellers; by 1992, that proportion had nearly doubled (INE 1992). The largest concentration of Aymara speakers is La Paz's sister city, El Alto, a rural-urban border zone where adobe is interspersed with brick and tin housing. As the principal point of arrival for rural migrants, El Alto grew from just under 100,000 inhabitants to over 400,000 between 1976 and 1992 (INE 1992). By 1988 it was the fourth largest urban center in Bolivia (after Santa Cruz, La Paz, and Cochabamba) and was officially declared a separate city. In character it is more Aymara, more working-class, more closely connected to the surrounding rural communities, and more removed from metropolitan cultural pursuits than is "La Paz proper" and is home to much of the light industry and cheap labor on which the latter depends.

Social scientists only recently have turned their attention toward this vital urban expression of Andean culture. Archondo (1991:23), in one of the few book-length treatments of the urban Aymara, notes that "when one looks for studies about things Andean, one finds that the majority have chosen rural or agricultural settings as their point of observation . . . Investigation of the urban environment of Andean migrants has yet to spark great interest."[13] In the *altiplano*, links between city and country are vital to the economic survival of both. One might consider urban-rural ties a modern extension of the Andean "archipelago" subsistence strategy described by Murra (1972), in which ecological niches at different altitudes are exploited in complementary fashion; the city can be considered yet another "level" of economic niches and resources.[14] Due to the importance of the urban-rural interchange, Aymara cultural patterns have melded with urban influences to form a unique way of life that in many ways still manifests the cultural and economic logic of more traditional highland communities (Albó 1988, 1990; Archondo 1991; Farthing 1991). As Muñoz (forthcoming) has noted, conceptions of migration as a "modernizing" force have had to be revised or discarded. Correspondingly, in addition to the growing penetration of Aymara culture by urban influences, migration has also given rise to a powerful indigenous cultural presence in the very heart of the metropolis.

Popular Culture and "The Language Problem"

The popular culture of urban La Paz spans a continuum from exclusively western-oriented to traditionally Aymara, with many combined and syncretized forms in between. Many upper- and middle-class Bolivians, especially youth, take their cue from the United States for fashion, music, and leisure pursuits. Children's products display images of Ninja Turtles and Power Rangers, and video jockeys on the Latin American version of MTV drop English phrases ("Hey, what's up?" "That's right!") into their between-song patter. Madonna and Michael Jackson are popular radio fare, and movie marquees advertise the latest films of Arnold Schwarzenegger and Kevin Costner. Nevertheless, there is a thriving folkloric music scene, and Aymara and bilingual radio stations are nearly as common as Spanish ones. La Paz's biggest festival is the Dia de Nuestro Señor de Gran Poder, which attracts thousands of spectators with a parade through the historically Aymara neighborhoods; many of the 80,000 dancers and musicians are Aymara, either native *paceños* or rural immigrants.[15] Another event produced by and for the popular sectors is the annual Cholita Paceña contest sponsored by Carlos Palenque's Canal 4—a sort of beauty contest for the *de pollera* set, but focusing more on personality, eloquence, and skills such as dancing and singing than on physical attractiveness. Just as noteworthy is the cultural production of indigenous and *indigenista* intellectuals. Prominent among these is film director Jorge Sanjinés, whose considerable output (most of it combining Aymara and Spanish language) dominates modern Bolivian film, focusing on themes of Aymara identity, *mestizo* and Yankee exploitation, and urban-rural linkages. In music, indigenous elements appear in the repertoires of formally trained jazz and classical composers. There is also a growing body of scholarship by Aymara social scientists (including vice-president Cárdenas), and as Aymara linguistics continues to advance, occasional Aymara newspapers such as Juan de Dios Yapita's *Yatiñasawa* and Felix Laime's *Jayma* have appeared on the scene. There are plans to initiate an all-Aymara television station by the year 2000.

The emergence of Aymara in the mass media reflects a broader change in language attitudes. Disdained as a mark of low status since colonial times, Aymara is now enjoying a revitalization; rather than denying knowledge of the language for fear of being socially stigmatized, many now express pride in being able to speak it. Organizations such as ILCA (Instituto de Lengua y Cultura Aymara) and THOA (Taller de Historia Oral Andina) pursue original linguistic and anthropological research under the direction of native Aymara speakers. Still, Spanish remains dominant in the upper levels of society. English, though rarely used in everyday communication, has even greater prestige; studying English is a popular pursuit among those who can afford it, and even in rural areas, schoolchildren bombard visiting foreigners with requests to teach them a few words. At present, the languages taught in public schools are more often English and French than Aymara or Quechua, though results are meager; teachers are seldom fluent themselves, and most students never get to use the little they learn.[16] Previously, bilingual education programs targeted only those students whose lack of Spanish fluency made them a necessity; but bilingual/intercultural education is a cornerstone of the current educational reform, which aims to halt the decline in indigenous language fluency in the younger generations and raise Aymara, Quechua, and Guaraní to the status of truly "official" languages. If this plan is maintained throughout the coming years, Bolivia should see significant changes both in language demographics and in language attitudes.

While "the language problem" has been identified by Bolivian policy makers as a crucial obstacle to national unity, and presents many pragmatic problems in terms both of pedagogy and of public policy, it has also served as a foil for ethnic rivalries and ideological debates that run deeper than linguistic difference. As Clifford Geertz argued, "The 'language problem' is only the 'nationality problem' writ small, though in some places the conflicts arising from it are intense enough to make the relationship seem reversed. Generalized, the 'who are we' question asks what cultural forms—what systems of meaningful symbols—to employ to give value and significance to the activities of the state, and by extension to the civil life of its citizens" (1973a:242).

In a sense, language is only one among numerous symbolic systems that vie for advantage in the public arenas of cultural production. But language is qualitatively different from other systems in the unique way that it structures both personal and group identity. Of those traits that provide a basis for communal relationship, a shared language creates the strongest bond among people who feel that they "belong together." "Common language and the ritual regulation of life . . . everywhere are conducive to feelings of ethnic affinity, especially since the intelligibility of the behavior of others is the most fundamental presupposition of group formation" (Weber 1978:389). The social gulf between Aymara speakers and Spanish monolinguals is partly due to the fact that they do not find each other's behavior intelligible; they lack the mutual understanding, the joint interpretation of interactive cues and contextual knowledge, that people who share a language and culture enjoy.

Furthermore, the high awareness of linguistic conflict makes it a likely point of attack in a wide range of social situations. Individuals are frequently ridiculed for their speech when it is their politics, social position, or cultural behavior that is "really" at issue. But as the epigraph that began this chapter suggests, virtually every time Spanish or Aymara is used in La Paz, a subtle but significant territorial claim is made: to the right to use the prestige language, although imperfectly; to the right to use the indigenous language in a public space, though it may offend some ears; to reinforce the boundaries of Spanish and deny the legitimacy of indigenous languages by refusing the latter a response in "official" domains. All of these situations and many others remind speakers on a daily basis that "for any speaker of it, a given language is at once either more or less his own or more or less someone else's, and either more or less cosmopolitan or more or less parochial—a borrowing or a heritage; a passport or a citadel" (Geertz 1973a:241).

Language is also the medium in which social categories and identities are defined. As such, it plays a unique role in the incessant "war of position" over what constitutes both the national interest and the national character. At stake is "not just the replacement of one language by another, but the taking over of both the public and the personal functions of language . . . the means of communication and the consciousness behind this communication, including self-concepts, identities, and voices" (Walsh 1991:43). In this sense, the pressure to adopt Spanish is crucial to the identity formation of indigenous peoples and to the construction of a collective national subject.

In mapping the respective positions and strategies of "Aymara culture" and "occidental culture" (taking these as two essentialized extremes that in reality flank a wide range of syncretized forms), it is useful to draw upon two abstractions often employed in nationalist debates: the "Indigenous Way of Life" and the "Spirit of the Age." Geertz (1973a:240) saw the problem of defining the collective national subject as revolving around the "content, relative weight, and proper relationship" of these two abstractions, one stressing local traditions, practices and institutions, the other oriented toward a more global history and direction. He designated these two perspectives "essentialist" and "epochalist," claiming that national language debates hinge on the tension between them. More than an intellectual rivalry between differering philosophies, this tension is a struggle between opposed social institutions and the human groups that control them (252).

In Bolivia, the essentialist/epochalist schism can also be read as a dynamic between "inward-oriented" and "outward-oriented" perspectives. The first is typified by the valorization of traditional cultural forms, such as indigenous languages, food, music, rituals, and other aspects of rural life; it finds its fullest expression in indigenous revitalization movements and the intense patriotism that is so marked in Bolivia. The outward orientation focuses on an external cultural ideal (usually the United States), assigning much greater prestige to foreign and/or urban products, languages, and lifestyles than to local ones; this view is often expressed in racist practices or the derogation of Indians and indigenous culture.[17] Language attitudes are thus one facet of a broader struggle in which *lo propio* and *lo ajeno* (the native and the foreign) are set in opposition to each other and constantly compared.

The cultural production and consumption characteristic of the inward orientation is likely to be considered "vulgar" relative to that of the outward orientation. The charge of vulgarity also appears frequently in attacks that are at their heart political, such as middle-class criticisms of political leaders whose constituency is indigenous or working-class.[18] The outward orientation is stronger as one moves up the class hierarchy; in this sense the two orientations roughly correspond to two "class cultures" (though this simplified view overlooks, for the moment, the significant divisions within classes, as well as the presence of contradictory elements within any one group's cultural repertoire). Each orientation is linked to macro-level phenomena that belie a more direct class interest; inward-oriented sectors generally oppose the political and economic trends favored by the outward-oriented, and vice versa. Still, the correspondence between class position and cultural orientation is far from complete, most notably in the adherence of working-class youth to outward-oriented cultural products. Personal economic strategies also play a part, as when ethnically indigenous, working-class individuals adopt an outward orientation for reasons of social mobility.

In addition to those cultural practices expressing one or the other orientation, there are second-order phenomena that can be read as reactions *against* each of them. For example, Farthing (1991) notes that the decline in the power of the urban proletariat (an indicator of an increasingly outward orientation) has led many Bolivians to turn back to the family as the principal economic unit, rejecting traditional union structures in favor of community-based organizations. Similarly, government attempts to eradicate coca, which can be read as an attack against inward-oriented religion and culture (at the behest of outside actors such as the United States), have spurred the revalorization of coca by opposition political parties. Another example would be the intense popular protest sparked by the (outward-oriented) privatization of state enterprises. One indicator that the New Economic Plan is popularly viewed in terms of outward vs. inward loyalties is the use of the term *vendepatria*— one who sells his own country to outsiders—as the archetypal political insult.

Reactions against the inward orientation tend to be more subtle and indirect, perhaps because few Bolivians are willing to state explicitly their cultural preference for the foreign. Such biases are often expressed in jokes that ridicule either indigenous culture itself—as in the extensive genre of "stupid peasant in the big city" jokes, which mock indigenous culture and people as inadequate to the demands of modern life—or the ideological stance of valorizing that culture. The following example of multilevel humor derides the inward-orientated stance *per se*:

> Jaime Paz, George Bush, and Mikhail Gorbachev schedule a top-secret meeting to be held in an airborne jet, to ensure maximum security. The meeting is in progress when the motor fails and the plane begins to descend rapidly. Bush, unruffled, says "Well, mine is a highly developed country and we have the technology to deal with any situation, so I'm not worried." He leaps from the plane and presses a button on his pen, which opens into a parachute and floats him safely to the ground. Gorbachev then says, "Well, my country also has a highly developed technology; maybe the economy is in crisis, maybe perestroika isn't working, but I too am unafraid." He jumps from the plane and pulls out a pocket calculator, which at the touch of a button opens up into a parachute, and floats safely to the ground. Paz then says, "My country has its own technology, handed down from our ancestors, which has served our people for thousands of years, so I'm not worried." He jumps from the plane and plummets to the ground like a stone. Bush and Gorbachev find his broken body with its fist tightly clenched around an object; upon prying it open, they find a little tin that reads "*MENTISAN—alivia todo: para resfríos, para quemaduras, para caídas . . .* "[19]

Appreciating this joke requires a familiarity with the product Mentisan, a petroleum jelly whose TV commercials state proudly and prominently that it is a product of *la industria boliviana*. The familiar green tin—which formerly carried a slogan like the one in the joke—is such a staple of the Bolivian household pharmacy that it can perhaps be considered the archetype of Bolivian small industry. It appears here as a foil for the "traditional science and technology of our ancestors" extolled by *indigenistas* and other inward-oriented types who are indirectly ridiculed in the joke.

More than simply a humorous jab at those of an opposing political philosophy, this joke is a rhetorical gambit in the promotion of a supposedly superior cultural strategy (the joke itself leaves little doubt as to which strategy has greater survival value). It serves as a metaphorical device in the service of a particular nationalist ideology. Further uses of popular humor to strengthen or subvert various nationalist discourses are explored below; but first, let us explore the origins of these discourses and the obstacles faced by those who pronounce them.

Obstacles to the Construction of a Unified and Unifying Bolivian Nationalism

Since the 1952 revolution, a major government concern has been how to forge a unified nation from a diverse melange of frequently antagonistic social groups. Bolivia is not well consolidated as a nation, and many see this as a primary cause of its underdevelopment. Some of its most characteristic features are also its most formidable obstacles to "national unity": linguistic diversity, a conflictive past, the persistence of indigenous cultures, a strong working-class consciousness, sharp social inequities, and marked regional differences. These features define *lo boliviano* for many, but also tend to pull any notion of a unifed "Bolivian society" away from a common center.

The notion of "Bolivian society" is itself problematic, given the formidable social barriers separating different sectors. Certainly, all societies display internal contradictions and antagonisms. But even defining "society" broadly—as a self-reproducing, socially bounded sphere whose members see themselves as parts of an entity which far exceeds the lifespan of any individual, yet provides an underpinning of continuity connecting them all—it is doubtful whether Bolivia can be considered a single society. For many rural dwellers, the idea of the nation is still a very marginal reality. Even those living in the geographic and semiotic heart of urban life do not all "think" the nation in the same way. They may share a belief in its existence and yet have very distinct conceptions of its history, its goals, its social cleavages, its achievements and frustrations. In other words, while the idea of "the nation" is generally accepted, even taken for granted, its specific ideological content varies widely. The notion of "Bolivian society" should be critically viewed as a fantasy that is collective but not unanimous, a discursive and ideological fabrication whose purpose is to make itself "real" in the private and shared imaginations of those whom it aspires to embrace.

In a sense, ideologically constructing Bolivian society is less complex than constructing "the Bolivian nation." Defining the precise contents of a society is not as crucial to its conceptual reality as is merely promoting the assertion that it exists (ideally, to the degree that this assertion becomes automatic); the more the notion of "Bolivian society" circulates unquestioned through the orbit of public discourse, the more "real" it becomes. But in the construction of nationhood, ideological and political differences are critical. The nationalist project is one of articulating the ways different groups "think" the nation, of creating and circulating a unified and unifying nationalist discourse around that conception of the nation promoted by the dominant social sector(s).[20] A look at the discourses and practices that express dominant as well as oppositional interests will reveal how the current vision of the nation has evolved, the major schisms that divide it, and the ways in which alternative and oppositional discourses are suppressed or incorporated (though never completely).

The forging of a nation in the popular consciousness of those who comprise it is a hegemonic project whose vulnerability to contestation varies according to specific social and historical factors. In Bolivia, three major fault lines cut across attempts to establish the nation as the most salient entity with claims on subjects' loyalty and identity. These are region, ethnicity, and class.

Bolivia's nine departments are intersected by deep cultural, economic, and political divisions, expressed in individuals' strong identification with their own department and frequent rivalry toward others. While this rivalry is often good-natured, it can also be overtly hostile; personal defects or social conflicts are often ascribed to one's opponents' place of origin. Given the different regions' geographic and cultural diversity, the difficulty of travel between them, and the incipient state of the national media, the scarcity of cultural symbols to represent them all or evoke feelings of identification as "Bolivians" (rather than as *paceños, cruceños,* etc.) is not surprising.

In addition, there are few public rituals that effectively reinforce a sense of nationwide belonging.[21] National holidays contribute to the fortification of patriotic feeling; yet the nationalist emphasis of Bolivian Independence Day is offset by the fact that each department has its own patriotic anniversary, celebrated with nearly equal fervor. Such ceremonies highlight regional divisions at the same time that they intensify nationalist feeling. Other major holidays either lack any specifically nationalist content (like Christmas or Mothers' Day), or trigger sentiments that run counter to an ideology of national unity (such as Día de la Raza or Día de los Trabajadores).[22]

Even more salient than departmental boundaries is the distinction between *cambas*—the fair-skinned, Spanish-speaking inhabitants of the eastern lowlands—and *kollas*, the indigenous and *mestizo* inhabitants of the western *altiplano* and intermontaine valleys. These categories perhaps come closest to Weber's notion of a generalized "communal relationship," based on "a subjective feeling of the parties, whether affectual or traditional, that they belong together" (Weber 1978:40). One might say that members of each group share a "primordial attachment," stemming from the "givens" of social existence, such as kin, religion, and cultural practices (Geertz 1973b:259).[23] Though the *camba/kolla* distinction is primarily regional, it refers to ethnicity as well, as is clear from the discrimination suffered by *kolla* migrants to the eastern city of Santa Cruz.

A complete study of ethnicity in Bolivia would also include the many lowland tribes that still retain distinct cultural identities, the Afro-Bolivians of the Yungas region, and more recent immigrant populations such as German Mennonite, Japanese, and Korean. Nevertheless, Bolivia's most fundamental ethnic division is the tripartite one between *indios/campesinos, mestizos*, and *blancos/criollos*.[24] These categories are more permeable than one might expect; individuals may be assigned to one or the other as much on the basis of speech, dress, and other elements of personal style as by actual descent or phenotype (see Luykx 1989a). Although "ethnicity" is often quite fluid and situational (Eriksen 1993:20), the perception of ethnic categories as clear-cut and easily definable is important in an ideological sense (Tambiah 1989:335). In popular discourse, ethnic labels tend to be reified as static categories, usually in opposition to the speaker's identity.

The social distance between *blancos* and *indios* may be the most formidable obstacle to fostering a communal sentiment inclusive of all Bolivians. Racism is manifest in many public and private contexts, from personal interactions to macro-level political and economic discrimination. At the same time, many Bolivians invest their connection to an indigenous tradition with a high degree of loyalty and identification. The term *indio* usually refers to the Aymaras and Quechuas; *indigena* more often refers to the smaller lowland tribes, many of whom see their relation to the state as more or less antagonistic (for those whose reduced numbers put them at risk of cultural and even physical extinction, it tends to be more). The habit of referring to all of these groups as *nacionalidades* points to their ideological construction as marginal subnations within, and competing with, the nation.

While the social dominance of light-skinned Bolivians is fairly secure, *mestizos'* position is more ambiguous. In a sense, *mestizo* is the unmarked category, neither obviously indigenous nor conspicuously white.[25] However, *mestizos* are fewer in Bolivia than in most Latin American countries, causing many to feel that they must identify either with the indigenous majority or with the small but prestigious "white" minority. The first option not only entails a step down in the social hierarchy, but may be difficult for one who does not speak an indigenous language, while the second option exposes one to accusations of social climbing and the corresponding slur *"cholo."*[26]

That ethnic mobility is seen as dishonorable is evident from the sanction it receives both in everday conversation and in numerous literary works. It is nevertheless a common phenomenon, due to the social barriers confronting those of indigenous background. The attempts by *indios* to pass as *mestizos*, and by *mestizos* to pass as *criollos*, create new categories in the interstices of the old; Corrigan and Sayer (1985:194–95) refer to "the attempted construction of aspiration, the internalization of bourgeois norms as constitutive of personalities." This internalization may occur more easily among *mestizos*; as nonindigenous, nonwhite Bolivians without a recognized cultural tradition of their own, *mestizos* are ethnically ambiguous. Many find a basis for identity in class-based movements or regional solidarities. But while perhaps less "well-defined" than other Bolivian ethnic groups, they are crucially important to the nationalist project. Internal migration, continuing intermarriage, and the move by increasing numbers of indigenous people into more advantageous social identities make *mestizos* the fastest growing category among those discussed. Additionally, their lack of a strong cultural identification with either the international elite or an indigenous tradition makes them the most promising ground for the cultivation of nationalist ideology.[27]

Race and Class in the Nationalist Project

If Bolivia's ethnic divisions pose one of the severest obstacles to national unity, the most significant attempt to paper over this schism dates from the 1952 revolution and turns upon the use of the terms *indio* and *campesino*. A brief look at the historical changes these terms have undergone will shed light upon the race/class intersection in Bolivia.[28]

In some respects, *indio* is comparable to the term *nigger* as used in the United States. Originally used by *criollo* elites to refer generally to the members of a phenotypically distinct, enslaved population, the 1952 revolution and subsequent enfranchisement of that population shifted its meaning to that of a vehement social insult. In the postrevolutionary era, the term was discouraged as racist and not in line with revolutionary goals. In official discourse (spoken and written), *indio* was replaced with *campesino* (peasant), a term that overlapped fairly neatly with the first in terms of referent but had a more positive connotation (especially as part of the ubiquitous political refrain of *"nuestros hermanos campesinos"*).[29] The shift in terminology also reinforced the salience of the land reform as the cornerstone of the revolution; a *campesino* owns a plot of land, while a *peón* or *pongo* (other terms previously synonymous with *indio*) works another's land in conditions of servitude. More important, it furthered the revolutionary aim of highlighting class over ethnicity or race.

In recent decades, cultural revitalization movements have argued that the term *campesino* is inadequate for referring to indigenous people in general. Not only has the proposed isomorphism between *indio* and *campesino* become unwieldy, as increasing numbers of indigenous people migrate to urban centers; the term also obscures, behind the reductionist rubric of class, the cultural differences that such movements wish to emphasize and valorize. As one indigenous leader put it: "Currently they call us 'peasants'; and those Aymaras who are workers, miners, professionals, students and intellectuals have been dispossessed of our personality as *Aymara* people."[30] While thirty years ago "Aymara" denoted simply the language, and was rarely used as an ethnic category, (Albó 1988:33), its use has accompanied the growing "ethnic consciousness" among such sectors.

The term *indígena* is also used as a polite alternative to *indio*, though some have attempted to reclaim the latter as a symbol of racial pride, rejecting *indígena* as a euphemism born of a colonial mentality. With the recent ascendance of "multicultural" discourse, *los pueblos originarios* has also come into use, denoting an explicitly antiracist stance. Among less politicized sectors, *campesino* remains the most commonly used polite term. Its inclusion of urban dwellers as well is facilitated by the fact that these often retain strong ties to rural communities. Albó (1988:33) also notes, "Many urban migrants continue to call themselves '*campesinos*' and affirm that they will never cease to be such. Behind this word continues to resound the term '*indio*' . . . [which] is still more evocative of people's experience and more forcefully expresses their feeling of being exploited and denigrated."

While he sees this subtext as indicative of migrants' interiorization of racism and exploitation, it can also be read as a collective refusal to reduce indigenous identity to questions of class or residence. Given the overwhelming influence of indigenous culture even in urban centers (and within the canon of "official" national culture), claims that indigenous Andeans have been "deculturalized" as a result of their proletarianization are unsustainable. Certainly, Aymara cultural practices are influenced by dominant *criollo* culture; but to infer from this that Aymara culture has ceased to evolve according to its own "internal dynamic" (Albó 1979) and has become essentially (though not immanently) moribund, both ignores the vitality of new, syncretic strains of indigenous cultural expression and implies a previous cultural purity and isolation that is largely mythical, not only for the Aymara but for most indigenous groups.

Albó's notion of Aymara as a politically oppressed language and culture is useful for analyzing its place in Bolivia's complex social scene. But to claim that this "impoverished subculture . . . will continue impoverishing itself by functioning in relation to the dominant structure" until it is reduced to being merely "the lowest social class within a 'more modern' national society" (Albó 1979:312) is to conflate class and ethnic oppressions, obscuring the internal dynamics of both, and no less significantly, their interaction.[31] To go even further and suggest that the "dual culture" model be replaced by a class model (Greaves 1972) jettisons cultural difference for the sake of theoretical (over)simplicity. Likewise, Calderón's (1977:218) claim that racial discrimination in Bolivia "is tending to disappear, leaving only class exploitation" is fairly incredible in light of the racist treatment suffered by many Bolivians on a regular basis, independent of social class.

More recent explorations of class and ethnicity (Norton 1984; Williams 1989; Albó 1990; Montoya 1991; Eriksen 1993) avoid reducing one to the other, focusing instead on their interaction. Theorists such as Hall, Laclau, and Mouffe, who likewise refuse to reduce multiple oppressions to a single axis, have explored their mutual articulation in the interests of capitalist exploitation and ideological hegemony. One can analyze Aymara cultural practices in terms of "class cultures" (Bourdieu 1984), but this does not mean that they arise from, or are determined by, actors' position in the class structure.[32] Despite the broad overlap between class and ethnic divisions, they are not the same; *indio* and *campesino* are not identical categories. Rather, their conflation is a discursive construction that, historically, has served specific ideological ends.

Reductionist class analyses have ramifications not only for scholarly work, but for political life as well. The failure of Bolivia's radical left to gain mass acceptance among what is unquestionably a deeply exploited and impoverished population is partly attributable to its adherence to this restricted perspective. Not that the left ignores questions of indigenous culture altogether; parties like the POR generally support education in students' native languages (in word if not always in deed) and often evoke the image of the indigenous peasant as a revolutionary archetype alongside that of the urban proletarian. But their recognition of indigenous people as such, rather than as strictly class subjects, is limited and often smacks of political expediency. While expressing solidarity with the peasants, the POR does not see them as capable of the type of revolutionary leadership provided by urban proletariat groups such as miners and teachers.

This position derives from a rigid Marxism that designates the industrial proletariat as the sole agent destined to transform society (regardless of its actual size relative to the peasantry). Still, this vision of "liberation" overlooks the fact that "it is oppressive to 'free' people if their own history and culture do not serve as the primary sources of the definition of their freedom."[33] Ethnic loyalties are highly salient for most Bolivians and must form part of any political agenda that aims to mobilize the active participation of "the masses." "The revolutionary process can not be restricted to a movement organised on strict class lines . . . It is, therefore, vital for the working class not to isolate itself within a ghetto of proletarian purism. On the contrary, it must try to become a 'national class,' representing the interests of the increasingly numerous social groups. . . This process of disarticulation-rearticulation constitutes in fact the famous 'war of position' " (Mouffe 1979:197).

While Bolivia's social divisions clearly cannot be reduced to the question of class, class differences are themselves a serious obstacle to forging a unified national identity. A multi-ethnic, pluralist nationalism is at least conceivable (if seldom achieved); but a sense of common purpose—of "belonging together"—is hard to imagine for groups divided by such vast inequalities as those separating Bolivia's rich and poor. The extremes of Bolivia's socioeconomic spectrum are conspicuously far apart, and the bottom ranks swollen with a greater proportion of the population than in most nations. Nationalist ideology depends largely on obscuring class divisions; in Bolivia, these are so glaring as to make this virtually impossible.

Bolivia's class schism has given rise to (at least) two distinct strains of nationalism. Expanding upon a distinction made by Atahuichi (1990), I refer to these as "revolutionary nationalism"—characteristic of the lower classes and the indigenous and *mestizo* people comprising them—and "bourgeois nationalism"—characteristic of the official discourse of society's elites.[34] Identifying the ideological foundations of each of these strains will help us analyze the ways in which nationalist symbols are claimed, and such claims contested, by different groups.

Tenets of Bourgeois Nationalism

• The essence of Bolivia is the cultural heritage created by Spanish-descended colonists in their unique New World environment; the defining event of Bolivian nationalism is the achievement of independence from Spain in 1825; the pantheon of national heroes includes Bolívar and other *criollo* leaders who "created the Bolivian nation."

- Patriotism means loyalty to the state as it is currently formulated; ideological compromise can be patriotic if it helps to preserve the stability of the state.
- Our common heritage and future destiny as Bolivians transcend class and ethnic divisions.
- What's good for the dominant sectors is good for the country; all classes rise or fall together.
- Class differences are submerged in favor of an interpretation that sees all Bolivians as having the same "class position" relative to countries such as the United States.
- The way for Bolivia to progress is to follow the path of the developed nations and ally itself with them politically.

Tenets of Revolutionary Nationalism

- The essence of Bolivia is the cultural heritage of its original inhabitants, subjugated by the *criollo* colonists; the defining event of Bolivian nationalism is the 1952 revolution; the pantheon of national heroes includes Tupac Katari and other martyred rebel leaders.
- Loyalty to bourgeois governments is a false and mystifying nationalism; "authentic" patriotism is identified with working-class and peasant interests.
- The history (and future) of the nation is seen as the gradual process of liberation of "true" Bolivians from antipatriotic (elite) interests.
- Social classes do not rise and fall together, but are diametrically opposed. The bourgeoisie's loyalty lies not with the nation, but with their class counterparts in other nations.
- The global division of labor by no means negates the class divisions within each country. Rather, class struggle is a patriotic struggle to wrest the country from foreign interests.
- "Alliance" with developed countries is simply the cooperation of First and Third World elites in the subjugation of the working class. True development and the culmination of national goals will come only through revolution.

North Americans accustomed to characterizations of the left as "antigovernment" and those with leftist tendencies as "anti-American" may be surprised to discover that, in Bolivia, accusations of antipatriotism are launched more frequently from the left than from the right. This is partly due to the strong discursive link between "nationalist" and "revolutionary" stemming from the 1952 revolution. Furthermore, the Bolivian left firmly supports the idea of a strong state, albeit one organized under a dictatorship of the proletariat. Their most common complaint about the ruling class is that it is "weak" and incapable of building a strong Bolivian state, being made up of *vendepatrias* who put personal and class interests above national ones.

Given that the alleged *vendepatrias* are in fact running the country, the theme of threatened national sovereignty is hammered on strongly by the left, usually with reference to U.S. influence on Bolivia's domestic policy. From this perspective, the major threat to the national interest is the semicolonial status imposed upon it by the United States. Borrowing from Marx, one might say that the leftist nationalist project is to make Bolivia a nation not only in itself, but for itself.

Official History and Popular Humor: Public Tropes of Ethnic and International Conflict

The superficially neat opposition between revolutionary and bourgeois nationalisms is complicated by the state's use of revolutionary rhetoric in its attempts to resonate with the "popular classes."[35] Official nationalist discourse is often explicitly or implicitly historical; Alonso (1988:50) notes that "national histories are key to the imagining of community and to the constitution of social identity." Examining official representations of key events in Bolivia's history will aid our analysis of official nationalist discourse and its attempts to construct a particular national identity.

Much of the MNR's credibility lies in its popular image as the vanguard of the 1952 revolution. The party's name, Movimiento Nacionalista Revolucionario, draws upon the strength of this association, combining the ideas of nationalism, revolution, and state power in a single insitution. The glow of this revolutionary tradition still adheres to the MNR, despite its current status as a firmly entrenched member of the political establishment.

As various authors have noted, the popular insurrection sparked by the MNR's coup attempt in 1952 brought about economic and social changes far beyond what its middle-class leaders had originally intended. Nevertheless, a central element of the MNR's hegemony is the idea that it was and is "the party of the revolution" and is thus entitled to take credit for the social changes that occurred during that period—changes actually due as much, if not more, to the pressure exerted on the MNR by the peasantry and the working class, through their political organ, the COB. More recently, the MNR's image as heroic vanguard has been tarnished by the contradiction between the two projects for which it is best known: the revolution itself (including nationalization of the mines, enfranchisement of the peasantry, etc.) and what many perceive as the rollback of revolutionary gains (privatization of the mines and other state enterprises, restructuring of the educational and health systems, etc.). Managing this contradiction has been the MNR's foremost challenge as it attempts to rebuild the popular support it once enjoyed.

If the relation between past and present is the shared object of both history and anthropology (Alonso 1988:51, Popular Memory Group 1982:240), it is also the object of politics—especially that brand of party politics that depends heavily on public image. Bolivia's political elites justify their policies of privatization and alliance with multinational capitalism by casting them in the rhetoric of popular control and efficiency, presenting them as a continuation rather than a negation of past revolutionary goals. Thus, while the revolution continues to be lauded in general terms, specific policies (such as state control of national resources) are portrayed as "failed experiments," digressions from the true path of national progress. The goal claimed by modern leaders is the efficient exploitation of the country's resources; the "inefficiency" that accompanied nationalization is portrayed as (1) an inevitable result of state control, and (2) inimical to the nation's best interest.[36] This portrayal has not been completely successful; despite the MNR's electoral victory, popular opposition to their policies remains strong. Nevertheless, their rhetorical strategy exemplifies the ways in which "national goals" are articulated around purposeful constructions of national history.

In addition to Bolivian elites' attempts to construct an ideological and historical continuity between themselves and the

1952 revolution, there is a simultaneous attempt to distance themselves from the intervening periods of repressive dictatorship. This is buttressed by official claims of having entered a new and democratic era that constitutes a clean break from the corrupt and violent past. Such claims are nevertheless threatened by the emergence of subversive, oppositional histories—such as the accusations that, for years, government leaders clandestinely harbored former dictator Luís García Meza (recently captured in Brazil), or the widely publicized campaigns to recover the remains of revolutionary martyrs Ché Guevara and Marcelo Quiroga Santa Cruz, executed under past military dictatorships.

For official representations of a more distant past, one can look to the national historical museums, where official ideology is displayed in its most overt form (with the possible exception of the school curriculum). La Paz's main historical museums cluster together in the genteel confines of Calle Jaén, a small cobblestone street surrounded by colonial architecture, giving the impression that one has stepped back in time. In line with the tenets of bourgeois nationalism, these museums' pantheon of national heroes is drawn almost exclusively from the war of independence. The 1952 revolution (which has no museum dedicated to it) is more often identified with an anonymous "victory of the masses" than with specific individuals (perhaps because many of them are still living, their foibles available to public view). Official portrayals of individuals from that period would inevitably evoke the factional disputes that they came to represent and that eventually led to the revolutionary coalition's downfall. History can be "a divisive rather than a unifying force" (Hobsbawm 1983:272), and any official portrayal of the revolution and its aftermath could not easily efface conflicts whose scars are borne by many still living.

Just as telling is the museums' treatment of ethnic conflict. Of the various indigenous leaders who led uprisings before and after independence, the only one usually recognized in official contexts is Tupac Katari (Julián Apasa), whose extended siege of La Paz in 1781 was put down only with the aid of 10,000 *criollo* troops.[37] Official portrayals of Katari are restricted to the solemn ambience of museums; his name is never evoked in official celebrations (but often is in popular ones). The museum images are themselves revealing; unlike the *criollo* heroes, usually shown in statesmanlike poses or leading military charges,

Katari is invariably shown at the moment of his execution (he was publicly drawn and quartered in the town square of Peñas). An ambiguous combination of savage bogeyman and popular martyr, Katari is never portrayed in his revolutionary strength, but rather naked, humiliated, tortured, and at the point of death—a mute warning to any future revolutionary aspirants.[38]

Another key site for the official represention of history is the Museum of the Littoral, dedicated to Bolivia's former coastline. Lost to Chile in the War of the Pacific over a century ago, the littoral is still a painful thorn in the national psyche, and the goal of its recovery is regularly emphasized in nationalist celebrations. A ubiquitous feature of Independence Day pageants is the procession of schoolchildren dressed to represent Bolivia's nine departments, with a tenth child veiled in black representing the Lost Littoral. The identificatory jingle of one La Paz radio station (Radio Mar) is "We will recover the sea, we will recover our coastline," sung to the strains of a military march; many schools begin the day by having students sing the same lines. The most notable feature of the Museum of the Littoral is the preponderance of historical maps prominently depicting Bolivia's coast, in evidence of its tenaciously held claim to the area. The theme of the littoral is a vivid distillation of besieged patriotism, with the Bolivian nation defined against the encroaching borders of external enemies.

Finally, there is the official representation of the pre-Colombian past, centered on the ancient civilization of Tiahuanaco. The main collections of Tiahuanaco artifacts are La Paz's Archeological Museum and the nearby archeological site of Tiahuanaco itself. The museum, a beautiful and rather ostentatious building whose architecture reflects indigenous motifs, is paradoxically tucked away on a small sidestreet around the corner from one of La Paz's major hotels. In it are various objects from pre-Colombian civilizations and a few from the colonial period; there is little attempt to show continuity between the ancient Andean societies and Bolivia's modern-day indigenous populations. The small, dusty museum at the archeological site suffers from this same lack of continuity, although it stands on the edge of the present-day Aymara community of Tiahuanaco. If one could reach Tiahuanaco without first passing through La Paz, or did not happen to venture into the adjoining town after exploring the impressive courts and megaliths of the site, one might think this was all that remained of its builders—the gorgeous remnants of a dead civilization, empty and in ruins. In La Paz, however, indigenous voices still clamor to be heard. As the folkloric group Norte Potosi asserted during a concert in La Paz, "They say the *chullpas* are mummies in baskets, but we are *chullpas*, and you can see that we are not mummies, but rather very much alive."[39]

In contrast to official representations, the realm of popular humor constitutes a treasure trove of implicit commentaries "from below" about past and present ethnic, class, and international conflicts. Jokes often reveal points of conflict in a society; like eddies in the flow of everyday discourse, they indicate rocks and breaks under the surface. Certain kinds of humor can be read as popular critiques raised against the multiple oppressions of everday life. The fact that such critiques are indirect and metaphorical, rather than overtly expressive of a revolutionary consciousness, does not negate their political significance. On the contrary, it shows that class and ethnic conflicts are not restricted to the strictly political or economic realm, but rather find expression—and, more important, are *partially constructed*—in everyday practice and discourse on the interpersonal level. Comaroff and Comaroff (1987:205) maintain that false dichotomies between fact and poetry, history and myth, serve only to obscure the role of such popular discourses in the construction of social reality: "The poetry of representation . . . is not an aesthetic embellishment of a 'truth' that lies elsewhere. Its puns and metaphors, jokes and irreverencies, are the stuff of everyday thought and action—of the human consciousness through which culture and history construct each other."

Given Bolivia's multi-ethnic character, popular humor about ethnic identity is to be expected. For example, a very popular recent recording by a Bolivian comedy team[40] contained a sketch in which two characters—an introverted, shy *kolla*, and an extroverted, brash *camba*—ask for the hand of their respective sweethearts. Even more charged than this essentially horizontal contrast are the boundaries between lower and higher social strata. Many jokes focus on exploitation, resistance, and status conflicts among different social sectors; common themes include greedy or lecherous priests, corrupt or incompetent politicians, unfaithful wives or domineering women, and ignorant *campesinos* stumbling in their attempts to enter *criollo* society. Such tensions are also expressed in more serious treatments;

these often revolve around the phenomenon known as *haciéndose q'ara* (making oneself white), whereby individuals of indigenous background try to distance themselves from their roots. Several Bolivian literary works turn upon the premise of a young person (usually female) who faces a moral conflict in attempting to deny her family background in her climb up the social ladder. Perhaps the best known is Antonio Díaz Villamil's novel *La Niña de Sus Ojos.*

Popular humor exploits not only the tensions between different social strata within Bolivia, but also those pertaining to Bolivia's place in the hierarchy of nations. Themes of Bolivia's dependecy and underdevelopment arise frequently in casual conversation, in expressions ranging from angry frustration to ironic cynicism to cheerfully self-deprecatory burlesque. Much national humor hinges upon the inefficiency and corruption associated with Bolivian institutions. In a reference to Bolivia's Kafkaesque bureaucracy, the comedy team mentioned above asserted that, just like the more advanced nations, Bolivia sent four "assault squadrons" to aid in the war against Iraq: the Customs Service, the Internal Revenue Service, the Municipal Government, and the Highway Patrol. In an example somewhat closer to home, I once came across a group of students milling around the normal school grounds when they should have been in class. When I asked Paco, a tall, graceful young man with a reputation as school comedian, why they were not in class, he heaved a sigh of mock despair and replied sadly, "Porque los bolivianos son así. Somos atrasados."[41]

Often, a negative view of Bolivians is used to foreground an even more negative view of foreigners. The following joke neatly combines the triumph of native common sense over supposed foreign superiority with a commentary on the upper-class practice of learning English: "A drunk is staggering alongside a pool of water. A big blond foreigner passes by, and the drunk accidentally bumps him into the pool. Not knowing how to swim, the foreigner begins to cry out 'Help, help!'; the drunk observes him gravely and then remarks, '¡Sonso! En vez de aprender inglés, ¿por qué no aprendiste a nadar?' "[42]

In this Bakhtinian inversion of the dominant/subordinate relationship between Bolivia and the United States, one might wonder why the Bolivian character is drunk; it is not essential to the foreigner's mishap in the pool, and indeed leads one to think that it is the other who is about to fall in. However, drunkenness is essential to the image of the degenerate Bolivian who nevertheless triumphs over the foreigner. The message is, "I may be alcoholic, backward, vulgar and uncivilized, but I'm smarter than *you!*" This burlesque fantasy of inverted power, in which it is the First World *Übermensch* who suddenly finds himself dependent upon "foreign aid," can be read as a small but significant guerrilla sortie against unquestioned First World dominance, a discursive dart meant to prick the hide of the leviathan without challenging it directly.

Willis and Corrigan (1983) claim that jokes about oppression, though often seen as trivial (or as a passive means of "making the best of a very bad job") are significant in their highlighting of social contradictions. A joke is like a knifeblade slipped into the interstices of an oppressive discourse: with a humorous twist, the discourse is disarticulated (albeit momentarily), and possibly rearticulated towards other, more subversive ends. In seeking out these interstices, jokes resist certain kinds of discipline; "forms of 'discourse,' or patterns of control over others . . . can be unlocked or reinterpreted by the joke" (96). In Bolivia, nationalist and ethnic ideologies are favored targets for this sort of unlocking.

Ethnic humor often contains a blend of the two extremes that Gramsci termed "philosophy" and "common sense." Even a political joke whose primary aim seems to be a racist jibe can suggest multiple meanings, as in the case of this widely circulated riddle:

Q: Why is President Sánchez de Lozada known as "The Lone Ranger"?
A: Because he always goes around with his Indian at his side.

Clearly, the riddle hinges on the suggestion that Vice President Cárdenas is little more than an indigenous token, along to provide some local color while the white hero takes care of the real political business. Nevertheless, the reference to the "Lone Ranger" might be read as a commentary on Sánchez de Lozada's political isolation as he attempts to push his unpopular policies past a wall of opposition. And the fact that the Indian in the Lone Ranger series is named "Tonto" (Spanish for "stupid") suggests an oblique commentary on the dubious political wisdom of any serious indigenous intellectual who willingly takes on the role of the president's subaltern sidekick.

In popular humor, individual characters often appear as stand-ins for entire sectors of society (or even entire societies), whether in the dozens of nationalist jokes that begin: "There was a Bolivian, a Peruvian, and a Chilean . . . " or in the numerous jokes that circulated during Jaime Paz's presidency, positing homosexual relations between him and either Ronald Reagan or George Bush. The following observation by the Popular Memory Group, though made in reference to oral histories, is equally applicable to humorous forms: "What marxism or an explanatory social history will wish to treat as social relations or as social classes, these accounts tend to treat as persons . . . social relations are understood through the qualities of persons who inhabit them. Structural determinations appear as relationships between people" (PMG 1982:244–45).

Or occasionally, between animals; the following example highlights the ambivalent nationalist feelings that inevitably arise when the image of the nation is so firmly wedded to images of backwardness, poverty, and corruption. Whether this should be read as evidence of some "national inferiority complex" is a question left to the following section. What it does clearly indicate is that Bolivian popular humor serves not only as a vehicle for resentment against ethnic, class, or international rivals, but also for frustration over the lack of solidarity among one's own compatriots. In this case, the age-old conflict of "Us against Them" is replaced by a dispirited jest on the theme of "Us against Us":

> A scientist is experimenting on a group of Bolivian crabs and another of North American crabs. To survive in their laboratory environment, the crabs must be moved occasionally while the water in their tanks is changed. While changing the water one day, the scientist's assistant moves the North American crabs to an empty tank and covers it with a board so they won't escape. When he goes to change the water in the other crabs' tank, he likewise moves them to an empty tank, but neglects to cover it. At that moment the scientist comes in and scolds the assistant: "Why did you leave the crabs uncovered? They could climb out and escape!" The assistant replies casually, "Don't worry, those are the Bolivian crabs. If one tries to climb out, the others will grab him by the foot and pull him back down."

Finding a "We": Defining Lo Boliviano against a Hostile World

Two questions seem to circulate constantly in Bolivia's collective consciousness. One is, "Who are we?" arising out of the conflictive diversity of co-existing cultures examined above. In the minds of many, indigenous people are not only the majority, but also the "true essence" of Bolivia. The fact that they remain socially and politically dominated by nonindigenous elites is a persistent and intrusive dissonance in the attempted construction of a transcendent nationalist harmony.

The other question plaguing the national psyche is, "Why are we unable to emerge from our backward condition?" A common answer is the very disunity evinced by the first question. Beyond this, however, is a pervasive awareness of Bolivia's "Third World" status, as central to Bolivian identity as membership in the "First World" is to that of the United States. The intense patriotism and ethnic pride characterizing so much of Bolivian nationalist feeling is perversely complemented by a self-deprecatory discourse in which speakers speculate on possible internal causes for their country's dependency, poverty, and underdevelopment. From this perspective, all things foreign are superior to anything produced in Bolivia, and Bolivians themselves are suspected of containing some fatal flaw that chains them to their underdog status. The student quoted below, in a parallel to the joke cited above, often lamented what he saw as Bolivians' tendency to hold each other back, rather than move forward together. He describes how some teachers, having reached a position of authority through personal and political connections, purposely try to thwart the best students:

Mateo: They try to screw you every time. They just try to kill you. Maybe because they don't want you to excel. That's how we Bolivians are, we're *selfish*, you know? There's a lot of egoism . . . The other guy always wants to be on top. He doesn't want the new generations to get ahead . . . This country could get ahead but those guys, they ruin it, because of their own ignorance . . . There's no awareness, everyone just seeks their own interest, their personal interest, everyone just dedicates themselves from morning to night to getting rich. No, this way the crisis will go on forever.

Without claiming that all Bolivians feel this way, I did hear several express similar opinions. Institutionalized corruption and incompetence are indeed widespread in Bolivia, and many Bolivians had difficulty ascribing all of their country's problems to U.S. exploitation when they were confronted almost daily with examples of exploitation by their own countrymen.[43] For many, the frequency of such incidents, both in the press and in their personal lives, was evidence of a generalized flaw in the national character.

While at least one Bolivian author (and former Minister of Education) refers to his country's "inferiority complex" (Baptista 1974:51), this cannot be uncritically accepted as evidence of some collective neurosis by which Bolivians passively resign themselves to their Third World status. Not only is there a complementary tendency to forcefully valorize *lo boliviano*, but the examples of popular humor examined above show that the key assumptions of the discourse of national inferiority are frequently subverted by speakers who deploy them with ironic intent. Still, the prevalence of this discourse points to an important contrast between First World and Third World nationalisms in general. The bulk of scholarship on nationalist ideology tends to operate under the assumption that the perceived "essence" of a nation or its people is, by definition, the best and brightest that the nation has to offer—be it the wholesome Swedish countryside (Lofgren 1989), the grandeur of England's upper-class architecture (Wright 1985), or the unpretentious acumen of "American ingenuity." This assumption is perhaps valid if discussion is limited to the developed nations' views of themselves, but it becomes problematic when applied to Third World nationalisms. It goes almost without saying that what is "essentially Swedish" or "essentially English" should be construed as those nations' unique distillations of "the good"; but for most countries, simplistic slogans along the lines of We're Number One can evoke only a pained irony, rather than the popular resonance found in First World nations ("first" by definition and by fiat). What of those nations whose defining collective experience is one of subjugation, poverty, and violence? What is the "national essence" of Rwanda or Guatemala?

In posing these questions, I do not wish to imply that one can only speak of "national genius" in reference to those few nations who are winners in the arena of global power struggles, nor that all Third World peoples suffer from some form of national inferiority complex. Clearly, more study is needed in order to form a comparative picture of Third World nationalisms from the wide range of historical and political experiences that such nations comprise. I do maintain, however, that nationalisms that are built slowly, whose symbols accrue gradually from a history of conquest, expansion, and assumed racial superiority—that is, those that have been the main focus of study to date—are fundamentally different from those nationalisms that emerge painfully and suddenly from a past that is traumatic rather than nostalgic, whose symbols must be drawn from a "national heritage" of centuries of colonialism. Upon emerging into nationhood, such nations are faced with the dilemma of at once embracing their history and distancing themselves from it.

There are a few prevailing ways of going about this task, which are not necessarily mutually exclusive. One is to situate the national genius in a posited precolonial "Golden Age," exemplified by Chicano visions of Aztlan or Andean collective "memories" of a just and harmonious Pax Inkaica. Another is to extract an image of national virtue from the traumatic past itself—a morally superior heritage of resistance, perseverance, and martyrdom—such as might be argued for Poland, Czechoslovakia, or Bolivia itself. But despite these and other strategies, it must be recognized that in nations with a long history of subjugation and underdevelopment (and the term "Third World" is perhaps nothing so much as a shorthand for these conditions), many of the ideological elements seen as comprising the "national essence" will be very negative. Centuries of racism, violence, and poverty leave an ideological residue that even the most fervent national pride cannot erase overnight. Thus it should come as no surprise that the popular image of *lo boliviano* includes not only bravery, shrewdness, and militant tenacity, but also factionalism, self-interest, and imitativeness. In the pantheon of national archetypes, the revolutionary underdog, the heroic martyr, and the subaltern trickster must vie for dominance with the alcoholic, the peon, and the cheat. These are the sorts of contradictions with which subjugated nationalisms must contend.

Bolivians share an awareness that not only is their country not a global winner, it is also rather far down on the list of losers. Despite a popular revolution that raised nationalist hopes to great heights, they have had to face the fact that such victories are not won once and for all, but are constantly subject to betrayal, attrition, and outright reversal. The influence of for- eign entities such as the World Bank, the International Mon- etary Fund, the Drug Enforcement Agency, and the U.S. Embassy is so great that, for many Bolivians, it belies the notion of national sovereignty. The question now dominating national debate is to what degree international pressures will succeed in reversing or redefining the achievements and goals of the revolution. Also present in the back of the national mind is the fact that, since independence, Bolivia has lost more than half its territory to the ambitions of its neighbors. Thus, a major theme of Bolivian nationalism is the attempt to hold on to that which is being insidiously and inexorably plundered.

The pervasive sense that the national heritage is slipping out of Bolivia's collective grasp gives rise to a national solidarity defined in terms of a common external enemy. The theme of "the nation in peril" takes many forms: from historical griev- ances such as the Spanish plunder of Bolivia's mineral wealth or Chile's usurpation of its coastline, to more recent threats such as encroachment by Brazilian settlers and Chilean oil and gas explorers, the absorption of national industries by multina- tional corporations, and the plundering of rural communities' symbolic riches by foreign anthropologists. There is a perceived need not only to protect Bolivia's economic resources, but also to "defend our customs," lest they be swept away by hostile forces.

In unity there is strength; thus constructing a unified nationalism is popularly viewed as crucial to Bolivia's future. Central to this task is the question of defining the collective national subject broadly enough so that it will resonate with all Bolivians, despite their conflicting interests and loyalties. A related problem is creating an ostensibly organic bond between this subject and the state—a state toward which many pres- ently feel distant, alienated, and disillusioned, if not overtly hostile. Geertz (1973a:240) saw this as nationalism's primary challenge: "defining, or trying to define, a collective subject to whom the actions of the state can be internally connected . . . creating, or trying to create, an experiential 'we' from whose will the activities of government seem spontaneously to flow." Any scenario in which the activities of government are imag- ined to "spontaneously flow" from the will of a collective national subject contrasts sharply with Bolivia's current situation, where the most common image of a collective subject is that of "the people" locked in a zero-sum game with a government whose interests are categorically opposed to their own.

It is not my intention to conjure up visions of a reified state imposing a hegemony solely of its own making upon an ideologically subjugated people. Ideology is not disseminated exclusively from above or below; rather, it is structured in the space between those extremes. Official nationalisms almost always have something of the popular in them, and vice versa; they are joint constructions of the popular sectors *and* the political leadership. It is more useful to view the state/civil society distinction as an interface, rather than a partition; drawing too sharp a division obscures the ways in which the state intrudes into popular practices and personal subjectivities. A fully elaborated conception of hegemony must recognize that "the state apparatus is by no means the only site of state power, even if it is its most visible manifestation" (Alonso 1988:54).[44]

Clearly, any "authentic" Bolivian nationalism must take ethnicity into account; no articulation of ideological elements will resonate with the majority of Bolivians if the indigenous element is not prominently included. Of course, the hegemonic solution to competition for subjects' loyalties by rival attachments is not eliminating these attachments, but incorporating them; not "wish[ing] them out of existence by belittling them or even denying their reality, but domesticat[ing] them" (Geertz 1973b:277). Thus the indigenous elements that find a place within official nationalisms most often do so via "historical tourism" (Starn 1991:67) or a valorized folkloric tradition. While Bolivia's *etnias* cannot be ignored, they may be encapsulated as a merely "cultural" phenomenon.

Nationalist ideologies are built from the cannibalized remains of other collective loyalties; to speak the national subject is to silence another. In the words of Corrigan and Sayer (1985:195):

> To define "us" in national terms (as against class, or locality, or ethnic group, or gender, or any other terms in which social identity might be constructed and historical experience comprehended) has consequences. Such classifications are means for a project of social integration which is also,

inseparably, an active disintegration of other focuses of identity and conceptions of subjectivity. They provide a basis for construction and organization of collective memory—the writing of history, the manufacture of "tradition"—which is inseparably an active organization of forgetting.

In the hegemonic organization of collective memory and forgetfulness, there is perhaps no site more crucial than that which I shall take up next: the school.

2

RURAL SCHOOLING IN BOLIVIA

> *The problem of public education cannot be studied without con-*
> *sidering its intimate relation with the forms of economic devel-*
> *opment of the country, of which the school is the result and the*
> *reflection, since, as an instrument of transmission of the cul-*
> *tural heritage of the people, its structure, ends, and ideology*
> *can be no other than those directed towards the conservation of*
> *the society in which it operates.*
>
> —Carlos Salazar Mostajo, *Warisata Mía!*

Roots of Aymara Education: The Struggle for Land and Literacy

Despite the political and social transformations Bolivia has undergone since first emerging as a nation, Bolivian schooling displays strong continuities with the past, both in its surface methodologies and in its underlying aims. The current educational reform is undoubtedly the most comprehensive effort to date to break with the civilizatory project that defined the destruction of indigenous identity as one of the school's central objectives. Bolivia's new educational philosophy officially recognizes linguistic and cultural diversity as a resource to be fostered, rather than a problem to be eliminated, and proposes a methodology and epistemology clearly opposed to the ethnocentric, mechanical pedagogy of the past. Still, these efforts at change face formidable obstacles, not the least of which is the resistance of teachers themselves. While the progressive vision embodied in the reform raises hopes for a truly liberatory, critical education, the rigid, memoristic models of the past are deeply entrenched in teachers' classroom practice. Since the discourses and subjectivities generated by current school practices derive, in part, from those of the past, the analysis of Bolivian education must begin by unearthing its historical roots. A review of the social conditions under which the current system evolved will provide "a historical lens through which to view the present" (Walsh 1991:27) and a sense of the historical depth of struggles that continue to be waged.

Before assuming that schools "don't work," we must delve through the layers of rhetoric, deposited over decades, to discover what they were actually intended to do. Educational theorists often overlook the fact that the "hidden curriculum" started out as a very explicit political project. Carnoy (1974), Bowles and Gintis (1976), Apple (1979), and Bourne (1988) have shown, via the early writings of educators, sociologists, and historians, that public schooling was purposefully designed around aims of social control and the reproduction of a particular division of labor, rather than the expansion of democratic participation or the intellectual betterment of the population. Levinson and Holland (1996:16) note the importance of schooling to contemporary state formation, as the crucible of a (supposedly) shared national culture. How these aims became obscured by a very different rationality—that is, how public education's underlying agenda came to be "hidden"—is a story of class interests and ideological struggles whose pathways can be historically traced.

Analyses of the historical and ideological roots of mass schooling in the industrialized nations cannot be transferred wholesale to other cultural settings whose social and political histories are quite different. Yet they do provide a framework for analyzing how schooling works, and perhaps more important, for whom. This inquiry begins from the following questions:

- What were the major currents of social change when public schooling was implemented?
- What perceived problems was public schooling meant to address?
- What social sectors were perceived as the source of these problems?
- What social sectors were in charge of deciding the curricula and methodology to be used?
- How were these subsequently "naturalized" to the point of being perceived as inevitable and universal, rather than based in the political aims of a particular social group?

These questions provide the basis for a more informed and critical perspective on the current watershed in Bolivian education and the political discourses that it has generated. They also situate schooling within a larger political project: the consolidation of the nation-state via the construction of a collective national subject and the dissemination of nationalist ideology.

During the colonial period, conflicting interests of Church, Crown, and *criollo* elites gave rise to two centuries of shifting and inconsistent language policies. Originally, colonial administrators and clergy utilized the indigenous *linguas francas* already in place in the Andes to facilitate their control over the indigenous population. Convent-educated native elites were instrumental in the adminstration of colonial rule, a fact that led the Crown to take a liberal position toward indigenous languages. This policy had negative consequences for other powerful sectors of society, however. Bilingual clergy and *criollo* interpreters used their knowledge of indigenous languages to reinforce their own power, relative to the monolingual clergy and the Spanish-born *peninsulares*. Furthermore, the Council of Indies charged that many *criollos* who adopted the language of the Indians also adopted a far too liberal tolerance for their customs; in a sense, "what the Spanish had wanted to accomplish with the Indians (i.e., to convert them to their values and habits), the Indians were doing to some New World descendants of the Spaniards" (Heath and Laprade 1982:131).

Critics of this state of affairs petitioned the Crown to implement the "castilianization" (enforced learning of Spanish) of all indigenous subjects, so that they might learn "good customs" and be more easily governed. Still, factional conflicts created a gap between official policy and actual practice; royal decrees to establish schools filtered through a state and religious bureaucracy that was unwilling to carry them out (Mannheim 1984:301). Despite a general trend toward increased castilianization, the prospect of a subjugated but schooled Indian population was threatening to dominant elites. The resulting equivocal attitude is evidenced by a late-seventeenth-century decree making indigenous education compulsory until age ten and forbidding it thereafter (Mannheim 1984:298).

Independence from Spain in 1825 did little to improve the lot of the majority; rather, *criollos* exploited Indian labor with an even freer rein than before. There were scattered initiatives at founding rural schools in free communities, but education was denied to virtually all Indians living on *haciendas* (Carter 1965:43). Early curricula focused on hygiene, agriculture, and basic Spanish literacy; the use of indigenous languages in schools was unequivocally repressed. This period also saw the continuation of the rural rebellions that had reached their peak in the 1780s. Embattled landowners organized against rural education, drawing a (quite warranted) connection between indigenous literacy and threats to their political hegemony in the countryside. Yet, by the beginning of the twentieth century, rural elites had more to worry about than educational edicts promulgated by politicians, as indigenous people themselves began to organize clandestine educational networks, in an effort to resist exploitation by literate *mestizos*. These efforts, undertaken in the face of severe repression, predated by decades any serious government attempt at rural education.[1]

From the beginning, the struggle for rural education was closely linked to the struggle for land. During the Republican period, the legal assault on communal land ownership put intense pressure on the survival of Aymara communities. Illiterate, monolingual Aymaras had little recourse against land seizures legitimated in Spanish, in writing, and in the distant capital of La Paz. The related battles for the usurped lands and for rural schools constituted a cultural as well as an economic struggle—for the material survival of indigenous communities and forms of organization, and also for the preservation of cultural and linguistic diversity in the face of a rising nationalist ideology of castilianization and homogenization. The fights for literacy and against land seizures proceeded hand in hand, often directed by the same protagonists. The murder of indigenous teachers and the destruction of schools were often either the catalyst to, or retribution for, peasant rebellions. Under such circumstances, landowners' violent opposition to rural schooling is easy to comprehend.

Around the turn of the century, liberal politicians began to take an interest in schooling as a means of converting the indigenous masses into an effective labor force. This perspective, though thoroughly utilitarian and phrased in unabashedly racist terms, was strongly opposed by rural *hacendados*. Liberal laws were difficult to enforce where opposed by local authorities and often only exacerbated the turmoil in the countryside, provoking violent reprisals against indigenous educators. Conversely, indigenous leaders employed the discourses of liberalism and patriotism to present their educational demands as a step toward their conversion into dutiful state subjects (Conde 1992; Soria 1992). The use of such language to forge links with *criollo* society was part of a deliberate strategy by a relatively powerless sector, under attack by much more powerful groups.

Further impetus for the spread of indigenous literacy came, surprisingly, from the military. In 1907 obligatory military service was established for all able-bodied men, despite the strenuous objections of many *hacendados*, who warned that military training for Indians was a rash and dangerous policy, given the still-frequent rebellions in the countryside. Conscripts served for several years, rather than the current period of one year; the sacrifice for rural families was officially justified by conscripts' being taught to read and write (Mamani 1992:85). Thus the army produced a steady stream of literate Aymaras and Quechuas, many of whom went on to serve as teachers in the clandestine educational networks that began to operate soon thereafter. Military instructors also found their work easier if their charges were able to understand Spanish. The army thus had a stake in rural education and even helped protect some rural schools from attack (though in many areas landowners could still count on army support in quelling Indian resistance [Mamani 1992:86; Arze 1987]). In short, obligatory military service contributed greatly to the spread of Spanish fluency and literacy among indigenous people, as well as to their general integration into Bolivian national life (and continues to do so today).

The Chaco War with Paraguay (1932–35) also had a powerful impact on national educational policy. As thousands of indigenous conscripts were sent to the front, language barriers among Aymaras, Quechuas, Guaranís, and monolingual *criollos* impeded military operations, indirectly causing the deaths of many combatants (Soria 1992:54; Arze 1987). Bolivia's ultimate crushing defeat brought home to politicians the necessity of widespread castilianization of the country's indigenous population, if any large-scale national undertaking were to have hope of success.

Bolivia's most renowned educational experiment was the *escuela-ayllu* of Warisata, which combined socialist philosophy with Aymara cultural and organizational principles, inspiring similar experiments throughout Latin America (see Pérez 1962).

Unlike the clandestine efforts preceding it, Warisata was a high-profile undertaking that served as the organ of an entire community (from which the school took its name) in its struggle against exploitation by rural *hacendados*. Explicitly socialist and fiercely pro-Indian, Warisata was "a kind of liberated territory" (Salazar 1943:39). Its founders, *mestizo* educator Elizardo Pérez and Aymara leader Avelino Siñani, symbolized the union of two important intellectual currents of the time. Warisata introduced a curriculum and methodology decades ahead of its time, incorporating coeducation; bilingual education; community control over school decisions; communal labor; and elimination of grades, hourly schedules, and annual vacations (Salazar 1943:66–67). This project of "converting the school into a platform for struggle" brought swift and violent retaliation from the neighboring *mestizos*; the entire community became a target for kidnap, torture, arson, murder, and accusations of treason. After ten years of existence (1931–1941), the lifelines Warisata had drawn to a few powerful figures in Bolivian society could not save it; Elizardo Pérez was replaced by governmental fiat, and the experiment came to an end.

The discursive/ideological front of the long struggle for land and literacy is often overshadowed by that struggle's more tangible objectives, but proved to be equally important in the long run. While the movement slowed to some extent the usurpation of native lands and made significant gains in the spread of literacy, it also introduced into national political discourse ideas that previously had no place there. The dominant political rhetoric was explicitly, almost exclusively, racist; even liberal intellectuals who supported indigenous education saw it primarily as a means to "civilize" a backward race and transform it into a useful labor force. By the 1950s, however, themes of justice, racial pride, and solidarity with the "popular sectors" dominated public political discourse. They remain as central themes of political sloganeering by most parties even today.

There are few areas in which the dominant culture has a greater stake than public education. Where possible, counter-hegemonic meanings and practices are "reinterpreted, diluted, or put into forms which support or at least do not contradict . . . the effective dominant culture" (Williams 1980a:39). This is evident in the case of Warisata, which is still evoked as an official symbol of educational excellence, though its philosophical principles and methods have been largely suppressed. When incorporation is not possible, entire areas of subaltern experience may be excluded from national history, as occurred with the clandestine indigenous educational networks. In the construction of official history, "nationalist discourse has reshaped popular memories . . . by variously recoding, silencing and authorizing entire varieties of peasant practices" (Swedenburg 1990:28). The reconstruction of educational history must include the history of such practices, of the ideologies around schooling, and of the political currents that have shaped and reshaped them.

Rural Education in the Twentieth Century: Government Takes up the Reins

By the 1940s, a rudimentary system of government-sponsored rural schools was in place, with a curriculum emphasizing agriculture, vocational skills, and hygiene.[2] Literacy and math were secondary concerns, relative to the goals of "civilizing" the Indians and extending the reach of the state into indigenous communities. Schools were deficient in terms of infrastructure, salaries, and teaching quality, and only 11 percent of rural children attended (Burke 1971:329). Instruction was completely in Spanish, though most students had little or no knowledge of the language.

After the 1952 revolution, the number of students nationwide increased threefold and the number of rural schools fivefold (Carter 1971:144–45). This was largely due to the land reform, which broke the back of *hacendado* resistance to rural education. The MNR promulgated the Educational Reform of 1953, and the subsequent *Código de la Educación Boliviana* remained the central document of public education (though largely unfulfilled) until the present decade. By the 1960s, education consumed one-fourth of the national budget and indigenous people had begun to enter the system as teachers themselves. But with Spanish as the exclusive language of the classroom, dropout rates remained high, with only half of urban students and 6.5 percent of rural students ever reaching the sixth grade (Carter 1971:145). Female students remained marginalized in terms of both enrollment (Burke 1971:325) and school curricula and materials (Miracle 1973, 1976). Students were often beaten for their inability to pronounce Spanish words or for speaking their native tongue in the classroom. Rural teachers had little or no training in bilingual education and were usually Spanish-speaking *mestizos* rather than members of the communities they served. Neither linguists nor indigenous people had a voice in the planning of school materials or curricula. Lack of knowledge about indigenous languages and cultures contributed to students' frustration and a humiliating classroom atmosphere (Copana 1981; Yapita 1981).

Despite the populist rhetoric promoted after 1952, the knowledge, values, and history of the indigenous majority remained absent from the school curriculum. Nationalist ideology gains much of its strength by downplaying ethnic differences and solidarities in favor of a common national culture, and the school was the most important disseminator of nationalist ideology among the rural population. Postrevolutionary rhetoric directed somewhat more attention toward "the Indian problem," but did not significantly reformulate it in terms of the perceived problematic and the overriding goal of national integration.

The 1960s saw various attempts at bilingual education, beginning with the evangelical Summer Institute of Linguistics and continuing through the 1970s with the support of USAID and UNICEF. While some projects produced encouraging results, achieving some degree of literacy in both languages, most suffered from deficiencies in community participation, linguistic training of personnel, program coordination, funding, long-term planning, and evaluation (Briggs 1985; Amadio and Zúñiga 1989). Political instability made program continuity difficult; programs begun by one administration were often discontinued by the next, and laws containing basically the same objectives were passed by one administration after another (Carter 1971; Primov 1980; Briggs 1985). Despite some government coordination, there was no comprehensive bilingual education policy at the national level. In most cases, the aim was to move students into Spanish-taught classes as quickly as possible, not to maintain their use of native languages or incorporate indigenous culture into the curriculum. Such attempts seemed to derive less from any progressive sensibility on the part of government than from the growing realization that schooling "can fulfill its essential function of inculcation only so long as a minimum of adequacy is maintained between the pedagogic message and the receiver's capacity to decode it" (Bourdieu and Passeron 1977:99).

Despite the proliferation of rural schools, investigators lamented that this meant only "more education, not a better quality of education" (Burke 1971: 330). Still, though most rural schools remained decidedly substandard, the national literacy rate rose from 31 percent to 67 percent between 1950 and 1976 (Klein 1982:264).[3] Furthermore, classrooms have become gentler places in recent years; corporal punishment is rare, and teachers often use indigenous languages when necessary, rather than punishing children for speaking them. This change in attitude was partly due to the realization that the old methods were so oppressive as to drive children out of school altogether. Also, a large fraction of teachers today are themselves Aymara or Quechua speakers. Knowledge of indigenous languages is now officially recognized as a desirable trait for teachers and is given (minimal) attention in their training. By the beginning of the 1990s, the *Proyecto de Educación Intercultural Bilingüe* was coordinating bilingual education programs in different parts of the country, with some government cooperation (the proyect was integrated into the national educational reform in 1995).

Still, even after the more overtly cruel features were phased out, the hidden curriculum of schooling changed little, both in its underlying social aims and in the practices employed to achieve those aims. The curriculum remained centrally dictated, based on a set of official meanings that reflected the dominant view of society, with no input from teachers, students, or parents. Teaching remained a unidirectional process based on dictation, memorization, and copying. Classrooms continued to be organized around principles of regimentation and conformity. All in all, Bolivian schooling remained a far cry from the *educación democrática y liberadora* mandated by law.

A central problem throughout Bolivia's history has been the integration of the rural majority into the economic and cultural life of the urban minority. Rural dwellers' cultural and linguistic distinctiveness and their reticence in orienting their production toward "national" needs have been problematized as the primary obstacle on the road to capitalist development. As in many Third World countries, mass education first arose in order to bring indigenous people into the fold of the "national culture" and economy.[4] The "problem" of cultural difference has often been constructed as one of citizenhood; indigenous people are seen as insufficiently nationalized, inhabitants of

Bolivia but not quite Bolivians. Correspondingly, a central aim of rural schooling has been to fashion "Bolivian citizens" from "Indians."[5] As Archondo (1991:54) summarizes this view, "If the Indians have any rights that should be recognized, it is the right to stop being Indians so that they can finally belong to the national culture from which they have been separated."

Rural schooling created a limited but significant degree of social mobility, manifested primarily in increased urban migration.[6] While this migratory influx might be read as evidence of indigenous people's "integration into the national culture," so long sought by politicians and planners, it has not proved as advantageous as was perhaps expected. While some migrants manage to find regular employment, many more drift into the burgeoning "informal sector," and a significant number end up among the most marginalized of society, begging in order to survive.

The new social mobility provided by mass schooling proved problematic in another sense as well. As Hobsbawm (1983:294) notes, "secondary schooling provide[s] a broad criterion of middle-class membership, but one too broad to define or select the rapidly growing, but nevertheless numerically rather small, elites which . . . actually [run] the national affairs of countries." Simply raising the educational level of the population is clearly not enough to erase the social barriers in Bolivia's highly stratified society. As a more selective criterion of middle-class membership, language plays an important role. Previously, the broad division between Spanish speakers and non-Spanish speaking Indians constituted a fairly clear boundary between the legitimized and the marginalized sectors of society. More recently with the spread of Spanish fluency throughout much of the indigenous population, the *kind* of Spanish spoken has become a powerful marker of social position, as well as a basis for social discrimination. Consequently, much of Bolivian schooling has been dedicated not only to replacing indigenous languages with Spanish, but also to trying to eradicate (with little success) the influences of the former from students' speech. Not surprisingly, the delegitimation of students' language has often been accompanied by the delegitimation of their culture(s) and their persons. At the same time, what D'Emilio (1991:38) refers to as "the myth of schooling"—that is, the assumption of an automatic connection between education and economic progress—has been a powerful force in Aymara efforts to obtain greater access to education and has contributed to a widespread ideology that views education as the key to social and personal power.

Part of the ideological construction of Bolivia's "educational crisis" has been the assumption that schools were not fulfilling their function. However, looking beyond official objectives to the deeper social functions that schools fulfill, it would seem that, in many respects, Bolivia's public schools have accomplished their implicit social mission, if not always their stated pedagogical one. Though many children remain unschooled, Spanish fluency and basic literacy have spread throughout most of the population. Schools have carried the dominant values, meanings, consumption patterns, and modes of organization into many rural communities, these forms either displacing or syncretizing with indigenous ones. Urban migration, with its promise of greater academic opportunities[7] and the chance to put such learning to economic use, has increased, forming a growing pool of cheap, low-status laborers for the urban centers.

One might argue that the many rural children still marginalized from the educational system are evidence that schools are *not* fulfilling their mission; but this view ignores schooling's role in the stratification of society. Bolivia is still mainly an agricultural nation; while "integrating the peasantry into national life" remains an official goal, it would not be desirable for *all* peasants to achieve an educational level that would encourage their migration to the city. Some must remain in the countryside to perform the agricultural labor of the nation, and restricting access to education (or limiting it to the primary grades) is one of the most efficient ways of assuring this distribution of labor.[8] Though politicians speak of providing a high school education to all citizens, a highly educated peasantry would put severe pressures on the present economic and social organization of the country.[9] It would seem that today, as during the colonial period, "the linguistic barrier is both an impediment and a godsend for ideological and social control" (Mannheim 1982:302).

Schooling's role in the stratification of Bolivian society is manifested in its bifurcation into two parallel systems, rural and urban.[10] This division is reflected in teacher training as well, although graduates of rural normal schools can teach in urban schools and all public schoolteachers must put in two years of rural service before seeking a transfer to the city. But in general, the rural normal schools take in rural students and train them to teach in rural areas, while the urban schools reflect a more urban orientation both in their curriculum and in their student body. For many reasons (detailed in chapter 3), the normal school is often the only choice available to peasant or working-class youth (which, in the department of La Paz, is virtually synonymous with Aymara youth) who aspire to continue their education beyond high school. The division between the normal schools and the universities reflects a system of higher education still largely segregated by class.

Reverence and Resentment: Teachers and Rural Communities

As might be expected, given the conflicts and contradictions that rural education has traversed over the years, the popular ideology surrounding it is both powerful and ambivalent. Many rural parents place an almost religious faith in education, viewing it as the salvation that will lift their children out of poverty and into the middle class. Contrasting with this belief in the value of schooling is a clear awareness of its shortcomings: the limited utility of much of what is taught, the ignorance or active denigration of indigenous culture, the notorious inefficiency and corruption. A high school diploma and Spanish fluency undoubtedly broaden one's economic and social opportunities, but the costs have been high with regard to the devaluation of indigenous culture, changing relations within the family and community, and submission to the humiliating process of *castellanización.* While education is idealized in the abstract, the actual system and those it employs are subject to heavy criticism from parents, students, and educators themselves.

Schoolteachers occupy an ambiguous position within the rural community. Supposedly the hub of public life, most are occupational migrants without longstanding local ties. The idealized archetype of the rural schoolteacher as classroom instructor, town scribe, mediator, counselor, social worker, and community organizer is offset by the teacher's image as an agent of cultural imperialism and exploiter of rural communities. Rural teachers also suffer discrimination by their urban colleagues. The perception that rural teachers are less competent stems from various sources: prejudice against teachers who speak with an indigenous accent, the idea that rural teachers are cut off from urban intellectual currents, rural schools' reputation as less rigorous. Rural teachers react indignantly to such notions, pointing out that not only do they work more closely with students and communities, but their job involves demands and challenges not required of urban teachers: "We have to do battle in the countryside, not just within the four walls [of the classroom], but organizing in the community . . . The urban teacher simply shows up, signs his time card, goes into the class he's scheduled for . . . They don't give their all like the rural teacher has to . . . It's we who really bear the weight of this problem of education, educating the children of the peasantry" (interview).

While maintaining a critical attitude toward the belief that rural teachers are less qualified, the factors underlying it cannot be dismissed out of hand. Entrance standards for rural normal schools do tend to be more lenient than those for urban ones. Additionally, the rural service requirement for new teachers means that the ranks of rural teachers contain disproportionate numbers both of beginning teachers and of those who could not pass the exam required for promotion to an urban school.[11] Those from the city often have trouble adjusting to rural life. Their effectiveness may be hampered by lack of fluency in the language of their students, combined with the frequency of transfers in the middle of the school year. On the other hand, many teachers who do speak an indigenous language show marked interference in their use of Spanish; this is often interpreted as a sign of ineptitude, even by students and parents whose speech is similarly marked.

Rural schools often lack the most basic material resources, and teachers are often isolated in remote communities, teaching several grades at once. While lecturing, copying, and memorization are also the predominant methods in urban schools, the dearth of dialogic teaching is exacerbated in rural areas by the lack of materials, inadequate training, and language barriers between teachers and students (until the current reform, teachers' language abilities were not even taken into account with regard to placement). In many rural schools, personnel shortages require teachers to teach outside their subject area. Subjects such as English or French become a virtual charade when a teacher who does not speak the language in question is obliged to go through the motions. Students are aware that much of their instruction is of dubious quality, and this affects their image of teachers in general. On several occasions I found myself assailed by schoolchildren beseeching me to teach them a little English, because "our teachers don't teach well" or "they don't want to teach us."

Rural teachers often depend upon the community's generosity for part of their sustenance, and those who are perceived as competent and dedicated can count on such support as the accepted way of things. Not all teachers are equally well loved, however, and parents often complain about teachers taking advantage of their position to demand favors from the community or extract gifts of food from students on holidays. Though parents often sympathize with teachers' efforts to strike for better wages, one also hears disparaging comments about striking teachers simply not wanting to work. Male teachers' drinking is another common source of complaints. Grumbling about teachers' behavior can be heard even from villagers with teachers among their immediate relatives, though sometimes with the qualifier that "the ones from here are a bit more discreet."

With these observations, I do not wish to imply that substandard teaching is restricted to rural schools, nor to disparage the efforts of the many dedicated and effective rural teachers. In terms of community involvement, rural teachers are perceived as superior to urban ones. Urban teachers have little contact with students outside the classroom, and are often viewed as selling their labor by the hour, rather than dedicating themselves full-time to education.[12] The negative image of rural teachers is presented here, not in order to debate its truth value, but rather to analyze a popular conception that often makes for strained relations between school personnel and the communities they serve. These tensions, combined with the abundance of teachers in the area, led one parent to refer to a nearby normal school (not the one analyzed in this study) as "a teacher factory, that turns out products of poor quality."[13] Such attitudes contrast sharply with the extreme reverence reserved for schooling in the abstract. But given the school's ambiguous nature—simultaneously an avenue of social mobility and an agent of cultural domination—such ambivalence is hardly surprising.

On the Threshold of Reform

Summarizing the discussion thus far, we can identify two contrasting perspectives at work in Bolivia's language and educational policy. The first views the official language (spoken and written) as an avenue to political power; Spanish-speaking elites thus tried to deny education to indigenous populations, while those populations in turn strove for greater access to educational resources. The second perspective views the official language as a means to integrating the indigenous population into "national life," that is, the capitalist market economy and urban/*criollo* cultural values. Policies of cultural and linguistic homogenization implicitly recognized indigenous languages as "the source and pillar of cultural memory, in a situation in which what was wanted was forgetting" (Mannheim 1984:297). This perspective gave rise to the exclusive use of Spanish in schools and, in more recent years, has led indigenous populations to demand recognition of their cultures and languages within the educational system. Historically, national elites oscillated between these two perspectives in their search for the most efficient means of controlling the indigenous population. While the rural rebellions and land struggles characterizing the period up until 1935 gave strength to the first perspective, the disaster of the Chaco War, the rise of industrialism, and the populist nationalism of the 1952 revolution have brought the second perspective to dominance.

In 1992, a nationwide educational congress was held with participation from all relevant social sectors. Out of this congress came a comprehensive reform plan put forth by the government, as well as parallel proposals from other groups.[14] This plan embraces the entire system in both its pedagogical and its administrative aspects, giving central place to progressive goals such as gender equity, local input, and bilingual-intercultural education (largely through the initiative of vice-president Cárdenas). In contrast to past policies of linguistic and cultural homogenization, the reform emphasizes the maintenance of local languages and cultures and the incorporation of students' cultural knowledge into the curriculum. Although its administrative aspects have provoked bitter arguments, its pedagogical aspects seem to fulfill progressive educators' fondest dreams: a constructivist, student-centered approach designed to promote symmetrical classroom relations, a cooperative ethic, and toler-ance of diversity. With the reform already being implemented in 334 pilot schools, government efforts in the training of person-nel, production of materials, and building the theoretical ground-work for its pedagogical vision all seem to indicate a serious commitment to transforming the philosophical and practical underpinnings of Bolivian schooling.

Nevertheless, transformations of such scope are not made in a year, and perhaps not in a decade. The reform was initi-ated in the earliest grades; while there are obvious reasons for introducing the new system at the bottom-most level, proposed changes in teacher education have lagged behind. Most teach-ers are still trained via the traditional, stultifying methods of copying and memorization and have considerable difficulty adjusting to the new system. But the most formidable obstacle to the reform is political rather than logistic: the teachers' union has declared itself firmly opposed to the plan and has had mixed success in winning public support for its position.

On the pedagogical front, teachers' criticisms focus mainly on the transitional difficulties of adopting new methods and materials with inadequate retraining; in terms of pedagogical *principles*, there are relatively few complaints, given that the reform proposes changes that teachers and others have been demanding for years (valorization of students' language and culture, more dialogic teaching methods, etc.). The most in-tense opposition has been sparked by the proposed administra-tive changes, such as the decentralization of the school system, which had been highly centralized in practially all aspects. Under the new plan, financial, administrative, and operational responsibility for schools will shift from the federal to the deparmental level. This should eliminate excessive bureaucracy,[15] make school authorities more answerable to complaints, and permit curricula to be tailored to regional needs. Combined with the government's Popular Participation Plan, decentraliza-tion should give local communities greater control over schools.

Critics of decentralization claim that its primary aim is not to increase local input in educational decisions, but to shift financial responsibility for schools to the local level. This is likely to cause a severe drop in available resources in poorer departments such as Potosí and Pando; correspondingly, the plan's strongest support is in wealthier departments such as Santa Cruz and Cochabamba, whose taxes currently subsidize education in poorer areas of the country. Many schools may face a constant struggle simply to maintain operations (already a struggle in many areas), leading to neglect, deterioration, and the eventual shift of the financial burden to parents (in the form of charges for school supplies, maintenance expenses, entrance fees for exams, etc.). The government claims that money will be made available by the disbursement of federal funds to the departments, additional taxes at the departmental level, and "extra-budgetary funds." Large sums are currently being injected into the system (to produce new materials, retrain personnel, provide school libraries, etc.), but most of this money is foreign aid specifically earmarked for the transition to the new system and cannot be expected to continue indefinitely.

Furthermore, Bolivia's nine departments are neither administratively nor pedagogically prepared take on the burden of planning and running their own school systems. The development of administrative frameworks and pedagogical expertise at the departmental level is still in its initial stages. Ramos (1988) and others have also argued that before decentralization can take place, a "regionalization" of the country is necessary, redrawing departmental boundaries to coincide with the country's geographic, economic, and ethnic divisions. Teachers have also objected to the "interference" from parents that local community involvement in schooling entails.

Another objection to decentralization is the threat it poses to "national unity." This criticism runs deeper than the allegation that regionally diversified curricula and diplomas would no longer be compatible. The worry is that a decentralized school system will foster the formation of separatist regional identities, instead of a single national identity. The reform's commitment to bilingual/intercultural education explicitly includes the concern for maintaining local cultural identities, in contrast to the historical trend by which the school subsumed or erased indigenous bases of identity in favor of a homogenous collective national subject. Such proposals provoke serious concern in a nation whose political cohesion is already perceived as threatened by intense regionalist sentiments. During its 173 years of independence, Bolivia has lost over half of its original territory to the ambitions of its neighbors; one of its largest and wealthiest departments (Santa Cruz) has flirted with secession on numerous occasions. Thus a certain amount of trepidation over any policy likely to loosen the bonds of national unity is to be expected.

Beyond these nationalist anxieties, decentralization is assumed by many to be the first step toward the eventual privatization of education. Shifting the burden to the departmental or community level could conceivably lead to shifting it away from government altogether, onto the private sector. While such plans are not explicitly stated in official documents, public suspicion to this effect (fueled by the teachers' unions) has sparked heavy criticism and public outrage.[16] Once the flow of transitional foreign aid dimishes, rural areas will almost certainly be harder hit than urban centers. Not only are rural areas poorer, but deficiencies in infrastructure make school operations difficult. Paved roads are still relatively rare throughout much of Bolivia; many communities are accessible only by foot or by burro, requiring several hours or even days of difficult travel for the teachers who work there (and who must periodically return to the city to collect their pay, visit their families, etc.). Currently, teachers in remote areas receive extra pay; under the decentralization plan, however, such areas (already less attractive to prospective teachers) will be unable to offer salaries competitive with those of the wealthier departments and urban centers. While departmental governments could institute a rural service requirement similar to the present federal policy, their power to do so will diminish as the number of private schools increases and more teachers move into the open market. Even if local governments are able to provide schools in remote communities, the continued proliferation of private schools in urban areas will most likely continue the trend toward a two-tiered system of education, sharply divided along class lines.

Teachers' sharpest objections to the reform, however, spring from the threat it poses to their own economic interest. Currently, teaching is a state-supported profession, meaning that every normal school graduate is guaranteed a job. This accounts for much of teaching's popularity as a career, despite the low pay and difficult conditions. It also attracts many students who have little talent or even liking for teaching, but choose it in the face of limited alternatives. Some of the reform's proposed changes, such as the conversion of teaching into a "free" profession (with teachers competing for jobs like any other professional) and making union membership voluntary instead of automatic, succumbed to union pressure and were withdrawn. Attempts to provide specialized training or differential pay for teachers with specialized skills have been branded by the union as "attempts to turn teachers against each other."

Another sticking point has been the legislation of periodic competency exams for teachers. While union pressure resulted in a modification of the law, assuring that no teacher currently in service could be removed due to changes implemented under the reform, future teachers will have to demostrate their competence in order to keep their jobs. Introducing performance as a criterion of employability is likely to restrict the class mobility that a teaching certificate provides, reproducing the current distribution of "academic capital" by favoring candidates from families where a high level of education is already the norm. Many who enter teaching seeking upward mobility would be obliged to seek other employment (perhaps in vain, given the general economic situation of the country). A professor at the normal school expressed the following opinion: "I think it's necessary. I think it will improve our salaries. Because maybe then there would be some standards, no? Because our public education really isn't demanding . . . If we measured [teacher competence] in some rigorous way, concretely, fairly, then maybe a lot of teachers would be out of the system. Because I have to admit that, really, we rural teachers especially, we *aren't* well prepared." While more stringent academic requirements for teachers undoubtedly would improve educational quality, they fly in the face of teachers' collective interest; and predictably, when teachers' interests conflict with those of students, the former have tended to prevail.[17]

These issues raise important questions about the responsibilities of individuals and the state with regard to the less privileged sectors of society. From indigenous people's perspective, schooling might be considered a trade-off between economic sacrifice and submission to an alienating regime of knowledge, on the one hand, and increasing one's future economic and social opportunities, on the other. A decision to focus government resources on improving primary education would assure the continuation of schooling's ideological functions, while withdrawing support precisely when schooling begins to "pay off" in terms of students' future life chances. Another normal school professor evaluated the question in terms of the costs and benefits to the state, only to arrive at a discouraging conclusion: "I think privatization will happen, because the government considers us unproductive . . . in the material sense.

Not like mining, handicrafts, factories, oil reserves, etc... How can we generate economic resources? It's difficult, we only generate human resources." In later chapters, I will argue that schools *are* in fact productive, and that the human resources they generate are just as essential to the maintenance of state power as are factories and mines.

Clearly, Bolivia's educational crisis is as political as it is pedagogical. While educational quality is undoubtedly poor enough to justify drastic and far-reaching measures, this itself is not sufficient to explain why the government should choose this particular moment to implement such measures; certainly, education has been in desperate straits for decades. An analysis that goes beyond the pedagogical reveals other forces at work as well. In addition to the progressive goals the federal government has set for itself in terms of reconceptualizing educational practice and its relation to Bolivia's multicultural reality, restructuring the system also has clear advantages in terms of managing political pressures, both internal and external:

- by partly divesting itself of the financial burden of schooling, the federal government can more easily meet the demands of the World Bank and the IMF to reduce public spending (notably, international lending institutions have had a prominent voice in how reform funds are to be spent);
- by shifting responsibility for education to the local level, the government removes itself from the line of fire of dissatisfied parents, teachers, and other critics of the system;
- by decentralizing administrative decisions, it disperses the collective power of the teachers' union, thus defusing one of the most serious threats to its political stability.

The teachers' union is a major thorn in the side of government, with its ability to close schools department- or nationwide, bring traffic in La Paz to a standstill, and frustrate government efforts to carry out unpopular policies with a minimum of social upheaval. Many teachers argue that a central aim of the reform is to disarticulate one of the most powerful and militant sectors of a labor movement that has become increasingly resistant to government containment. The weakening of the teachers' union must be viewed in the context of the neoliberal wave sweeping over all of Latin America. Economic and educational reforms accompanied by declining union power are not unique to Bolivia; such processes are underway throughout the continent (largely due to pressure from the developed nations). While Bolivia cannot help but be caught up in these global trends, it is worth noting, in this period so decidedly shaped by the global decline of socialism, that traditional Marxist-Leninist ideals and rhetoric are very much alive here, in educational as well as in other debates.

Traditionally, the backbone of Bolivia's labor movement was the miners' union. Legendary for their militancy and tenacity, miners were a strong symbol of working-class power, winning important concessions from a series of administrations. Since 1985 they have been severely weakened by the New Economic Plan; hard-won gains have been rolled back and nearly 20,000 miners laid off. Consequently, teachers moved to the fore to spearhead the battle against the NEP. Their frequent strikes and demonstrations often draw in other sectors as well, severely hindering business in the capital and causing a massive headache for government officials.

The crux of teachers' political power is the Federación Departamental de Trabajadores de Educación Urbana de La Paz (FDTEULP). While ostensibly representing only urban La Paz public school teachers, the FDTEULP serves as the *de facto* leadership of all public school teachers, due to its large membership, tight organization, and proximity to the center of government power.[18] In times of conflict (that is, most of the time) the FDTEULP provides organizational leadership for La Paz teachers in general, urban and rural. When conflict reaches the national level, it coordinates the actions of the various departmental unions, though there is not always consensus between them. The FDTEULP is conspicuously dominated by the Partido Obrero Revolucionario (POR), and there is considerable overlap between the leadership of the two.[19] A Trotskyite party from the extreme left of the political spectrum, the POR's influence is greater than its actual size, due to its strength within the miners' and teachers' unions. This influence is evident in the degree to which virtually all public debates over education are cast in the rhetoric of revolutionary socialism.[20]

Although the ideologically rigid POR is regarded with distaste by many rank-and-file teachers, it enjoys a fair degree of support, due to its reputation for dedication, discipline, and steadfastness in the face of government pressure. During union elections in 1992, I was surprised to hear friends who habitually complained of the POR's domination admit that they had voted the POR slate as well. When asked why, they replied with a shrug: "They're the only ones who won't sell us out to the government." In a country where corruption is rampant in organized labor as well as in business and government, sincerity and effectiveness may win out over ideological differences.

Nevertheless, the teachers' union, and by extension the POR, suffered a major blow in 1995 as a result of a largely unsuccessful month-long strike against the reform. A similar strike in 1996 resulted in a salary hike of 13 percent, but did not significantly impede the reform's progress. While school strikes have been a frequently used weapon in Bolivia's labor disputes, often supported by parents, peasant unions, and other citizens' groups, many parents have grown frustrated with the difficulties of educating their children within the public system.[21] Strikes are increasingly perceived as holding students hostage to union or party interests, and as this perception spreads, public support has waned. Furthermore, as the reform moves ahead, it continues to gain adherents; correspondingly, the union is increasingly perceived as the major obstacle to bringing about real change in the system, and while the *kind* of change necessary is hotly debated, there is little argument over the *need* for change. The early stages of implementation have shown that many teachers are eager to be integrated into the reform; while some schools have resisted inclusion, many more are clamoring to be part of the pilot group. Despite an intensive propaganda campaign against the reform, opposition seems to be concentrated mostly in the cities (where the unions hold greater sway); in rural areas, teachers working under the most minimal of conditions are more optimistic that the promised changes may bring them some relief.

Thus, the promise of reform evokes both anticipation and worry. Despite official assurances that a renovated, restructured school system can reach all of Bolivia's children, many parents remain unconvinced, fearing that improved quality will mean decreased access, especially in poor and rural areas. Others are simply skeptical of any government promise of substantial change. One thing is clear: without some semblance of social consensus—sorely lacking at this point—such an immense undertaking will achieve its goals only at a high social cost, if at all. Ultimately, the reform's chances for success will depend upon the willingness and capability of teachers (as they themselves point out), since they will be the ones who implement it—or refuse to do so.

3

STUDENT LIFE AT THE NORMAL SCHOOL

Donde hay educación, no hay división de clases.

—Confucius
(Plaque hanging at the entrance to the girls' dormitory)

"Peor que nada es quedarse . . . ": Career Choices and the Lack Thereof

The Research Site and Subjects

The Escuela Normal Rural "Kollasuyo"[1] sits on the edge of Los Pozos, a small farming town in the heart of the Aymara culture area. Its three-year program trains rural teachers specializing in primary education. During the first half of the research period, there were 337 first- and third-year students; there were no second-year students, due to the government's moratorium on admissions the previous year. Halfway through the research period, the third-year students graduated, leaving 220 second-year students (135 male and 85 female). Due to another moratorium on admissions, no new students entered at the beginning of 1992. Nearly half the students were from the surrounding area; 87 percent were originally from rural communities dedicated to mining, fishing, or agriculture. Of these, 12 percent had relocated to La Paz or El Alto during childhood or adolescence.[2] Students ranged in age from eighteen to thirty-five, with most around twenty. Nearly half of them lived in dormitories on the school grounds, thirty or forty sharing one large room. The rest lived either with relatives in the area or in rented rooms in town. These *externos* were almost all male, since female students were strongly encouraged to live in the dormitories.

School personnel included twenty professors; the rector and the academic director; the secretary; the librarian; two dorm inspectors (male and female); the administrator; and the kitchen, grounds, and agricultural staff. Faculty members were graduates of similar institutions, who had subsequently taught for several years in rural schools and then completed a year of postgraduate study in the Instituto Superior de Educación Rural (ISER), specializing in a particular subject area. A few had some university training as well, usually in education or administration. All staff members were male except for the librarian, the secretary, the girls' dorm inspector, and the home economics teacher. The other professors were middle-aged or older men, except for two in their early thirties, who had been invited to attend ISER after showing particular promise in their university work. Several (including the rector) were from the area, and most spoke fluent Aymara as well as Spanish. Though most of their contact with students took place in the classroom, faculty lived on the school grounds and thus were accessible to students outside of class as well. Aside from the two dorm inspectors and the health professor, faculty members did not enter the dormitories.

Most students were of rural origin, though several were of the urban working class. A general indicator of class, ethnic, and regional origins in Bolivia is the *pollera*, the full, multilayered skirt worn by Aymara and Quechua women. When asked whether their mothers wore the *pollera*, 93 percent of those surveyed answered affirmatively, and over half of the female students indicated that they themselves wore the *pollera* when not at school. On weekends, most went to La Paz, some to stay with relatives, and others to catch buses for their home communities. Students who were short of money or who lived too far away to go home on weekends often spent weekends at the school.

Many students came from peasant families; 30 percent listed their father's occupation as agriculture, while 17 percent put "schoolteacher." Other responses included laborer, bricklayer, carpenter, baker and musician. Of those listing an occupation for their mother, 75 percent put "housewife,"[3] while others put farmer, teacher, weaver, or market or street vendor. Two-thirds of the students had themselves worked before entering the normal school, mostly in domestic labor, construction, agriculture, vending, driving, or factory or office work. At least two (men in their early thirties) had worked as interim teachers before deciding to pursue certification at the normal school. Twenty had traveled to other countries, most to work,[4] though eight mentioned "study" as well. In Bolivia, teaching tends to run in families; over half the students counted at least one teacher among their close relatives, and 15 percent had a relative or godparent on the faculty of the normal school itself. There were several sibling pairs among the students, and several had siblings at other normal schools.

It has become common practice in school ethnographies to focus on members of a particular peer group, as they position themselves in relation to the institution and to other groups: Willis's "lads" (1981a), Foley's "vatos" (1990), MacLeod's "Hallway Hangers" and "Brothers" (1987), Everhart's junior high buddies (1983). Such is not the case here, for several reasons. One is simply that the normal school did not contain such clearly defined groups as one finds in urban U.S. high schools.[5] Aside from affinities arising from place of origin, residence (on or off school grounds), and the urban/rural distinction, students did not differentiate themselves into small groups, and since most local students lived in town, the above-mentioned factors overlapped to a significant degree. The smallest bounded student group were the twenty to thirty who lived in the boys' dorm—far from the tight-knit small groups characteristic of so many school ethnographies.

While the lack of small-group focus was a drawback in some respects—such as the lack of group interviews, which proved so fruitful in the works mentioned above—it had its advantages as well. The "buckshot" approach to interviewing provided insight into the lives of a variety of students—male and female, married and single, urban and rural—and was invaluable for examining social divisions and conflicts from a variety of perspectives.[6] This variety was limited, however, by the fact that all students interviewed lived on the school grounds. This was mostly for logistical reasons; living on the grounds myself, I had greater access to and rapport with the dorm students, so that interviews with them were much easier to obtain. Furthermore, the dorm students were better suited to serve as expert consultants for many of the things I wanted to know. Living under the school's control to a much greater degree than the others, they were "subjects" of the institution in a much more complete sense.

While the female students I interviewed covered a fairly wide range in terms of their social status within the school, male interviewees were all among the most popular of their fellows—part of a vaguely defined "core group" that took most responsibility for student programs, meetings, and so on, though they did not form a cohesive, exclusive group of friends among themselves. I did not set out to interview only the "big men on campus," but the fact that they were more extroverted and expressed more interest in my presence yielded basically this result. Since females did not enter the boys' dormitory, I was unable to spend as much time inside their social scene or get to know many of them as well as I did the girls. I did look for variety when seeking interview subjects, but those I ended up interviewing were more often chosen for reasons of accessibility, personal affinity, or follow-up to previous informal conversations, than demographic balance of the sample.

Roads to the Rural Normal School

Most students whose parents were not teachers themselves were from peasant or working-class backgrounds; many were the first in their families to enter "the professions." Not surprisingly, their reasons for choosing a teaching career were largely economic. Personal preference was a factor in many cases, but the idea of choosing a career solely on that basis was a middle-class luxury out of reach for most. Many, as children, no doubt dreamed of being sports stars, scientists, artists, or business tycoons; but such aspirations were soon leveled to reflect the real-life opportunities available to them.[7] By the time they graduated from high school, the careers they aspired to were more along the lines of taxi driver, electronics technician, or radio announcer—and in many cases, even these hopes had been relinquished as grand illusions born of youthful naiveté.

Some saw teaching as a stepping stone, a way to earn money and/or academic credentials that would enable them to continue studying, usually at the university. Several cherished career plans that had nothing to do with teaching, and 22 percent of those surveyed said they did not intend to begin teaching after graduation. Given their economic situation, only a handful could probably hope to fulfill such aspirations. Indeed, most seemed to realize the unlikelihood of their dreams becoming reality, while at the same time maintaining an attitude of "anything is possible if you really want it."

The normal school professors were well aware that many students had not chosen teaching, as they said, *"por vocación."* Professor Torres, the sociology teacher and later academic director, summarized the kinds of considerations that draw rural youth into a teaching career:[8] "Most of them are children of teachers. And, one has to be realistic, even if they don't have the vocation or the aptitude, since their parents are teachers they send them to the normal school . . . It's the shortest course of study, and the least expensive . . . There also isn't much work [required of students]. Here we don't have the means, there isn't much in the way of research or teaching materials, so students are pretty content to just do what we give them."

Family pressures, combined with the meager but steady paycheck that teachers receive, were important factors in the choice of many. Mateo had varied work experience and many practical skills, but these did not offer the guarantee of steady employment and a retirement pension. Already thirty-two, he was of necessity receptive to such logic:

Mateo: More than anything it was the pressure from my mother and my sister. They said, "You think you're going to be young all your life? At any moment your strength will give out, and you'll be tired and unable to work. At least [teaching] you'll have something, enough to live on." And I said to myself, "They're right." That's why I decided to do it; it wasn't really my vocation. It was like an imposition, I'd say, from my sister and my parents. Or rather, I was compelled to come.

The following excerpts describe students' reasons for entering the normal school, and reflect the similar concerns faced by thousands of rural youths every year. While some mention a personal affinity for teaching, financial and family pressures were most often the deciding factors.

Diana: I wanted to study in the university, and I did, I was there for about a month. Then they re-opened the normal school, and my friends said, "Let's go there, what do you want to spend more money for?" . . . My father could barely support me . . . there's also my brothers who are studying. So, since I'm the girl, I had to come here . . . Before, I thought teachers had studied [in the university], were children of rich people . . . Then I found out children of peasants could be teachers. So I decided, "Why can't I go too?" And I came.

Roberto: Maybe it was because of my family's influence, that I chose this career. Because, to begin with, my father is a teacher. And my eldest brother too. And my sisters, they're teachers too . . . And I like the profession, being a teacher; it's what I most like, in life.

Faustino: Since I was a kid, in high school, I really liked this career, teaching. That was always my intention . . . to help the peasants, work with them, impart what knowledge I had to the community . . . It's a short course of study, fine, but I'm not going to stop there. I plan to go on, at least set foot in the university, no? Work for two years, one can do it, you know, studying and working too. So as to have, at least a little more, to complete oneself—

AL: For a rural teacher it's a little difficult to continue studying, isn't it?

Faustino: Yes, there's that, because one works mornings and afternoons. For urban teachers it's different; one works straight through, from morning until 1:00, but in the after-noon one can do what one likes. One can go to an institute . . . But in the case of the rural teacher, no, that's true. Maybe during vacations, no?

Antonia: I was never one to stay behind; I wanted to continue studying, and I was working too as an interim teacher . . . It's the career I most liked since way back then. That is, since it's sort of general knowledge. It's guaranteed too, it's se-cure, although the salary is low . . . When my father was teaching, I'd think, How I'd like to work like that, like my father. There are holidays too, celebrations, Teachers' Day—they really have fun then! [laughter]. I liked that most of all, and so I chose this career. It's also the shortest . . . My father says now, "Don't keep studying that, they're going to privatize it." Oh well, like people say, when you start something you have to finish it.

Carlos: I came here kind of by accident. Life in the mines is sad; how one works, how one lives; you can't stay there, it's terrible. And, by chance, a friend said to me, "You could go to the normal school, at least be something . . . " There, one can at least earn one's daily bread, without sacrificing oneself like in the mine. Because imagine, if you stay in the mine, though it's great, much better [than here], but if you stay, what happens? You could die, catch some disease maybe, most miners have silicosis. That's why a lot of people leave . . . I also wanted to seek new horizons here in Bolivia, so I came to the normal school.

Among all the students interviewed, Carlos presented the widest gulf between personal aspirations and actual career choice. He expressed an unequivocal dislike for teaching, and yet a combination of personal and social factors seemed to leave him little choice. The following was recorded after he revealed his plans to return to the mine after graduation:

AL: But why study three years to be a teacher, if you don't plan to do that afterwards?
Carlos: Yeah, that's the thing. It's like I told you, it was by accident. I never wanted to be a teacher . . . It was to satisfy my family. I don't like it. I want—something else, I don't know, I can't figure out what . . . Create something, invent something that doesn't exist yet. I want to discover, I don't know, maybe some things, but I don't know what. I think that's my calling. Not being here . . . I really don't like children that much. I know someday I'm going to get mad and I'm not going to want to teach them, and if I'm going to be teaching them, maybe, no, that's not good . . .
AL: Did you ever think of going to the university, instead of the normal school?
Carlos: Mmm, I never tried.

AL: Why not? If your calling is to discover things—
Carlos: Because, no one ever said to me, "Try the university"
   or "There you could be something." And also, I never told
   anyone I had those ambitions . . . Because my father, my
   relatives, they're very strong people. They talk loud. They're
   very different . . .

A frequent theme in such conversations was students' desire
to continue studying beyond high school. For young people of
their background, this is practically synonymous with entering
the normal school.[9] The university, though cheap by U.S. standards, is beyond the reach of most (due as much to the cost
of urban living as to strictly study-related expenses). Agricultural and technical institutes are scarce in the countryside. For
Aymara youth seeking an escape from farming, the mines, or
the "informal economy," the normal school is the obvious and
often the only choice. Nevertheless, a student's personal reasons for entering the normal school seemed to have little bearing on his or her academic success, or even on what kind of
teacher he or she would become. Those who were most ambitious and, consequently, most frustrated with the normal school
program, often seemed destined to become the best teachers,
by virtue of the very intellectual restlessness that made them
dissatisfied students.

Students' Expectations: The Ideology of Teaching and Teachers

Most students shared a well-defined set of ideas about
teaching as a profession. Trujillo (1996) notes that educational
subjects' "teaching ideology" is formed largely on the basis of
(1) the image of teaching they have formed as students, and (2)
the ideological orientation they receive during their professional
training. The normal school students' previous school experiences deeply influenced what they hoped to accomplish as
teachers themselves. Their interviews displayed sharp criticisms
of teachers in general, offset by a profound idealism about the
profession in the abstract.

Soledad: Before, I wasn't really sure this was the career for me,
   but as the year went on, I came to see that it is. Before, I

thought about becoming a nun . . . [in church] they told us, "You must put yourself in the service of others, to help them." And I thought, "Being a teacher will give me that opportunity" . . . I know that I have something of value, maybe not everything, but I know I have some knowledge at least. To contribute my little bit, for them, you know? And, that way I can help them, so they can know too.

Faustino: One doesn't earn much teaching, but it's a noble profession all the same. Because of teachers there's everything, there's engineers, there's—if it weren't for teachers, there would be nothing.

Diana: Some teachers make the parents hate them . . . There are good teachers who really deserve respect, right? Then there are those, for example, who take advantage of the female students. They talk to the girls just like any guy would, they don't respect them; that kind of teacher they hate. In my village it happened several times, teachers who were single, we found out, they even had a baby with some of the girls . . . The parents hated those teachers. But others no, when a teacher behaves well, why should we fight with him, hate him too?

Mateo: In rural schools you have to do everything, that's why I wanted to come . . . My logic is always, contribute what I can for the good of education. Education first, the fundamental base of any country, right? But unfortunately these days our education is upside down. Sometimes with colleagues, principals I've talked to, they tell me, "Gee kid, I'd like to think like you, it sounds nice, but I know your thoughts will change." "But why, Sir?" I say. "Because once I thought that way too," they tell me. "Like you, but I got into all this corruption, and now I'm already dead, I'm just another thief . . . " Hell, sometimes I think—maybe, no? Could be! Could be the very environment will lead me to it.

Some saw education as a way to change society, via teachers' power to shape the values of the next generation. For these students, education was the potentially transformative element in a broader philosophy of social change.

José: I would like there to be in Bolivia, for everyone to enjoy
a little part of something. Not some living unhappy, crying,
with tears in their eyes, the rest laughing, happy, with their
children taken care of . . . I want to instill that idea in my
students, for them to carry that idea from childhood. That
a thing should be for everyone, not just for oneself. That
there shouldn't be this exploitation. That things like natural
resources are for everyone, not just for a part of the population who can take it for themselves . . . If there's no education, if we're all going to be illiterate, we're just going to stay
the same, out of ignorance . . . The fundamental thing is to
orient people somehow, so they realize . . . How great it would
be, if the teachers who graduate in the future would have
that aim, to orient people, to make people *understand* . . . to
give them an idea of how we can emerge from this backwardness.

Actual teaching experience often dispelled such idealistic
hopes. Mateo—a relatively young man posesssed of a strong
moral sense, who had seen the results of trying to maintain
such ideals in a system of compromise and corruption—
fluctuated between a passionate, revolutionary optimism and
bouts of discouraged, even cynical, resignation. Recalling his
years as an interim teacher, he described how one's own colleagues can constitute an obstacle to the pursuit of excellence:

Mateo: So many children could be taught, but what happens?
The teachers themselves . . . they look at you like, "Ah no!
That teacher, what's he doing?" saying you're against them,
they exclude you, isolate you . . . They meet among themselves and get you transferred . . . I want to speak the truth,
teach the children conscientiously; but the same thing happens, they do you the same way. The whole profession is
like that . . . So, what do you do? All alone you have to try
to placate them and adapt yourself to them. Live with them,
in that environment. What else can you do? . . . The peasants recognize and acknowledge conscientious people who
try to help the village progress with their teaching, who
speak the truth. They know. They come in secret to see if
that teacher's worth his salt, if he teaches well, and by
asking their own children . . . In this region they produce
potatoes, eggs, right? So the kids bring them; they say,

"Here teacher, have some" . . . [The others] say, "Hey, what's going on? Why is that teacher treated so well? Why do they love him so? How come they bring him stuff and they don't bring me anything?" . . . They grab you, kidding around they say, "How's it going professor, how ya doing, what's up? Let's fry up some eggs, let's cook some potatoes" . . . Yeah, in that situation [intake of breath], desperate, you feel uncomfortable, you know?

Teachers with years of experience often display a cynical humor about the profession; such humor is a central element of teachers' occupational culture. I once accompanied Rosa, a professor at an urban normal school, to a job orientation talk she and a colleague were giving to a group of high school students. On the way, they joked, "We'll begin by saying, 'If you want to be victims, badly paid, abused by parents and by society' . . . " After the talk, during which few students asked any questions, Rosa remarked, "We discouraged them by telling them how little one earns!" but laughingly added that this was good, since students should be warned, "so they don't go get involved [in teaching]." Such mocking disparagement occurs within many professions, as a way of marking group boundaries, expressing solidarity, and commenting on the flaws and limitations of one's own field. Among Bolivian teachers, however, it also seems aimed at calling attention to the lack of respect and remuneration for those who carry out a difficult and important task, as well as at deflating the idealized version of the profession that constitutes the "official line."

Students—even quite young ones—are aware of the resignation and cynicism with which many teachers approach their job and the criticisms to which they are subject from parents and the community. As Rosa remarked to me, the teacher may be the highest-status person in the rural community and yet be resented and looked down upon by parents who perceive such status as undeserved. Teachers' poor reputation is exacerbated by the fact that, despite schooling's numerous shortcomings, virtually all educational struggles over the last decade have focused not on the quality of training, curriculum, or materials, but on salaries. The current conflict over the reform may be an exception (although even in this case the threat to teachers' economic interests accounts for much of their opposition), but even this wave of protest was sparked, not by the abysmal conditions of the status quo, but by plans to change it. Despite the union's revolutionary rhetoric, Rosa claimed that "teachers are a highly conservative sector," because "the work lulls you into a routine." Teachers who actually attempt radical changes in the classroom are very few.

When the normal school graduates enter the world of teaching, they enter a maelstrom of heated political debate that occasionally erupts into violence. They will be called upon to strike, to confront riot police in the streets of the capital, and to weigh the interests of their students against those of their colleagues. They enter a profession whose future is uncertain, where the rules of the game in effect when they begin their training may have changed drastically by the time they finish. Those studying in the rural normal school follow closely the political battles taking place in the capital, for those battles are deciding their future even as they move ever closer to graduation.

This, then, is the social and ideological environment from which students choose teaching as a career. Despite the mixed messages they receive about teachers and teaching, the combination of idealism, ambition, a desire for economic security, and lack of alternatives is strong enough to attract thousands of Aymara youth to the possibilities that the normal school holds for them. Many arrive with expectations of self-actualization and intellectual growth within an institution whose aim is nothing less than their own personal and professional fulfillment, through service to country and community. What they actually encounter there, and how the experience reshapes the visions they have brought to it, are the subject of the rest of this chapter and the following one.

Students as Regulated Subjects

Daily Life at the Normal School

Except for those students from Los Pozos itself, there was little contact between the normal school and the town. Unofficial contact between students and town residents was strongly discouraged (mainly to avoid romantic liasions and students' drinking in town). Official contact was mostly limited to student holiday parades and events such as graduation or Mothers'

Day, when students's relatives in town were invited to the school to observe the ceremony. Occasionally there were visits by educational authorities, for which the school grounds were spruced up and students instructed to be on their best behavior. These visits often occurred on national holidays; a meal would be served in the guests' honor, usually followed by several hours of drinking and conversation between the visitors, the rector, and the higher ranked (male) teachers. Other visits (decidedly less festive in tone) were prompted by more serious events, such as the conflict over admitting new students. Visiting authorities sometimes held meetings, inviting students to share their concerns; but students were generally hesitant to express their grievances in public, and had little opportunity for private access to the authorities.

Each member of the normal school community occupied a fixed place in a social hierarchy that can be described as follows: rector; academic director; the two dorm inspectors; male professors with several years of seniority; newer male professors; female professors (the home economics teacher and the librarian); administrative staff; students (boys before girls, older students before newer ones); and lower level staff (kitchen, grounds, and agricultural workers). Visiting authorities, when present, effortlessly took their place at the top of this hierarchy.[10]

Though there was relatively little class differentiation among students, those differences that did exist were a source of considerable tension, particularly among the girls. The most significant divisions among students (aside from gender) were between those from the country and those from the city (more salient among the girls), and between those from Los Pozos and those from elsewhere (more salient among the boys). The dynamics, conflicts, and alliances created by these divisions are explored later in this chapter.

Since primary education was the only specialty provided at the school, all students followed the same program of study, in classes (paralelos) of about fifty students each (reduced to thirty-five during the second half of the research period). On a typical day, the dorm students rose at 5:30 or 6:00 in the morning, at which time they were required to sweep and mop the floors, and afterwards run laps, sweep the grounds, or clean the latrines. After completing these tasks, they were free to play basketball or volleyball, hang out around the school grounds, or relax in the dorms until the breakfast bell rang at 7:30.[11]

Those students living in town arrived at 8:30 for morning assembly; on Mondays, this included *hora cívica,* a brief program (produced by the different *paralelos* on a rotating basis) that began with the raising of the flag and the singing of the national anthem, followed by music, dance, proverbs, speeches, or readings on patriotic and educational themes, and a *tribuna libre* ("open mike" period) during which a student or staff member might speak briefly about some historical anniversary or matter of public concern. Other days, assembly consisted of a short period of marching and turning to military-style commands called out by the inspector or a designated student; announcements were made, roll was called, and the *paralelos* marched off to class. Students had classes until noon (with recess from 10:00 to 10:30), followed by lunch and free time until 2:00; there was another brief assembly, during which roll was taken again and any further announcements were made, and then classes until 5:00 (with recess from 3:20 to 3:40).

On Mondays there was one more brief assembly at 5:00 for the lowering of the flag, and then students socialized, played basketball or volleyball, knitted, or studied until the dinner bell rang at 6:30. Those who lived in town were free to leave after classes, but many stayed to play sports or rehearse for upcoming *hora cívica* or holiday programs. After dinner, most students retired to the dorms, though often several boys stayed outside playing basketball until 10:00 or 11:00. A tighter rein was kept on the girls, who usually had to enter the dorm by 8:30 or even earlier. There they passed the time studying, chatting, knitting, eating, or sleeping until the lights went out, often not until the wee hours of the morning if some were studying late. Sometimes they celebrated a birthday, listening to music, dancing, and sharing some modest refreshments together. Nighttime activities in the boys' dorm were similar: studying, chatting, horsing around, the occasional birthday celebration. Many boys played musical instruments and would occasionally play, sing, and stomp until 11:00 or later, sometimes getting fairly raucous. Friday evenings, students and faculty left for La Paz in a bus regularly contracted for that purpose, and the school remained relatively empty and quiet, with only the janitor and a few students, until the rest returned Sunday evening.

Institutional Control and the Microphysics of Power

The various aspects of students' daily life were subject to a network of stringent regulations, though this network was not without flexibility. Students lived within an intimate regime of control that not only governed their behavior, but also cast them in the role of regulated subjects, via a particular ideology and set of practices.[12] There was a specific disciplinary procedure for those who broke school rules, but more important to the institution's regular functioning were not those rare occasions when its corrective mechanisms were brought to bear, but rather the everyday controls that regulated and constrained students' actions on a continual basis. A disciplinary system may be most visible when rules are broken, but it is when they are observed—that is, most of the time—that its effects are most cumulative and pervasive.

A useful framework for interpretation is Goffman's (1961) analysis of "total institutions" (such as asylums, prisons, and the military), in which virtually every detail of inmates' existence is subject to regulation and control. The normal school differed from such institutions in several ways. Students were not competely isolated from the outside world; some lived off school grounds, and all were free to leave on weekends. There was not a "basic split" between inmates and staff, in that staff also lived on the grounds and were subject to many of the same restrictions as students. Social mobility between the two was not restricted; rather, the normal school's explicit aim is to train one group to occupy the social position of the other. Still, the similarities between "total institutions" and the normal school make many of Goffman's observations apropos to this context.

The most obvious similiarity is, of course, the power difference between students and faculty, manifested in the minute regulation of the former's behavior according to prescriptions and constraints determined by the latter. Other similarities include the social division between teachers and students (or in Goffman's terms, "staff" and "inmates") and the sense that the institution "belonged" to the staff, by virtue of their control over its functioning. "Two different social and cultural worlds develop, jogging alongside each other with points of official contact but little mutual penetration. Significantly, the institutional plant and name come to be identified by both staff and inmates as somehow belonging to staff, so that when either grouping refers to the views or interests of 'the institution,' by implication they are referring ... to the views and concerns of the staff" (Goffman 1961:9).

These features are related, in that (1) students live in an environment that does not belong to them, in which the most intimate details of their behavior are externally controlled, and (2) this control is justified as being in the interests of "the institution." This last term was deployed within the normal school in various ways: sometimes it referred to the school and its staff, as distinct from students; at other times, it included the student body as well. Rules existed so that the transgressions of a few might not impugn the reputation of "the institution" and, by implication, all students (of course, the other side of this reasoning dictates that the behavior of all be curtailed because of the potential misbehavior of a few). While some rules were arguably "for students' own good," most of them transparently served the convenience of "the institution," that is, the staff.

Students' experiences of institutional life were far from uniform, partly because they received differential treatment, especially with regard to gender. But just as important to one's experience of institutional control is the past experience that one brings to the institution. The boys' previous military service was key to how they experienced the discipline of the normal school. The regimented aspects of dorm life that most irritated the girls tended to be taken for granted by the boys, most of whom carried recent memories of much stricter treatment. They had, in Goffman's words, been "immunized" to institutional living; for them, it was "just another total institution, to which they can apply the adaptive techniques learned and perfected in similar institutions ... they make uncomplaining [inmates] because from their point of view they have little to complain about" (Goffman 1961:65–66). While the girls often complained about the crowded living conditions and the indignity and inconvenience of being locked in at night, the boys mostly experienced life at the normal school as a period of relative freedom, compared to what they had undergone before.

Student life was similar to army life in many respects: students lived barracks-style; their activities conformed to a strict schedule marked by the ringing of the bell; they had to go through a series of military drills every morning before heading off to class. The boys' military experience helped them accept this regimen with equanimity; indeed, the normal school was a place of liberty and ease compared to the harsh training (including physical beatings and other strict punishments) they had already passed through. Even the methods of instruction, which to my eyes appeared remarkably rigid, were described as fairly lenient, relative to lessons in the *cuartel:*

Arturo: The difference is that [here] one learns many things . . . In the *cuartel*, one follows orders. They tell you, "You're going to learn this," and you have to learn it, word for word . . . Here, although they teach us, we can debate them, or just accept it; it depends on the individual student. But there no . . . You have to learn it, till you get it right. If not, they keep at you, insisting. But here, if you can't, if your capacity only goes so far, fine, they leave you alone . . . It depends on the student, if one can learn, if one feels like learning or not.

Whereas the boys had already been socialized as institutional subjects, the girls faced this difficult process for the first time (aside from grade school, which allowed them much greater freedom than a live-in institution). Still, one aspect of institutional control was a particularly sore point with the boys. Of the five areas examined below, we will look at this one first.

Sexuality

With regard to most aspects of students' behavior, there was some flexibility within the limits set by the institution: schedules contained blocks of "free time," some types of speech were unregulated, certain areas of personal adornment were left to individual choice. The margin of personal freedom was much narrower with regard to sexuality. Many disciplinary routines, such as the constant checking of attendance and the confining of students to the dormitories at night, were directly linked to official attempts to limit students' sexual contact.

Given two hundred to four hundred young people, most between the ages of eighteen and twenty-three, living in close quarters far from the watchful eyes of their parents, the emergence of sexual interest would appear inevitable. And given the generally conservative nature of *altiplano* social norms with regard to premarital sexuality, one would expect the school to take measures to control that interest. Actual intercourse or pregnancy outside of marriage was viewed as the most serious sort of delinquency and treated accordingly. The position of "the institution" on such matters was elucidated by Professor Torres, through the example of two student couples who had been discovered cohabitating in town:

PT: They came to take their final exams . . . and [the girls] showed up in a family way. But we told them, "Marriage certificate" . . . We have to maintain the prestige of the institution at least minimally, no? Fine, they fell in love, all that, but to come here like that, expecting a baby, and say to us, "There's nothing going on here," that's no good. So we asked for marriage certificates, and, lamentably, in spite of all their declarations that they had them, they haven't presented them; we've had to suspend their exams up to the present time . . .
AL: That can also be cause for expulsion, can't it?
PT: It can. At least, if the crime is, say they're "caught in the act," if it's very, that is to say, they've been seen, it's proven, then it's expulsion, immediately.

This episode shows that surveillance of students extended beyond the bounds of the school itself. There was other evidence of this as well, such as the mandate that all female students move into the dorm due to "problems with the [town] population" and threats by the rector to send "patrols" into town to apprehend students who drank or engaged in other illicit behavior. One morning at assembly it was revealed that some students had been leaving school Thursday rather than Friday, with the excuse that they were needed at home, and then spending the night in town with their sweethearts. This brought stern assurances that the administration would be cracking down on such activity and keeping track of students' whereabouts even more strictly than before.

Many parents no doubt demanded the kind of control that the school provided, and one could perhaps argue that it benefitted students as well. Several female students expressed satisfaction with the restrictions on sexual activity; many probably felt that the strict regulations protected them from situations they were not ready to control themselves. But the prohibitions on sex found few defenders among the boys, most of whom felt that the staff were overly strict and that students could be trusted to control their own behavior.[13]

Faustino: It's forbidden, to meet, hugging, kissing, all that. They'll even expel you . . . We're already adults; one can control oneself. One isn't a, a chicken, an animal, [having sex] at any moment. Falling in love is normal, kissing, all that, right? This is the only place where they think badly of it. It's as if hugging were the same as having sex. Here they reprimand you, say you're disrespectful; really it's a very rigid control . . . When the girl has her period, we know the story, right? You control it, you can make love then and nothing happens! One is aware, you don't just do it any time. I don't know, that's what I think. And not just me; the girls think the same way. But here it's as if it were a sin to fall in love.

Indeed, some of the girls did feel the same way, though Remedios was far from typical among the girls, in this as well as other aspects:

Remedios: They don't even let us go into town. And any girl that has a boyfriend, she's already marked . . . I don't know why they think so badly of it, if it's just part of life. They've been through the same thing that we're going through; they've had boyfriends and girlfriends. I don't know why they shut us in so much and don't understand us. It's unfair.

Some older students felt that the constraints imposed upon them denied their adult status and prevented students from developing adult sensibilities. Carlos, who at twenty-eight already had a fair amount of "life's experience," felt confined by institutional life. He viewed many of his classmates as naive and provincial and felt that the school exacerbated rather than corrected this tendency. Remedios, who even at twenty-three displayed remarkable independence and self-confidence, voiced similar sentiments:

Remedios: We're adults, we can govern ourselves. Because, when there's more control, there's more misconduct. If we're going to be teachers, why are they looking after us so much like little children? We're going to go out to work, and we won't know how to develop ourselves. We'll never be able to, if they're submitting us to this strict control with regulations and all.

Students who had studied at other normal schools said that Kollasuyo was stricter than most—that elsewhere, male and female students could visit each others' dormitories or form couples and were trusted to keep their sexual activity within the limits of safety and discretion. In contrast, at Kollasuyo even holding hands or conversing habitually with the same boy or girl was seen as warrant for disciplinary intervention. Despite official disclaimers to the effect that "falling in love is not a crime," it seemed that any expression of romantic interest was considered, if not a violation of the rules, dangerous activity that could lead to such a violation and thus was better avoided. Faustino and Arturo described to me their encounters with the school's disciplinary apparatus, provoked by actions that they clearly considered undeserving of such sanctions:

Faustino: They suspended me from classes for having talked with a girl; like, we were talking, holding hands, and then we went into the cafeteria, and we sat down like that, and just for that . . . they gave me a punishment. I have to work in the fields down there . . . It happened the other day, in the cafeteria. She'd hug me, kiss me, but I didn't do anything. We were just like, having our breakfast. Even that they take the wrong way! . . . They kicked me right out of there. I regretted it.

AL: I can't believe that.

Faustino: Seriously, it surprised me . . . I'm used to the city, you know, because in the city it's normal to go around like that, holding hands, or walking with your arms around each other. But here, sometimes I want to act the same way, [laughter] but here it's very different; I can't get used to it . . . Sometimes it makes you want to laugh, no? . . . Because of that girl—if they'd seen me like, hugging, or whatever— shit, I don't know what they would've done to me, expelled me probably.

Arturo: Often they'll see us talk [frequently] to the same girl, and so they call us into the Department of Orientation . . .

They say, "Look, what are you doing? Why are you always talking to her? We see you talk to her all the time, why?" . . . Lots of us, even if we're boyfriend and girlfriend— we *are* going out, right? But we say "No, Professor, she's not my girlfriend, we were just talking" . . . They say, "Yeah, you two are dating, and you shouldn't date because you're going to go down the wrong path and forget about your studies" . . . They take note of us, like. The professors comment on it in meetings, saying that "such-and-such boys and girls are dating, lots of students are falling in love" . . . They called me in, they say, "How come you're going steady?" or, "Why do you always have to talk with that girl?" I finally said, "Professor, we've always shared things, she helps me when I have homework or I can't do some assignment, she lends it to me, or I lend it to her; we help each other out." We explained it to him like that, and he said, "Fine, but don't overstep anymore. It's okay that you help each other. Go ahead and talk, but not all the time, because the professors suspect something, or, they think something else." So we said, "Okay, Professor."

The strictness with which such matters were treated contrasted sharply with the laxity around academic requirements. In the above episode, for example, Arturo defends himself with the excuse that he and his girlfriend were simply exchanging homework, an excuse accepted by the professor with no comment about the propriety of students copying assignments from each other.

The usual justification for the prohibition on romance was the protection of female students. The specter (and occasional reality) of unplanned pregnancy, and its possible consequences for the reputation of the school, were frequently evoked in discussions of the tight rein kept on students.[14] Whereas some students felt that the risks were exaggerated and they could be trusted to take care of themselves, many girls agreed that some measure of control was necessary. McLaren (1986:219) has noted students' tendency to view school rituals that "rigidly reify the social world" as "nurturant and protective, providing them with a sense of order and security," and this was certainly true for some of the girls. This perspective was often combined with a view of sexuality, especially female sexuality, as dangerous and threatening, even pathological. The opinions expressed below by Juana were in line with her unofficial role as a sort of house mother among the dorm girls, but somewhat surprising in light of her own status as a married woman with children:

Juana: I think it has to be that way in an institution. Because if they let everyone just police themselves, really, it's a negative process . . . The girls are young, the guys are young, they go to certain limits that they shouldn't, and the girls get pregnant, or they have, like, conjugal problems. It's for that reason more than anything, that there's someone to guide them, watch over them, watch over us . . . If one starts to, say, go into the other dorm, one loses respect . . . Sometimes among the girls, you come in and they're undressed, or some are in bed, doing whatever. And the boys always have one eye peeled . . . and then outside they want to be more, how can I say, without any fear of the girls, without that respect . . . I don't know what it could be, a sickness, a sexual attraction . . . Like they say, a woman is always weak . . . You know the saying, "The devil never sleeps," because a man, say, a woman tempts him . . . All over the world, a woman is a woman. And a man always has other thoughts, and the one who runs the most risk is the woman. For that reason.

Soledad: There's a lot of control. Where there's more control, there's more rebellion. They say, "You're *not* going to talk to your boyfriends, you're going to make bricks!" But the heart often commands the head, though it should be the other way around . . . If they have that need to converse, however they can, in secret, they're going to go on talking. That's why, I think, to make us not talk with the boys, they tell us so many things that can happen to a woman. Yes, they can happen—but where there's more control I think it's worse.

AL: And it seems like there's more [control] over the girls.

Soledad: Yes, because—sincerely, we women are the ones who, it's more dangerous for us, more risky. Although each one knows how to take care of herself, all that, but often, like they say, the devil never sleeps. At any moment, one isn't safe from some misfortune; at any moment one can fall.

Oddly, the institution itself sometimes displayed a rather bizarre mixture of repression and titillation. Perhaps in an effort to increase students' attention and participation, class discussions occasionally veered into provocative territory. One class on differences in social structure included a digression by the teacher on the subject of Arabian harems, inciting a buzz of excited giggles throughout the class and prompting Sergio to call out, "Let's go to Arabia!" Another teacher's lecture, ostensibly about biology and health, included a list of various sexual perversions (necrophilia, pedophilia, bestiality) and their definitions. One might interpret these self-conscious attempts at unabashed urbanity as piecemeal efforts to "modernize" the curriculum by broaching hitherto prohibited topics of discussion. But as isolated fragments in a context of overwhelming sexual conservatism, such verbal forays did more to reinforce an image of foreign decadence and exoticism than to provide any really useful information. In perhaps the most paradoxical of such incidents, the health professor one day distributed free condoms in class (probably left over from some foreign aid project). During the giddy commotion that ensued, no one chose to point out that actual use of such an item by a student, if detected, would be grounds for immediate expulsion.

Time

Jackson (1968), Willis (1981a), Everhart (1983), and others have described how schools manage time according to the exigencies of formal classroom dynamics, so that much of students' time is spent waiting or in "busy work." In the normal school, the dorm students were subject to the regimentation of time not only in the classroom, but throughout the entire day. They got up, assembled, marched to class, took their leisure, and had their meals not when they chose, but when the ringing of the bell dictated that they should. Adapting to this externally dictated routine was part of students' adjustment to institutional life.

Organizing one's activity by an external timetable, imposed for another's convenience, affects subjects' relation to their own practice. Rather than becoming fully absorbed in a given activity, subjects must be prepared to suspend what they are doing and hold it in abeyance until the next block of scheduled (or unscheduled) time. Conversely, if a scheduled activity is insufficient to fill the time alloted, it is drawn out in order to "fit," or some arbitrary activity is contrived to fill the remaining minutes. The notion of efficiency becomes meaningless when students are forced to go through their day in unison; any time saved by finishing a task quickly must be spent waiting for the signal to go on to the next.[15] This removal of the temporal organization of one's actions from the realm of personal autonomy is a defining feature of institutional life.

> [In civil society], one can with overall profit schedule one's activities to fit into one another—a kind of "personal economy of action," as when an individual postpones eating for a few minutes in order to finish a task, or lays aside a task a little early in order to join a friend for dinner. In total institutions, however, minute segments of a person's line of activity may be subjected to regulations and judgements by staff . . . Each specification robs the individual of an opportunity to balance his needs and objectives in a personally efficient way and opens up his line of action to sanctions. The autonomy of the act itself is violated. (Goffman 1961:38)

Enforced timetables, beyond whatever other purposes they serve, also function to undermine this personal economy of action; to borrow a phrase from Oscar Wilde, "Punctuality is the thief of time." Correspondingly, the degree of autonomy with which one manages one's time is a measure of social status within an institution.[16] In the normal school, this "status hierarchy of time" was evident not only with regard to subjects' control over their own time—teachers had more leeway than students, and administrators more than teachers— but also in terms of whose convenience was seen as legitimately determining the schedules of others. Students waited for teachers to arrive and awaited their signal for class to begin, not vice versa. Teachers consulted with the rector at his convenience, not their own. And when educational authorities scheduled visits (for which they often arrived hours late), the entire school population killed time in "wait mode," with classes suspended and the elaborate meals and ceremonies put on hold until the guests arrived.

Students and staff often seemed locked in a constant battle over time, from the ubiquitous stragglers at morning assembly to the occasional meal smuggled to a fellow student who chose to stay in the dorm rather than responding to the dinner bell. Students rarely arrived late for class—having, after all, nowhere else to go—but teachers frequently did. Although teachers' resistance to their work conditions is not the main focus here, these "stolen moments" accumulated throughout the workday can easily be viewed as a kind of resistance to institutional discipline.

As in the area of sexuality, the administration's control of students' time extended beyond the bounds of the institution itself. The dorm students were free of school-controlled time only on weekends. Yet even these were not inviolate; though there was a bus from La Paz that left early enough Monday morning to deliver students to school in time for assembly, those who lived on the grounds were required to return Sunday evening (this also helped discourage romantic liasions). Failure to comply resulted in "fines" of labor or materials.[17] Since most male students lived off the school grounds, this was one more rule that applied more strictly to female students.

AL: It seems there's more control over the girls than over the boys, no?

Antonia: Ooooh! They control us a lot. You have to be everywhere on time; you can't be late. You have to arrive Sunday; you can't arrive Monday, or you have to bring a light bulb [sigh]. Or carry rocks. You can't be late, or miss even one day; that's how it is. Those who miss a day have to buy sand; I think now they've added forty rocks, no? For the construction of the new dorm.

Remedios: I agree with the rules, but not with all of them, not the way they carry them out . . . Why should we bring a light bulb if Saturday and Sunday are free days? . . . And if we say something, they start to yell at us. They say, "Well then, Miss, why didn't you arrive on time?" They give us a whole sermon.

As with many such regulations, it was often not the rule itself that rankled student sensibilities so much as its perceived arbitrariness. Students frequently concurred with the need for strict controls, but felt that these were not implemented in a way that was reasonable or beneficial to their professional formation. Of course, as both Goffman (1961) and Jackson (1968) have shown, institutional regulations are designed more for the efficient functioning of the institution and the convenience of staff than for the benefit of inmates.

Space

The organization of space and of actors' movements within it is fundamental to institutional life and the exercise of power. The normal school was divided into "personal space," such as the dorms, and "institutional space," such as the classrooms; each kind of space was off limits to students during the time they were supposed to be in the other. A common complaint among the girls was the lack of space in the dorms, as well as their confinement there at night; this was further complicated by the location of the school latrines outside. Sometimes the dorm key was entrusted to a student, who could open the door in case of emergency, but just as often it was kept by the *inspectora*. Not only was this sometimes a cause of major discomfort—as on one occasion when several girls suffered from food poisoning and were unable to go out to the latrines—it also raised the specter of potential tragedy, given the jury-rigged condition of the building's electric wiring.

However, it was the lack of privacy and the subjection of all of one's activities to the gaze of others that the girls found most irritating. There was a corresponding lack of control over one's personal possessions; not only was the loss or theft of small items a common source of annoyance, but the empty dorm was locked during classtime, so that a student who had forgotten a needed item could not easily retrieve it. In the evenings, the background noise of forty or fifty students made studying difficult and frustrating. Though group living had its pleasures as well, most of the girls at one time or another felt it to be not only inconvenient, but intrusive and undignified.

Remedios: There's a lot that could be said about the dorm, you know? In the first place, it's uncomfortable. We're *packed*; we're closed in like animals in a pen . . . Why do they have to lock us in, like we were some kind of delinquents?

AL: Sometimes they close the girls in at 8:00, and the boys stay out playing football till 10:00 or 11:00.

Remedios: And that's not fair. Not even at 8:00, by 7:30 they're already yelling at us, "Girls, inside!" No? And we have to go in.

Those female students who were married and thus allowed to live *externas* provoked considerable envy, not only for the greater comfort they enjoyed, but for the lack of constant surveillance by fellow students and the *inspectora*. As Soledad observed:

We have to scrub the floor, sweep, clean out the bathrooms, get up early to run . . . The married ones have the advantage of living off grounds. They have all the comfort; they can study, get up when they want, sleep when they want; God alone knows how they live.

The lack of privacy and of control over one's immediate environment, while on one level necessitated by the scarcity of resources, can also be viewed as techniques for dislocating inmates from their past identities and preparing them to take on new ones:

Beginning with admission [to the institution] a kind of contaminative exposure occurs. On the outside, the individual can hold objects of self-feeling—such as his body, his immediate actions, his thoughts, and some of his possessions—clear of contact with alien and contaminating things. But in total institutions these territories of the self are violated; the boundary that the individual places between his being and the environment is invaded and the embodiments of self profaned. (Goffman 1961:23)

Like the above-mentioned personal autonomy of time, autonomy of space is a marker of status. Control over a personal living space, free from the contamination of others, distinguished teachers' lifestyle from that of students. Each dorm student's living space consisted of the area surrounding his or her bunk, with a trunk to hold personal possessions and a few nails in the wall for hanging shawls, cups, and other items. Teachers, by contrast, each had a private room in a duplex-style arrangement, which students were officially forbidden to enter (though this rule was not always observed). The rector not only had an entire duplex to himself (the other half of which was used for visitors), but an office as well.[18] Though teachers' rooms were rather spartan, they afforded a degree of privacy and personal expression far exceeding that of the dorm. A few enjoyed the luxury of a private bathroom, and virtually all chose to personalize their living space with pin-up girls, political or religious homilies, or hand-drawn sketches of admired artists or thinkers.

Aside from personal space, institutional space was organized so that there was hardly anywhere for students to be alone or unobserved. Those living on the grounds were only supposed to leave on weekends (except for short trips to the nearby kiosks), and "special function" areas such as the auditoriums, the garden, and the gate leading to the agricultural fields were locked when not in use. Students were expected to remain within prescribed spaces at all times, and these were organized so that it was easy to spot a student who dared to stray beyond their limits.

An exception to this rule was the small wooded area behind the classrooms, known as the *bosquecillo*. It was virtually the only area on school grounds that provided some protection from staff members' gaze; consequently, students were discouraged from entering there, especially at night. The spot was legendary as a hideaway for trysting couples, so that the mere mention of it elicited conspiratorial giggles from the girls and sly grins from the boys. It was a common topic of classroom banter, guaranteed to liven up a dull lesson with laughter and scandalized glances. The *bosquecillo* was the only part of the school landscape not molded to institutional purpose. With its popular mystique of resistance and eroticism, it constituted a wild, liminal place outside the administration's control, a tiny but essential territory where sensual nature held forth against bureaucratic culture. For students, it symbolized the subversive presence of sexuality within the walls of the institution, one of the few chinks in the disciplinary regime in which they lived.

The Body

Inmates entering a total institution undergo a process that Goffman (1961:14) called "role dispossesion." Many of the techniques of role dispossession target the body, as a crucial (though certainly not the only) site of identity formation. Foucault refers to this process as "the way in which the body itself is invested by power relations . . . a certain 'political economy' of the body." Though focusing mainly on the use of pain, he notes that even in more lenient systems of punishment "it is always the body that is at issue—the body and its forces, their utility and docility, their distribution and their submission" (Foucault 1977:24–25). Many of the disciplinary techniques mentioned above relate to the body and its activity, but there are others concerned less with subjects' activity in time or space, than with docility as an end in itself. These aim to create a mental and physical disposition toward obedience and conformity, which, as various critics of formal education have pointed out, are central to students' preparation for the world of work. Once again, many of these measures were applied more stringently to female than to male students.

One of the most obvious mechanisms of role dispossession is the uniform. Bolivian schoolchildren habitually wear the *guardapolvo*, a white garment similar to a lab coat. Generally by high school, and certainly in postsecondary education, boys cease using the *guardapolvo*; in the normal school, however, the girls continued to wear it. In addition, those girls accustomed to wearing the *pollera*, that characteristic marker of Aymara femininity, did not wear it at school, though many continued to do so on weekends.[19] Through the regulation of dress, individuals are prevented from presenting their usual image to others; for female students, this "loss of identity equipment" (Goffman 1961:21) meant that yet another avenue of personal expression, another aspect of the individual's control over her public self, was shut off.

Avineri (1968:106) mentions personal adornment and the organization of dwelling space as areas of expression where human beings are "freely active" and unalienated. The lack of room for creative expression in students' dwelling space has already been mentioned; as for personal adornment, this is not exhausted by the question of clothing. Some of the urban girls wore jewelry and makeup, but such embellishments often were looked upon with scorn by the boys (and some faculty members) as evidence of vanity and frivolity. There seemed to be few outlets for students' personal creativity: arts and crafts class; participation in *hora cívica*; the enjoyment of music and the playfulness of dorm life; the decoration of notebooks with TV and pop star images; and the rare (but much-anticipated) student variety productions.[20] There were no interest groups or clubs to speak of, aside from several boys who played musical instruments and performed at school events or during late-night carousing in the dorm. Aymara women do not usually play instruments, and the normal school girls were no exception, though a few did sing on occasion. Still, musical performance was not part of female students' "image," as it was for several of the boys.

Central among schools' disciplinary techniques is the physically restrictive setting of the classroom itself, graphically described by McLaren (1986:163) as a "culture of pain": "The pain of being a student was often considerable—manifested in the bland, dreary impotency of instructional rituals and routines, the grinding, drudging familiarity, the deadening, mechanical applications of instructional rites, the unremitting banality of the subject matter, the bleak inevitability of repetition and invariance, the tedious succession of unrelated episodes, and the wearisome wait for instruction to end." While the physical discipline of the normal school entailed more discomfort than actual pain, that discomfort was often considerable, as students were forced to sit in unlit, unheated classrooms or stand through interminably long assemblies. Beyond the generally conservative atmosphere regarding physical expression, there were specific exercises aimed at disciplining the body, such as the military drills that initiated every morning assembly and students' rising to attention when a teacher entered the room. Those who left assembly in disorderly fashion risked having the entire *paralelo* called back to line up again. The sense that one's physical comportment was under constant scrutiny extended even to those contexts that were supposedly relaxed and informal:

Carlos: I'd like for there to be complete freedom, for everybody to be free . . . For example, I don't know, have you ever been to a party here? But what a party! I don't understand it at all, I hate it . . . It doesn't seem like a party, they don't even let you smoke a cigarette . . . There [another normal school] it's much more fun, ooh, they really move. If they want to dance, they *really* dance. Not like here, "Maybe the teacher's looking at me" [surreptitious glance over the shoulder], and yow! "You were dancing like that, you're going to flunk!"

Students' obedience was frequently sluggish and reluctant, but on no occasion did I observe a physical attitude signaling open defiance. While students' tendency toward automatic compliance may be partly due to the deference shown to teachers in Bolivia (and a fairly strict cultural standard regarding young people's respect toward adults in general), it was also a function of institutional life itself. For those students living on school grounds, virtually all activities were realized in ways organized by the institution. They ate institutional food, according to the cafeteria schedule; slept in precisely arranged bunks; relieved themselves in school latrines; spent their productive hours on tasks assigned by the institution; and took their leisure as they were allowed in the hours scheduled by the institution. Activities taking place outside institutional structures and surveillance were reduced to a minimum. If it is true that individuals tend to identify more strongly with subject positions that claim a greater proportion of their time and activity, one might expect to find a greater degree of obedience, and a stronger personal connection to the institution itself, among the *internos* (dorm dwellers) than among the *externos*, and this in fact seemed to be the case.

Speech

Attitudes toward the use of indigenous languages in schools have improved as more indigenous people have themselves moved into teaching. While the situation is still far from ideal, Bolivia has thankfully left behind the days when rural children were punished for speaking their native language in class, and the use of indigenous languages should increase greatly within the planned educational reform. In the normal school, official use of Aymara was restricted to the weekly Native Languages classes; but Aymara was used frequently in informal conversations among students (more often among girls than boys) and (very occasionally) among professors as well.

Increased tolerance does not mean that Aymara has achieved equal status with Spanish, despite official rhetoric valorizing it as "part of our cultural heritage." Even the rector—himself a fluent Aymara speaker—saw fit to reprimand students the morning after their Independence Day parade through town, not only for general horseplay, but also because their banter during the supposedly silent procession had been "not even in Spanish!" He reminded them that they should constantly be practicing Spanish, since it was destined to become a universal language, whereas if they spoke Aymara when they traveled to other countries people would not understand them. Whatever the validity of this assertion, the unmistakable implication was that students' behavior during the parade had been even more vulgar and reprehensible for having utilized Aymara.

Still, what bothered students much more than the restrictions on speaking Aymara was their feeling that they had no right to express grievances or verbally defend themselves against teachers, in any language. One incident, which provided a rare glimpse of actual "backtalk" from students, occurred during agriculture class, while they were in the fields threshing beans from their pods. The teacher criticized the students' technique and tried to correct them; to my surprise, the usually retiring Diana dissented, replying, "No, beans are done like this." The two argued back and forth until the teacher told her to be quiet, to which she replied even more boldy (though lowering her eyes to the beans), "Why should I shut up?" The teacher continued to reproach her, contending that students were always complaining about something, and that Diana complained most of all (an accusation with no basis in fact as far as I could tell). Diana continued to argue (which seemed to surprise her classmates as well), threatening to denounce the professor to the rector for always yelling at them; he replied that she should go ahead and do it.[21] Some students began to chant, only half in jest, their own version of the popular refrain: "*¡El curso—unido—jamás será vencido!*" ("The class—united—shall never be defeated!"). This seemed to break the tension; the professor backed down and occupied himself with something else, while Remedios turned to me and remarked with a devilish grin: "Here we have the old style of work, the *patrón* and the Indians." The students, still working, continued talking among themselves in conspicuously loud voices about how they had no rights, but the professor refused to take the bait, and things eventually settled back down.

Agriculture may have been the one class where such a dispute could take place, in that students (rural students at least) had a substantial store of first-hand knowledge that they could draw upon to challenge teachers. But, in general, such incidents were rare; while the familiar moans and complaints associated with homework and tests sometimes resulted in compromises over deadlines, and so on, few were willing to openly challenge a teacher's authority. Students complained to me repeatedly over what they felt to be a wide array of injustices, but did not feel at liberty to lodge any official complaints. The outspoken Remedios, in an interview recorded shortly after the above incident, was more than willing to talk about the stifling of student grievances:

Remedios: We have a lot of complaints. Here they treat us, not like people, but like animals . . . They yell at us whenever they feel like it. If we express our opinion, many of them think we're out of line. If we complain about something, they think we're calling them thieves, that it's unfair. I'm not saying all the professors, but that's the reality . . . The students don't have any right to say anything. We say we live in a democracy, but as I see it we don't . . . We don't know who to complain to. Because in the end, all of them will treat you badly, or they'll want to expel you. And there's no trust. Right now there isn't anybody to confide in really. Nobody. It's as if we were here all alone, without any recourse, you know? Sometimes it seems like a reformatory more than anything else . . . If we protest, they look upon us badly, and then we're already marked, we're already on the blacklist.

While Remedios's claims may seem extreme, there was evidence to back them up. One afternoon, prior to student elections, a special assembly was called so the student fronts could present their platforms. One student got everyone's attention with a call for "unification against discrimination" and the claim that the *inspectora* discriminated against the dorm students (drawing indignant cries of "That's a lie!" from several). The next morning, the rector announced that the agitating student had been replaced as front leader, and gave a short talk on the undesirability of liars, demagogues, and factionalism, and how important it was that all work together with the staff and not try to manipulate groups against each other for personal gain. In the *inspectora's* defense, he added, "Is it discrimination, that we make suggestions and that they be carried out? I think not!"[22] At election time, the controversial front won, to the surprise of many (allegedly due to the preponderance of third-year students on their slate). Still, the point with regard to free speech had been made.

As is typical of social situations marked by an imbalance of power, the types of speech used and received by students and teachers contrasted sharply. Students' overall attitude toward staff was one of deference, marked only subtly, if at all, by that "attitude of discreet rebellion" that often accompanies compliance in controlled settings (Goffman 1961:36). The contrast with U.S. public schools, where teachers must face outright defiance from students as a matter of course, was striking. In general, students' behavior toward teachers was almost uniformly respectful; rude or disparaging commentary might be shared in the dorm in the evening, but was never made to a teacher's face. Correspondingly, I rarely observed teachers publicly humiliate students in class. Nevertheless, students felt strongly that something was lacking from their interactions with staff. They shared a desire for a more dialogic education, in which they would have some input, in which rules would be negotiated (or at least explained) rather than simply imposed.

Sergio: They shouldn't prevent us from going steady and all; rather, they should teach us what things are dangerous. That way, the girls themselves would be more aware . . . When we tell a kid that something is dangerous, what do we do? Simply pique his curiosity . . . One should tell him in another way instead, orient him.

Diana: It's okay that they control us, but I don't like when they exaggerate. If [the *inspectora*] is a counselor, I think she should counsel us, but it's not like that; when she comes to the dorm, she scolds us about everything, she yells at us. And we just keep quiet, what are we going to say? Because, if we try to argue, she'll go to the administration and give us a sanction. Or take us to the Department of Orientation . . . We're afraid of her. Always, all the girls, when the *inspectora* comes, it's "Look out, the *inspectora!*" and we all go silent . . . She should advise us, she should be—she's a counselor, no, in an institution, but really, I can't remember that she's counseled us, ever.

José: A counselor really should be like a mentor, no? . . . but no, instead she spends her time catching people, looking in the shadows, scolding them, taking them to Orientation and there she just scolds them some more. She doesn't guide them, they tell me.

AL: And is [the boys' dorm inspector] more like a counselor to you all?

José: No, he's just the same . . . One of the guys used a term, "I've fallen into the wolf's mouth" [laughter], talking about how the two of them were waiting for him, they scolded him, they wouldn't get off him for anything, he said! . . . The counselor should have charts, a blackboard, advise us well, like we've never had from Orientation, since grade school, primary school, through high school . . . He should at least come to the dorm now and then, to explain the rules, how one should act—we don't get any of that. Not even once! When he does come, he just posts some papers. Who's going to read so many pages? Four pages, no, it's too hard to read. They should teach us, come to us, or take us to the Department of Orientation and orient us, in detail, point by point. That would be great. But they don't act like counselors, no way. They function more like inspectors, like judges, punishing us.

The purpose of most disciplinary techniques is not mere compliance. Compliance is of course necessary to the institution's smooth functioning and the continued legitimization of its authority, but the deeper function of discipline is the formation of a socialized subject. The ultimate goal is not perfect surveillance, but self-regulation; ideally, inmates should internalize institutional standards, making surveillance and coercion unnecessary. Despite students' rejection of many of the school rules, most agreed that *having* rules, and giving staff the authority to enforce them, was a good and necessary thing; even the self-reliant Sergio tempered his complaints with the assertion that "things here should be kind of strict, because that's what makes up one's personal formation." The emphasis on students' internalization of school standards contrasts with those institutions where discipline is primarily a means toward the efficient functioning of the institution itself, and where staff may have little concern for how inmates retain such standards when they leave (Goffman 1961:118). Schools aim to socialize, not merely compel; it is students' incorporation of institutional standards that is the institution's primary function.

Discipline, Habitus, and Hegemony: The Production of
Docile Bodies?

How do mundane phenomena such as schedules, routines,
barracks-style living, deference in speech, and so on, socialize
students in the interests of the dominant social order? In other
words, how does daily practice accumulate to form a guiding
ideological conception of that practice, an "accepted way of
doing things" that sets the cognitive limits of future activity? A
brief look at some powerful models and their accompanying
critiques will provide us with a framework for analyzing the
socializing and resistant practices described in this and later
chapters.

Foucault (1977:25–26) speaks of the body as enmeshed in
a "political field," in which "power relations have an immediate
hold upon it; they invest it, mark it, train it, torture it, force it
to carry out tasks, to perform ceremonies, to emit signs. This
political investment of the body is bound up, in accordance
with complex reciprocal relations, with its economic use; it is
largely as a force of production that the body is invested with
relations of power and domination." The body is subject to this
political field in all social contexts, but in institutional life the
disciplinary forces trained upon it are refined and focused to a
higher degree, and for more explicit purposes. Disciplinary techniques are often related to the "economic use" of the body, but
they are just as closely tied to its ideological use. If ideology is
manifested in concrete practices, at once producing and reproduced by them, one might infer that the compulsion of particular practices fosters the formation of particular ideologies. This
has been the oft-unstated assumption underlying many analyses of the "hidden curriculum"; certainly the organization of
classroom practice around the principles of "crowds, praise,
and power" (Jackson 1968) instills in students (and in teachers) a coherent, if not always conscious, mental schema of
what "education" entails.

Schools often operate under the implicit assumption that
habituation to a ritual will lead to the absorption of its symbolic content, even (or perhaps especially) when children are
only vaguely aware of this content. What better explanation for
the daily Pledge of Allegiance that U.S. schoolchildren are trained
to recite, hand over heart, at an age when many of them have
trouble telling their right hand from their left? (And what better

proof of how deeply this ritual is ingrained in the body than the practice of many children, when asked which is their right hand, to assume the Pledge of Allegiance stance as a mnemonic device?). Though the link between practice and ideology is rarely so direct as such rituals might imply, the *existence* of such a link is the basis of many disciplinary practices that fall outside the realm of the merely coercive. "Docile bodies" are molded in the hope that docile minds will follow.

The connection between the rules and rituals imposed upon students and the ideologies produced in them is a manifestation of the power/knowledge equation that is the fundamental axiom of Foucault's calculus of social existence. The net of power relations in which students are enmeshed generates a knowledge about the nature of work, leisure, language, sexuality, the need to set limits, and even the desirability of living within limits set by others. This knowledge in turn serves as a framework for the interpretation and organization of daily practice.

Foucault (1977:178) revealed how institutional life is subject to a whole "micropenality" of time, activity, speech, sexuality, and so on, and how apparently neutral elements of the disciplinary apparatus serve a punitive function by making the slightest departure from correct behavior subject to sanction. But Foucault's scheme, while illuminating the mechanisms of power and the body as the terrain on which they operate, lacks a sense of agency, failing to examine subjects' responses to the controls exercised upon them. A conception of power as undifferentiated and diffuse as his is inadequate to teasing out the specifics of race, gender, and other co-occurring oppressions.[23] Furthermore, Foucault's model ignores the essential concept of *resistance* to power; there are no chinks in his regime of surveillance, no crimes that escape punishment, no *bosquecillo* in his Panopticon.[24] And if "knowledge" is itself the product of power, there is little need to make explicit the processes by which bodily dispositions are translated into cognitive ones (or to take note of what may be lost in the translation). Nevertheless, these questions are crucial to examining the socializing processes characteristic of schools.

More useful in this regard is Bourdieu's model of ideology and practice in social reproduction, and his concept of *habitus* as "a system of lasting, transposable dispositions which, integrating past experiences, functions at every moment as a *matrix*

of perceptions, appreciations, and actions" (Bourdieu 1977:82–
83; original emphasis). Rooted in the shared material conditions of existence, the habitus is class-specific and collectively
experienced, operating as "a subjective but not individual system of internalized structures, schemes of perception, conception, and action common to all members of the same group or
class" (86). Bourdieu postulates a circular, dialectical relationship between habitus and practice, in which the "dispositions"
that make up the habitus regulate and structure everyday
practice without recourse to fixed rules of behavior; human
activity is thus "collectively orchestrated without being the
product of the orchestrating action of a conductor" (72). These
"dispositions" share a number of characteristics, synthesized
by Thompson:

> Dispositions are acquired through a gradual process of *incul-*
> *cation* in which early childhood experiences are particularly
> important. Through a myriad of mundane processes of train-
> ing and learning . . . the individual acquires a set of disposi-
> tions which literally mould the body and become second nature.
> The dispositions produced thereby are also *structured* in the
> sense that they unavoidably reflect the social conditions within
> which they were acquired . . . the dispositions are *generative*
> and *transposable* in the sense that they are capable of gener-
> ating a multiplicity of practices and perceptions in fields other
> than those in which they were originally acquired . . . The
> habitus also provides individuals with a sense of how to act
> and respond in the course of their daily lives. It "orients" their
> actions and inclinations without strictly determining them . . .
> The practical sense is not so much a state of mind as a state
> of the body, a state of being. It is because the body has
> become a repository of ingrained dispositions that certain
> actions, certain ways of speaking and responding, seem alto-
> gether natural. (Thompson 1991:12–13; original emphasis)

Bourdieu, like Foucault, placed great importance on the
body as the site of socialization. Although I will later draw upon
his equally important work on language, Bourdieu claimed that
the most important elements of the habitus bypass language
and consciousness, operating via the apparently insignificant
practices of everyday life. The habitus's structured dispositions
are hard to resist precisely because they are "silent and insidious, insistent and insinuating" (Bourdieu 1977:51). By circum-

venting language and consciousness, they remain invulnerable to challenge or critique; they cover the tracks leading from their material foundations, becoming "history turned into nature, i.e., denied as such" (a phrase that might also serve as a concise definition of ideology). Their strength is in the naturalization of their own arbitrariness. "It is because subjects do not, strictly speaking, know what they are doing that what they do has more meaning than they know" (78–79).

Viewed from this perspective, the disciplinary practices lived by students are part of a process of inculcation. Accumulated bits of training eventually crystallize into more generalized, durable, and transposable dispositions, which orient students' future perceptions and actions in accordance with the habitus that originally generated them. This model has some advantages over Foucault's: it makes explicit the dialectic, mutually reproductive relationship between objective and cognitive structures and is broad enough to incorporate those kinds of learning/training experiences that are neither specifically focused on the body nor institutionally regimented. However, this model also has its shortcomings—once again centered around the areas of heterogeneity and conflict—which limit its usefulness for analyzing the socializing processes that concern us here.

The homogeneity of the habitus within a given group or class and its corresponding power to produce a shared consensus of meanings are central to Bourdieu's scheme; it is this homogeneity that permits the unquestioning acceptance of practices within the group (80). But, as we have seen, students do *not* take for granted many of the practices required of them; there is a difference of perspective between students and teachers which (assuming their shared class background) cannot be accounted for by differences in the habitus (since within Bourdieu's model the habitus is not internally differentiated). Bourdieu provides an escape from this dilemma in the form of the "hysteresis effect" or "structural lag" between the habitus shaping students' dispositions and the one in which their teachers' generation was formed. One can also argue that not all disagreement occurs at the level of the habitus; conflict can exist above the bedrock of a shared world view. Bourdieu explicitly posits the existence of both a field of unquestioned *doxa* and one of opinion, where orthodox and heterodox beliefs vie for supremacy. If we locate student-staff conflicts in this latter realm, however, the notion of habitus is of little use in examining them.

But there is a more serious flaw in the habitus concept that is even more relevant to the present discussion. Positing a homogeneous class habitus leaves no room for intra-class variation along the axes of race, ethnicity, or gender; unlike differences of age, these cannot be accounted for by a temporal "structural lag." According to Bourdieu, one of the habitus's principal effects is a "consensus on the meaning *(sens)* of practices and the world . . . the harmonization of agents' experiences and the continuous reinforcement that each of them receives from the expression . . . of similar or identical experiences" (80). Yet few would be willing to argue for either a consensus of meaning or a fundamental similarity of experience across race and gender lines. Inasmuch as Bourdieu's model reduces multiple oppressions (and bases of identity) to the question of class, it is of little use in examining how overlapping systems of oppression interact.

In addition to eliding intra-class differences, Bourdieu dimisses the psychological realm and its impact upon subjects' class-being, claiming that individual history is merely a particular specification of the collective history of one's group or class; the system of dispositions guiding each individual is simply a "structural variant" of the class habitus (86). But these "structural variants" may be highly significant to the ways in which struggles over class (and ethnic and gender) meanings are played out. The habitus concept cannot account for the difference in world view between two female students of peasant background, one of whom prefers to dress and act like an urban *mestiza* and one of whom adopts a more traditional style, nor can it address the bitter contest over ethnic meanings that goes on between the two. These fundamental differences over questions of meaning and identity cannot be dismissed as mere structural variations on a theme. The individual factors that lead one girl to one position and her classmate to the other are beyond the scope of this work, but the discrepancy itself, and its prevalence among girls of this class, point to the existence of ideological conflicts within the supposedly homogenous habitus.

While Bourdieu's model of the habitus in its "normal" state makes no provision for such conflicts, being fundamentally static, it does allow for moments in which *doxa* becomes vulnerable to questioning. This occurs in times of objective crisis, when "the immediate fit between the subjective structures and the objective structures" is broken. At such moments, the arbitrariness of dominant classifications is revealed, and the relationship between language and experience becomes visible; "the everyday order is challenged, and with it the language of order" (168–70). While Bolivia's regular proximity to crisis might make it an attractive candidate for such an interpretation, this view ignores the *constant* struggle over meanings that introduces a certain amount of slippage even into the everyday relationship between language and experience. It would seem that, for Bourdieu, signs are fairly fixed entities, undergoing major shifts only during times of objective crisis, rather than multivocal entities constantly subject to negotiation, as Bakhtin (1986) suggests. While Bourdieu (1977:164) grants that the naturalization of arbitrariness, necessary to all established orders, is carried out "to very different degrees and with very different means," he has little to say about the degree to which it *fails*. These failures are not only a structurally significant part of any social system; they are also a source of potential transformation of that system.

Correspondingly, Bourdieu's model fails to acknowledge a category of resistant or oppositional practices that are not immediately incorporated into the habitus or reduced to only that which can be imagined within the boundaries of its structured dispositions. At the very least, contact with individuals whose habitus differs from one's own should expand the realm of the imaginable. Still, on the subject of subaltern struggles, Bourdieu (1977:164–65) claims that "social categories disadvantaged by the symbolic order, such as women and the young, cannot but recognize the legitimacy of the dominant classification in the very fact that their only chance of neutralizing those of its effects most contrary to their own interests lies in submitting to them in order to make use of them."

Aside from denying the reality of resistance by disadvantaged groups, such a statement falsely implies that "submitting" to the dominant classification as a means of survival is equivalent to recognizing its legitimacy. Submission is not an all-or-nothing phenomenon; interviews revealed students' recognition of the need to "submit" temporarily in order to graduate, even while striving to maintain the autonomy of their own symbolic order—no easy task, but one that many considered crucial to their own sense of identity. In summary, the habitus model is not only inaccurate in its assumption of homogeneity within classes, it also leads to a pessimistic view of the potential of human agency. Bourdieu provides a dialectic between structure and practice, but it is not a dialectic of conflict. His "theory of practice" is basically apolitical,[25] since any theory that sees itself as part of a transformative politics must leave room for agency in some form or another; it must posit a regular source for the emergence of alternative practices and maintain a grounded optimism with regard to the potential of those practices to affect ideology, and eventually, objective structures.

Gramsci's notion of hegemony, especially as developed by Williams, Hall, and Laclau and Mouffe escapes many of the above pitfalls. Rejecting the notion of fixed relations between experience and ideology, these scholars share a view of hegemony as "a more or less adequate organization and interconnection of otherwise separated and even disparate meanings, values, and practices, which it specifically incorporates in a significant culture and an effective social order" (Williams 1977:115). An interpretive framework based on the concept of hegemony allows for the operation of mutually reinforcing but distinct forms of oppression, rather than reducing all of these to class. It also recognizes the eternally incomplete nature of the hegemonic project, taking into account both the practices that resist or escape its grasp and the attempt to repress or incorporate such practices. Not only does this model provide a more accurate picture of that contradictory ideological realm that Gramsci (1971) labeled "common sense," it also provides a theoretical basis for the agency of groups and individuals in articulating disparate meanings, values, and practices around their own interests (including, but not limited to, class interests).

As regards the shifting nature of these meanings, values, and practices, Williams claimed that

> it is the reduction of the social to fixed forms that remains the basic error. Marx often said this, and some Marxists quote him, in fixed ways, before returning to fixed forms. The mistake, as so often, is in taking terms of analysis as terms of substance. Thus we speak of a world-view or of a prevailing ideology or of a class outlook, often with adequate evidence, but in this regular slide towards a past tense and a fixed form suppose, or even do not know that we have to suppose, that these exist and are lived specifically and definitively, in singular and developing forms. (Williams 1977:129)

Bourdieu's notion of habitus is open to precisely this charge of "reduction of the social to fixed forms." Also, by operating solely at the unconscious level, his sets of dispositions suggest an unbridgeable chasm between conscious and unconscious thought (and action). Williams' notions of "practical conscious- ness" and "structures of feeling" bridge that chasm, and also suggest a source of alternative meanings and practices: the tension that results from bringing the two realms (conscious and unconscious, received knowledge and practical experience) into proximity.

Historical moments of flux and displacement give rise to contradictory and ambivalent ideologies within groups, even within individuals. Aymara students' values may coincide with those of teachers in many aspects, and be violently opposed to them in others. Even those students who concur with institu- tional standards may attempt end runs around the control of their sexuality, attendance, drinking, and other aspects of their lives. They may see through some of the ways that the domi- nant social sectors attempt to present their specific interests as "natural" and be blind to others, while at the same time offer- ing naturalized rationalizations in support of their own inter- ests. While Bourdieu noted the importance of the naturalization of arbitrariness to any established order, the concept of hege- mony allows for the full play of competing groups' efforts at naturalization and denaturalization.

Many of the grounds on which Bourdieu's early work can be criticized concern his view of discourse; one might suggest that the habitus model is better suited to the analysis of em- bodied dispositions, deeply ingrained and unconscious, and the hegemony model to the analysis of discursive ones, which are more vulnerable to social contestation. Both kinds of disposi- tions are crucial to the process of socialization—which, aside from constituting education's primary aim, can also be defined as the incorporation of individuals and communities into hegemony.

Dormitory Life

The Girls: Conflict in Close Quarters

An important part of students' socialization is learning to negotiate the social environment of the school itself. How stu- dents meet this challenge depends largely on their previous socializing experiences, themselves structured by factors of class, residence, and especially gender. Student interviews revealed strong gender differences in the level of conflict students faced in living together. Whereas the boys' dorm was fairly peaceful, with only a modicum of interpersonal conflict, social friction among the girls was intense, if not always conspicuous. Underneath the routine complaints about noise, lack of privacy, and crowding lay a deeper hostility. Its source was the rift between urban and rural girls, or (and these conflicts tended to be even more bitter) between rural girls whose demeanor clearly reflected their background and the daughters of rural-urban migrants who adopted urban dress and mannerisms and were thus seen as "putting on airs" or trying to distance themselves from their peasant origins. That these class/ethnic tensions were interpreted as such by the girls themselves (and not as merely personal animosities) is evidenced by their labeling of both actual incidents and vaguely present hostilities as "discrimination."

The topic of discrimination sparked a wide range of responses in interviews. Some girls denied it existed; others unleashed a litany of affronts suffered at the hands of others. Some admitted discrimination on the part of their classmates and asserted their own disgust at such behavior, while others lamented having become the innocent targets of such accusations. When the topic was raised, voices often dropped to a conspiratorial whisper; speakers would falter and hesitate, searching for words to express what was for them a complex situation, fraught with pain and misunderstanding. Less important than the degree of "actual" discrimination is the fact that the *perception* of discrimination was very real for many girls and sharply affected how they related to others.

Juana: There's a certain discrimination, because a girl from the city knows how to speak a little better, dress a little better, they're a bit more sociable, in certain terms more civilized, in every aspect . . . In contrast the country girls, in the very way they dress, in skirts, with braids, sometimes they can't pronounce things, or they confuse /i/ and /e/, /u/ and /o/; for that more than anything they criticize each other. One says, "Why don't you know how to dress?" and then the other says, "Where are you from, what are you discriminating for?" . . . For example [another girl], she's always been like that, apart, as if to say that she's from the city. But her mother wears the *pollera*, her father is the same, people of that class . . . But still she feels superior, she likes to discriminate . . . We've clashed several times.

Clara: There's discrimination by the provincial girls—they're the ones that set themselves apart. On the part of the city girls—yes, there's a little bit there too, but personally, I at least like to share with everyone, I don't consider myself, to say, "I'm better, I can't be with her" . . . But the rural girls are like that. Sure, once they know you, they share a bit too, but they're always like, a little bit apart. They just keep to themselves . . . Are they discriminated against? Well, they feel like they are, but—sometimes, there are people who really do too. I think some do, but myself, I don't discriminate against them, at least I try not to because really we're all equal. Maybe in some aspects there might be a difference; maybe we have a bit more knowledge, that sort of thing. But after that, it's all equal.

Diana: There's a lot of fighting among us in the dorm. Last year, you knew [two other girls], right? They would criticize us, say things to us, insult the rural girls . . . say that we were peasants, provincials, we don't know how to dress, stupid stuff. So, I always like to stick up for people because I'm from the country. Why should they discriminate against us? If they think they're so great, why don't they go study in a university? . . . They say to us, "I graduated from such-and-such high school, *Liceo de La Paz, Liceo de Señoritas*" . . . Those two didn't come back this year; hopefully there won't be that kind of fighting now . . . I don't like when they criticize me like that, saying I'm a hick, a peasant . . . I've always stuck up more for my classmates from the country. Not for the city girls.

Soledad: I won't tell you who, but I've heard them say, how is it? *"Mamakas,"*[26] those sorts of words, vulgar . . . It bothers me, but—I don't like to get involved . . . Just today they told me, "When you first came here, they said about you 'Huh, who does she think she is? Little Miss Perfect' . . . " I cried, I went in the dorm and said, "Why? Why does my name always have to be dragged in, what did I do to them?" . . . We city girls, our parents are all from the country too, we're all descendents of Aymaras, right? But they think that we think we're ladies, superior to them . . . There's always someone who says, "Oh, those girls think they're something special, don't talk to them . . . " But it was never our intention to isolate anyone or discriminate . . . We talk about our high schools, etc., we have that in common, while they have other things in common . . . My mother wears the *pollera*, my grandparents are from the country, so I don't like to discriminate . . . In the end we're all equal, but they don't think that. No, they think we think we're something special.

Clearly, these personal hostilities reflect larger structural issues (as the girls themselves were well aware). What appear as personal antagonisms are often manifestations of class and ethnic conflict (Scott 1985); Bourdieu (1977:81) maintained that "'interpersonal' relations are never, except in appearance, *individual-to-individual* relationships." In his later work, he analyzed expressions of taste (in dress, music, etc.) as markers of class identity, noting the strong reactions they can provoke when perceived as threatening the integrity of the group (1984:380–81). Thus girls of rural origin who adopted urban styles drew even sharper criticism than the urban girls themselves; the reproach, "What does she think she is?" *("¿Ella qúe se cree?")* was a literally worded challenge to those making identity claims that implied disdain for another's identity.[27]

This is not to imply that the girls' dorm was a constant hotbed of seething ethnic tensions. Many spoke of the pleasures of shared activities: birthday parties, joking and cooking together, bedtime gossip, help with schoolwork. The rural-urban division itself was a source of new learning, for students on both sides of the divide:

Soledad: What we learned from [the country girls] was how to dig potatoes. Sure, our mothers did it, but we ourselves hardly at all . . . They knew how to make *k'ispiña*; that's something I didn't know how to do. We pick up little things like that. Maybe not doing it ourselves, but watching, at least we have an idea of how it's done . . . They pick up things from us too, like how to be more sociable and talk without being timid. And how to dress, sometimes—like, somebody always brings something new, you know? She says, "Look, this goes like this, with these clothes, it's nice like that." So you see, one picks up lots of things . . . things that, who knows, maybe before you hadn't known.

The normal school was a place where young people with different lifestyles and different conceptions of Aymara identity were able to share experiences, ideas, and cultural practices, at times clashing, at times learning from each other. Aside from learning new skills and styles, many girls expressed satisfaction at having learned "how to get along together, for better or worse." Nevertheless, the fact that learning to get along was such a struggle, entailing defense of one's identity against perceived attack, reveals the considerable strain involved in constructing a generalized Aymara identity from such heterogenous particulars.

Why were such tensions so strong among the girls and not among the boys? Part of the answer lies in the general sexism of Bolivian society. Lesley Gill (1988), in a study of La Paz maids and the upper-class women who employ them, suggested that the latter "took advantage of class and ethnic differences to mitigate their own gender subordination." Few groups in Bolivia are more subordinated than young indigenous women. Those who can gain some measure of personal power by differentiating themselves from others even lower in the hierarchy are likely to do so, given the lack of other means of empowerment and claims to social status. The difference is also due to male students' previous passage through another key site of socialization, one that helps them adjust later both to the diversity of the dorm population and to the normal school's version of institutional life, with considerably greater ease than did the girls.

The Boys: Negotiating Personal Relations after the *Cuartel*

Before entering the normal school, male students were subjected to another intensive process of identity formation, entailing a year-long immersion in a environment that is heavily and overtly ideological, and relatively isolated—geographically, culturally and communicatively—from the rest of society. The socialization boys undergo there deeply affects their attitudes toward their country, their fellow students, institutional life, gender roles, and their own ethnic background. It is a fundamental rite of passage for peasant and working-class youth, from which females are excluded (or exempted, depending upon one's point of view). It is *el cuartel*—military service.

In Bolivia, all able-bodied men between the ages of nineteen and twenty-one are supposed to do a year of military service. In practice, fulfillment of this obligation depends largely on class; many middle- and upper-class youth manage to avoid it through bribes, family connections, or spurious medical exemptions, while working-class and peasant youth seldom have access to these options. Even if they did, many would no doubt forego them, given the *cuartel's* importance to their construction of masculine identity. One can imagine the difficulties faced by a rural youth, perhaps leaving home for the first time, speaking imperfect and self-conscious Spanish, who is thrust suddenly into a regimented environment where failure to comply quickly and correctly brings immediate (often physical) punishment. Racism is reputed to be even more intense in the army than in civilian society—but here as well, it tends to focus on language rather than skin color per se.

AL: Do you think the *cuartel* is worse for those from the country?
José: It's worse. They suffer more. Because, they can't talk like the others. So the officers, they realize right away that one is from the country. And the military guys are more racist. One who can't talk [Spanish] can't learn theory, he just gets punished all the time . . . If one knows a bit, he's good, a high school graduate, he doesn't have to suffer too much. I didn't suffer much. Of course, I realized that, with the high school graduates from the city, and me from the country, I got up to their level more or less . . . I had rank, I learned fast, so they coudn't humiliate me easily. But sometimes, even among rural folk, among one's fellows, we mistreated each other . . . There's abuse . . . One guy can't talk, he's timid, he's afraid. And the other guy knows how to talk, and, well, there you are . . . There's that scorn that peasants receive. But I've always fought for my people, for the peasants, for them not to be so abused . . . Because, sometimes, I feel

bitter when some country kid doesn't know how to talk. He's like, poor guy, all humble. Those guys—sometimes it makes you sad.

Rural schools were historically used to facilitate indigenous youth's conscription into the army; conversely, the army often serves to accomplish what the school failed to. "Civic instruction"—the building of a nationalist consciousness—is one of the *cuartel*'s principal functions. For recruits with little or no schooling, it is the first institution that trains them to think of themselves as Bolivians; for others, the nationalist ideology already inculcated in childhood is driven home even more forcefully. A former interim schoolteacher described his military service in the 1970s:

> They have classes, civic instruction, what is the flag, the coat of arms, all that. One has to learn to read and write . . . They teach subjects like geography, how many departments does Bolivia have, which one are we in now, everything. The colors of the flag—there are some, from the country, who have never been to school. They don't know "the emblems of our nation," as they say. You ask one, and he doesn't know. In the *cuartel*, he learns. By the time he gets out, he knows how big Bolivia is, its population, how many cities it has, everything. But before going to the *cuartel*, he doesn't know anything. He doesn't know where he is, where's Pando, Beni, Cochabamba. But there, in the *cuartel*, they take the map, "This is such-and-such a place; this is the river, the biggest river in the country."

In those sectors from which Kollasuyo's students were drawn, the *cuartel* is close to a universal male experience. Indeed, the certificate of completed military service was required from all male students (except the physically handicapped). But other reasons for their compliance, perhaps just as compelling, are found in the ways that these young men socially construct the idea of military service, the attitudes they bring to their conscription, and its role in their achievement of adult status.[28] Among Aymara youth, military service is anticipated as often with pleasure as with dread. It is a chance to expand one's horizons, see other parts of the country, and escape from the restrictive environment of the home (albeit to an environment that is in many ways even more restrictive). Friends from the same peer group often enter the *cuartel* together; Sergio, who graduated from high school at only fifteen, expressed disappointment at not being able to enlist with his friends. Military service also provides a new kind of masculine camaraderie and consolidates one's gender identity in the eyes of one's peers. Arturo, who recalled the *cuartel* as challenging but not particularly onerous, observed: "It's not exactly obligatory, but between friends, or between classmates, one is looked down on—'you haven't gone to the *cuartel*,' they start to humiliate you." José, who also remembered his military service as both intellectually and personally rewarding, nevertheless saw this process of masculine affirmation as less than benign:

José: We peasants more than anyone are obligated to go. Because, even within ourselves, there's this defect that people have, of criticizing, of humiliating. Like, they say you're just not a *man* [if you haven't been], so for that reason, one automatically has to say that he's been. Otherwise, at some party, where people are sitting around drinking, he'll just have to be, you know, held back, humiliated.

In rural much more than in urban areas, military service is a requisite of adulthood for young men. The most important transition to adult responsiblity and identity is marriage, and rural parents are unlikely to accept a prospective son-in-law who has not yet been to the *cuartel* (Carter 1977). But while a young man who still owes a year of his labor to the state is certainly not well positioned to begin the joint undertaking of supporting a family, the *cuartel*'s significance is as symbolic as it is pragmatic. It marks the end of childhood and the initiation into manhood; it is a site of differentiation and bonding, of separation from the feminine and consolidation of the masculine. It was a crucial part of male students' life histories, strongly affecting their relationships with each other and with the physical and social environment of the normal school. Many had fond memories of the *cuartel*; their accounts revealed a wide variety of experiences, many of which had a transformative effect on their behavior, personal philosophy, and identity.

AL: It must be a bit frightening, no, a kid of eighteen, nineteen, entering the cuartel?

Carlos: Hell no . . . It was easy for me, serving my country. Of course you suffer too, but it's great. You cry, you laugh, you have fun, you dance—you do eveything, you are everything there. Because there's no mom and dad there . . . I was fine. Sure, sometimes they beat me. But it wasn't my fault; I was the squad commander, and so, if my comrades couldn't do something it was . . . "Boy, it's your fault this one doesn't know it!" They'd give it to me good, but I'd just laugh . . . No, it was like, like a family.

Arturo: Life in the *cuartel* is good. One learns a lot of things there . . . one learns to share. When one hasn't gone to the *cuartel*, maybe it's like, he doesn't know what it is to suffer, no? But there—sure, you suffer some; it's not that you don't suffer, you suffer a little.

AL: But together.

Arturo: But you suffer together! [laughing]. Seriously, that's the truth.

José: The *cuartel* was really enjoyable too, for me . . . I liked being a soldier. I have that voice of command, and I learned quickly. I was a good soldier, I'd say . . . Of course, one suffers there sometimes. We're humiliated, beaten, mistreated, insulted . . . but one learns good things. One's temperament for example, one's character, changes. At home, in civilian life, one gets angry, one gives vent to one's anger, you argue with your father or talk back to him, or whatever. But there, they do everything to you, and you can't say anything. You swallow your anger, you just have to take it . . . If you argue, you get more beatings; maybe all the soldiers will beat up on you. It's like that. Maybe in other places the *cuartel* isn't like that; here there's a lot of bullying, a lot of abuse. On the part of the officers.

AL: Some have told me it can be almost traumatic, going to the *cuartel* for the first time.

Mateo: Aah, no no, not for me. It was just normal.

AL: And do you think your service did you any good?

Mateo: No good, absolutely no good at all. I think it's just a waste of time, and with the obsolete weapons, you don't learn anything . . . It's just boring . . . I think instead there should be some guidance . . . They should teach us, at least, how to use a computer.

Mateo, the only student interviewed who claimed to have gained nothing of value from his military service, had spent years working, traveling, and gaining life experience before entering the normal school. For the others, the *cuartel* was clearly a place to mature emotionally and learn new relational skills. Despite the different ways that *cuartel* life is experienced and remembered, there are important commonalities that not only form the basis of masculine sharing during the year of service, but also prove useful later on. For some, the value of the *cuartel* experience was evident upon their first arrival at the normal school. Most of the girls described this as an anxious and lonely time, arriving at a strange place without friends, separated from family for perhaps the first time, tightly controlled, living in close quarters with so many strangers.

Diana: At first I was really sad. I even got sick, I'd cry . . . I'd want to leave and go to the city every weekend. But then, there are old classmates; I came with two or three others [from my village], and we got used to it, and now we're already in our second year, so now we're okay . . . I was used to living with my father, with my family back home, in the countryside. So I miss that the most, my father, my brothers and sisters. Also, here we're locked in, like I never was when I was in high school. We always played until late, but here, the *inspectora* locks us in at bedtime, so that too was strange for me.

Antonia: It cost me, getting used to it. More than anything, I missed my family . . . I'd say to myself, "Oh no, why? Why did I come here?" I regretted it after I arrived. And the older students, when we got here, they mistreated us . . . They'd get us out of bed at 4:30, 5:00 in the morning, to run . . . Since we didn't know anything about the normal school, we'd do it, shivering . . . We all went out; since we were new, we were afraid [to refuse].

In contrast, most of the boys had little difficulty adjusting to the normal school regimen. Dorm life shares many similarities with army life; in negotiating personal and group relations, male students drew upon social skills developed during their military service. Faustino described his ease at adjusting to the normal school as a direct result of his *cuartel* experience:

Faustino: We arrived at night. There were just three of us, we slept in the dorm. I said to myself, "What am I going to do?"—there was nothing, nobody I knew. I didn't have anyone to talk to . . . The next day the other students arrived, bit by bit; I felt just like in the *cuartel*, all the bunks. Bit by bit they familiarized us with the rules, why it was strict, all that. But it wasn't hardly that strange for me, the environment itself, not really. It was just like being in the *cuartel* for me. It was okay . . . [referring to the abuse suffered by new recruits] It's like we have here with the third year students, you know? We're the first years, so the third years would abuse us, "mangy new kids," all that. In the *cuartel*, they fuck with you more . . . They abuse us, make us come up with things to give them—we mess with each other a bit.
AL: You say it's like that here with the third year students?
Faustino: Here, not much. In the beginning they wanted to, no? But since there's a lot of us . . . it's hard for them to fuck with us.

The *cuartel* was a helpful precedent for male students in their new institutional context; they shared the experience of having crossed a similar threshhold in the past and survived it, each with his self-image intact (if somewhat altered). The value of this experience was even more evident in light of the tensions over ethnic and class loyalties (as well as issues of space, privacy, and personal habits) that simmered in the girls' dorm. While the boys tended to dismiss the cliquish behavior and hurt feelings of the girls as stupid, petty, or unfathomable, they were a very real source of unhappiness for many girls, most of whom were facing such a pressurized living situation (and such close contact between rural and city dwellers) for the first time. The boys had already learned to negotiate such conflicts, often under threat of physical punishment, and most had done so successfully. The boys themselves agreed that learning how to get along with others of different backgrounds had been a valuable part of their *cuartel* experience.

Arturo: It helps us a lot that we've gone to the *cuartel*; we already know how to get along, for better or worse, no? While the girls, they arrive here, maybe it's the first time they've lived all together like that. Maybe that's why they feel kind of irritable, get annoyed with each other. They're a bit—they don't live well together. There's animosity, all that.

José: [The city girls] spend their time discriminating against the country girls, hating them, instead of teaching them the good things they've learned in the city . . . I think among guys that can't exist. I'm from the country myself, but I think someone from the city wouldn't have an easy time trying to humiliate me that way. If someone wants to be, say he's from the city, he tries to discriminate; we kick him out, isolate him. So far there isn't anyone. That doesn't happen among us . . . Sometimes we treat each other like in the *cuartel*. We give each other shit, we treat each other every which way. But it's just kidding around. There are some who are kind of whiners; we don't say much to them. The others know when to joke with them, but if a guy gets mad, then all together they reproach him, they hate him, so he catches on. What's the good of making the others hate you? One has to adapt.

No doubt, part of what boys learn in the *cuartel* is simply to become more thick-skinned; by the time they leave, they are no longer such vulnerable targets for the class and ethnic put-downs to which the girls were so sensitive. More important, they learn to negotiate tensions within groups and to defend themselves against threats to their identity. Some perhaps never learn to do so successfully, and emerge from their year of service with a cultural identity warped by constant abuse. But whether the memory of military service is fond or painful, it provides a degree of maturity and preparation for the future. All in all, the boys arrived at the normal school much better prepared for institutional life than the girls; the conflicts plaguing the girls were ones that the boys had already learned to accept or work out among themselves. Nevertheless, divisions among the boys were not totally absent; rather, they fell along different lines than those separating the girls.

Regional Rivalries: *Lugareños* and *Forasteros*

The preceding discussion may give an impression of seething resentment and hostility among the girls, contrasted by good-natured solidarity among the boys. This impression is quickly dispelled if we examine another axis of inter-student rivalry: that between students from Los Pozos (or nearby communities) and those from farther away. In contrast to the class and ethnic rivalries so prevalent among the girls, regional conflicts were stronger among the boys, for reasons closely linked to students' living arrangements. Students from the area normally lived at home, rather than on school grounds. Early in the year, however, the rector announced that all female students were to live in the dorms, due to rumored "problems among the population."[29] No such rule was imposed upon male students, and thus most of the local boys continued to live in town, as did several who were not from the area but did so out of personal preference.

These students were markedly set off from the tight-knit community of the boys' dorm. The dorm boys, urban and rural alike, viewed themselves as *forasteros* ("outsiders"), collectively opposed to the *lugareños* (those "from here"). Among the girls, the division between local and nonlocal students did not correspond to any division between *internas* (dorm dwellers) and *externas* (nondorm dwellers). Even if it had, the social rifts already present among the original dorm girls probably would have precluded their closing ranks against the new arrivals. Regional rivalry was not totally absent among the girls, but it was clearly not their primary source of conflict. For the boys, however, the division between *forasteros* and *lugareños*, corresponding closely to that between *internos* and *externos*, was a sharp one. The solidarity that the *internos* felt for their dorm community was expressed by several.

Arturo: It's good to live all together, to share. Like brothers. Because, if we were to live off the grounds, in rented rooms, there couldn't be that sharing between us.

Faustino: That's the advantage there is in the dorm, you know? Here we're always horsing around, it's just normal. While among the *externos*, no, closed up in their rooms, who is one going to talk to? There's nobody, you see? Whereas here, at least we have fun.

The causes of the tension between *internos* and *externos* were various, but generally centered on the former's perception of preferential academic treatment of the latter. Many considered this a potentially serious obstacle to their academic careers; some *internos* wanted to organize a trip to another town for their final evaluations, where at least the teachers of the elementary classrooms in which they would demonstrate their expertise would be free of regional favoritism (not surprisingly, such a trip never materialized). José's sentiments reflected the complaints of a number of students:

José: The disadvantage is . . . most of the students are from right here . . . And what's worse, the teachers are from here too. They're the same people, their uncles, their fathers, who knows . . . Say my uncle is a teacher here; he's not going to flunk me if I don't do my work . . . Even if they're not relatives, they're from the same place, they know each other well . . . It's only the ones from far away who are outstanding students. From here, there isn't even one . . . They're sure they're going to pass. There's no sacrifice, no interest in their studies . . . Those from here don't know what it is to suffer. It's no hardship for them. But us, when we go to work, we already know how one lives, coming from far away . . . We're already prepared for that. One can foresee the things he's lacking. But these others who are just now getting ready to leave home, they'll soon find out what it is to suffer.

Nonlocal students also felt outnumbered in elections and other areas where students had limited decision-making powers. Soledad (who despite her comments was later elected to the student government) summed up several grievances adding to regional tensions within the school:

Soledad: This regionalism . . . it's with the aim of running things here where they live. Making it so those from far away can't hold any office . . . All so the town will look good . . . Those of us from far away also have that desire to stand out; we say, "Look, they can't force us, why can't we do something?" . . .

but since we're so few, it's impossible for the few to win out over the many . . . In class, *they* want to be the presidents . . . In sports, they're the *first* to say, "All those from here, on one team!" You see? So it's just total disunity . . . Lots of the teachers I think have their godchildren here, their nephews, their grandchildren, who knows. In so many things, they have a lot of influence with them. And those of us from far away, often the teachers don't pay us much mind. All because, they too, the teachers themselves, want those from here to stand out . . . so that one day they can hold them up, saying, "Look, those from our town are good."

This divisiveness was especially evident during student elections; the slates formed by the boys (who generally dominated such matters) crossed rural/urban lines, but neatly reflected the *interno/externo* division. Personal disputes[30] resulted in the splintering of the *interno* ticket and its narrow defeat by the *lugareño* front, causing José to remark bitterly:

The voters didn't really focus on the capacity of each one . . . They don't see the experience one has, that one could manage well the future of the students. No, that doesn't count; it's just regionalism, all for themselves. They don't want other people to get ahead . . . Other people could have good intentions, do good things for the normal school, but those from here—since the rector is from right here, and the student federation is from here, what can the others do, just among themselves? Go argue with the rector? Who knows, the rector could be the guy's uncle. So, it's a little difficult, you know?

As the following year's elections drew near, another incident occurred which deepened the rift between *internos* and *externos*. A soccer team from the city visited the school for a match, during which several *externos* were observed loudly cheering the visiting team, rather than that of their classmates, which was made up exclusively of *internos*. At assembly the following morning, the academic director reprimanded the students for their unseemly behavior, for giving the visitors the impression of *divisionismo* among the student body and for reflecting badly upon the school. Soon after, those *internos* who had previously taken an active role in student politics withdrew from the campaign, feeling outnumbered, discouraged by their previous defeat, and disgusted with what they perceived as the corruption and incompetence of the incumbent student government. The day of the election neared, and still no student fronts had registered. Half an hour after the deadline, a slate of local students came forward to register their ticket; however, the electoral committee (made up of professors) charged with the task of ratifying the student fronts contained one student representative, and that one happened to be José. Claiming unwillingness to set a standard of laxity that might then prevail in student affairs throught the year, José refused to bend the rules to admit the belated ticket. Not only did this cement hostilities between the competing parties, but the resulting lack of official contenders forestalled the election altogether. In the end, each class chose three representatives, and this group then elected a governing body from among themselves. Not surprisingly, those elected to the highest positions were *lugareños*.

4

CURRICULUM AND IDENTITY

It is not even possible to talk about the political dimension in education; it is political throughout.

—Paulo Friere

The Reproduction of Ideology in Schools: Socialization as the Interpellation of Student-Subjects

In the Introduction mention was made of the frequent breach between macro-level and micro-level analyses of schooling. This breach is unfortunate, because schooling is one of the most vivid examples of how macro-level social structures are reproduced through the accumulation of minute, micro-level practices; it is, more than anything, the routinized details of school life that socialize students as particular kinds of subjects. While the socializing effects of specific classroom practices and interactions are examined in chapter 5, this chapter analyzes the nationalist, ethnic, class, and gender images that formed part of the normal school students' "professional formation."

"Socialization" is commonly understood as that early period of concentrated cultural learning by which the child is integrated into society. In this sense it is universal, though its content depends on the specific culture in which it occurs. However, Williams (1977:137) points out a weakness (or rather, a mystification) in this concept: by emphasizing the universality of the processes involved, it obscures the fact that "it is precisely the historical and class variations of 'socialization' which need to be studied."[1] The cultural learning that enables children to speak the language of their community, understand and be understood by its members, and function as social

123

beings is not distinct from that which fixes them in particular positions within society (with regard to class, gender, ethnicity, and so on).[2] A concept of "socialization" that emphasizes only its abstract and universal elements serves to conceal the processes by which hegemony is maintained.

> What is abstracted in orthodox sociology as "socialization" is in practice, in any actual society, a specific kind of incorporation. Its description as "socialization," the universal abstract process on which all human beings can be said to depend, is a way of avoiding or hiding this specific content and intention. Any process of socialization of course includes things that all human beings have to learn, but any specific process ties this necessary learning to a selected range of meanings, values, and practices which, in the very closeness of their association with the necessary learning, constitute the real foundations of the hegemonic. (Williams 1977:117)

We must reconceptualize socialization, not as a set of skills and knowledge unproblematically transferred to the next generation, but as a dialogic process in which hegemonic structures are absorbed, resisted, and transformed in unpredictable ways. It is the combined product of structural factors and individual circumstances, beginning but by no means ending with the child's location within the matrix of family and community relations. Children undergo not one socialization, but many, through their encounters with various social institutions (cf. Walsh 1991:36–47). The influences of family, community, school, and other institutions act simultaneously and at times contradictorily, mirroring the complex cross-currents of hegemony and the multiplicity of subject positions that social identity entails for each individual. These contradictions are not resolved in adulthood; "There is no essential, unitary 'I'—only the fragmentary, contradictory subject I become" (Hall 1985:109).

This perspective replaces the traditional view of socialization with a clearer picture of its actual functioning in society. People's incorporation into structures of social stratification and "a selected range of meanings, values, and practices" is not completed in childhood, but continues through adolescence, as young people grow into their roles both as adults and as particularly positioned social subjects. This "secondary socialization" involves the mastery of new communicative competencies, exploration of various ideologies, and experimentation with various social personae—in short, the construction of an adult identity and habituation to the practices that it entails.

The re-negotiation of identity that accompanies the emergence from childhood involves an increasing awareness of, and identification with, the various subject positions available in the adult world. The subject positions available to any individual are, of course, limited by factors such as ethnicity, class, and gender (though some may serve as avenues *out* of a particular ethnic, class, or even gender position).[3] Subject positions are never simply "given"; rather, they are constructed in the discourses and practices that make up one's social environment. "The question of identification is never the affirmation of a pre-given identity, never a *self*-fulfilling prophecy—it is always the production of an image of identity and the transformation of the subject in assuming that image" (Bhabha 1994:45). One of the principal institutions charged with creating the discourses and practices that prepare young people to take on certain subjectivities is, of course, the school.

A conception of socialization that goes beyond early childhood places much of its burden on the school, and this burden has increased with the widening cultural rift between generations. In Bolivia, the 1952 revolution opened new routes of social mobility for rural dwellers; people aspired to greater things for their children than had ever been possible for themselves.[4] Parental pressure for children of peasants is no longer to continue in an agricultural lifestyle, but rather to find a way out of it, with schooling the most likely avenue. Thus the school has come to rival even the family as a crucial site of socialization. The cultural learning necessary to function in society is changing and expanding too rapidly to be contained within the bounds of the family; "the sort of trans-generational stability of knowledge which was presupposed in most theories of [socialization] can no longer be assumed" (Appadurai and Breckenridge 1988:17).

Thus, the knowledge and practices learned in school play an increasingly important role in shaping individuals as particularly positioned social beings. Still, "schools encourage some aspects of the self more than others" (Luttrel 1996:94). In early childhood, schooling molds students to fit the behavioral and ideological parameters of governable subject-citizens, emphasizing the national and gender dimensions of identity.[5] Later, those more specialized institutions that serve as protracted rites of passage into adulthood—the military, the university, and, in some cultures, the monastery—prepare the young person for a more specific adult role: one defined by a particular type of work and by coming to identify oneself with the kind of work one does.

Both formal and hidden curricula contribute to schooling's socializing function. The normal school plays a special role in this process, due to the geometric multiplication of the socialization that occurs there; not only are students interpellated as particular types of subjects, but they also learn to carry out this same process with their future students. Powerful messages delineating the subject positions offered to students (including that of "student" itself) are encountered both in and out of the classroom. These subject positions are selective and purposeful, but a crucial part of their representation is that they are made to appear natural. It is this obscuring of both their historical roots and their role in maintaining structures of power that makes such representations ideological.

The reproduction of ideology need not involve heavy-handed "indoctrination" or conspiracies of domination by the powers that be. Rather, subjects are produced—and hegemony reproduced—through the gentle tyranny of everyday practice. "If ideology were merely some abstract, imposed set of notions . . . the result of specific manipulation, a kind of overt training which might be simply ended or withdrawn, then the society would be very much easier to move and to change than in practice it has ever been" (Williams 1980a:37). Rather than something imposed at the surface of our minds, ideology is embedded in material practices that permeate our existence, becoming so ingrained as to define the limits of apparent possibility. The gradual evolution of these practices from something that people *do* to something that they *are* interpellates individuals as particular kinds of subjects and simultaneously naturalizes the selective character of this interpellation. Following Gramsci and Althusser, Mouffe (1981:226) defines ideology as a practice producing subjects via the mechanism of interpellation; ideology's material nature is evidenced by its operation in the realm of concrete practices by which subjectivity is produced. This practical realm also includes language, which itself "offers a series of subject positions, a range of discourses out of which historical understanding develops and particular forms of knowledge and social practice become legitimated" (Giroux 1988:215).

Signs, symbols, and rituals are central to the construction of a student subjectivity and to the interpellation of students within it (McLaren 1986). The transformation of identity that students undergo in the normal school is largely symbolic—not in the sense of "less than real," but inasmuch as it occurs through discourse and other symbolic practices and is aimed at students' acceptance of a particular symbolic order and their own (and others') place in it. A change of identity entails a move out of one symbolic construction (a subject position or set of subject positions) into another and adoption of the symbolic practices associated with the new identity. Students' socialization consists largely of learning to recognize and use the symbols associated with particular subject positions; especially, to manipulate particular styles of language. At the same time, the learning and performance of practical skills are also crucial to identity formation—especially when such skills are strongly associated with modernity, and are incompatible (or perceived as such) with the skills and knowledge characteristic of more traditional cultural identities (Rival 1996).

While the process of interpellation is essentially hegemonic, to suppose that it might be avoided, or that a revolutionary project should adopt such an aim, fails to grasp the ubiquitous nature of subjectivity. Interpellation as some sort of social subject (i.e., into some constellation of subject positions) is an indispensable part of being human. It is what makes individual and collective identity possible and invests human existence with meaning. Nevertheless, the subjectivities encouraged in schools are often those which dominant groups endorse for others, according to specific historical interests of their own (Levinson and Holland 1996:24). Our aim should be, not to remove ourselves from the process of interpellation, but to gain a critical perspective on it and on the subject positions involved; in other words, to "denaturalize" them and penetrate the ideological veil that obscures their origins in human-made structures of power.

With this aim in mind, I turn to the nationalist, class, ethnic, and gender images that form part of the normal school curriculum. As we saw in the discursive shift from *indio* to *campesino* (chapter 1), the subjectivities produced by state institutions are not static, but change with the changing needs of the state. To see them in historical perspective, a kind of "geneology of representations"[6] is necessary, as a first step in discovering how these ideological elements have been articulated. The cross-section of school life examined here can yield only the general contours of such a geneology, revealing points of turbulence in the stream of discourse, places where traditional and emergent ideologies clash. By analyzing the conflicts and ambivalences contained in institutional messages, it is possible to deduce the past (and perhaps even the future) direction of certain ideological shifts. The rural normal school's position at the crossroads of these ideological currents makes it a crucial site in the continuous redefinition of national and other identities.

The Citizen in the Nation, the Nation in the World

The production of subjects in ideology includes certain orientations toward the social structure those subjects inhabit (Levinson 1996). Correspondingly, schools transmit a selective and purposeful image of the individual's relation to society; this relation is usually represented as "citizenhood." It is the school's task to construct a bond between students and the nation, to embrace students within a network of meanings and practices that define them as "Bolivians" and make this relationship an enduring part of their ideological repertoire.

This is accomplished via the selection and articulation of different ideological elements; from a vast range of possibilities, certain meanings and practices are emphasized, others excluded, and yet others "reinterpreted, diluted, or put into forms which support or at least do not contradict other elements within the effective dominant culture" (Williams 1980a:39). Where consolidation of the nation-state is a relatively recent (and still incomplete) project, schools are even more crucial to building a self-identified citizenry. Various strains of nationalism compete with class and ethnic solidarities in an ideological "war of position" played out across a wide range of public contexts. In many of these contexts, the identities of the collective protagonists are taken for granted; that is, the content and boundaries of socially constructed subject positions are naturalized, and it is mainly the state's prioritization of their respective demands that is debated.[7] In schools, these identities are presented in explicit form, to a captive and (at least initially) naive audience; here the groundwork is laid for the more public ideological battles in which students will participate upon reaching adulthood.

The hidden curriculum often involves a particular orientation to metropolitan cultural influences (Hannerz 1987:554); the same is true of the explicit curriculum, where official images of urban/*criollo* and rural/indigenous culture transmit a model of the social world and of students' place in it. Such images constitute conscious and semiconscious attempts by teachers, administrators, and curriculum designers to convey a map of Bolivia's human landscape—the landscape that peasant and working-class Aymara youth must traverse on their way to becoming rural teachers.

Although most of the social reproduction literature has focused on schools' promotion of bourgeois/middle-class values, in Bolivian schools both "bourgeois" and "revolutionary" currents operate simultaneously. While many teachers see their task as leading students to "identify with the institutions and ideals of the society that sponsors the education system" (Murray 1983:25), many others see it as the cultivation of a revolutionary class consciousness in the young. Despite the inexorable drift toward neoliberalism, Bolivian nationalism's engagement with socialist ideology and the key role of teachers in this debate continue to find powerful expression in the classroom.

Furthermore, many students enter the normal school already armed with a vaguely socialist orientation, though rarely identifying with a particular political party. Years of exposure to school ideology cannot erase rural students' awareness of their place in the social hierarchy; in contrast to the United States, with its dominant discourse of individual success and failure, the ideological context in which Aymara youth live allows and even encourages them to locate the cause of their frustrations in a system of class and racial oppression. As encouraging as this may sound to radical education theorists, however, the leftist orientation of many Bolivian classrooms is far from sufficient for the nurturing of creative or critical debate on students' place in this system.

Stromquist (1992b:5) claims that schooling "fulfills a critical role in the transmission of representations and beliefs about the 'appropriate' and 'natural' social order," solidifying students' acceptance of and respect for social institutions. This would seem to hold true even for school systems professing a critical and even revolutionary stance. Much of the normal school's curriculum could be considered "revolutionary"; students were assigned topics such as "World Syndicalism" and "The Education of Socialist Man," class discussions frequently focused on Bolivia's dependent and oppressed status, and teachers often criticized the government in class. Several were given to impromptu monologues on official corruption, the persecution of peasants, the lenient treatment of criminals with government or military ties, the repression of public protest, and, especially, the educational reform. Nevertheless, this oppositional perspective was accompanied by exhortations on the importance of obeying the laws, paying one's taxes, and working hard, as the good citizen's keys to success and social mobility— specific manifestations of the "bourgeois ideology" that was so regularly criticized in the abstract. Similarly, the rhetoric of class conflict was frequently employed side-by-side with an implicitly functionalist view of society, in which social institutions were represented as working for the common benefit of all citizens.

The contrast between these two perspectives could have served as a catalyst for class debate, but hardly ever did. Rather, contradictions passed without comment; lesson content was met with undifferentiated acceptance by students concerned mainly with copying down what the teacher said. There were a few students who regularly made cogent critiques of material presented in class, and occasionally some topic provoked strong reactions even among the usually quiescent. But such incidents were isolated eddies in the near-stagnant flow of lecturing, note taking, and questions launched by professors only to fall into dead air. The infrequent class discussions had a self-contained quality; after serving their purpose of filling class time and "getting through" a particular topic, they were put aside, and their relevance to any subsequent material was not evoked.

An examination of one afternoon's sociology class will illustrate this pattern.[8] Class began with a discussion of "Social Groups," defined as institutions that aid the individual's integration into society; groups acting against or outside this function were dismissed as operating "on the margin of society." Professor Torres initiated a discussion of the mass media, asserting that "most media encourage individuals to adopt the rules of society; naturally they are not going to work against the interests of society." One boy asked if the media always fulfill their function in a fair and objective manner, to which the professor responded, "What do you all think?" After one boy quipped, "I don't have a radio," provoking laughter from the class, talk turned to the political stances of various La Paz radio stations. Students spoke of how some stations supported indigenous people's concerns, while others only gave the view-point of the upper class. Professor Torres remarked that this often depends on the ideological perspective of the station owner; some provide a forum for public grievances while others try to create the impression that everything is fine. One student mentioned a reporter with a reputation for "telling the truth"; the professor praised this reporter and criticized those who gloss over unpleasant facts. He then returned to his prepared lecture with a definition of "Society: a large number of human beings who work together to satisfy their social needs and who share a common culture," giving the United States and China as examples.

While this rather facile definition would seem to have been debunked by the discussion preceding it, as soon as the teacher resumed lecturing all heads went down and the definition was copied without comment. No one challenged the assertion that the United States, China, or Bolivia for that matter each con-tains a "common culture" shared by all inhabitants harmoni-ously working together to satisfy their common needs, despite the class and ethnic conflicts debated moments before.

The juxtaposition of Marxist and functionalist perspectives was observed in a number of classes and with a number of different teachers. At times it seemed to reflect discrepancies between teachers' own views and the received curriculum, as when one teacher introduced a lecture by stating: "Individuals have different levels of intellectual and physical ability, and this places them in a determined social position." While it seems unlikely (one would hope) that the students assiduously copy-ing down this statement would consider their own social posi-tion a direct result of their intellectual and physical abilities, none bothered to dispute it. And yet a moment later the teacher was expounding on the poor's limited possibilities for improving their status, as opposed to the rich who can send their children abroad to study (rather than to the normal school). When the lesson reached the topic of social mobility, however, examples were limited to individual overnight successes, such as lottery winners; no mention was made of social mobility (or its absence) as a group phenomenon, nor of the students themselves as examples of same.

Educational reform was the subject of bitter critiques in a number of classes, as were the government's alleged efforts to weaken the teachers' union and sabotage the regional and national educational congresses with delaying tactics and political machinations. However, these critiques did not preclude the presentation of a placid, "official" view of society and government in general. During a lesson on customs, Professor Torres remarked that "customs should be respected by all of us, or it would be total chaos, people robbing and killing, acting like wolves." When a student asked, "What about bad customs?" he replied that society punishes those, though this answer seemed to miss the point the student was getting at. When the discussion turned to laws, these were defined as "rules established by those exercising political power, enforced by the state apparatus . . . the state can do whatever is necessary to assure that the laws be obeyed." Professor Torres explained that since the ADN-MIR were currently in power, they were entitled to establish laws "that naturally are for the benefit of the entire society, not just for a limited sector . . . thus we should obey them"—despite the fact that he had severely criticized the government's education plan on many occasions and later joined a hunger strike with some of his colleagues in protest of it.

Teachers' "progressive" political views did not always translate into a revolutionary perspective in the classroom. Often the way debate was framed proved as significant as the opinions being expressed, as was shown in a lesson on the decline of socialism in the wake of the Soviet breakup. After reviewing the rise of *perestroika* and independence movements in Eastern Europe, Professor Torres challenged students to reconcile the failure of socialism with the Marxist model of the linear evolution of society. He mentioned Cuba as the last bastion of socialism, remarking that even there Castro was "lamentably" in his last years and would probably not be in power much longer. He then asked if a transition from capitalism to socialism was possible in Latin America. Students muttered among themselves, but none wanted to take the floor. Finally, one boy said that it was not possible, because the entire socialist system is deteriorating; isolated revolutionary movements are still active, but it is hard to build consensus behind an ideal that is having such setbacks worldwide. After comments from two others, the professor concluded by saying, "For the moment it is impossible to think of any other system, any other alternative besides capitalism." If any students disagreed, they kept their opinions to themselves.

In general, the political framework employed by students was extremely vague, centered on a narrow range of oft-repeated slogans and ideas. In its rigidity and unexamined assumptions, it was comparable to the sort of individualist work ethic that goes unchallenged in classrooms where the national consciousness is based in expansionist capitalism, rather than in class struggle and a collective awareness of exploitation. With rare exceptions, the "revolutionary" content of lessons and student presentations did not imply a more critical perspective than one would find in any "bourgeois" classroom. Many students learned to manipulate basic socialist rhetoric with little real understanding of the concepts involved. A topic such as "Factors impeding the industrialization of the country" would provoke denunciations of the iron control wielded by the bourgeoisie and the powerlessness of the workers, but a query as to how this impedes industrialization drew only blank looks. When one teacher asked the class, "What is 'the crisis' and where does it come from?" the automatic answer was "From the United States, who are capitalists," followed by a string of politically charged catch phrases culled from a pamphlet that students had used to "research" their topic. During one class, Arsenio, a high-achieving student who took such discussions more seriously than most, called the presenting group's bluff and asked them *how* Bolivia's crisis is caused by the United States. After some confused fumbling by the others, Arsenio adeptly answered his own question.

Meaningful discussion was not totally absent from the classroom; a topic such as the foreign debt could spark an outburst of indignation over governments who borrowed huge sums that then had to be repaid by the sacrifices of the working class, though the loans seldom benefitted them. Many such outbursts had a single source, an older student named Eulogio. Unfortunately, Eulogio's monologues tended to dampen discussion rather than provoke it; other students seemed put off, less by his ideas (an incongruous blend of revolutionary socialism and fundamentalist Christianity) than by the tireless zeal with which he promoted them. During a discussion of the importance of studying history, Eulogio challenged the class: "Are we going to go on dancing like puppets for Monje,[9] for Paz Zamora? . . . We have to decide for ourselves if we agree with the history that's taught, Simón Bolívar as the liberator of Bolivia, those things . . . The teacher should be anti-imperialist, a factor for change." There were a few giggles, but no one took the bait. Several students expressed similar ideas in private, but none seemed to consider the classroom a fitting place for such blunt and impassioned debate, and Eulogio's attempt to provoke it fell flat.

In contrast, similar sentiments expressed during *hora cívica* were well received, but in a context that did not allow for discussion. Here, students held forth on the hazards of privatization, the sacrifices of long-dead indigenous martyrs, and the need for unity and courage to transform Bolivia's history of exploitation. In these speeches, students reworked and challenged official conceptions of nationalism, implicitly raising the question of how "one's own people" should be defined.[10] Rather than simply accepting the category of *bolivianos,* students often defined their "we" in class and/or racial terms. One boy, speaking on the anniversary of Tupac Katari's death, suggested that political movements bearing his name (e.g., the "Kataristas" of the 1970s) were not really Marxists, but simply "disguised" as such. He asserted that the true path to justice was neither the right nor the left, but rather that of "the [indigenous] race." Another speaker urged listeners to reflect on "who we are and why we are here," asking: "When we leave here as teachers, do we forget who we are, forget our class? It is a lie that liberty has come to our Aymara people." By rejecting the dichotomy of right and left in favor of an essentialist ethnic nationalism, students held out an alternative to the nationalist ideology dominating the school system. *Hora cívica* provided a space where students could express such opinions freely and even earn official praise for doing so. Nevertheless, this space was exempt from spontaneous feedback; ideas could be broadcast but not debated. And, as in the majority of such public contexts, female voices were all but absent.

The upper class, the military, hypocritical politicians, and U.S. imperialism were frequent targets of criticism by students and teachers alike. But, for reasons that can be traced to the organizational principles and pedagogical methods that dominate Bolivian schooling (examined in detail in chapter 5), real classroom debate was rare. Furthermore, students who expressed such opinions seemed to have arrived at the normal school with their political ideas already defined; these were not formed on the basis of classroom analyses, nor were they offered toward the fulfillment of academic obligations. These obligations were met instead by one-page homework assignments copied out of books and the strung-together catch phrases that served as class presentations, seldom linked to the political and social concerns that many students felt strongly.

A large part of the normal school curriculum (like that of primary and secondary schools) was dedicated to defining national goals and transmitting a selective, legitimized image of the nation itself (laid out explicity in a class artlessly dubbed "National Reality"). The picture of domestic and international relations painted in the classroom contained contradictions similar to those described above, which students usually copied down without comment. When they did comment, their opinions were more often dismissed than encouraged. In 1992, Bolivia carried out a national census for the first time since 1976. Many rural communities and some leftist parties opposed the census, on the grounds that it would enable the government and multinational corporations to exploit the peasant and working classes more efficiently. The language teacher began one lesson by mentioning this opposition, but followed with the assertion that "all Bolivians" supported the census. Sergio objected, arguing that it could be used to take advantage of the population; the professor defended the census as necessary for "a dependent nation such as Bolivia," and after a brief exchange the matter was closed, without any other students having participated.

Somewhat paradoxically, many classroom portrayals of Bolivia's "national character" were overwhelmingly negative. Pedagogy class, dedicated mainly to reading Franz Tamayo's *Creación de la Pedagogía Nacional,* invariably adopted Tamayo's turn-of-the-century ethnic stereotypes and essentialist analyses as given, rather than using them as jumping-off points for critique. Much of the class consisted of professorial confirmations of Tamayo's derogatory portrayal of Bolivia. The repeated assertions that Bolivia's social problems spring from national defects such as laziness and alcoholism were met not with criticism or debate, but with statements such as: "We don't have many scholars, nor do we have great works of art, and alcoholism is an aspect of our national character... We must educate ourselves; we must reform ourselves."

This self-deprecatory discourse was present in other classes as well, not only within official lessons but as part of the general atmosphere in which lessons were received. One teacher, lamenting students' failure to complete assignments, declared: "We Bolivians are characterized by this; we make promises and don't keep them." Even less explicit comments often contained an implicit slur, such as Professor Torres' assertion during a sociology lesson that "a country progresses because its inhabitants work." Leaving unspoken the implication that Bolivia's underdevelopment is due to its citizens' unwillingness to work, the professor went on to compare English and Spanish colonial policies. The English, he said, worked and colonized North America, whereas the Spaniards simply plundered South America of its riches; furthermore, there was no race mixture in the United States because the English exterminated the indigenous inhabitants. Given the negative portrayals of *mestizos* that students received in their other classes, one wonders whether the conclusion to be drawn was that Bolivia would have been better off if all of its native inhabitants had been eradicated during the Conquest and replaced with hardworking Europeans.

Despite disclaimers that "every society is culturally distinct... it isn't possible to compare them," the model underlying classroom discourse about Bolivia's place in the world was that of a graded hierarchy of development.[11] At the top of this hierarchy was the United States; at the bottom, those few nations viewed as even more backward than Bolivia, to whose level Bolivia was in constant danger of falling. A lesson on Bolivia's infant mortality rate (the worst in Latin America) prompted the teacher to exclaim, "Comparable to Africa, imagine!" The factors determining Bolivia's position in this hierarchy were seldom debated; underdevelopment was ascribed either to inherent national flaws or to vague, gargantuan forces of capitalist exploitation that did not receive close analysis.

The theme of beseiged sovereignty discussed in chapter 1 was also present in classroom discourse. The review of current events that began each Language class typically might include alleged Chilean incursions into Bolivian territory and the importance of staying informed in order to guard against such threats. In National Reality class, discussion of Bolivia's native fauna predictably led to the topic of the recent U.S. importation of Bolivian llamas and speculation over how this might intensify First World exploitation of Bolivian resources. In Sociology class, Professor Torres evoked the specter of hostile forces plotting the disintegration of the nation, in a lecture on decentralization and its potentially fragmenting effect on Bolivian society: "In Santa Cruz, not to speak badly of the *cruceños*, but they're very regionalistic. There was even a time when they burned the Bolivian flag . . . They wanted to raise just the *cruceño* flag, imagine . . . You all know there are countries that like to think of Bolivia as a historical error, to say that it shouldn't exist! That each one should take over a piece of Bolivia. That's what's happened throughout our history; all our neighboring countries have always taken something from us."

Thus, Bolivia's image as a backward and threatened nation—already a common theme in popular culture as well as primary education—is reinforced yet again at the normal school level. Its presence here contains a subtle difference, however; as future teachers charged with molding the opinions of the next generation, students were invested with a certain responsibility toward the nation that was presented to them. Teachers, they were repeatedly told, must be agents of change and stalwart defenders of the national interest. Nevertheless, the scenario presented to them portrayed the prospects for social change and national progress as discouraging in the extreme.

Proletarian Professionals: The Ambiguous Class Identity of Bolivian Teachers

The class identity of Bolivian teachers is fraught with contradictions. The dominant rhetoric of the profession assigns teachers a self-consciously combative stance that assumes a revolutionary solidarity with the working/peasant class. In the array of subject positions that make up rural teachers' identity, the class element is particularly strong, as the activity of regional and national unions demonstrates. As mentioned earlier, the working-class militancy of Bolivia's teachers historically has been surpassed only by that of the miners. But while miners constitute a virtual archetype of the revolutionary industrial proletarian, teachers' class position is more problematic.

Bourdieu (1984:103) notes that a social group's "collective trajectory" may be progressively masculinized or feminized, grow older or younger, etc. In this sense, teaching in Bolivia has been both "Indianized" and "proletarianized." In earlier decades, it was a middle-class occupation, but indigenous people's increased access to education has led to an influx of peasant/ working-class youth into the field. Yet, while this (along with falling salaries and the rise of militant political activity) did much to "proletarianize" teaching, teachers are still seen as "professionals."

While the cultural capital associated with professional status is an important part of the normal school's allure, teachers' political alignment with workers and peasants requires them to identify with those whose fate they have managed to escape. John Kenneth Gailbraith (1968:179) captured this dilemma with the observation that "a lurking sense of guilt over a more pleasant, agreeable, and remunerative life can often be assuaged by the observation 'I am a worker too.' " Of course, teachers' low pay and standard of living give them some basis for their proletarian identification. The escape from a life of manual labor, while significant, is not accompanied by as great a rise in social status as that usually associated with entry into the professions (this is especially true of rural teachers).[12]

Teachers' status as simultaneously the most "proletarian" of professionals and the most professional sector of the proletariat places them in an ambiguous position with regard to class struggle. While the Trotskyite union leadership portrays itself as the socialist vanguard of an urban proletariat, teachers' own membership in that group is questionable.[13] Declaring teachers' work equivalent to that of the laborer means downplaying its intellectual nature and its personal and professional rewards. The idea that teaching is personally fulfilling and engages the highest philosphical ideals is central to both bourgeois and revolutionary ideologies, but is not strictly compatible with the role of "exploited labor." While working-class solidarity is easily assumed, extending this to a feeling of identification is hampered by the "professional" element of teachers' collective self-concept.

The conflict between working-class solidarity and professional identity is manifested in teachers' attitudes toward the type of work they do and the type of work they have left behind. Union rhetoric espouses the unity of mental and manual labor and schools' incorporation into social processes of work and production, in contrast to the current focus on texts and hypothetical treatments of problems.[14] But while many teachers supported this view, the normal school used manual labor mainly for disciplinary purposes.[15] When students guilty of tardiness or other minor offenses were made to haul rocks for the construction of a new dormitory, the punishment seemed to consist not only of the physical exertion involved, but also of the public indignity of the act. This contrasted sharply with the descriptions (read by students in Pedagogy class) of cooperative labor between students, teachers, and peasants during the heyday of Warisata, the *escuela-ayllu*. Instead of being approached as a cooperative task in which all labored together for the benefit of the institution, manual labor was used to isolate those students who were officially in disgrace.

Despite students' broad experience in manual labor, such work was viewed as inappropriate to their future status. One teacher lamented the prevalence of this attitude among his colleagues: "We're ashamed of our [manual] work . . . For example, a teacher might make bricks. But if someone sees him, his colleague perhaps, making bricks, selling them maybe—he starts commenting, saying 'I saw my friend doing that, poor guy.' So then, people look down on him and don't allow him to get ahead . . . Bolivians are like that. It makes me very sad."

Much of the normal school's appeal lies in its promise of escape from a life of toil, and the prestige associated with the image of the "professional." Adoption of these values is an important part of students' identification with the role of teacher. The emphasis on professionalism was evident in the classroom as well as in students' more personal disclosures. In Native Languages class, after one student recounted (in Aymara) the tale of two industrious brothers and one idle one (who, predictably, comes to a bad end), the professor declared the moral of the story to be the importance of having a profession, since "a person without a profession isn't worth anything." Antonia (whose father was also a rural schoolteacher) expressed a similar view in her explanation of why she chose a teaching career: "Worst of all is to stay back, that's worse than anything. If I didn't go on studying, I would just be like nothing there, suffering in the countryside, or unemployed."

In contrast to the union's valorization of productive labor as a necessary part of education (and of the awakening of a revolutionary class consciousness in the student), some students saw their training as precisely opposed to such activity. Carlos, for example, considered the manual chores required of students as beneath the dignity of one forming himself as a "man of ideas":

Carlos: For example, you see students sweeping the grounds, sometimes they're out there painting something . . . I think there are janitors for that, to take care of keeping things clean, those things, right? I believe if a man wants to be a professional, he has to dedicate himself to study. Completely to study, no? And maybe he has to have fun also.

Teachers' identification with the proletariat is threatened by the break with manual labor that higher education implies. Related to this is the social distance between the teacher and the peasant community. While students were taught that rural teachers should be democratic and culturally sensitive, they were also supposed to command a healthy respect from those they served.

Faustino: Sure, we play around, have fun, but when one shares with another person, or with a professor, one becomes a bit serious, responsible. And aside from that, one doesn't share like that with just anybody, you know? He looks for that quality, one who speaks well. One changes . . . When you're a kid, you horse around, here among the guys we play, but when we graduate it's very different. One feels like, I'm here in the normal school, I'm going to be a teacher. That always happens; I've really felt it. And that way, people are afraid of you . . . They talk to us with respect, with awe. Thinking that one really knows, you know? And one has to reciprocate in the same manner.

The relationship between the teacher and the rural community was portrayed to students as one of both solidarity and social distance. The paternalistic terms in which it was described left little doubt that teachers are socially apart, with and for "the masses" but no longer of them. Rearticulating students' identity from the peasant community itself to the cadre of professionals who supposedly lead that community was part of the normal school's hegemonic function. "No mere training or pressure is truly hegemonic. The true condition of hegemony is effective *self-identification* with the hegemonic forms: a specific and internalized 'socialization' " (Williams 1977:118; original emphasis). This socialization was as crucial to students' training as was the information they absorbed about pedagogical methods, child psychology, and bureaucratic skills.

The Teacher in the Rural Community: Solidarity and Social Distance

The teacher's relationship to the rural community was specifically addressed in those subjects dedicated to questions of teacher practice, but advice on teachers' proper role showed up in other classes as well. The most common image was that of the teacher as a civilizing and modernizing force, a leader (though not a member) of the rural community. The rural teacher was portrayed not only as classroom instructor, but also counselor, mediator, translator, town scribe, public health worker, and community organizer. The teacher was said to be the center of the community, the one to whom residents turn in times of trouble or dispute. His or her behavior therefore should reflect the highest moral standard, serving as a model for others. The teacher should initiate and participate in community events, teaching "enthusiasm, admiration, respect, and patriotism" for Bolivia's national culture, as well as understanding and regard for its regional cultures and customs.

Numerous official documents contain long lists of desired qualities for schoolteachers, from optimism and emotional stability to a critical perspective and the fortitude to stand up to authorities. Teachers are charged with "forming the type of man needed in society" and "preparing individuals to participate actively in the process of social change." This means working with communities in a democratic and cooperative manner; correspondingly, students were taught that projects must be organized with input from parents and local authorities, so as not to foster resentment. They were advised to gain the community's confidence before undertaking projects, and warned against making demands for food, housing, and beer before they had even started working.[16] Pupils were to be treated gently and with affection; corporal punishment and other traumatizing practices were strictly discouraged. "Consideration of the psychological aspects of the child" was a progressive advance upon which the normal school prided itself and distinguished itself from the old, oppressive style of education.

While some aspects of the teacher's job—like the steps for building a medical post or ordering new desks—were covered in excruciating detail, the treatment of others was vague, mystifying, or simply absent. There was no mention of relations with one's fellow teachers, administrators, or authorities, nor of the local political conflicts in which teachers and communities frequently become embroiled. Sexual harassment, a problem for some female students and undoubtedly for some teachers as well, constituted one of the "structured silences" of the school curriculum. Platitudes such as "we are forming ourselves to be teachers with a new ideology, a new kind of training" were common, but less so the specifics as to what this new ideology and training entailed.

References to the teacher's role in the community usually appeared in teachers' offhand comments, rather than as part of the official curriculum. Much more class time was dedicated to the bureaucratic and ritual practices of teaching than to the social relationships involved. Entire class periods were spent on such skills as marking attendance, figuring grades, and record keeping. One class included a lengthy outline of various school ceremonies and their corresponding documents; in another, students copied sample letters written in the formal style required for official school business. Students found such lessons boring, but their content was far from insignificant. On the contrary, they emphasized the importance of bureaucratic rituals over other aspects of school life.

Professors sometimes made a conscious effort to combat discrimination and elevate the low opinion of rural teachers. Professor Torres took advantage of a class discussion to chide those rural teachers who, upon moving to urban schools, forget their origins and look down on their former colleagues. It was frequently asserted that the superior scientific training of urban teachers was offset by the superior pedagogical understanding of their rural colleagues. In one class presentation, students cited the lack of scientific preparation in rural normal schools as a cause of the discrimination suffered by rural teachers, but also claimed that these "valued our traditions" more than urban ones. The professor broke in to assert that there was really no difference between urban and rural teachers, except perhaps with regard to social class. However, after re-marking that the idea that rural teachers "didn't know any-thing" maintained a certain currency in urban circles "up until the 1980s" (a rather optimistic assessment perhaps), he reiter-ated the students' point as to urban and rural teachers' respec-tive superiority in scientific/theoretical vs. "practical" areas.

At other times, the notion of rural teachers' inferiority was reinforced. After summer vacation, when there was some con-fusion over exactly when classes were to resume, the rector addressed students to deplore the lack of discipline of those who had still not arrived. It seemed, he said, as though they were only preparing themselves to teach in the countryside; they were not up to the standards of their urban colleagues, and a change of attitude was urgently needed. In a discussion of the competition that would result from privatization, Profes-sor Torres told the class:

It's unfortunate, but we have to be realistic. Teachers forget about continuing their training, continuing to read, to inves-tigate. They forget because they go to remote places, where one can't even buy a newspaper. There, the teacher starts to forget about everything. He becomes routine . . . He doesn't give his full attention to education. He only dedicates a few hours to his work; after that he goes to his field, to work the soil. What is he doing? He's producing students who are altogether badly educated!

Students inevitably measured official images of the rural teacher against their own observations and aspirations. Some-times the ideology of teaching was so far from students' own experience that it simply fell flat (such as a visiting professor's declaration that "in the nuclear schools there are good teachers and average ones; there are no bad ones because if they're bad they don't graduate from the normal school"). On rare occa-sions, however, class discussion turned to the cracks in the professional mythos that dominated official school contexts. Although such discussions usually took the form of pejorative remarks about students' actions or motivations, they did pro-vide a small gleam of relevance in the morass of remote infor-mation that made up much of the curriculum.

When class discussion focused on students themselves, it was usually about cheating, failure to complete assignments,

or lack of sincerity in their aspirations to become teachers.
Only twice did I hear teachers bring up in class students' reasons for entering the normal school. One discussed what it
meant to have a "vocation" for teaching, asking students if they
had it; several responded, "Some do," and the teacher went on
to discuss the factors that lead students to enter teaching (similar
to those mentioned in chapter 3). Another spoke to the class of
students who come to the normal school with no clear idea of
why, or for economic or family reasons, following with a discussion of why students drop out. In another class, this teacher
told of an incident in which a student doing her practicum
was unable to divide twelve by three for the third graders she
was trying to teach. He lamented: "This is the reality in our
country . . . We don't want cheap teachers . . . This way we are
deceiving the children." He suggested that some students in the
normal school were similarly unqualified, that they could better
pursue some other career and would one day say to themselves, "Thanks to that teacher who made me reflect on things,
I'm now making a lot of money (as a bricklayer, etc.)." The
possible accuracy of the teachers' sarcasm with respect to students' qualifications was not matched by his assessment of the
actual possibilities open to them; as interviews with students
revealed, many had themselves calculated the costs and benefits
of a teaching career and decided that the normal school was
their best choice among limited alternatives.

Cognizant of the shortcomings inherent in the mythos of the
model teacher but unwilling to abandon the ideals that had led
them into higher education, students walked a fine line between
aspiration and resignation. Many held a low opinion of teachers
in general, but were determined to be different, to transcend the
mediocrity that had characterized much of their own schooling.

Mateo: From what I've seen, sometimes I think "My God, the
     people who get into teaching." Sometimes I say to myself "I
     would die for the sake of education," but sometimes . . . it's
     like I'm going to be—pardon the expression—one more
     lunthata[17] working for the state. [laughs] Yeah, like, some-
     times I ask myself, I say to my friends, "We're all just going
     to be one more *lunthata*, no?"

AL: What kind of teacher do you think you'll be when you
     graduate?

Diana: [laughing] A mediocre one . . . [seriously] I don't want to be like, for example, those mediocre teachers who don't teach well. I don't want to be like that. I don't want to cheat people. When I graduate from here, I'd like to always continue learning, although I won't leave here a great scholar, but with time I think I'll improve.

Students' experiences, ideals, and notions of where they fit in the social universe factored heavily into their conceptions of teachers and of what they hoped to accomplish as teachers themselves. Also important to the evolution of their professional identity were their conceptions of their own ethnicity. While questions of class, nationality, and gender presented their own problems for students' ideological formation, the question of ethnicity was the most complex. As future "agents of change" in rural communities, students' orientation to both traditional Aymara culture and Bolivian "national culture" was key to their initiation into professional status. A large part of the normal school curriculum was thus directly or indirectly dedicated to shaping this orientation.

Uneasy Positionings on the Field of Race—or, "We Have Met El Hermano Campesino and He Is (not?) Us"

Indians in the Modern World: Stereotypes and Mutability

Before 1952, the subject positions available to indigenous people within the dominant society were largely restricted to positions of servitude. The supposed equivalence between the categories *indígena* (a person of indigenous descent), *indio* (in the sense of a racist epithet), and *peón/pongo* was virtually impossible to challenge within the racist hegemony of the era.[18] In contrast, recent decades have seen various attempts to disarticulate indigenous and peasant identities from the deeply entrenched image of the despised *indio*. New subject positions have appeared, into which indigenous people are moving in increasing numbers. They now face the question of what it means to be indigenous within social categories that were previously incompatible with that status.

Rural education and the rise of the normal school as a key institution of social mobility expanded the subject positions available to indigenous people. Yet, while mass education served to partially desegregate the middle class, it intensified class stratification within the indigenous community itself. First, access to primary schooling created a large stratum of literate rural dwellers, offset by a large stratum of illiterates, since "universal public schooling" is seldom truly universal.[19] Second, limited access to secondary education provided some with an avenue out of agricultural life. However, not only is this avenue limited in the numbers it can accomodate, it also entails a rejection of the way of life that, until fairly recently, was the unquestioned underpinning of Aymara cultural identity. The rise of alternative identities has been accompanied by conflicts over which of these are desirable, advantageous, and morally acceptable. Now that "Aymara" does not automatically mean *"campesino,"* many are left unsure as to what it does mean, and the resulting differences of opinion take on the bitterness characteristic of questions that threaten one's personal identity. Education has ameliorated (somewhat) the racial divisions in the nation's class structure, but it has created new divisions within indigenous society itself.

Although multiculturalist rhetoric has largely replaced the racist ideology and aggressive assimilation policies of the past, ethnic stereotypes persist within the normal school curriculum. Sweeping generalizations about the innate characteristics of *campesinos* and *mestizos* appeared frequently in classroom lectures, as did matter-of-fact assertions of the "backwardness" and "primitiveness" of nonliterate societies.[20] The widely accepted notion that *altiplano* dwellers are reserved and timid, while people of the *oriente* are extroverted and carefree, was repeated often in the classroom.[21] In a lesson on reading, one teacher linked the higher literacy rates among urbanites to a "linguistic and mental maturity" supposedly lacking in rural areas. At other times, the indigenous stereotypes encountered in the classroom were superficially laudatory, but dovetailed with more racist discourses in their narrow conception of indigenous character.

In contrast, the classroom stereotype of the *mestizo* was openly disparaging. While Indians were described as honest, hardworking, introverted, passive, and suspicious, *mestizos* (or *mistis*) were allegedly more intelligent and sociable, but also opportunistic, idle, imitative (due to their lack of an essential racial character), and prone to decadence and degeneracy.

Lacking both the simple purity of the Indian and the rational nobility of the European, *mestizos* were untrustworthy exploiters and charlatans, always ready to betray their indigenous cousins in their grasping efforts at personal gain and their futile aspirations toward the social prestige enjoyed by their natural betters.[22] These images were sometimes accompanied by pseudo-scientific explanations of race mixture, such as that the offspring of a white man and an indigenous woman will have the physical traits of the mother and the intelligence of the father (thus the craftiness of the *misti*). The teacher who offered this statement qualified it by stating that the child "will retain the physical features of his mother, but not completely; he will be better-looking, although not as white as his father."

In class discussions in various subjects, a deficit model of indigenous culture predominated. Students as well as teachers were likely to characterize indigenous people as conservative and superstitious, and to ascribe their marginalization to a "lack of culture." In one class, students were asked "Which is more intelligent, the *mestizo* or the Indian?" A few boys answered *"el indígena,"* but this was not the "correct" answer. Yet in another class the same teacher asserted that "no one is incompetent. We all have the capacity to learn . . . It's not a question of race." These occasional disclaimers could not negate the restricting effects of a discourse, constructed over so many similar lessons, that sharply delimited the official view of Indianness. When valorized, Aymara culture was usually referred to in terms of a past "golden age"; there was little mention of it as a modern-day phenomenon, or of its urban manifestations (except in the context of derogatory comments about *cholos*). When asked what culture was, students responded with "the customs of our ancestors" and references to the ancient civilization of Tiahuanaco. Aymara religion, marriage customs, and land tenure patterns[23] were presented as anachronisms, of no use in contemporary society. This was brought home to students in a more personal way during morning assembly after the Day of the Dead, when the rector reprimanded students for leaving school Thursday when only Friday had been given as a holiday. He declared that the staff had been very tolerant with regard to students' homesickness and ritual obligations toward their deceased, but asserted, "We're in a time of change; when there are responsibilities, one must leave behind . . . the customs of our grandparents." Those who had left early were barred from their Monday exams as punishment.

My intention is not to paint a black-and-white picture of racist teachers imposing a reactionary world view over the resistance of ethnically proud Aymara students. Teachers as well as students strongly identified themselves as Aymara, and confusion over what this implied in the context of the contemporary nation-state was common to both groups. Positive images of indigenous culture were not totally absent from the curriculum; in Native Languages class, students were instructed to collect Aymara proverbs and stories, while in Language class they analyzed a series of children's books containing public health lessons embedded in culturally sensitive portrayals of rural life (as noted approvingly by the more attentive students). Sometimes it was students, rather than teachers, who seemed most ready to relegate Aymara culture to the dustbin of history. During a group presentation of a sample elementary school lesson, in which the two themes used as examples were Life and Customs of the Aymaras and Man's Voyage to the Moon (themselves forming a rather provocative opposition), some students wanted to correct the prepared materials to read "What *was* the name of the god of the Aymaras?" rather than "What *is* the name . . . ?" This was argued solely as a question of wording, not of the current viability of indigenous religion.[24]

The "integration" of indigenous culture into the curriculum often constituted an exercise in contradiction, a superficial valorization of a stereotyped ideal of indigenous identity which cloaked a deeper discourse of denigration. The normal school's tendency, even when ostensibly glorifying indigenous culture, was to weaken rather than strengthen students' identification with it, presenting it as a romanticized past with little positive bearing on students' present ambitions, and positing a stereotyped indigenous subject from which students had to distance themselves in order to become true professionals. Woolcott (1974:420) views this process through the metaphor of students as prisoners of war, with teachers as representatives of the enemy culture: "The purpose of instruction is to recruit new members into society by encouraging prisoners to defect, and . . . giving them the skills so that they can do so effectively." While this view may be a bit extreme, the classroom discourse of teachers and students does reveal a conception of two opposed cultural alternatives; the next section examines how speakers locate themselves with regard to these alternatives.

Self-Situating Discourses: Staking a Claim in the Bolivian Ethniscape

Viewing the unstable scaffolding of ethnic and national ideology that is cobbled together in the classroom, we might ask: Where do students and teachers locate themselves on the ethnic map? As a relatively new social entity—indigenous professionals—their very existence throws into sharp relief (and deep confusion) the categories in which Bolivian society is conceived. The difficulty of remolding these categories to fit one's identity—or vice versa—is evidenced by the contradictory statements such efforts produce. Clearly, most students and professors located themselves firmly within the category of *los aymaras, los indios, el pueblo indígena.* This was evident not only from markers like language, dress, and explicit affirmations of identity, but also from the generalized use of first-person pronouns when speaking of this group: "Before the Spaniards arrived, we were lords of the land. The Spaniards disinherited us"; "Elizardo Pérez always identified with our cause"; "Before, there was no education for us"; "our indigenous race"; "our Aymara language." In class terms, students and teachers identified strongly with the working class, both in expressions of political ideology and in their use of pronouns (as when one professor explained that, "Before, teachers were of the petty bourgeoisie, they weren't people of our class").[25]

The picture is complicated, however, by the term *campesino.* As we have seen, the term's use in official discourse has political and cultural implications that run far deeper than the simple gloss *peasant.* Its use in the postrevolutionary period as a politically correct substitute for *indio* aimed not only to disallow a key marker of racism from official discourse, and to discursively reinforce the new labor relations in the countryside, but also to de-emphasize ethnicity in favor of class.[26] As part of a national project of ethnic homogenization, ethnicity was gradually delegitimized as a basis for collective claims. However, since the ethnic difference between indigenous rural dwellers and nonindigenous urbanites was and is quite salient,[27] the rhetorical drawing of attention toward class and away from ethnicity was not completely successful. Instead, the substitution of *campesino* for a term that signified race/ethnicity (*indio*) resulted in the former's partial disarticulation from a strictly class meaning and its re-articulation with a particular ethnic identity.

During the period immediately following the revolution, the ethnic boundaries demarcating indigenous Bolivians (at least in the *altiplano*) conformed fairly neatly to the contours of the *campesino* class; most indigenous people *were* peasants, or at least had strong ties to the rural economy. But in time, the fit between these two categories became increasingly uneven. More rural migrants took up permanent residence in urban centers, and the expansion of schooling gave rise to a cohort of rural youth whose aspirations did not include a life dedicated to agriculture. Class and ethnic subject positions that were previously isomorphic subsequently diverged, while others that were mutually exclusive came to overlap. The normal school students were constructing their adult identities—national, ethnic, class, professional, and gender—precisely in the historical disjuncture between the categories of *indio*, *campesino*, and indigenous professional.

The term *campesino* came up frequently in class discussions, in ways that revealed speakers' ambivalence. Most often, the *campesino* was spoken of in laudatory but not self-identificatory terms, typically as *el hermano campesino* ("our peasant brother"). In one class discussion, a boy spoke of discrimination, referring to "we ourselves, our race"; a girl then denounced the way "*el hermano campesino*" is treated in city offices, making a subtle but definite shift away from the first-person pronoun. She asserted that without the *campesino* there would be no food for the cities, but she also spoke of his defects in language, education, and cultural level, maintaining that while some *campesinos* have moved to the cities and improved themselves in this regard, those who stay in the countryside are unable to do so. When I asked where she and her classmates fit in this scheme, she replied simply that not all were "from the provinces" (she herself was from a mining area).

Those students who *were* from the provinces tended to be less equivocal about their relation to the *campesino*. Diana, with rare eloquence for a rural female student, spoke of the *campesinos* as "we," the ones who work for the homeland and are first in war, while the whites avoid military service. She indignantly recounted how "the politicians deceive the Indians in their campaigns and then forget all about us." The professor's reply displayed the familiar combination of solidarity and distance, as he related how, during the war of independence, the illiterate Indian was incapable of analyzing the political situation and was thus utilized by forces on both sides of the conflict.

Balancing the linked/opposed discourses of *"el hermano campesino"* and *"nuestro pueblo campesino"* was a touchy business, often provoking strong reactions from students (unlike most other classroom topics). In one class, the teacher claimed that *campesinos* habitually sleep late and go to their fields in the morning having hardly washed. This incited a rare clamor of protest from the students, who asserted (many from first-hand experience) that *campesinos* must often rise at four or five in the morning. The teacher refused to cede the point, responding that students did not know all areas of the country. Another teacher introduced the topic of "factors impeding national development" by asking, "Why do the *campesinos* not pay their taxes?" This also drew an outcry from students, who argued indignantly that it was a bad question; the *campesinos* **do** pay, it's the upper class that doesn't. The professor, taken aback by the forcefulness of their reaction, hastily concurred, agreeing that "we have always paid, because they have always exploited us."

The "discourse of distance" remained present in a variety of guises, however. Sometimes it reflected an awareness of the very real social barriers between peasants and teachers; thus, advice for new teachers entering rural communities included: "With the peasant brother one never imposes, one should only suggest." One professor cautioned students against building schools near cemeteries, since "in the Aymara culture people believe very strongly in the soul"—as though he and his students were not themselves products of "the Aymara culture." On the other hand, the term *campesina* was often employed for hurtful ends within the girls' dorm. Teachers also occasionally fell into such usages, as when one, after several minutes of rebuking the class over the disarray of the classroom, exclaimed: "The *campesino* has just one room, with his stove, etc.; he has no idea of what tidiness is, what organization is—but we are *high school graduates.*"

Despite students' and teachers' awareness that they constituted a new social phenomenon (evidenced in comments such as "Before, teachers were not of our race"), the topic of their ambiguous social position remained submerged. In class discussions on discrimination, development, exploitation, and so on, the question of their own identity frequently seemed on the verge of being addressed, but never was. One day in Sociology class, a boy asked about the difference between *indio* and *campesino*; the teacher replied that it was merely a difference in terminology. Another then asked if, when a *campesino* goes to the city, he stops being a *campesino* or goes on being one; the teacher answered resolutely that he goes on being one. The first student took issue with this, but the teacher overruled him, reiterating that the *campesino* might adopt urban customs, but he cannot change his essence no matter how much he imitates the city dwellers. The implications of this for the students themselves—many of them children of peasants, supposedly in the process of becoming professionals—lingered in the realm of the unspoken, and the discussion ended there.

Language: The Golden Past and the Corrupt Present

Students' ambivalence about the *campesino* contrasted with their unequivocal identification of themselves as Aymara. Though generally supported by the school's official discourse, this shared identity was not without its problems. One of the strongest markers of ethnic identity is language; it was largely because students spoke Aymara that they considered themselves natural members of this group. Students' Aymara identity received most of its official recognition in Native Languages class. Still, the school's treatment of the Aymara language, and of students as Aymara speakers, was fraught with contradictions, though these were due less to ambivalence over identity *per se* than to the school's uncertainty as to how to integrate indigenous language and culture into its curriculum.

While the inclusion of a native languages component in the normal school curriculum was an important step toward the official recognition of indigenous culture,[28] the pedagogical goals of the class were never clear. Some considered it a response to students' need for Aymara fluency, since they might be called upon to teach monolingual Aymara children; but most of the normal school students already spoke fluent Aymara. Others felt the aim was to teach students to read and write in Aymara, and something of the language's structure and history. But dedicating most class time to these ends meant that the few students who did *not* in fact speak Aymara were not taught how. The result was a disjointed mix of pedagogical aims and methods that failed to fully satisfy any of these goals.

The Native Languages teacher, Professor Ramírez, took great pride in his Aymara identity and even claimed to be writing a book about the language. He was vexed by students' failure to take his lessons as seriously as he did, and sometimes had trouble maintaining order. At such times, he exorcised his frustrations by presenting students with large amounts of complicated information, rapidly and with little explanation. At other times, students responded eagerly to the chance to speak and joke with a teacher in Aymara, and he was able to use this atmosphere of excitement and good humor to actually teach them something. Professor Ramírez's classes provided some of the most frustrating and most rewarding moments of teaching that I observed at the normal school.

The class consisted mainly of two kinds of activities: lectures on linguistic or sociolinguistic topics, and language drills. Students might be asked to recite proverbs or short narratives in Aymara, or work blackboard exercises in Aymara morphology. While the exercises were useful for teaching morphological processes, students found them difficult because they had not yet been taught to read or write Aymara. The language drills consisted of simple questions of the type one might encounter in any first-year language class, even though most students were fluent Aymara speakers for whom such drills served little purpose. On the other hand, the drills were not regular or comprehensive enough to provide any real grounding in the language for those who were *not* fluent. Their main purpose seemed to be to have students speak a little Aymara in the classroom, however minimal the actual content. When I asked Professor Ramírez about those students who did not speak Aymara, he claimed there were none; but my talks with students indicated otherwise.

The class moved onto more hazardous ground when it turned to technical and theoretical topics in linguistics. Sometimes these were insightfully used to illuminate social phenomena; when a student asked the difference between *lengua* and *idioma*, Professor Ramírez took the opportunity to discuss how the term *dialecto* had been pejoratively applied to indigenous languages. He used a discussion on phonological errors to warn students against mocking Aymara speakers who do not pronounce Spanish correctly, pointing out that people whose Spanish shows interference from high-prestige languages such as English are not laughed at. He compared Aymara structure with Spanish, English, and French, showing students that their language was also complex, though different from these others (and thus of interest to foreigners like myself). At times, students seemed intellectually excited by this new perspective; some who rarely spoke in other classes would expound on the importance of knowing about one's language, the discrimination that Aymara speakers suffer, the difficulties of learning to write a language one has known only in its oral form, and so on. At such moments, students became involved to a degree rarely seen in their other classes, perhaps feeling that here was an area in which they had some expertise.

Just as often, however, Professor Ramírez's explanations were partial or inaccurate, leaving students confused or worse. During a lesson on diglossia, he explained that languages are "functionally" differentiated into "type A" languages (such as English, Spanish, and French), considered superior and prestigious, and "type B" languages (such as Aymara and Quechua), considered inferior. He did not mention social context (Spanish, for example, would be a type B language in the United States), nor did he explain how this distinction was "functional." He said that linguists do not classify languages this way, but by another method, which he did not elaborate. In another class, he defined diglossia as speaking two languages, either "with interference" (when a speaker is ashamed to speak his language and prefers a more prestigious one), or "without interference" (when a speaker alternates between the two without difficulty, "as we do"). Students seldom questioned such information; as far as grades went, copying down the right terms was more important than understanding them, and in any case, the professor tended to get annoyed when inconsistencies in his lectures were pointed out.

While the confusion of linguistic concepts was particularly frustrating for me to witness, from the students' point of view it differed little from all the other classes in which they took extensive notes on material they did not understand. More significant was the attitude toward their own speech. Professor Ramírez was a stickler for speaking Aymara "correctly," that is, as it was spoken before the Spanish Conquest. He was fond of statements such as "Before the Spanish arrived, people spoke Aymara well" and "The Aymara language is becoming completely distorted," and he frequently lamented that Aymara was losing its structure and "essence" in the mouths of speakers who corrupted it with Spanish borrowings.[29] A common technique of his was to ask students how to say something in Aymara (something that seemed deceptively easy to them as native speakers), reject their responses as examples of Spanish influence, and then give them the "correct" form. Not only were these often unfamiliar to students, most of whom had spoken Aymara all their lives, but some of the forms he rejected were extremely common even among monolingual speakers.[30] Though students were often frustrated and perplexed by the rejection of what seemed to them obviously correct Aymara, they seldom challenged the professor. But when he told them that the word for "potato" was not the familiar *ch'uqi*, but rather *amka*, some found this impossible to swallow and insisted that in this region it was *ch'uqi*. Generally, however, this technique made students reluctant to speak, feeling (with some justification) that the drills were designed to trip them up.

Many students had heard all their lives that they spoke Spanish badly, and their teachers regularly reminded them of this; one even told them that if they did not improve their speech, the parents of their future students would demand their removal: "If we don't speak well, every year we'll be going from one school to another, because no one's going to accept a teacher who talks that way." Many students had a marked Aymara accent and tended to confuse the Spanish phonemes d/t, k/g, e/i, and o/u (which are not significant contrasts in Aymara). But instead of receiving ear training or language drills to overcome this, they were simply reminded on an ongoing basis that their Spanish was deficient. The language teacher once told the class that they would do "a little test, to see which of you have problems and how these can be corrected" (no doubt sending a shiver of apprehension down the spines of many). The test was not carried out during the length of my stay, however.[31]

After a lifetime of being told that they spoke Spanish badly, students entered Native Languages class, introduced for the purpose of valorizing and legitimizing their native language, only to be told that they spoke Aymara badly as well. The Aymara language was praised enthusiastically in class, but students as speakers were not. In other classes as well, they were likely to hear that "We don't speak our own language well, nor do we know how to speak Spanish correctly." Code-switching was considered a result of linguistic deficiency, rather than creativity. Bilinguals were perceived, not as versatile and linguistically skilled, but rather as lacking full competence in either language.[32] As evidenced by students' verbal proficiency in a variety of contexts, this perception was due more to the fact that they spoke nonstandard varieties of both languages, than to actual lack of communicative competence.

Although Professor Ramírez extolled the beauty of Aymara, emphasizing that it was in no way inferior to other languages, it always seemed to appear as the "deficit case" in his examples. He spoke of Spanish phonemic distinctions that are absent in Aymara, but never of the Aymara ones that Spanish lacks; it was always the hypothetical Aymara child who did not understand because of his lack of Spanish, never the converse. Aymara was presented as a noble and highly developed language whose contemporary speakers were incapable of doing it justice; rather, they were characterized by "an anemic cognitive capacity, due to the limited linguistic conduct of the inferior social strata, where mothers pass their inadequate speech habits on to their children, leaving them unprepared for the middle-class linguistic environment of the school."[33] In such a context, the linguistic "shame" felt by some students is hardly surprising:

Sergio: The girls are ashamed to say that they know Aymara. In class they deny that they can speak it well, or they abstain [from speaking]. But when they leave, in the dorm, or in the street, they'll be talking with their friend, all in Aymara. It's a huge defect, one that hurts the person himself, hurts our own class. We're denying our own culture. If I know something, I have to say so . . . But, I think it's also a product of how, since grade school they've taught us that way . . . molding one's character to despise what is one's own.

Central to the ideological environment of Native Languages class was a theme that I mentally entitled "The Bilingual as Neurotic," after the image repeatedly evoked in Professor Ramírez's lectures on bilingualism's social and psychological consequences. While his attempts to address language loyalty and related issues in class might be applauded, his handling of what Wilfredo Kapsoli calls "the *mestizos'* drama of defining their linguistic identity" (in Arguedas 1986:12) often left the impression that bilingualism was an inherently pathological condition. In one class, Professor Ramírez cited various authors on how speakers' negative feelings toward their language lead them to reject their own identity and believe themselves inferior—quotations that seemed disturbingly apropos to his own comments on his students' defective language habits. Encouraging students to reflect on the dilemma of conflicting language loyalties, Professor Ramírez asked them, "When we speak two languages, how do we feel? On the side of Spanish, or on the side of Aymara?" One girl whispered, "Aymara," but most of the boys answered, "Spanish," one adding, "because we do our schoolwork in Spanish" (a better answer might have been that it depends on the situation). The professor explained that "this psychological complex affects the bilingual, while nothing happens to the monolingual . . . Bilingualism is a kind of solution, a compromise, an alternating between situations, when there are conflicting loyalties in the individual." These "conflicting loyalties" could lead to "linguistic self-hatred," whereby:

> the individual rejects and detests his own language. There is a restructuring of the personality in accordance with the patterns of the new group into which he wishes to integrate himself. He will abandon the values and ideas of his original culture . . . That is why we, being Aymara, no longer want to be Aymara, we want to be Spanish . . . Similarly, the Spaniards want to be English . . . An Aymara comes to exploit his fellow Aymaras, to hate his own language. (Excerpt from a class lecture)

In contrast, monolinguals were portrayed as untroubled and serene, free from the "psychological ruptures, tensions, and readjustments" suffered by bilinguals upon denying their group of origin. And in the event of a race war—Professor Ramírez asked the class—where will the bilingual stand? With his own people, or with the oppressors? "He must define himself . . . For this reason the bilingual exists in two worlds. He is unstable; he is in conflict."

Few would deny that bilinguals in a country like Bolivia do in fact confront social and psychological conflicts of the type described above. Still, one must question the effects of such a one-sided portrayal. Aside from occasional references to the rural teacher's function as translator for the indigenous community, bilinguals were never portrayed as skilled, adaptive, versatile individuals whose broad range of linguistic resources provides access to a wide variety of social contexts. Bilingualism was never described as advantageous—either economically, socially, or intellectually—though myriad examples from Bolivian society would be easy to enumerate. Instead, bilinguals were portrayed as conflicted, unstable, and potentially treacherous, though comment was never made on the relevance of such judgements to students' own condition.

After one day's lengthy exposition on the bilingual malady, Professor Ramírez turned his attention to a girl in the second row and addressed her in Aymara, asking her opinion of this sad state of affairs. In response, he received only the customary bashful silence. After a few seconds, the tension was broken by the laughter of the boy sitting next to her. "Self-hatred," he joked.

Gender Ideology in the Normal School: Frozen Images and Structured Silences

The previous chapter examined how male and female students relate to their peers outside the classroom; we now turn to the gender images they encountered within the classroom. The masculine constituted the "unmarked" form in school discourse; any hypothetical subject whose gender was not at issue was automatically assumed to be male.[34] Thus, the majority of "gendered" statements referred to females. Such statements reinforced particular ideas about feminine (and, by implication, masculine) character and behavior. As will become clear, however, the gender ideology of educational settings has as much to do with what is not said, as with what is said.

While academic opportunities for Bolivian girls have expanded in recent decades, increased participation in education does not always lead to increased participation in other areas of social life (cf. Stromquist 1992a), nor does it preclude the persistence of sexist ideology in educational institutions themselves. As Rosenberg (1992:34) observed for Brazil, "Sexual discrimination in education has shifted . . . rather than hindering women's access to the educational system, it now affects those within the system."[35] While female students in Bolivia have yet to reach numerical parity with their male peers, especially in rural areas, institutionalized sexism currently finds expression less in girls' physical exclusion from school than in their symbolic exclusion from the curriculum and school life. Girls often end up as spectators in an educational enterprise that is largely male-oriented; though able to study and obtain a degree, they are seldom full participants in the exchange networks of linguistic and cultural capital under which "learning" is organized. When their concerns are addressed, it is often in a derogatory or trivializing manner. In light of this shift from physical to symbolic exclusion, one must question the effects of female students' engagement with the school upon the formation of their own identities and ideologies.

In order to analyze the newer, more subtle forms that sexism takes within schools that are nominally egalitarian, Bonder (1992:236) suggests that we shift our emphasis from quantitative approaches focusing on how much education women get, to qualitative analyses of what, how, and for what purposes women are taught. Academic sexism's greatest significance may no longer be in effects that can be measured numerically, but rather in the construction of gender identities and hierarchies, the internalization of social norms, and the expectations placed upon male and female students.[36] Such effects are subtle but powerful, and may be all the more insidious when they occur under a cloak of superficial equality. Unlike many quantitative indices of sexism, symbolic discrimination must be sought at the level of specific classroom practices. Both quantitative and qualitative inequalities feed into macro-level processes of social reproduction, but they are also "the end products of a long chain of subtle and relatively small processes that occur through the daily interaction among teachers, administrators, students, and parents" (Stromquist 1992b:4).

Many of these processes are influenced by the fact that, in rural Bolivia, the shift from physical to symbolic exclusion is fairly recent and still incomplete. While nearly half of students are female, this is not true of teachers, administrators, and educational authorities. Female teachers are the minority in all but the earliest grades, and their presence decreases as one moves up the educational hierarchy. Students' strongest link with the school apparatus, aside from fellow students, is the teacher; teachers thus play a key role in the transmission of gender ideology, shaping students' notions of femininity and masculinity via their daily interactions with them. The most obvious feature of such interactions in the normal school was that almost all teachers were male; the only women on the staff were the secretary, the librarian, the *inspectora*, and the *Hogar* (home economics/family life) teacher.[37] This dearth of female role models meant that by the time they reached the normal school, girls were unlikely to find many teachers who could address their specific concerns or serve as models for their own professional behavior and identity.

This was also a likely factor in the normal school's failure to address women's position as teachers and in Bolivian society generally. As Stromquist (1992c:153) notes in her analysis of gender politics in the Peruvian university, lack of female faculty can have a "dampening effect" on the identification and academic exploration of women's issues; and when faculty refrain from addressing such questions, students are not likely to raise them either. It was hard to imagine the reaction a normal school student might receive if she tried to raise such issues in class or openly challenge the institution's patriarchal ideology. Students were generally wary of being labeled "troublemakers," fearing reprisals by teachers or the administration; as a result, the ideological terrain of gender was thoroughly dominated by the official messages emanating from the faculty. When students did challenge professors' statements, it was only on "safe" subjects (such as the extension of a woman's social status to other family members), not on topics directly involving the school (such as sexist behavior by professors). Even in these cases, discussion usually was dominated by males. There was little in the way of popular challenges to the gender images of the curriculum, both overt and hidden.

Earlier studies (Miracle 1973, 1976; Luykx 1989b) have revealed gender bias in Bolivian educational materials for the primary grades. Textbooks and class lectures tend to portray males as leaders and problem solvers, while females are portrayed in passive or dependent roles. Almost exclusively, women are shown in a narrow range of domestic activities, belying the reality of many Aymara women who are farmers, merchants, entrepreneurs, teachers, etc. This restricted view of acceptable female roles persists at the normal school level as well. Most of teachers' explicit statements about women referred to the family, reinforcing the image of women as nurturing, self-sacrificing, needful of male protection, and subject to male authority. Such statements seldom turned up in the context of talk about gender issues, but rather "in passing" during discussion of other topics. For example, one teacher, in order to illustrate the verb *administrar* ("administrate"), gave the example of a husband deciding how to distribute his salary to cover his family's necessities—although in Aymara households it is more often the wife who controls the family budget. In another class, a discussion on "the disintegration of the family" was cast entirely in terms of the disastrous psychological consequences of divorce on children. There was no mention of the possibility that divorce might be the best solution for a failing marriage, nor of the related problems of male alcoholism and domestic violence, both notoriously widespread in Bolivia.

Those rare occasions when women's status was directly addressed were telling in their own way. During a lecture on social status, Professor Torres explained that a man's social status extends to his wife and children as well. Paco argued that any family member who achieves high status, even a woman, can elevate the status of the entire family. The professor agreed and then sought input from a female student, but received only silence. He moved on to another girl, but got the same response. A boy volunteered, but Professor Torres put him off, continuing to solicit the second girl's participation; after some coaxing, she answered well, if briefly. José offered the example of a female ambassador's status extending to her entire family; Paco countered that in such a case, her status could extend beyond her family to all women in Bolivia, for instance if a woman became president.[38] The discussion continued between Paco, José, and the professor, while the girls doodled distractedly in their notebooks or looked on in silence.

Gender ideology also was revealed in teachers' offhand comments. In Native Languages class, Professor Ramírez once exclaimed (during a digression about government corruption): "A peasant, simply for having hit his wife, gets thrown in jail . . . while all the corrupt politicians are free . . . the jails are full of innocent people." Despite the psychological and medical (sometimes fatal) consequences of domestic violence, it was never treated as a subject worthy of discussion, not even in National Reality or Sociology class, where social problems were often discussed (I never heard it mentioned in Hogar class either, but I did not observe all lessons in that subject). When mentioned at all, it was only to trivialize it in comparison to truly "serious" issues.[39] Other comments can be read as examples of backlash against women's entry into a formerly male sphere. The curriculum teacher once described to the class those remote, sparsely populated areas where the teacher must adapt to a solitary lifestyle, with only the radio and perhaps a guitar for company. Recalling a former teaching post, in which the school and his own quarters were located next to a graveyard, he remarked, "Even worse if [teachers] are young ladies, they could die of pure fright."

Student opinions on such matters tended to be more progressive than those of professors:

José: It persists in the countryside, that idea that "she's just a woman" . . . Women didn't matter. Now it seems to me the world is changing, I've noticed that it's changing. But in those places it continues. "She's just a girl, why should she study? Only boys have to study," they say. But no, I don't believe that, for me it's like, everyone has the same rights. To education, to better oneself, to excel. That shouldn't hold a woman back.

Nicolás: I think that shouldn't exist, at any moment, difference between the sexes, between men and women. I believe we both have the same aspirations, the girls as much as the guys, you know? We're all equal. We have the same capacity, everything.

Whether the verbal expression of such a perspective corresponds to actual practice is another question, but the fact that it has gained currency as an accepted (perhaps even preferred) viewpoint among students is itself significant.[40] Nevertheless, students seldom expressed such views in class when faced with teachers' expressions of a more reactionary ideology. While derogatory statements about *campesinos* often provoked indignant reactions from students, similar remarks about women were tolerated without comment.

In the one class expressly charged with instruction in the domestic realm, Hogar, a somewhat more progressive view prevailed. Most visibly, the segregated curriculum of the past has disappeared; both boys and girls now learn domestic skills such as cooking and knitting (though in "real life" these tasks are still performed almost exclusively by females). The professor (the only female classroom teacher in the school) tried to provide students with an image of marriage as a partnership whose success or failure depended on the contributions of both husband and wife. She corrected students who discussed child care only in terms of the mother, reminding them that both parents were equally crucial to the child's well-being. She stressed the importance of choosing a mate on the basis of inner qualities and compatibility, rather than physical beauty. Hogar was one of the few official contexts where students could discuss subjects such as love, sex, and family relationships. Their pleasure at exploring such important "taboo" subjects in a school setting was evident from their participation and from the nervous giggles that accompanied the incongruously formal group presentations on topics such as romance and marriage.

Not that Hogar was an ideology-free oasis in an otherwise hegemonic curriculum. One of its central aims was the transmission and legitimization of a narrowly defined ideal of marriage. Students were taught that engagements should be neither too long nor too short; women should be at least twenty before marrying, and men twenty-five; a large discrepancy in age between partners was undesirable; a successful marriage should produce at least one child, preferably more; divorce was to be avoided at all costs. Topics such as homosexuality, abortion, and nontraditional roles within marriage were beyond the pale of acceptable classroom discussion. The point is not whether the ideal presented was inherently good or bad; simply that Hogar, like other subjects, was largely about the exclusive sanctioning of a narrowly selected range of human practice.

Outside the classroom, the version of femininity ratified in institutional practice was even narrower. The control exercised over students' movements and behavior was more stringent for females than for males, reflecting a more limited range of what was deemed acceptable feminine behavior. This was evident in the reproach students received from the rector one morning after drinking during a town celebration. The rector singled out female students especially, exclaiming: "How shameful that a young lady should be fond of alcohol! I can understand with the boys; sometimes they need to share, to unburden themselves, but the girls . . . What man is going to want to marry a girl who likes to drink?"[41] His scandalized reaction was no doubt partly due to concern for the reputation of the institution, to which female license constituted the far greater threat.

Female students usually took a back seat in the ceremonial life of the school, but there were two events constructed specifically around celebrations of femininity: Mothers' Day, when those students who were mothers were feted along with mothers of students who lived nearby, and Students' Day, coinciding with the first day of spring and the Bolivian equivalent of Valentine's Day. The high point of Students' Day was the coronation of the elected student "queen," attended by "princesses" representing Spring, Scholarship, Athletics, Happiness, Beauty, and other feminine and scholarly virtues. The coronation was preceded by hours of preparation in the girls' dorm as the princesses readied their hair, makeup, and dresses—elaborate confections of white taffeta, lace, and sparkles, in dazzling contrast to the enforced drabness of their usual school attire. The queen was made ready in a separate sanctum, aided by the *inspectora* and a few privileged attendants. Finally, their beautification complete, the princesses were promenaded by their highly polished male escorts through a corridor of their classmates. This interminably long procession (arranged to build up maximum suspense for the entrance of the queen) was provided with comic relief by two clowns (played by male students) who burlesqued and bothered the princesses as they approached in all their finery, the clown's buffoonery contrasting with the glamour and solemnity of the royal entrance. Through it all, the girls did not smile or even let on that they were aware of being mocked, but continued their slow, stiff approach, eyes straight ahead, in an attitude reminiscent of a "proper" lady's response to appreciative or vulgar remarks by unknown males on the street. Except for the clowns, the escorts, and the apparent prohibition on smiling, the event seemed choreographed along the lines of a beauty pageant; all attention was focused on the girls, whose role consisted of little more than walking up to the "throne" and then sitting or standing on display. After the queen was crowned, she danced the requisite waltz with the rector, and then the dance floor was opened up to all present for the remainder of the evening.

The official messages transmitted to students both in and out of the classroom reveal a definite gender ideology at work. Those events focusing specifically on females offered the same narrow range of subject positions that have become so tiringly familiar to feminists: wife/mother and beauty queen. On the other hand, the idealized teacher with whom students were trained to identify was invariably male. As Bourdieu (1984: 102–3) has observed: "The common image of the professions . . . takes into account not only the nature of the job and the income, but those secondary characteristics which are often the bases of their social value (prestige or discredit) and which, though absent from the official job description, function as tacit requirements, such as age, sex, social or ethnic origin . . . so that members of the corps who lack these traits are excluded or marginalized."

Symbolic representations of the Teacher were nearly always male, from the noble figure lauded in school hymns to the statue in La Paz's *Plaza del Maestro*. Casual remarks by teachers—such as the one who speculated that women were too timid to teach in remote areas—reminded female students of their inherent unsuitability for the role. These practices suggested a mutually exclusive relationship between the essentialized notion of "the feminine" and that of "the teacher." Those characteristics and behaviors presented as archetypically feminine (dedication to home and family, modesty, timidity, and passive beauty) were incompatible with those of the archetypal teacher (dedication to career, assertiveness, eloquence, and masculine cameraderie). The conflict is similar to that noted by Bruno Bettelheim, in reference to the problems youth face in finding professional fulfillment under changing social and economic conditions: "In this respect the fate of the girl can be even harder than the boy's. It is impressed on her from an early age that her main fulfillment will come with marriage and children, but her education has nevertheless been the same as that of boys, who are expected to realize themselves mainly through work and achievement in society" (Bettelheim 1968:18). General sympathy with this statement should not blind us to the fact that girls' education is *not* the same as that of boys, even when both share the same classroom. Though exposed to the same curriculum, male and female students are differently positioned with regard to that curriculum, and thus experience it in different ways. Female students are likely to have difficulty reconciling the school's gendered atmosphere to their professional aspirations, whereas boys do not.

The above examples address explicit gender messages both in curricular and in extracurricular school contexts. However, the very obviousness of such examples may obscure an equally crucial area of gender ideology in schools: the structured silence around most gender issues. The incidents described above are not particularly subtle; their very explicitness highlights the ideology from which they arise, making it at least potentially vulnerable to critique. But most issues concerning gender discrimination remained submerged and suppressed; proscribed from legitimate school discourse, they were seldom if ever subject to challenge or debate. In this way, the assumption of a superficially egalitarian stance by school authorities can serve to preclude actual critique of the issues involved. "In education the most effective method of transmission of gender relations is not through explicit reference to the prescribed conditions for men and women but through the avoidance of these issues, while in practice—through everyday discourse and ordinary events—building gender asymmetries. In other words, by making the curriculum officially gender-neutral while genderizing the social practices of the school" (Stromquist 1992b:4).

The most effective ideological messages are found, not in what is asserted, but in what is assumed. Incidents and statements such as those described above may be less important than the silence around women's issues that suffuses the school curriculum. To uncover the real substance of institutional gender socialization, we must analyze not only the most blatant examples of sexism, but also the unspoken, pervasive "genderizing" of school practices.

Such "genderizing" is often manifest in the organization of institutional tasks and is especially notable in ceremonial/ritual contexts. In the normal school, an implicit sexual division of labor assigned females those tasks carrying less prestige and requiring less skill, while more prestigious tasks were reserved for males.[42] With regard to staff, the overwhelmingly male composition of the faculty made this rather a foregone conclusion. With regard to students, however, the pattern took on greater significance, especially in light of the supposed gender neutrality of the curriculum.

This division of labor was evident in the weekly *hora cívica* programs. While male and female students participated in roughly equal numbers in the dances, virtually all major speaking roles were filled by boys. If a girl spoke at all, it was usually to recite a brief proverb or (less frequently) a poem. Longer speeches were presented by male students; I never saw a female student or staff member speak during the *tribuna libre*. In other school rituals as well, there was a near-exclusive predominance of male students in roles involving any kind of authority or public speaking, while female students were assigned those tasks whose chief requirement was manual labor.[43] A boy led students in singing the national anthem, while a girl raised the flag; in the cafeteria, a boy read the names of latecomers and dismissed students after eating, while girls cleaned the tables; of the two "class leaders" chosen each month to lead the morning assemblies, the girl rang the bell calling students to formation, and the boy then led them through the sequence of military-style commands. Only twice did I see female students take charge of this last task, and one of these times, the assembly was so disorderly that after the girl had finished, a boy came up to lead students through their paces once again (with much better results). There was also evidence that student teachers passed on this pattern to their own students; observations of students' practice teaching revealed such habits as handing out rhythm instruments only to boys when teaching children to dance.

The sexual division of labor is evident in many areas of school life, but is most significant in the realm of language, since so much of what students do and learn in school involves the manipulation of specialized linguistic registers. Much of the "cultural capital" produced, legitimated, and distributed in educational institutions consists of mastering the discursive styles (spoken and written) characteristic of such institutions. Evidence indicates that competence in these registers is unevenly distributed by sex, and that normal school training fails to remedy this discrepancy. As we will see in the following chapters, the sexual division of labor governed students' verbal activity not only in school ceremonies, but also in the classroom and in the expressive practices generated by students themselves. These areas together comprise the "linguistic economy" of the school, in which discourses, ideologies, and (ultimately) subject positions are produced.

Conclusion: Rural Education and the Race/Class Intersection

The stresses and schisms running throughout Bolivian society are reflected within the micro-community of the normal school—in the curriculum, in face-to-face interactions in and out of the classroom, and in personal declarations of ideology. In this moment in Bolivian history, social definitions are being reformulated and new subject positions created, especially those constellating around collective constructions of indigenous identity. This process of redefinition is accompanied by conflict, as groups and individuals struggle to negotiate shifting social boundaries and promote their own views of the cultural and political terrain such boundaries inscribe. The unfolding changes in the country's class/race structure give rise to new kinds of social subjects; in the process, individuals take on new identities and attempt to reshape them from the inside, while they simultaneously try to struggle free of the ideological straightjacket of outdated stereotypes.

Teachers and students live out these contradictions in their daily practice, though at what level of consciousness it is hard to say. The ambivalence manifested in teachers' oscillations between praise and denigration of the *campesino* and students' difficulties in defining their own identities reveal a certain ideological discomfort. This is partly due to the necessity of cannibalizing old discourses in order to construct new subjectivities; as Caryl Emerson describes it, "One makes a self through the words one has learned, fashions one's own voice and inner speech by a selective appropriation of the voices of others."[44] Those other words and voices may speak past realities better than present ones, making them less than ideal as materials for the construction of identity.

Still, "ideological discomfort" is visible only in its social-interactional manifestations; what forms it takes within the "inner speech" of individuals is much more difficult to discern. How much do Aymara students really worry about whether seeking higher education means "denying, abandoning, concealing their origins, their roots, betraying ther own"? (Oliart 1991:212). To what degree can a Professor Ramírez distance himself from the psychological disorder he ascribes to the anonymous, generalized bilingual? Do rural schoolteachers privately question the heroic image that casts them as the saviours of *el hermano campesino*? Or their own capacity to fulfill such a role?

Although these questions cannot be definitively answered here, it is clear that the normal school constitutes a fulcrum for ideologies of ethnicity, nationality, class, and gender. Where various ideologies are lived out in the same social space, they cannot remain separate; they form an interlocking system, and change in one inevitably affects the others. Students engaged a patchwork of conflicting interests, positions, and identities on a daily basis; on the one hand, each had to construct and defend his or her own sense of self amid the antagonistic jostlings of class ambitions, ethnic loyalties, and gender images that formed the social environment of the school. On the other, they responded to the social categories presented to them, alternately incorporating them, challenging them, or withdrawing from the academic encounter. Beyond this, students had to contend with the ambiguity of their role as prospective rural schoolteachers. That role is an ambivalent one no matter who fills it, but when teachers are of the same ethnic group as the inhabitants of the communities they serve—and yet so markedly different from them in other ways—the ambiguity is doubled. Part of students' socialization involved coming to grips with the fact that the achievement of professional status distanced them from their ethnic origins.[45] Differing reactions to this fact accounted in part for the friction over "discrimination" in the girls' dorm.

Furthermore, students' transformation from captive subjects of the educational system into its active agents means incorporating themselves into a system that traditionally has threatened the integrity and value of indigenous culture. As future teachers, they will be called upon to disseminate a world view that is opposed to the one with which they are encouraged to identify as Aymaras. The position presented to them as the sole moral and legitimate choice is that of maintaining these two ideological loyalties simultaneously, despite the cultural and historical incompatibilities between them. It may not be an exaggeration to suggest that this constitutes a collective cultural-psychological crisis that indigenous teachers (and all upwardly-mobile indigenous people) must pass through on their journey toward personal and professional identity.

One solution to this dilemma is to embrace the teacher's role as a position of power from which to advocate a conscious solidarity with indigenous culture. As precarious as this stance may be at times, it is a necessary one if indigenous people's move into "the professions" is to be a force for their collective political empowerment. Breaching the ethnic divisions in the class structure is a hollow victory if subjects must cease to identify with indigenous culture as soon as they earn their diploma. Many indigenous intellectuals are attempting to construct new subjectivities whereby the appropriation of literacy, western science, and the other benefits of "development" need not imply a rejection of indigenous culture. While some critics may interpret the incorporation of indigenous teachers into the middle class as a palliative, serving only to blunt the sharpness of ethnic and class struggle, it may also provide a site for consciousness-raising and empowerment among a broader (and still impressionable) young audience.

Issues of class, gender, and ethnicity are central to the formation of students' personal and professional identities, emerging in virtually every aspect of normal school life. The question that must now be asked is why classroom discourse works to discourage students from grappling with such issues directly. Official documents repeatedly stress schools' obligation to help students become politically conscious critics of their social milieu—"agents of change" in a nation trying to free itself from the vestiges of colonialism and the encroachments of imperialism. A crucial part of this process is helping students situate themselves as social actors. Yet the pedagogical instruments for addressing these issues seem to block rather than foster debate. Why should this be?

I shall argue that the answer lies in the ways that students' linguistic expression is commodified in school contexts—that, despite the superficially revolutionary stance of the institution, the production of ideology within its walls is governed by a political economy of discourse whose logic is essentially conservative. Though focusing on micro-level structures of classroom interaction, this view is by no means intended to deny or disregard the existence of a hegemonic nationalist project whose ultimate aim is the homogenization of potentially subversive diversity. On the contrary, this analysis is undertaken precisely in order to expose the concrete, everyday practices by which hegemony is reproduced. Schools have long been recognized as crucial sites of cultural and ideological production; the task now is to examine the means, mode, and relations of that production, which takes place largely in the realm of discourse.

5

COMMODIFIED LANGUAGE AND ALIENATED EXCHANGE IN THE NORMAL SCHOOL

Half the professors... would arrive at class twenty minutes late; they'd spend ten minutes taking attendance, and the rest of the time yawning or lecturing on some ancient subject that we students had to copy throughout the entire year. The other half would go over all the questions indicated in the Official Plan, they stuck to the plan with military precision... In the five years of Secondary Instruction that I had, we never read a book in class... Year after year, the professors labored in order that the students might learn, at least until the final exams, the myriad questions contained in the Official Plan, neglecting one of the fundamental obligations of teaching: to awaken in one's students the enthusiasm to investigate on one's own.

—Peruvian novelist and educator José María Arguedas, recalling his own school days

Pedagogical Praxis and "School Knowledge"

Classroom Interactional Structures

Chapter 4 examined the subject positions presented to students via the *content* of school discourse; this chapter examines those arising from the ways school discourse is *structured*. Subject positions generated from content cluster around axes of *identity* (ethnicity, nationality, occupation, class, and gender); those deriving from classroom interactional structures pertain more to *activity*, interpellating students as particular

171

types of learners, workers, and language-users. By legitimating certain forms of knowledge and naturalizing certain social practices, the school constructs a selective notion of what it means to be a "student" and what kinds of activity constitute "learning."

We can draw a practical distinction between classroom content (or "curriculum") on the one hand and interactional structures ("methodology") on the other, but in reality these are so closely linked that studying either one in isolation from the other results in a partial or distorted interpretation. McNeil (1986) shows how the forms and methods of conveying school knowledge shape the knowledge itself and students' responses to it. While she ascribes students' lack of intellectual engagement to the fact that their classroom participation is subordinated to the demands of institutional efficiency and control, I aim to show that the causes of students' alienation run deeper than the school's institutional dynamics, engaging wider processes of social reproduction.

Murray (1983:19) claims that a chief function of schooling is students' political socialization, noting that the array of power relations within the school's microsociety may be more important in this regard than academic content *per se*. Official conceptions of "education," and the power relations underpinning them, construct a particular view of the world and of students' place in it. This view of both learning and social relations is virtually inextricable from the academic knowledge and skills whose transmission is more readily recognized (Williams 1977:117–18). It constitutes an implicit ideology which, embodied in certain pedagogical practices, comprises what we might call "meta-teaching": that which is taught and learned about teaching and learning.

Despite Bolivian teachers' sharp criticisms of government, that critical spirit is seldom applied to the school itself or to the ideologies produced there. While teachers' collective political stance is increasingly oppositional, the vast majority of classrooms are ruled by a rigid methodological conservatism. Teaching is rarely dialogic; much of students' time is spent copying lessons or reciting memorized texts, despite evidence that such methods are less effective for intellectual development than a balance of speaking and turn-taking between teacher and students (Cazden 1988).[1] Student "participation" usually takes the form of one-word unison responses to the teacher's questions. Earlier studies (Buechler and Buechler 1971; Carter 1971;

USAID 1975) indicate that these rote methods were used generally throughout Bolivian schools, and my own more recent observations (Luykx 1989b) did not reveal much change in this regard.[2] If schools train students in particular "ways of knowing," setting their expectations of themselves as "people who can learn, ask questions, contribute new answers, or who must be dependent on others to tell them what they need to know" (McNeil 1986:207), one can only surmise that Bolivian schools are designed to produce passive student-subjects rather than critical and active learners.

While the range of pedagogical techniques and the opportunities for participation are broader at the normal school level, the emphasis on copying and memorization persists. The most common structure for classroom speech events was for the teacher to dictate a lesson that students copied verbatim and later reproduced in fragmented form on the exam.[3] On exams, deviation from exact wording was discouraged; thus, students' questions more often concerned the exact manner in which information was to be copied, rather than its meaning. Students had few opportunities to express their own ideas in writing. For presentations involving the "analysis" of some topic, their usual procedure was to copy the information out of a book and then recite it in front of the class. They were sometimes encouraged to put things "in their own words," but most had considerable difficulty doing so. This was partly due to their lack of reading comprehension and to the school's emphasis on the "correctness" of written sources. Years of schooling in which "speaking in one's own words" was discouraged no doubt also took their toll on students' analytic and expressive abilities. Another factor was the deliberate withholding of verbal participation. In an attempt to break down students' resistance to speaking in class, some teachers required group presentations on assigned topics; below is an account of one such class. Of note are both students' lack of engagement and the way in which the discourse styles of the classroom enabled them to fulfill the teacher's demands for "participation" regardless of their comprehension (or lack thereof) of the material.

National Reality Class, August 26, 1991. Ten minutes are lost to confusion and stalling as the first group gets ready to present. They finally come forward, and the first boy reads the objectives for the unit on natural resources. A student interrupts him to ask: "First the *objetivos* or the *contenidos*, professor?"[4] The first boy's entire presentation consists of reading the objectives that the teacher dictated to them last week. The next boy discusses the exploitation of Bolivia's resources by foreign interests; his presentation is confused, repetitive, and brief. The next girl reads hers, with some difficulty. It is only a few sentences long, but does sound like she wrote it herself—unlike that of the next boy. The class pays scant attention; there is considerable murmuring that the teacher does not attempt to control. All the presentations are very general and very short, the entire group taking only ten minutes.

The professor gives the class a chance to comment, but no one does; he complains about the lack of questions (but not about the presentations themselves). He then expounds briefly on the topic himself, defining "renewable resources" as those that can be substituted by others—such as coca, which the government hopes to replace with less controversial crops. "Nonrenewable resources" he defines as minerals. When he calls up the next group, a few students ask, "Is that all, professor?" (for the exam). He answers sardonically, "It's better for you all, isn't it, if it's short?"

For the next group, Laura writes on the board: FACTORES QUE INFLEYEN EN LA EXTINCION DE LA FLORA Y FAUNA. Several students mistakenly correct *extinción* to *extensión* before anyone notices the actual misspelling (*infleyen*); the girls next to me write down "FACTORES QUE INCLUYEN . . . "[5] Laura fluidly reads the *objetivos*, mentions the colonization of the Yungas area, and ends abruptly. She is followed by Eva, who speaks well if briefly, also mentioning the 1906 relocation of colonists "who just exploit the land without any methodology or knowledge." No one mentions any modern causes of extinction (though just last week the air in La Paz was heavy with smoke from the burning of forests in the Yungas). A boy then tackles "Fauna"; he speaks clearly but reads straight from a monograph, not even from his own notes. He gives a biological classification of animal families, but does not relate it to Bolivia or to the question of extinction. After a couple of sentences about organisms' adaptation to particular climates, he steps down. The next boy reads from a monograph about the local flora and major crops and their economic importance. After a long pause, he says, "That's all" and sits down.

The teacher asks for questions, but gets none. He asks the class what notes they have taken and makes a few recite the semicoherent fragments they have written, prompting derisive laughter from the others. He asks for factors influencing extinction; one student mentions climate. He asks another to elaborate, but her response is inaudibe due to scuffling in the classroom. Another mentions colonization; the teacher cites the burning of forests, prompting a brief discussion about pollution. He claims that burning is a bad way to clear land because it kills the organisms in the soil, making it unproductive; "We in the *campo* are wrong to do this." He then changes tack and says that *campesinos* know burning kills the soil, while the big companies with all their scientists do not.

Moving on to "Fauna," he asks what is implied by the recent exportation of llamas to the United States. One girl answers cogently, until she is interrupted by a boy. There is some general carping about the United States, followed by a comment from Sergio that perhaps the *gringos* have discovered some new benefit from llamas, that Bolivians don't know about.

The teacher keeps the class after 5:00, so the last group can present; they stall, hoping to be put off until next time, but finally get up when he threatens to give them no credit. Their topic is "Advantages and Disadvantages of the *Latifundio, Minifundio,* and *Parvifundio*" (they are unsure of how to spell the last term). The first boy defines *latifundio* and gives the number of people living under this system, but says nothing about its advantages or disadvantages. The next reads confusedly out of a book for about a minute, defining *minifundio*. The first boy explains that this refers to the *campesino* class. He then presents again, defining *parvifundio*. The other girl and boy in the group don't speak at all. The teacher reads the objectives out loud and asks, "What have you all done? You've barely explained what *latifundio, minifundio,* and *parvifundio* are." The group says they didn't have enough time. He asks the class about the results of the Agrarian Reform; Faustino answers briefly and fluidly, though with little actual content. The teacher tells the group they did poorly, then talks about Aymara forms of land tenure. He briefly goes over how the *latifundio* arrived with the Conquest, while the Agrarian Reform gave land to the *campesinos*; he does not mention the disruption of indigenous land use patterns caused by both of these policies.

A student asks the difference between *latifundio* and *minifundio*, though the terms have already been defined at least twice. Faustino asks if all *minifundios* are the same size (no).[6] The teacher asks, "If our farming techniques are already insufficient, what will happen to Bolivian agriculture twenty years from now, when we have children? That's why our parents send us here, to give us a profession, since the land is running out." There is no more discussion; he lets the class go at 5:30.

This class is typical of what happens when teachers (1) feel pressured to cover large amounts of detailed material despite insufficient time and resources, and (2) routinely control students' output by imposing strict discursive parameters. "Such a context governs teachers' and students' behavior so rigorously that efforts to set up a dialogue immediately turn into fiction or farce. The lecturer can call for participation or objection without fear of it really happening: questions to the audience are often purely rhetorical; the answers, serving chiefly to express the part the faithful take in the service, are generally no more than *responses*." (Bourdieu and Passeron 1977:109; original emphasis)

Witte, referring not to the school but to the workplace, provides a parallel that reveals the similarities between the two institutions and their attempts to provide a democratic veneer to a set of relations that are ultimately determined by the distribution of capital (economic or cultural). Witte claims that an overriding concern for efficiency leads to simplified jobs devoid of decision-making and output measures geared to the individual rather than the group; we can easily see how the same tendency operates in schools, and apply to schooling Witte's (1980:9) question: "In this situation, can participation be anything more than a ritual, without real substance or effect?"

The Complicity of Misunderstanding and the Production of School Knowledge

Characteristic of classes in the normal school was what Bourdieu and Passeron (1977) call "a complicity of misunderstanding" between students and teachers. If students could produce a reasonably coherent string of discourse containing key terms from the lesson, they were seldom required to demonstrate any deeper understanding of the material. Their responses to teachers' questions were often little more than pastiches of buzzwords and generic "academese," belonging "less to the logic of cultural apprenticeship than to the logic of acculturation" (Bourdieu and Passeron 1977:111). Students' near-total dependence on copying left them at a loss when asked to summarize a lesson; one boy began a presentation, after much hesitation, with, "Educational psychology is a science that studies educational psychology . . . " and went downhill from there. Nevertheless, such utterances usually were accepted by teachers as fulfilling the requirements for "participation."

Students' verbal difficulties can be ascribed partly to their long passage through an educational system that excludes their own language from the realm of legitimate academic discourse (while exalting and ratifying authorial language, regardless of intelligibility) and partly to professors' reluctance to demand anything more.

> The conditions which make linguistic misunderstanding possible and tolerable are inscribed in the very institution; quite apart from the fact that ill-known or unknown words always appear in stereotyped configurations capable of inducing a sense of familiarity, magisterial language derives its full significance from the situation in which the relation of pedagogic communication is accomplished . . . the institution confers on professorial discourse a *status authority* tending to rule out the question of the informative efficiency of the communication. (Bourdieu and Passeron 1977:108; original emphasis)

Teachers' lectures and students' presentations stressed the definition and classification of terms far more than relationships, processes, or the logic of given categories. Lesson content, whether consisting of relatively straightforward information or of highly debatable opinions and interpretations, was presented in the same undifferentiated style, as more facts to be copied, and was rarely challenged by students. The origins of ideas usually went unacknowledged and unquestioned; there was an assumed sacredness about the written word that precluded interrogation of its validity or value.

Williams (1977:170) contends that reading, in anything more than its most literal sense, must include questioning the identity, position, authority, and intentions of the author. Both in students' own reading and in teachers' paraphrases of written sources, there was little such questioning, if any. Rather, the mere fact of *having been written* seemed to confer any text with sufficient authority as to make challenge or critique almost unthinkable. On the rare occasions when such challenges did arise, they usually failed. For example, Sergio once pointed out to Professor Ramírez that his statistics on Bolivia's linguistic demography contained contradictions and errors (such as that only 20 percent of the population of La Paz spoke Aymara). The professor seemed affronted by Sergio's criticism and defended his figures, which he had gotten out of a book. He had students copy them down as written, though all present knew that the majority of *paceños* are Aymara speakers. Such "facts," presented in order to be memorized regardless of their relation to students' own knowledge, are examples of what McNeil calls "school knowledge":

> . . . an artifact of facts and generalizations whose credibility lies no longer in its authenticity as a cultural selection but in its instrumental value in meeting the obligations teachers and students have within the institution of schooling . . . it is there to be mastered, traded for a grade and, as some students have said, deliberately forgotten afterward. When school knowledge is so divorced from the lively cultural content of societal experience, students receive it, but do not understand where it comes from, nor how, nor why, it became a part of school requirements. (McNeil 1986:191)

In classroom reading, not only do students fail to question the text, they also fail to let themselves be questioned by it (Muñoz forth.). As seen earlier, students and teachers tended to divorce lesson content from issues directly connected to their own lives, even when such connections were available. While many students held well-defined opinions on political and other matters, and could discuss them with insight and facility outside of class, for them the social and political aspects of lessons had less in common with these "real-life" ideas than with other, similarly commodified academic "facts"—they were to be copied, memorized, and repeated on command, but not necessarily understood. Not only did students have little faith in the validity of the information they received, it was of little concern to them relative to the goal of passing their classes. Of course, they were well aware that much of their schoolwork consisted of exercises in suspended disbelief, forays into a self-contained realm of pseudo-information with little connection to the rest of their lives. In a meeting of a group preparing a presentation on "The Education of Socialist Man," I listened to a student read notes he had copied from a book, citing one author named "Gramsa" and another named "Marx Engels" or "Max Engels," he wasn't sure. When I corrected his spelling of Gramsci, he claimed it was written that way in the book, which prompted another boy to jokingly insist, "The books are true!" Everyone laughed, and the first boy dutifully changed the spelling.

A common method of transforming "real world knowledge" into "school knowledge" is to fragment it into lists, outlines, and other isolated units determined by bureaucratic logistics and classroom organizational structures, rather than by the content itself or students' reactions to it. The copying of lists and outlines was common practice in the normal school, in line with McNeil's (1986:168) observation that "the list is not an aid to remembering the details from a complicated study of a topic; it *is* the study of the topic." The content students were responsible for consisted not of the logical relationships between elements of the subject matter, but simply the *taxonomic* relationships between terms. Once we recognize how classroom methodology functions to restrict and even determine content, it is easy to understand the co-occurrence of ostensibly revolutionary, socialist-oriented content with a passive, noncritical, and (as I shall argue below) essentially capitalist mode of learning. The type of integrated treatment that might have fostered a truly critical understanding on the part of students was replaced by abstract outlines, disjointed lists of topics and facts, abbreviated explanations, and hollow political slogans. Political content was denatured, becoming simply more inert, disengaged "school knowledge."[7] Despite the importance of socialist themes to many students' personal philosophies, these were not presented in such a way as to make this connection, but simply to serve a bureaucratic function as commodified information.

McNeil (1986:13) holds that "after being processed through worksheets, list-filled lectures and short-answer tests, the cultural content, regardless of whose interests it may have served before, comes to serve only the interests of institutional efficiencies." A National Reality exam about the planned decentralization of education provides a vivid example. Although the topic had been discussed at length (if not particularly deeply) over several class periods, the exam consisted of only ten short questions of the true/false or fill-in-the-blank type (e.g., "Decentralization will lead to national [*regionalization*], therefore the country's development will be hindered"; "Privatization is not synonymous with [*decentralization*], but rather with eliminating the people's right to education."). One question captured succintly the essence of the normal school's political formation: it read, "Would you say decentralization can solve the current problem in education?" The "correct" response consisted of one word: "No." For students who were sincerely concerned about the issue, the question was a betrayal of what normal school training should be.

José: In those subjects, that don't have a concrete answer... there shouldn't be yes/no questions, don't you think? Last year on the exam, one had to answer with one word, two words... I said to the professor, "This isn't an exam; if we're analyzing the national reality—flora, fauna, exploitation of natural resources, renewable and nonrenewable, all that—how are we going to ask those questions?"... One has to give his point of view, his critique, his opinion, what he thinks, right?... If I were the teacher, I'd give *that* kind of test. And evaluate, pull out the major points. That way the teacher can learn too. But this way, he's just imposing his opinion... Here they don't formulate abstract questions. That way there could be some reasoning. But always it's concrete questions, the professors want correct answers, answered exactly... The correct question would have been: "What do you think of the decentralization plan?" That should have been the question, right? Or, "What are the advantages and disadvantages?" That way one really has to think.

Many students were no doubt glad not to have to expound at length on the topic of decentralization, at least not on a graded exam. Still, the test highlighted the schism between "school knowledge" and "real world knowledge," by maintaining that division precisely in an area where the two should have overlapped (and where teachers made much of the fact that they were dealing with a "real" issue, of direct importance to students' lives). While the short-answer questions made it easier for students to earn a good grade on the test, they also exposed the fact that students were getting little out of the class *aside* from a grade. Generally speaking, teachers' demands for "correct answers" in such cases reduces evaluation of students' understanding to the mere reflection of teachers' understanding (Muñoz forth.). Students adopt this orientation as well, giving verbal responses that resemble steps in a guessing game, where the aim is to arrive at the conclusion already held by the teacher. The teacher listens only long enough to verify students' "comprehension"; classroom language loses its communicative value (in the Habermasian sense) as teachers, students, and texts engage each other, not to better understand themselves or the world, but with the instrumental aim of bringing others' opinions into line with one's own.

The Examination and the Ritual of Simulated Learning

The clearest example of how particular "ways of knowing" produce school knowledge is the examination. Exams were frequent at the normal school, and students' note-taking was geared primarily toward successful exam performance, which consisted mostly of reproducing memorized terms and phrases from teachers' lectures. Since exams for all subjects were scheduled together, students had to engage a formidable amount of material all at once, and spent the week before exams studying their notes late into the night. Afterward, there were "recuperation" exams for the many students who had failed, and a few weeks later, the whole cycle began again.

The emphasis on "covering" all the material before the exam, with relatively little concern for whether students had understood it, revealed a pedagogical model in which "the inputs and outputs are more important than the processes in between the two or the effects not predefined as outputs" (McNeil 1986:xviii). By emphasizing verbatim answers rather than students' comprehension, exams ceased to be reliable instruments for measuring what students had really learned. Rather, their usefulness lay in serving as the final step in the commodification of lesson content, and in their easy translation of complex material into "the quantitative language of accountability" (13).

The exam also served as a material manifestation of the ideology of control—both over students' behavior and over their productive activity—that is such a crucial part of the school

experience. As *the* central ritual of schooling, the exam constitutes an ideologically charged moment that is constructed as
the culmination of the formalized learning process. In the exam,
knowledge is both created and ratified; the value of students'
labor is realized in exchange; and students are fixed in a network of writing that is also a field of surveillance:

> In all the mechanisms of discipline, the examination is highly
> ritualized. In it are combined the ceremony of power and the
> form of the experiment, the deployment of force and the estab-
> lishment of truth. At the heart of the procedures of discipline,
> it manifests the subjection of those who are perceived as objects
> and the objectification of those who are subjected. The super-
> imposition of the power relations and the knowledge relations
> assumes in the examination all its visible brilliance . . . in this
> slender technique is to be found a whole domain of knowl-
> edge, a whole type of power. (Foucault 1977:184–85)

By structuring classwork around exams rather than around
dialogue between teachers and students, both became co-
participants in a *simulacrum of learning* that never required
them to actively engage content or their own relationship to it;
more important was "the ritual of seeming to deal with the
topic" (McNeil 1986:175). Class discussions were vague and
general, repeating the same basic points over and over; student
presentations were built upon passages copied out of the recommended texts, with key terms repeated frequently to create
an impression of mastery. In most cases, professors accepted
such performances as fulfilling the requirements of the assignment. The regularity of such practices revealed "both the ritualistic manner in which students viewed work and the limits to
which the institution would go to accept anything for the sake
of legitimizing the demands it made of students and having
students accept those demands" (Everhart 1983:162).

The ritual nature of class discussions, and students' frustration with them, were demonstrated in an anthropology class
comparing evolutionary and creationist theories of the origin of
Homo sapiens. The previous week, the class had divided into
six groups; each was to review a small amount of written
material, come up with a position, and present it to the class,
which would then debate the two theories. Since all groups
were assigned the same material, students were hard pressed
not to simply repeat what previous groups had said. Further-

more, they were unfamiliar with the sequence of hominid evolution and basic evolutionary theory, and the assigned material did not cover these topics. Despite a greater-than-usual interest in the topic, students thus lacked the information necessary for any real debate to take place.[8] A few pointed this out, with evident frustration. When they asked the professor to go over the stages of human evolution for them, however, he demurred; given the general lack of scientific texts and the fact that he was teaching out of his subject area, there was little he could offer them in the way of concrete information.

This topic generated more participation than usual, but discussion was dominated by a few students, as per the usual pattern. Questions were raised, but few answers offered. Due to the lack of actual information to be covered, the teacher seemed content to let students speak as long as they wished, in order to fill up time; as he said, "The important thing is that there should be participation." At the end of the "debate," he told each group to decide which theory they supported and offer their "conclusions." Several students objected, protesting that they had little on which to base such conclusions and that, in any case, such a question could not be decided collectively. The teacher brushed off their objections, claiming that the technique being used decreed that they do it this way, and if the group could not agree as to which theory was correct they should take a vote.

This incident shows how students' participation, while nominally encouraged, was actually sharply restricted. Given a topic that evoked strong opinions in many of them, students were offered two polarized positions and forced to declare collective support for one or the other, despite the lack of information necessary to weigh both sides and the impossibility of reaching consensus on such an issue. Yet, even in a debate this close to the heart of hegemony—a debate (in a Catholic country) on religious and scientific views of human origins—it was not direct repression by church or state that restricted student participation. Rather, "school was functioning in a way that attempted to socialize students into consensus history, into passive learner roles. Yet there were no overt community pressures, no external elites insisting the school take on this social control function. The controlling function stemmed from the way the school as an organization worked, not from outside pressures" (McNeil 1986:xx).

I would reject McNeil's implicit claim that "outside pressures" are irrelevant to the processes she describes; the way
schools function does not, after all, arise out of nowhere, and
in many cases *has* been designed by "external elites" precisely
for purposes of social control. Nevertheless, it is notable how
students' real intellectual concerns were completely subjugated
to the "logic" of curricular and methodological constraints. What
might have been a lively debate was rendered meaningless by
the artificiality of having to resolve, in the space of a class
period, a question that has engaged humankind for over a
century. Yet the teacher viewed this class as extraordinarily
successful, due to the high level of student "participation." It
mattered little that the participation consisted mostly of misin-
formation and frustrated criticisms of the class itself. Such
incidents demonstrate that choosing "relevant" subject matter
is of little use in transforming classroom practice if the methods by which it is treated remain undemocratic and intellectually stifling. A topic of intense interest to students may only
arouse sharper frustration for lack of adequate treatment, causing students to become cynical about the course or about school
knowledge in general (McNeil 1986:208).

To be sure, the ritualization of classroom practice is not a
unilateral phenomenon; under the pressure of assignment deadlines and professorial scrutiny, students are as likely as teachers to glean what short-term benefits they can from situations
of simulated learning.

> Students can always concoct, at least for the teacher's pur-
> poses, a semblance of sustained discourse . . . a second-order,
> second-hand *ars combinatoria* which . . . can only produce
> strings of words mechanically linked . . . Often their only course
> is a rhetoric of despair, a regression towards the prophylactic
> or propitiary magic of a language in which the grandiloquence
> of magisterial discourse is reduced to the passwords or sac-
> ramental phrases of a ritual murmur. (Bourdieu and Passeron
> 1977:113–14)

Students collaborated in such rituals, but did not freely
choose them; rather, they were the last resort left them by a
system that precluded genuine engagement. Many students
recognized this "rhetoric of despair" for what it was: a verbal
performance whose acceptability was judged according to magi-
cal rather than scientific criteria; an arbitrary effect between

word and value that was routinely ratified in lieu of a well-formulated argument. School discourse was cast in a sort of "second-order language" in which signifiers became detached from meaning or signification (Foley 1990:184). Combining insights from Habermas and Goffman, Foley describes how "a person's everyday discourse practices become reified. Increasingly, people . . . come to believe that their discursive practice of impression management *is* reality. They become less reflective about the gap between their words and their deeds. Consequently, traditional normative ideals about doing what one says and being sincere and truthful become less of a constraint on communicative action" (185). Thus "school knowledge" becomes progressively distanced from the truth standards governing "real world knowledge." But while the communicative constraints on classroom performance may be loosened with regard to truthfulness, it is also a more restricted discourse, constrained within the parameters that define the ritual language of the school.

"The Path of Least Resistance": The Teacher-Student Pact to Minimize Effort

Why should teachers, many sincerely dedicated to their profession and to students' intellectual development, resort to such stultifying methods? The answer requires a multilevel analysis of what goes on in the classroom. Without denying the impact of broad forces of social reproduction, evoking these vast, abstract processes is insufficient to explain the ways that classroom practice is structured; what is required is a delineation of the connections between on-the-ground cultural forms and diffuse, overarching social forces. McNeil approaches such an explanation with her claim that school practice is mediated by individuals' attempts to deal with institutional constraints. She views restrictive pedagogical structures and superficial "school knowledge" as the results of staff's pragmatic strategies for managing student behavior; teachers buy students' compliance by promising that lessons will be simple. Exhausted by the antagonistic relationship in which they are positioned—teachers demanding work, students attempting to fulfill these demands with as little exertion as possible—the opposing parties find common ground in a strategy that allows both to ease their workload. Overworked, bored, and perpetually behind in the race to cover content, teachers and students meet in a path of least resistance (McNeil 1986:174–76).

For McNeil, the main motivation for producing "school knowledge" is the desire to control student behavior; but this explanation is less compelling when applied to postsecondary students, who seldom constitute "behavior problems." Here, the fragmented treatment of complex issues, the clichéd phrases that serve as substitutes for real understanding, and the ratification of empty verbiage in fulfillment of class assignments are traceable to the control, not of students' *behavior*, but of their *production*; these techniques not only allowed teachers to cover quickly large amounts of material, they also provided the basis for a method of evaluation that placed few demands on them. One can imagine the difference in the amount of labor required to grade the National Reality exam described above, with that needed to grade a hundred thoughtful essays about the effects of decentralizing the school system. Teachers who already feel unsupported, unappreciated, and underpaid are unlikely to put in extra hours pursuing teaching strategies that are more meaningful for students but more time-consuming for themselves. Even if a teacher felt so inspired, most of the normal school students would have great difficulty producing such an essay, having passed through their entire primary and secondary education without ever having to research a topic on their own, express their thoughts in essay form, or write anything longer than a single page. Thus, the tacit pact by which obedience is exchanged for leniency is not the only (or even the primary) one engaged in by students and teachers. Also at work is a "complicity of misunderstanding"—the mutual agreement to pretend that "teaching" and "learning" have in fact taken place.

> Students and teachers have a duty—to themselves and to each other—to overestimate the quantity of information which really circulates in pedagogic communication . . . [The teacher] could not measure exactly the students' understanding of his language without destroying the fiction which enables him to teach with the least effort . . . As for the student, it is necessary and sufficient for him to follow his bent in the use of language to which his whole training predisposes him . . . keeping the teacher at arm's length with the pseudo-generalities and prudent approximations which are "not even wrong" and will win him [a passing grade], in short, avoid[ing] having

to reveal, in the clearest code possible, the exact level of his understanding and knowledge, which would condemn him to pay the price of clarity. (Bourdieu & Passeron 1977:113)

This arrangement has advantages for both parties: students receive passing grades while avoiding the difficulty of decoding a discourse that is largely opaque to them; teachers' workload is reduced, and the authority of their discourse goes unchallenged. Since schools are tailored to precisely this kind of exchange, attempts to break with routine and create a truly critical dialogue must struggle against the weight of power and tradition. Not that all were content with this arrangement; students objected when it was applied to an issue about which many of them truly cared (such as the origin of human beings). Some teachers expressed similar frustrations with the shallow treatment of classroom material; in an interview, Professor Torres employed terminology echoing that of Paulo Freire's *Pedagogy of the Oppressed* (1970).

Professor Torres: Unfortunately, the system itself makes it so the teacher simply has to go along depositing [information] in the child's mind, as if it were a bank, no? He fills it up and fills it up, and when exam time comes, he draws a check and the student has to give it back. It's a banking sort of education, we go along making deposits, and when we want to we take out what we've put in. Personally, I don't agree. But that's the system . . . The programs they give us, we simply use them like they tell us to, right? Along comes a program, they say, "You have to cover this," and we work from that, and sometimes we don't even get around to analyzing a topic, what's going on in reality . . . We have to break that tendency, be a bit more flexible, I think. Try not to be a bunch of bureaucrats that have to follow the program and the contents and [say] "There, our problem is solved; our work is done." I think we should relate it more to reality, to what we live, and try to make the class more dynamic. At least we could change in that regard, right? There should be participation, discussion.

I once observed another professor ask the class to evaluate the recently ended semester, telling them, "It's good for me [to hear your opinions], so I can improve my methodology." Paco led off with a critique of "some other teachers" who were inept and students who refused to participate for fear of making mistakes. Another boy remarked, "We haven't made good use of our time this semester; really most of us have hardly learned anything." He also claimed that some teachers were not up to teaching in a professional institution and simply lectured without giving students a chance to participate. The teacher broke in, claiming that failure to achieve all of the semester's objectives had been due to lack of time, rather than to deficiencies in personnel or methodology. When he asked for suggestions on how to organize the coming semester, several boys suggested working in groups of two or three; others recommended reviewing the conclusions from last semester; one criticized the dependence on photocopied handouts. Evidently, students (at least male students) were willing to critique classroom practice, given the opportunity. Nevertheless, the conditions they criticized remained unchanged the following semester. While teachers frequently promised (or threatened) to adopt new methods when students failed to turn in homework or respond in class, these plans were never actually carried out, to my knowledge.

Native Speakers and Native Readers: The Asymmetry of Informal and Academic Registers

In addition to the quest for "efficient" transmission of content and the minimizing of both students' and teachers' workloads, there was another reason for the superficial and fragmented treatment of subject matter: the disparity between the linguistic codes of the classroom and the linguistic repertoire of the students, evidenced in their low reading comprehension. Whereas several students had difficulty reading at all, even those who had mastered the technical aspects often read with only minimal comprehension. Students' Spanish was quite different[9] from that of academic texts, whose unfamiliar words and complex grammatical constructions constituted formidable obstacles to comprehension. The breach between oral and written forms of Spanish constitutes a "crisis of communication" for many indigenous students, impeding their critical engagement with texts even when the rudimentary aspects of literacy have been mastered (Hamel 1983; Michenot 1985; López and Jung 1989; Muñoz forth.).

Reading was not a natural, casual activity for most students; while many were native speakers of Spanish, very few were "native readers" of Spanish or any other language.[10] I use the term *native reader* to refer to those whose mastery of reading is nearly as fluid and ingrained as their mastery of their mother tongue in its spoken form. More specifically, a native reader is one who:

• has mastered basic reading skills in early childhood, so that literacy is not only an adjunct to the physiological and cognitive processes of the child's primary language acquisition, but is also an integral part of his or her primary socialization within a community of readers.
• belongs to a speech community where literacy plays an important role in daily life for all full members, rather than being restricted to a group of specialists or elites.
• reads naturally and automatically, having integrated into his or her mental structure the processes involved in deciphering written texts, so that these processes are no longer consciously evoked. The written message is thus perceived in "gestalt," as a meaningful message, rather than as a string of isolated elements and mental operations.
• can extend generalized reading (and writing) skills to new kinds of texts and contexts, eventually differentiating among a range of distinct written registers (analogous to spoken registers) which themselves carry social information.

The normal school students' relationship to written Spanish (and to those spoken registers stylistically derived from written ones) was in many ways similar to a person's incomplete mastery of a second language. Many carried dictionaries with them to class, like visitors in a foreign land. The gulf between spoken and written Spanish—or, more accurately, between informal and academic registers, both spoken and written[11]—was difficult for students to bridge. They could read, but had difficulty putting what they read into their own words. They could copy from a text or take notes on a professor's lecture, but were often unable to extract the relevant points from their notes. This was a major factor in the tendency of their written work and oral presentations to consist of little more than copied passages. José, himself a successful student, located this difficulty in the fact that reading was not an integral part of students' lives:

José: I have difficulties too. I can't easily summarize a book, I can't easily understand it. We *campesinos* have that defect . . . It goes back to high school, to grade school. In rural areas, there are no books, there are no libraries . . . You never learn how to sum up a book, or how to present it or discuss it just like that . . . One prefers just to copy it from someplace, easy.

Students' limited vocabulary (in the academic register) and their reliance on copying tended to reinforce each other. When assigned a topic to present in class, they went to the school library for the recommended texts. Finding these hard to understand, they composed their handout by copying what seemed to be the relevant passages. When this was distributed to the class, the others found it equally incomprehensible. During the oft-used "Philips-66" technique (in which groups of six discuss a topic for six minutes and then present their conclusions), students often spent most of the allotted time looking up unfamiliar terms and trying to understand the handout. When the time came to present, they were seldom able to recast the information in their own words, and so recited selections from the handout instead (one skill of such presentations being the ability to read aloud from the handout without appearing to look at it). The other students copied down these same words, which appeared again later as the completed homework assignment or the answers on a test. It was thus possible to "learn" the material, passing through the entire cycle of academic obligations, without ever having to engage the content or confront the fact that one had actually understood very little. "Learning" occurred at the very surface of intellectual activity; this surface was disturbed only when a teacher asked what was meant by a particular passage (often something the student had just read aloud, with deceptive fluidity). The usual response was simply to repeat the relevant passage; if pressed to reformulate it in their own words, most students retreated into an awkward silence.[12]

The Primacy of Form and the Dependence upon
External Knowledge

The common thread running through these observations is
the privileging of form over content, ritual over substance. The
ratification of students' work depended not on the depth of
their understanding, the clarity of their writing, or the eloquence of their oral presentations, but rather on the neatness
of their cover illustrations, the verbatim precision of their answers, and their ability to fill an allotted amount of time or
paper with words. When such considerations are allowed to
rule classroom life, they effectively determine content; in McNeil's
(1986:193) words, "The hidden curriculum becomes the overt
curriculum." Teachers and students are pressured to minimize
rather than maximize the potential of their interaction. Teachers place few demands on students, in exchange for acceptance
of their authority and of the school's way of organizing and
producing knowledge. Discouraged from going beyond the reified
"facts" of the official program, students adopt a client mentality, in which all approved sources of knowledge lie outside
themselves.

It is essential to recognize this as a structural, not an
individual phenomenon. Professor Torres provides a useful
example in this regard, precisely because he was one of the
most dedicated and talented teachers in the school. Of all the
faculty, he was the most liked and respected by students, largely
due to his dynamic teaching style, based more on his own
analysis and engagement with the subject matter than on dictation from written sources. Students remarked that he "made
himself understood" in the classroom, whereas other teachers'
lectures were often confusing. He was skilled at generating
discussion, finding something to valorize in almost any student
comment and building upon it to encourage participation by
others. Nevertheless, close analysis reveals many of the same
restrictions on debate in his classes as in those of other teachers. This suggests that the alienating environment of the school
derives less from the actions of individuals than from the way
teaching itself is structured.[13] It is deceptively easy to lay the
blame for oppressive schooling on corrupt or incompetent teachers; but if similar conditions are found in the classrooms of
skilled, sensitive, well-intentioned teachers, the causes of

alienation must be sought at a deeper level. As Giroux notes, it is quite possible for teachers to work from sound ethical and theoretical principles and still end up pedagogically silencing students. "What is at stake here is not simply the issue of bad teaching, but the broader refusal to take seriously the categories of meaning, experience and voice that students use to make sense of themselves and the world around them" (Giroux 1992:95).

The tendency of academic content to skate along the surface of linguistic consciousness, rather than being absorbed and reworked, is closely linked to the emphasis on copying and memorizing. This emphasis is partly due to the fact that most students, lacking fluency in the academic register, would find it difficult or impossible to extract lesson highlights and construct an impromptu written text while listening to teachers' lectures. But this explanation justifies the traditional methods only if we assume that the academic register—and, by implication, official school knowledge—is the only one worthy of being taught and learned. If students' voices and knowledge are excluded from legitimate pedagogical discourse, all other concerns—from the development of a critical dialogue to students' linguistic ease and self-esteem—must be subjugated to the transmission of official forms of knowledge. This has been, in effect, the guiding principle underlying Bolivian education.

In Bolivian schools, copying is more than just a pedagogical method; it is the double-sided *dybbuk* of school discourse and ideology, orienting the bulk of classroom practice while educators unanimously call for its exorcism. Franz Tamayo's *Creación de la Pedagogía Nacional*, the centerpiece of Bolivia's pedagogical canon, is a long diatribe against schooling's derivative nature, and a call for the creation of an "authentically Bolivian" national pedagogy.[14] In the normal school, weekly *horas cívicas* were peppered with aphorisms such as "The smallest creator is greater than the greatest copier of others' knowledge." Yet this discourse is embedded in a practical milieu in which copying holds central place and is implicitly regarded as the fundamental activity of "learning"; students are told that copying is the most despised form of intellectual labor, and yet it is their verbatim reproduction of external knowledge that is regularly and exclusively ratified by the school.

Bennet Berger warned of the social conflicts that ensue when the situations that a society typically engenders are not those its value system prescribes; one such conflict is "alienation from work" (Berger 1968: 204–5). In Bolivia, official documents repeatedly call for teachers and students possessed of intellectual fervor, a capacity for independent critique and inquiry, and a zeal for substantive debate on those questions central to national identity. Nevertheless, Bolivian schools do not produce such individuals (which is not to say they do not exist, simply that they are usually formed in spite of, rather than because of, their schooling). Schools exhort students to develop a critical consciousness, yet require them to subjugate their critiques and concerns to an external regime of knowledge. Copying is publicly and privately disparaged and yet is the primary road of access to school knowledge, the principal currency of the classroom economy. In a portentous passage, Berger (1968:204–5) predicts that "a culture which has not learned to honor what it is actually committed to produce creates an uneasy population." The discrepancy between what Bolivian schools honor and what they produce is evident, as is the social unease engendered by this schism. Below, I examine the "alienation from work" that is this pedagogy's inevitable result.

The Capitalist Mode of Symbolic Production: Schoolwork as Alienated Labor

Language as Productive Work

We have seen that the way classroom practices are structured gives rise to an assemblage of abstract information ("school knowledge") disconnected from students' real-life concerns. But what is it that structures these practices? The regular pattern of nondialogic interactions, across a variety of teachers and subjects, suggests a common model of teaching and learning underlying all such interactions. What follows is an outline of this model and its functioning.

It was asserted above that copying constitutes "the principal currency of the classroom economy." While not strictly accurate, neither is this merely a metaphor. What is exchanged in the acts of copying, recitation, and test-taking are *linguistic forms*—specifically, those forms officially accepted in fulfillment of institutional requirements. This linguistic exchange takes place within a micro-economy of knowledge and discourse that is governed by specific rules. I will argue that these rules are essentially those of capitalism—the dialectic dynamic between the production of value and its appropriation toward the strengthening of capital. Students' schoolwork is a form of labor; this labor is linguistic in nature, as are its products, but this does not exclude it from the realm of production *per se*. The mode of schooling examined thus far is essentially "a capitalist mode of consuming knowledge" (Lesage 1988:424);[15] it is also a hegemonic mode of producing subjects. Students' labor is doubly productive, generating linguistic forms on the one hand, and a range of subject positions and ideologies on the other.

Various authors have posited an analogy between the factory and the school, usually based on similarities in their regimentation of time, space, and behavior. The resemblance goes beyond the controls imposed on workers and students, however. Both factories and schools are *sites of production*, extracting labor from subjects whose lack of capital (economic or cultural) obliges them to sell their labor-power. Both commodify the products of labor, alienating them from their producers; and both appropriate a portion of the value produced toward the strengthening of capital. The fact that in schools the capital, labor, and commodities in question are primarily symbolic/ linguistic does not alter the fundamental relationships involved. Thus, when Foley (1990:113) claims that "the key similarity between schools and factories is that academic work can be as boring and alienating as industrial work," we should recognize that these similar effects are not coincidental, nor even simply a matter of preparing future workers for the regime of the factory; rather, they are the results of a similar process at work in both settings.

Indeed, the distinction between material and symbolic production grows ever less distinct. Material production is imbued with a symbolic aspect that ideologically binds subjects to the regime in which they labor; similarly, symbolic production depends upon a scaffolding of material practices. Ideology is effective precisely because it is embodied in material life; its corporeal existence allows it to be actively lived and internalized by human subjects.[16] One of Gramsci's principal contributions to social theory was his recognition of ideology's material nature, of its presence in practices and apparatuses that play an indispensable role in all societies (Mouffe 1981:227). This allowed him (and later scholars) to develop a concept of hegemony in which language, politics, art, and other phenomena previously relegated to the realm of "superstructure" are recognized as crucial elements in the production and reproduction of social formations.

To analyze how ideologies are constructed in material practice—in other words, how hegemony works—we must transcend the classical Marxist view that excludes symbolic behavior from the sphere of productive activity. It is easy to construe the famous passage from the *Grundrisse* that claims the labor of the piano maker as part of the productive base, while relegating that of the pianist to the superstructure, as some sort of scriptural axiom on the nature of symbolic activity. But Marx was analyzing a particular kind of production; for the analysis of cultural activity, in both its ideological and economic aspects, such a view is an unequivocal dead end (Williams 1980a:35). Concurrent with classical Marxism's failure to address questions of language and culture was "a specialization of the whole material social process to 'labour,' which was then more and more narrowly conceived" (Williams 1977:33). More recent theorists (Althusser, Williams, Hall, Laclau, Mouffe, etc.) conceive "productive forces" more broadly, rejecting a simplistic division between determining base and determined superstructure. As Giroux (1922:121) observes, "The production of meaning has become as important as the production of labor in shaping the boundaries of human existence."

This view arose from the dual realizations that (1) within late capitalism, questions of cultural production are inseparable from any analysis of large-scale economic activity[17] and (2) consciousness and its products are inevitably implicated in and realized through material processes. Cultural activity—including language—does not merely reflect an underlying socioeconomic formation; rather, it is directly involved in that formation. Excluding it from the category of productive forces gives an incomplete picture of the productive activity necessary to human life. "What then is a 'productive force'? It is all and any of the means of the production and reproduction of real life . . . [including] a certain mode of social co-operation and the application and development of a certain body of social knowledge . . . In all our activities in the world we produce not only the satisfaction of our needs but new needs and new definitions of needs" (Williams 1977:91).

Schools produce and disseminate, not only certain types of social cooperation and knowledge, but also new "needs" (and—sometimes—the means to fulfill them): the need to speak Spanish, to have a profession, to disassociate oneself from stigmatized identities. Aside from these individual needs, the school also produces collective ones: the need to build a unified citizenry bound by a supposed "national culture," to incorporate the peasantry into the national economy, and to spread formal schooling throughout the population, thus establishing itself as the ultimate foundation of all claims to individual and collective worth. The symbolic practices generating these needs take place within a material regime that includes the school infrastructure, texts and written assignments, the recruitment and physical organization of teachers and students, and so on; indeed, they have no existence apart from this material regime. Language, simultaneously a material and a symbolic activity, is the principal medium through which these ideological products are created.

Corresponding to the idea of language as a productive force is the notion of linguistic work: "Between the absence of any particular human product or result and the presence of the same product or result, there is a difference that can be explained . . . only in terms of the work expended by [people] in order to attain it . . . words and messages do not exist in nature; since they are produced by [people], we can directly derive that they are also products of work. It is in this sense that we can begin to speak of *linguistic human work*" (Rossi-Landi 1983:35–36; original emphasis). In schools, linguistic activity is also clearly perceived as work by both students and teachers, and is implicated in economic relations comparable to those governing other forms of work.

If signification is a kind of productive activity, it follows that technologies of communication are themselves means of production (Williams 1977:54, 1980b). The rise of mass education and literacy constitutes a paradigm shift in the mode of symbolic production, comparable (and historically related) to the Industrial Revolution's transformation of material production. What are often referred to as "patterns of teacher-student interaction," "participant structures," and so on, are nothing less than *relations of production*. Schooling is organized so as to inculcate and solidify those relations corresponding to the mode of (symbolic) production that rose to dominance with the establishment of the school as a primary instrument of hegemony. Schools impose a particular style of verbal interaction, thus incorporating students' linguistic work into the productive apparatus of the educational system. Students are, in this sense, linguistic workers in the educational institution. Their defining characteristic, within the relations of production under which they labor, is their lack of control over the means of production—that is, the linguistic codes in which schooling takes place, the discursive parameters by which their work is evaluated, and the policies governing the school itself.[18] Their situation is similar to that described by Rossi-Landi for his linguistic Everyman:

> The speaker is, so to speak, employed by the society in which he is born. He is asked and obliged to expend his linguistic labor power and he has no choice but to learn the modalities of expenditure which are taught to him; he must use already existing products and consume them, while unconsciously reproducing them according to models that are thus confirmed and perpetuated. In the event that he succeeds in rejecting these models, the price he must pay consists in nothing less and nothing more than expulsion from the linguistic society. If he does not learn to speak, or speaks a language with personal deviations, he is no longer understood and cannot make himself understood. (Rossi-Landi 1983:63–64)

Missing from this picture, however, is any sense of differentiation among speakers with regard to their "employment." While it is true that individual speakers do not control the objective (i.e., purely linguistic) aspects of communication, some groups do in fact control the social aspects, while others do not. As Fiske (1989:34) points out, "Linguistic resources are no more equitably distributed in our society than are economic resources." Differential value is ascribed to different types of language (and groups of speakers), in specific social and productive relations. Speakers who reject the dominant linguistic models (or, more likely, are simply less fluent in them), are unlikely to be "expelled from linguistic society"; rather, they are forcefully relegated to its lower ranks. Such speakers are less likely to suffer from "personal deviations" in speech than from *social* deviations that mark their speech as nonstandard and therefore of low prestige. Rossi-Landi's model lacks a notion of cultural capital—those skills, tastes, credentials, and knowledge (including linguistic knowledge) that are accepted as legitimate by dominant cultural standards, and are unequally distributed in (indirect) relation to the distribution of economic capital (Bourdieu 1984, 1991).[19] To understand how symbolic power is exercised and reproduced, we must examine the institutional mechanisms that assign different values to different products, allocate these products differentially, and inculcate a belief in their value (Thompson, in Bourdieu 1991:24).

Foremost among the institutional mechanisms that carry out these processes is, of couse, the school. Bourdieu and Passeron's description of how schools stratify students via the distribution of linguistic capital is especially applicable to language-minority students like the ones in this study:

> The unequal social-class distribution of *educationally profitable linguistic capital* constitutes one of the best-hidden mediations through which the relationship . . . between social origin and scholastic achievement is set up . . . The academic market value of each individual's linguistic capital is a function of the distance between the type of symbolic mastery demanded by the school and the practical mastery he owes to his initial class upbringing. (Bourdieu and Passeron 1977:115–16; original emphasis)

Subaltern students, lacking linguistic capital, are wage workers in the discursive factory.[20] The practices generated within the normal school's micro-economy arise from the mode of production in which students and teachers labor. The incorporation of students' linguistic activity into the productive process gives rise to certain meanings and values around language and learning, which in turn give rise to the detached, ritualized pedagogy that was examined earlier. These phenomena ultimately can be traced to the nature of students' schoolwork as *alienated labor*. To support this contention, we can trace students' linguistic production through the the circuits of Marx's theory of labor and value. The aim is not to view all of human practice through a traditionally conceived Marxist lens, but rather to use this lens (among possible others) to shed light on the role of the school and school discourse in the construction of ethnic, nationalist, and other identities.

To extend Marx's theory into the discursive realm, we must show how language serves as a medium for the production of use values, how these are commodified as exchange values, and how surplus value from this process is appropriated toward capital. Other theorists laid the groundwork for this task, but did not, in my opinion, go far enough. Marx himself gave notoriously short shrift to questions of language, cultural production, and symbolic value.[21] Since then, the symbolic realm has become even more important within the workings of late capitalism, and questions of symbolic production have moved to the center of social theory, largely due to the work of Williams and Bourdieu. Still, these authors failed to treat adequately the notion of *value* in regard to symbolic production. Bourdieu's concept of "cultural capital" was a major step forward, but was not explicitly linked to a theory of labor and value; he demonstrated the relationship between cultural/linguistic capital and economic class, but failed to see that specific class relations also govern linguistic production and commodification. In contrast, Williams moved language into the realm of material production, but did not show how linguistic production creates value. If linguistic work is a kind of productive labor, it should be subject to the same constraints, transformations, and appropriations as other kinds of labor; and if the meanings and practices of the dominant sectors of society do in fact constitute a kind of cultural "capital," then there is an implied opposition beween this capital (and those who control it) and those whose labor is appropriated toward its fortification. If the theoretical connections between language and political economy are not explicitly rendered, in ethnographic accounts of real-world discursive economies, they run the risk of being interpreted as merely metaphorical, when actually they are much more than that.

The Alienated Character of Schoolwork

Most of students' academic activity is linguistic: answering questions, reciting in front of the class, copying written or dictated information, reading silently or aloud. The products of this work are also linguistic: verbal performances and written texts. Students exchange their work for grades, which are then exchanged for a title, which in turn guarantees them a job and a salary. The economic exchange is less direct than that of the wage-laborer, but the principle is essentially the same.

This in itself does not make students' labor "alienated"; at issue is not whether one's work is remunerated, or its inherent ease or difficulty, but rather what (and whose) purposes it serves—"whether the work serves man as a mere means for existence or becomes the very contents of his life" (Avineri 1968:104). In the normal school, students' work was not an end in itself, but a means to an end (earning grades), and was structured in a way that precluded their engaging its content. Furthermore, it met Marx's litmus test for the determination of labor's alienated character: "As soon as there is no physical or other compulsion, it is avoided like the plague" (EPM:74).[22]

To determine the alienated nature of schoolwork, we can analyze the mode of production under which it is organized and see whether it conforms to Marx's description of alienated labor. First, a clarification of the term *alienation* is necessary, since its use as the keystone for our hypothesis depends on a more precise reading than it has often enjoyed. While Marx's concept of "alienation" was rooted in the concrete conditions of social life, by the latter half of this century the term was being applied to virtually any feeling of existential anomie or social discontent.[23] Though Marx criticized conceptions of alienation as a primarily psychological or spiritual phenomenon, he was not blind to its psychological aspects. Still, he saw these as resulting from workers' economic exploitation—a subjective manifestation of their objective position in the productive process, "subject to elimination only in the real sphere of object-related activity" (Avineri 1968:97–98). His rejection of the notion that alienation exists primarily in the mind was one of his major departures from Hegelian idealist thought. Nevertheless, some authors (Schacht 1970; Seeman 1975; Witte 1980) used his polemical position to posit an opposition beween "objective" and "subjective" (or economic vs. psychological) alienation—failing to recognize the connection between the two—or viewed "alienation" as inclusive of a variety of conditions that they saw as unrelated.[24] It was perhaps this tendency that led Althusser to declare himself "an avowed enemy of the concept of alienation," viewing it as "anthropological speculation" and "ideological and antiscientific nonsense," incompatible with what he considered to be the scientific nature of Marxism (Schaff 1980:5).

Ollman (1976:203), however, views the very attempt to compartmentalize alienation in this way as "a symptom of the 'disease'"; he claims that such an interpretation "alters the very character of the theory; from an analytical theory about capitalism, which integrates a description of people with an explanation of how the entire system works, it becomes a psychological theory, simply describing people's subjective reactions to their life conditions, and an ethical theory that finds this situation wanting" (253). Attempting to free the concept from the existentialist baggage that has adhered to it, he explains:

> Marx does not use the theory of alienation to understand the individual in capitalism but to understand capitalism from the standpoint of the individual. This is achieved by focusing not only on the individual but on those elements of his nature over which he has lost control and which are now controlling him. The whole process is then thoroughly mystified by the operations of the capitalist market, and this mystification too is an integral part of what is meant by "alienation." (252)

While our main focus here is on the objective conditions of students' alienation, rather than its subjective effects, understanding the causal and integral relation between the two is crucial to understanding the ideological consequences of capitalist linguistic exchange. Marx's objective aspects of alienation contain the seeds of such subjective phenomena as feelings of powerlessness, meaninglessness, and isolation. Paraphrasing from Marx (EPM), the worker is "alienated" from:

1. the products of his/her labor; these become alien objects belonging to another and exercising power over the worker, manifesting his/her estranged relationship to nature and the material world.
2. his/her own productive activity, which becomes activity controlled by and exploited for the benefit of another. The worker's life-activity becomes merely a means to the maintainance of physical existence, manifesting his/her estranged relationship to him/herself.
3. his/her species-being; social existence becomes a means to individual existence. Others are perceived as competitors rather than as partners in free, cooperative activity, manifesting the worker's estranged relationship to his/her fellow human beings.

Each of these factors is traceable to the antagonistic relation between labor and capital, under which producers do not control the means of production, the conditions under which they labor, or the fate of their products. Their lack of capital forces them to sell their labor, thereby increasing capital and its power over them (WLC). These conditions also apply to the normal school students:

1. Students do not control the products of their labor, nor choose what they will produce. Their verbal performances and written work are produced according to specifications dictated by others, using linguistic resources that are not their own, but rather are imposed upon them. This is true both of the language itself (Spanish instead of Aymara) and of the specific lexical and stylistic materials from which they must construct their products if these are to be deemed acceptable for exchange. The fate of their products—whether they will be accepted, rejected, placed in the school library, or destroyed—is not up to them. The products of their labor exercise power over them, serving as the basis of evaluations that will determine their future within (and beyond) the institution.

2. Students do not control the conditions under which they labor; these are structured as teachers and administrators see fit, and reflect institutional demands and teachers' convenience rather than students' needs or desires. Students thus spend much of their time in labor that is meaningless to them; their work is not an end in itself, but a means to future economic survival.

3. Students are placed in an antagonistic relationship with teachers, attempting to evade their control and fulfill their demands with the least amount of work possible. They are also placed in a competitive relationship with their fellow students, their opportunities for cooperative work severely restricted by the pedagogical norms of the institution.

With regard to the producer's perception of his or her own alienated activity, Marx's description can be easily applied to the student: "He does not even reckon labour as part of his life, it is rather a sacrifice of his life. It is a commodity which he has made over to another. Hence, also, the product of his activity is not the object of his activity. What he produces for himself is not the silk that he weaves, not the gold that he draws from the mine, not the palace that he builds. What he produces for himself is *wages*" (WLC:205; original emphasis). Similarly, what the student produces for him/herself is not the class presentation, the written assigment, or the completed exam, but *grades*. As for the assertion that students' labor is reckoned, not as part of their life, but as a sacrifice of their life, we need only recall how many of them choose the normal school precisely because it is the shortest course of study. The alienated nature of their labor is also evident in its abstract character; students' work is evaluated, not on the basis of content or quality, but by the amount of time or paper filled with words. It is reduced to a quantitative abstraction, exchangeable for another quantitative abstraction: points toward a grade. It is this that renders students' labor power a commodity and allows certain types of discourse to serve as the "currency" of the school economy.

Given that human beings are by nature linguistically creative, why should students have nothing to offer in linguistic exchange but their commodified labor? The answer is that, within the school economy, students are capital-poor. Lacking the linguistic and cultural capital that it is the school's job to transmit, their only asset (like the laborer's) is their labor power, which they must exchange for grades (wages), thus increasing capital and its power over them (WLC:211). What does this linguistic and cultural capital—whose production and distribution, it might be argued, constitute the primary *raison d'être* of the school—consist of? The values, meanings, and practices of the dominant social group, that is, urban-centered *mestizo/criollo* culture. For example:

- knowledge of and identification with nationalist emblems and practices: patriotic hymns, the flag, holidays, regional stereotypes, and so on.
- acceptance of the official version of key historical events, such as the war of independence and the 1952 revolution.
- familiarity with urban life and its corresponding social skills.
- familiarity with the political culture of the urban center (party politics, the mass media, etc.).
- adoption of the tastes and styles of the dominant group (in music, dress, etc.).
- knowledge of the academic canon of ideas, persons, works, and events that an educated person (as defined by the dominant group) is expected to know.

• mastery of the linguistic codes and styles associated with formal education (particularly, but not limited to, standard Spanish).

Significantly, these themes—the foundation of Bolivian "cultural capital"—also constitute a thumbnail sketch of the school curriculum. They are precisely the values, meanings, and practices that were analyzed in the previous chapter as being key to the construction of certain subject positions (citizen, professional, etc.), which in turn combine to form a particular national/ethnic/class identity among students. Conspicuously absent from the list is students' personal and local knowledge (even more so for rural than for urban students), which has no value within the school economy. This explains why students have little to bring to the educational exchange aside from their labor power, and also why most of their schooling is a one-way process, based on nondialogic methods such as lecturing and memorization. Teachers' role as the guardians of academic capital is to transmit it to those who lack it, not to engage in debate and social critique with students. There can be no free exchange of knowledge when knowledge is seen as something on which teachers hold a monopoly.

Not that the school is the sole producer of academic capital; Bourdieu (1984:23) defines it as a product of "the combined effects of cultural transmission by the family and cultural transmission by the school," but notes that the efficiency of the latter depends on the amount of cultural capital inherited from the family. Urban students' greater familiarity with urban culture, Spanish, the mass media, etc., gives them an advantage over rural students, in terms of the cultural capital they bring to the school setting. Not surprisingly, on those rare occasions when there was a dialogic exchange of ideas in the classroom, it was usually urban students who dominated the discussion.

Bourdieu and Passeron (1977:125) note that "pedagogic action must always transmit not only a content but also the affirmation of the value of that content"; every pedagogic interaction is, in this sense, a Trojan horse of ideological messages.

> The mere fact of transmitting a message within a relation of pedagogic communication implies and imposes a social definition . . . of what merits transmission, the code in which

the message is to be transmitted, the persons entitled to transmit it or, better, impose its reception, the persons worthy of receiving it and consequently obliged to receive it and, finally, the mode of imposition and inculcation of the message which confers on the information transmitted its legitimacy and thereby its full meaning. (109)

By defining as worthy of transmission only that information transmitted *from* teachers *to* students, via the legimitate channels and codes, the school defines students as consumers rather than producers of knowledge. Though students' labor drives the motor of social reproduction in schools, they are portrayed as mere clients in a system that appears to exist prior to and independent of their participation; "living labour appears as a mere means to realize objectified, dead labour, to penetrate it with an animating soul while losing its own soul to it" (Grund.:252). By exchanging their labor for academic capital, students increase that capital and its power over them; to the degree that they accept this as natural, they fortify the hegemony of the curriculum, laboring under conditions that, in Marx's words, "assume an ever more colossal independence."

The Commodification of Linguistic Products: Use Value, Exchange Value, Surplus Value

If students exchange their labor for a title and the deferred wage that title represents, what value does their labor have for the proprietors of capital? How is capital increased by this exchange? To answer this question, we must examine schoolwork from two perspectives: that of *exchange value* and that of *use value*. One might deduce, from the hollow, abstract character of school knowledge and the ritualistic nature of students' participation, that a defining feature of students' labor is its importance as an exchange value rather than a use value. Indeed, complaints of the uselessness of much school knowledge are so common that they have become cliché. McNeil (1986:208) claims that "simplified, mystified content becomes so artificial that it loses its credibility of substance and retains only whatever value it has in the exchange of student effort for course grade or graduation credit," and many students would undoubtedly agree.

This is not to say that schoolwork has only exchange value and no use value. Such an argument would be nonsensical in terms of Marx's theory; two exchange values are comparable precisely because they represent the mutual measurement of use values between two commodities. All exchange values are reducible to some quantity of Labor/Value (two sides of the same coin within Marx's schema [Cap1:304-5]). Students' academic products have use value, despite their surface appearance of uselessness; but to discern what these use values are, how they are realized, and for whose benefit, we must examine the actual nature and function of what students produce.

On one level, students produce lecture notes, written homework, test papers, and verbal performances. It is these that appear to lack use value, serving merely as the accepted currency of exchange for grades. What use values does this academic currency represent? Students' labor actually generates several different orders of products, and it is these other products whose use values are represented by the pieces of paper that students turn in for a grade. These other products include:

- *linguistic forms:* These include not only written texts and verbal performances, but also higher-level phenomena that persist over time, such as discourses and speech genres.
- *fluency in selected linguistic genres and styles:* Much schoolwork is assigned, not for its content *per se*, but to develop students' fluency in those registers (oral and written) associated with schooling. This fluency is a necessary component of the type of social subject schools aim to create.[25]
- *subject positions:* The production of certain subject positions, and students' interpellation into them, is part of the social reproduction of the "workers" themselves (in this case "transformation" might be more accurate, since the aim is to recreate students *not* exactly as they were before).
- *relations of production:* The first half of this chapter described certain dispositions toward teaching and learning that are embodied in the physical praxis of the classroom. Students' labor, in the way it is structured (with regard to classroom authority, speaking rights, control of content, etc.), continually reproduces the relations that govern it. In the case of teacher training, the relations produced are also reproduced later by graduating teachers with their own students.

• *ideologies:* All of the products mentioned above feed into the construction of ideologies around nationalism, ethnicity, class, gender, education, and language (outlined in the previous chapter), which are fundamental to the consolidation of state power.

Once we take into account the full range of what students produce, the question of use value springs into focus. The more tangible products of schoolwork may have little or no use in themselves, but this does not obviate the use values produced at other levels as a *result* of the production of schoolwork. Part of schoolwork's use value is realized in its consumption (that is, when assignments are turned in, read, and graded by the teacher), since this provides the basis for the system of evaluation in which students are caught like fish in a net. But *schoolwork's primary use value is realized in the process of its production, via the changes that the act of production works on the producers.* The production of schoolwork is in a sense a foil for the production of student-subjects. Within the realm of symbolic production, "the most important thing a worker ever produces is himself" (Williams 1980a:35). Thus, schoolwork's use value derives from its role in the production of discourses and subject positions and its positioning of students within them.

Clearly, language is central to this process, as the principal medium through which schools construct subjectivities and subjects interpret their experience. Language functions "to both position and constitute the way that teachers and students define, mediate, and understand their relation to each other and to the larger society" (Giroux 1988:99). It is language's power to define those who use it and their relation to their social environment that makes it a crucial site for the maintenance of hegemony. The value that students generate via their linguistic labor is the production of themselves as certain types of subjects; this is the use value that is exchanged for the comparable use value of academic credentials (which, in addition to providing a wage, also allow the subject to function in society in the manner for which he or she has been produced). Inside "the citizen factory," students are simultaneously producers and product.

If what we have described is in fact a "capitalist mode of production" in the realm of language, this assumes that surplus value is appropriated from students' labor and applied to the expansion of capital. The question of surplus value is closely linked to that of *commodification*. A thing becomes a commodity when its use value is transferred to another through exchange (Cap1:308); it is this surrender of control over the product's use value that implies its "alienation" from the producer (Ollman 1976:193). By exchanging their labor for grades, students transfer its use value to the institution. Their linguistic products serve them not as use values, but as exchange values. "In capitalism, no commodity is a use value for the workers who make it. A worker does not produce what he wants, but what will earn him sufficient money to buy what he wants . . . his product becomes a use value only after it is exchanged, and must contain such abstract and general labor as qualifies it for exchange" (183).

The tailoring of schoolwork to the use values desired by the institution, rather than to students' own aims, is evident from its abstract nature; assignments serve as exchangeable commodities first, and only secondarily as vehicles for intellectual growth. Since only the reified language typical of "school knowledge" is deemed acceptable for exchange, students' production is oriented to these specifications (and thus alienated from the students themselves) from the beginning. It is in this sense that the products of capitalism control their producers; if students controlled the use values produced by their labor, rather than having to trade them away for grades, these could be realized by and for students themselves and students' personal and local knowledge could be meaningfully integrated into their work. This would entail a very different set of subject positions than those that currently define students as producers of linguistic commodities and consumers of other people's knowledge.

Schoolwork, designed to satisfy institutional needs and solidified by tradition, eventually "attains an independent life," is "carried by a social dynamic of its own," and "takes on 'needs' which the individual is then forced to satisfy" (135). "In this situation, the very character of man is at the mercy of his products, of what they make him want and become in order to get what he wants" (146). In other words, the commodification of students' labor power positions them in certain relations to their products, to each other, to their teachers, and to the cultural capital for which they strive. These subject positions are "what they must become in order to get what they want";

the use value of their labor consists in their own interpellation, not only as ethnic, gendered, and national subjects, but also as subjects in particular relations of production.

Many things can be made into commodities, but it is the commodification of labor power, the transfer of its use value from those who labor to the owners of capital, that makes possible the appropriation of surplus value. This is because labor power is the only thing whose use value (labor) produces values greater than its own. In other words, labor's products have an exchange value greater than that of labor itself; it is this difference that is referred to as surplus value. To show that surplus value is extracted from students' labor, we need only show that the value of what they produce is greater than the "wages" for which their labor power is sold; this is evident from the state's continued willingness to engage in the academic exchange, to accept students' labor in exchange for a title, and indeed to enforce this relation by making schooling compulsory.

What value does the students' labor hold for the state? On one level, schooling's value to the state is economic in the traditional sense, in that it helps integrate rural dwellers' productive activity into the national economy (one of the original incentives for the expansion of rural education). It also serves as a necessary escape valve for class-based pressures and conflicts, by providing a certain degree of social mobility into which working-class aspirations can be channeled without threatening the overall social hierarchy. But given that schooling is organized around symbolic production, we should expect its value to derive primarily from the symbolic realm; and so it does, in the form of ideological support for the state and the accumulation/expansion of cultural capital. Students' accumulated labor fortifies cultural and academic capital and expands the national culture's sphere of influence, not only through the material expansion of the school system and its institutionalized practices, but also through the creation of subject positions and the interpellation of new subjects (children) into them. Indeed, Marx himself on one occasion defined "use values" as "*the reproduction of the individual* in certain definite relationships to his community."[26]

Schooling's ideological influence extends far beyond the walls of the school itself. Bourdieu (1984:23) argued that general dispositions toward "legitimate culture" are first acquired with respect to scholastically recognized knowledge and practices, and later applied to other areas of life as well. In Bolivia, the school is the primary disseminator of an ideology that defines "legitimate culture" as that emanating from the urban metropole. By expanding the reach of this cultural capital and making it the dominant criterion for the measurement of human worth, the school acts as a central organizing force in the consolidation of nationalist hegemony. The school's value to the state—value created by students' (and teachers') labor—thus lies in its function as the primary articulator of ideology for the majority of the population.[27] Not only does the school fill the demand for education, it does much to create that demand, establishing itself as the sole source of cultural capital for those who do not possess it by virtue of birth.[28] Since cultural capital is based on the values and practices of the already-dominant social sectors, the school provides key ideological support for the continuation and expansion of that dominance, by legitimizing and naturalizing what is, in reality, a very selective set of norms and practices. The school creates subject positions that coincide with certain interests of indigenous students and communities and articulates those interests with those of the state. It is in the expansion of cultural capital (via subjects' incorporation into the dominant ideology), and in the articulation of potentially oppositional elements toward dominant interests, that the state realizes its most significant profit from schooling. This is hegemony in action.

Implications of the Alienated Labor Model for Classroom Discourse

Having laid out a framework for the interpretation of micro-level school practices in terms of macro-level social processes, the question arises: What have we really achieved with this model? Is reading linguistic and pedagogical practice through the lens of Marx's labor theory of value merely a theoretical exercise, or does it reveal something new and significant about the nature of schooling and the role of academic discourse in the construction of identities and ideologies?

Ethnicity and nationalism are important issues in Bolivian public discourse. What does our analysis have to say to these issues? First of all, school is a central (if not *the* central) site in which such conflicts are played out. The fact that schools channel students' speech into alienating modes of expression, while suppressing nonalienating modes, means that *critical debate about ethnic, national, class, and gender identity is disallowed in the primary arena where such identities are formed.* If students' verbal expression were free to follow its own path and its own forms, school could be a place where identity is openly questioned and (at least in part) consciously constructed. Instead, students' speech is commodified in institutional forms for institutional ends, which take precedence over students' desire for critical dialogue. At least some students were aware of the school's potential in this regard, and frustrated over its failure to realize that potential:

José: I know all about that [discrimination among the girls]. It's terrible. Once I was talking to the *inspectora*, I said, "I'm from the country and those city girls think they're something special. I challenge them to a debate." A public debate, so I could ask them questions, openly. In the first place, "Where does your father come from?" And maybe she'll tell me that her father is from such-and-such a place, and her mother wears the *pollera*—so what does that make her? She's just the same peasant still! [laughter] . . . That's why I proposed a debate, but the *inspectora* told me no, "You just have to act with high morals." But what kind of morals are they going around with? To have it out face-to-face would have settled it for me. I have such a desire to clear these things up, but I can't do it all alone. It's hard.[29]

Schools' appropriation of students' linguistic labor constitutes, to borrow a phrase from Rossi-Landi (1983:155), "a tendency to take possession of them as *speakers*." Not only does this mean constructing students as certain *kinds* of speakers (defined by their mastery, or lack thereof, of the discourse styles the school demands), it also means that their discursive production is unavailable for their own ends. Issues of ethnicity and nationalism are clearly of concern to students, as their frustrated efforts at debate both in and out of the classroom reveal. A significant amount of (unalienated) classroom discourse no doubt would be dedicated to these issues, were it allowed. What prevents the school from being a space for open debate on questions of real concern to students is not a prohibition of such topics by teachers or administrators; no such prohibition was in evidence in the normal school, and teachers repeatedly expressed their desire for more critical class-room discourse. What prevents it is the school's organization of linguistic activity according to a particular mode of production. And, as Marx made clear, the influence of the mode of production extends far beyond the simple reproduction of material life:

> [The] mode of production must not be considered simply as being the reproduction of the physical existence of the individuals. Rather it is . . . a definite form of expressing their life, a definite *mode of life* on their part. As individuals express their life, so they are. What they are, therefore, coincides with their production, both with *what* they produce and with *how* they produce. The nature of individuals thus depends on the material conditions determining their condition. (GI:150; original emphasis)

This passage may seem to espouse a vulgar economism, but in fact it implies only what has been claimed thus far: that relations of production interpellate individuals as particular types of subjects, and that these subject positions are the building blocks of identity. While one's position in the productive process is not the only factor from which subjectivities are created, it is a crucial one. And with linguistic production, the effects are twofold: the relations under which students labor not only interpellate them as subjects within the productive process; they also severely limit their possibilities for addressing their own interpellation within *other* types of subject positions as well.

Hence the connection between "objective" and "subjective" alienation. The appropriation of students' linguistic labor prevents them from relating their productive activity to other areas of their life; that part of their identity that is defined through work/study is sealed off from those (previously existing) aspects of identity that they bring to the productive process. From here it is a small step to what is often referred to as "psychological" alienation. This compartmentalization of identity is a gradual process; part of the socialization involved in schooling is learning to accept the commodification of one's linguistic expression, indeed to view it as normal and natural. Not that all students do; many arrive at the normal school expecting to find an institution dedicated to their own professional and personal growth. Confronted with a regimen of academic production that divorces schoolwork from the areas of meaning most important to them, they are alienated in both the "economic" and the "psychological" sense. Their realization of the gap between their initial aspirations and the grind of meaningless assignments is often bitter:

José: When I came here . . . I thought it would be, that I'd be among students who were really good, better than me. I thought "I'm going to learn good things there, I'm going to gain more experience." But after I'd been here a few weeks, [I saw] there was no such thing . . . Next year I'd like to go somewhere else, where there are more qualified people; that way one also learns more . . . Here, we don't even want to go up in front of the class; we can't even read; we can't even look straight out at the other students . . . I thought it was going to be something different, that it would be demanding. But it's not, up until now, for me. I myself am disappointed with my grades, that I have good grades; sometimes it surprises me, because I'm not that great [a student], to have such excellent grades as I do.

AL: Since you arrived here, is the training more or less what you expected?

Sergio: No. They had always told me that the normal school was—really I've been quite disappointed . . . We ourselves cause people to look down on teachers. Because really, it should be, if they're going to graduate as teachers, they should graduate as *good* teachers. But, what do we see instead? Of those that entered in eighty-nine, not even one was held back. All of them are teachers now, but not many really know how to express themselves like teachers. And now the ones who came in ninety-one, it's the same thing . . . I had another idea of what the normal school would be like. More than anything I wanted them to prepare us scientifically much more. Pedagogically. That's what's needed. The professors who teach here also graduated from here—they were inculcated with the same methodologies, and now they do the same to us, but scientifically there's nothing. Nothing.

Several students expressed desires for a more demanding education, one that would be personally challenging and allow them to put more of themselves into their work. Of course, for every José or Sergio, there was another student who was reasonably content (if not particularly enthusiastic) with things as they were. But this is not surprising, given that students' earlier school experiences were generally even more restrictive and divorced from their personal concerns. By the time they reach adolescence, most have come to expect nothing more; the self-contained quality of school knowledge and the commodification of their own activity have become so routine as to be hardly worthy of comment—or of attempts at change when they themselves become teachers.

Complacency may also arise out of self-defense; a student who holds doggedly to a dialogic ideal of education is likely to experience such frustration as to make school life nearly unbearable. Others may deliberately enter a state of "suspended alienation"—like Mateo, who expressed near-total disgust with his normal school experience, but was determined to finish in order to satisfy his family. Until then, he recorded his complaints about the normal school and the educational system in general in a clandestine manuscript that he had vague plans for making public "someday."

One element has been left out of the preceding discussion (a casualty of polemics, perhaps): what students receive in return for their labor, *aside* from a title (and its implied wage). Students do receive some kind of training, though it may not be precisely the kind they were seeking. Aside from academic skills, they acquire new social skills: command of a set of middle-class practices and meanings that will serve as a passport to levels of the social hierachy that would otherwise be closed to them (though the levels accessed by virtue of rural normal school training are still fairly low on the status scale). These serve as markers of legitimacy precisely because they comprise the core meanings and practices of the dominant "national culture." This in itself does not make them antithetical to students' interests; some skills (literacy for example) are useful for a variety of ends and can be articulated to alternative or even oppositional ideologies. In general, though, it is hard to completely disarticulate such practices from the hegemony with which they are already permeated.

Some may argue that students acquire these meanings, skills, and practices only at the cost of those they had previously embraced (if these derive from a different cultural tradition; otherwise, schooling serves primarily to ratify them). Those cultural practices that challenge the dominant tradition may be deemed at worst vices, or at best, anachronisms—"elements of the past which have now to be discarded" (Williams 1977:116). Either way, the perceived conflict between traditions is a cause of social and personal tensions for many young Aymaras attempting to enter the professional world. In the drive for social mobility, individual and collective interests are pitted against each other; in achieving professional status, the Aymara individual gains personally and perhaps weakens the ethnic barriers that partly define the social hierarchy, but also reinforces that hierarchy by embracing its standards. Bourdieu (1984:147) calls this "the specific contradiction of the scholastic mode of reproduction . . . the opposition between the interests of the class which the educational system serves *statistically* and the interests of those class members whom it sacrifices."

This contradiction is reflected in teachers who can authoritatively laud *el hermano campesino* precisely because they have escaped such status themselves. Having exchanged indigenous identity for cultural legitimacy, they now possess the cultural capital enabling them to romanticize (or denigrate) subaltern traditions in class. For students, the contradiction is manifested in the ethnic antagonisms that simmer in the dormitories or the occasional protest sparked by a teachers' offhand comment. Having chosen the road of higher education, many students still find more meaning in the practices of their home culture (and in newer practices arising from both the alienation and the solidarity of school life) than in the meanings and rituals imposed on them by the school. Those students possessed of a more critical perspective—that is, those holding most strongly to utopian visions of what schooling *could* be— are often led by the perceived meaninglessness of their academic labors to a cynical or resigned attitude toward schooling as it actually is, until finally (in words ascribed to expatriate Bolivian teacher Jaime Escalante in the film *Stand and Deliver*), "they've lost confidence in the system they're now finally qualified to be a part of." However, disillusionment also can lead to demystification, resistance, and the development of critique.

The next chapter explores how students resist the commodi-fication of their linguistic production, evading, challenging, and burlesquing the productive apparatus in which they are embedded.

6

STUDENT RESISTANCE TO COMMODIFICATION AND ALIENATION: SILENCE, SATIRE, AND THE ACADEMIC BLACK MARKET

> *Conflicts of a social, economic, cultural, linguistic, racial, sexual, and political character are made and fought in history; they are also internalized in language and in consciousness and reconstructed from generation to generation.*
>
> —Catherine Walsh, *Pedagogy and the Struggle for Voice*

Resistance in the Classroom

Classroom Weapons of the Weak

One of the most useful analyses of student resistance to date is Willis's (1981a) study of a group of English working-class "lads" whose antischool values and practices ultimately reproduced structures of inequality by channeling students into menial jobs. While his insights have proved invaluable to the study of student culture, Willis did not address those issues of greatest importance to the normal school students: bilingualism, nationalism, colonialism, and the intersection of class with ethnicity and gender. Willis's lads displayed a well-defined, explicitly antischool subculture that generated a cohesive set of resistant values and practices while serving as the wellspring for working-class student identity. Though central to much recent school ethnography in the First World, oppositional student subcultures are rarer in more recently schooled

217

populations, such as indigenous groups in Latin America.[1] Thus, First World models of student resistance are not wholly adequate for analyzing schools in developing nations (cf. Levinson, Foley, and Holland 1996). The sort of antischool subculture examined by Willis and others was conspicuously absent from the normal school, where students seldom constituted "behavior problems." There was no group styling themselves the "bad boys" (or girls) of the school, opposing institutional norms at every turn; nor was there a vibrant antischool counterculture with its own set of stylistic markers and expressive practices to provide a basis for students' identities. In Bolivia, respect and courtesy toward teachers is a cultural standard that few students dare to (or care to) challenge; there, my tales of the combat-zone conditions and overt battles for dominance that frequently characterize teacher-student relations in the United States evoked expressions of amazement and dismay.

Still, the normal school students had their own ways of responding to the institutional constraints and daily injustices that defined their subordinate role within the school. Their covert and fragmentary resistance was far from the brazen insubordination of Willis's lads, Foley's *vatos*, or MacLeod's "Hallway Hangers." Their strategies were less constant and confrontational, more subtle and situational, akin to what Scott (1985) has described as "weapons of the weak": gossip, covert ridicule, foot dragging, dissimulation, petty acts of noncompliance. Given Scott's characterization of these as "everyday forms of peasant resistance," one might draw a connection between students' preference for such forms and their own predominantly peasant background. They also engaged in other tactics more particular to the student condition: cheating, plagiarism, truancy, tardiness, withholding of participation, appropriation of school ceremonies for satirical purposes, and the sorts of classroom diversionary tactics described by Foley (1990) as "making out games."

These strategies held the same advantages for the students as they did for Scott's Malaysian peasants. Both groups experienced conditions making organized or confrontational action unlikely: low prestige, lack of political legitimacy, the difficulty of coordinating mass actions in dispersed rural settings. In contrast, everyday resistance requires little coordination or planning; makes use of implicit understandings and informal networks; often takes the form of individual self-help; and typically avoids direct confrontation with authority (Scott 1985:xvi). It is also usually anonymous, an advantage for the relatively powerless when faced with opponents who control their livelihood or hold the power of decision over their future plans. In lieu of anonymity, resistance may masquerade as compliance, as in the ingratiating student ploy of asking trivial questions in order to divert the lesson from its intended course or score points with the teacher. In such cases, "it is almost as if symbolic compliance is maximized *precisely* in order to minimize compliance on the level of actual behavior" (Scott 1985:26). Actors may insinuate the insincerity of such performances, while maintaining the deniability of any grudging or ironic intent. Reluctant compliance, such as students' slowness to remove their caps in assembly or their "inability" to march in step, is "an intrusion, however slight, of 'offstage' attitudes into the performance itself, an intrusion sufficient to convey its meaning to the directors but not so egregious as to risk a confrontation" (26).

What these subtle forms of resistance share with more dramatic or overtly combative forms is the goal of mitigating or denying claims made by superiors, or advancing subordinates' claims vis-á-vis those superiors (32). They are often quite effective in this regard; without challenging the structures of subordination, they set the parameters within which such structures can operate and almost always result in significant material and/or symbolic gains for those involved (compare this to the more confrontational resistance of Willis's lads, which ultimately served to reinforce the structures of inequality in which they were trapped). Certainly these tactics allowed students to expend less time and effort and enjoy a greater degree of freedom than they would have otherwise. Added to this was the less tangible but no less significant gratification that comes from controlling one's own meanings and actions, at least in some limited, "offstage" domain.

The habits of gossip and covert ridicule generate benefits primarily in this latter realm, though they may also provide students with information helpful in "working the system." Students clearly found the sharing of rude nicknames, complaints, and rumors about staff an empowering experience and gained subversive pleasure from it.[2] Still, "the politics of reputation is . . . something of a one-sided affair" (24); those in power, though easy targets for gossip and backstage derision, seldom have to worry about what subordinates think of them, while for subordinates, remaining in the good graces of the powerful is often a material necessity. While students could deride faculty only behind their backs, teachers scolded students to their faces, secure in the knowledge that students could not break the mask of deference even to defend themselves.[3]

For a skilled speaker, however, this may prove as much an advantage as a disadvantage. One day, students wanted to suspend Native Languages class to rehearse for a school program. They had permission from the administration, but this had not been communicated to Professor Ramírez, who refused to let them go or to put off turning in their homework, claiming that they had no authority to suspend class without his permission. Roberto and Sergio objected so deferentially and yet so persistently, simultaneously appealing to the teacher's authority and refusing to yield to it, that he eventually had to send for the academic director, who settled the matter in favor of the students. Despite his apologies to Professor Ramírez, the incident constituted a significant loss of face.

The success of one resistant tactic often gives rise to others. When Professor Ramírez left the room to get the academic director, students rushed to enjoin their classmates not to turn in their homework, even if they had it ready. This effervescence of "resistant mutuality" (350) was heightened by one boy's writing on the board "NO, janiw churatati" (sic) Aymara for "You will not give it to him." The others, while amused by this subversive use of both Aymara (in Native Languages class, yet) and the official space of the blackboard, made him erase it before the teacher returned.

Another mark of everyday resistance is its "implicit disavowal of public and symbolic goals . . . The success of de facto resistance is often directly proportional to the symbolic conformity with which it is masked" (33). This is perhaps nowhere more true than in classroom "making out games" (Foley 1990), such as the asking of purposely irrelevant or diversionary questions in order to redirect the lesson to students' own ends (avoidance of the teacher's questions or relief of boredom) while giving an impression of heartfelt engagement. While students played this game only occasionally, it formed part of their tactical arsenal, and they had a fairly good sense of which teachers could be taken in by it (or at least would not get angry). Such gambits often seemed groaningly transparent, such as one boy's query during an agriculture lesson on the breeding of guinea pigs (offered immediately after the teacher announced that he was giving points for participation) as to whether guinea pigs could be washed; or the girl who asked, during a Hogar class on the disadvantages of May-December marriages, "What if the couple are the same age?" This tactic could also backfire if teachers were made oversensitive to it; when the agriculture teacher explained that guinea pigs can mate at six months, Sergio asked "What about afterwards?" at which point the teacher snapped, "I'm going to throw out anyone who kids around!" The city-bred Sergio's puzzled look, however (and the fact that he generally disdained such tactics), indicated that his question had been serious, despite the amusement it caused his rural classmates.

These subtle tactics were complemented by the more obvious breakdowns in order commonly known as "goofing off." While the normal school students did not engage in boisterous classroom behavior nearly as often as the typical North American high school class, it did erupt from time to time. Students would take advantage of the teacher's inattention to throw things at one another, steal each other's notebooks or pencils, or jerk each other's chairs as if to cause a fall. Most often it was the boys who indulged in such antics, while the girls watched amid smothered giggles. Everhart (1983:176) claims, rather abstrusely, that "goofing off resembles a shared speech community wherein collective interpretations of the relationship of the student to the productive process demanded by the school gives rise to collective actions." Simply put, students become bored with the production of knowledge they deem irrelevant to their interests and join together to appropriate a margin of class time to their own purposes. "Goofing off" is not always collective (though its most conspicuous forms are); for example, the girls would often take out their knitting during a slow lesson and knit with their hands hidden under their desks. Aymara women typically carry their knitting with them so as to have something to do during spare moments or periods of waiting; the fact that the girls knitted during class was a clear indication of how they perceived their time there.

Different forms of labor generate different forms of resistance, such as the logical penchant of wage workers for slowdowns and of piece workers for shortweighting (Scott 1985:34). Schoolwork also generates its own forms of "counterappropriation," many of which are based on language. "Making out games" and the empty rhetoric of student presentations fulfill the formal requirements of linguistic production without the substantive work, like a craftsman who uses a well-made casing to hide the shoddy workmanship inside. The dawdling and delaying tactics typical of class presentations are comparable to the factory slowdown, filling time with a minimum of labor expended. Such tactics can be traced to the commodification of students' linguistic production; they aim to minimize the amount of labor expended in class, either by offering insubstantial products, substituting another's production for one's own, or withholding participation altogether.

Silence as Resistance and Oppression

The most elemental form of student resistance is simple withdrawal from the academic exchange. This may take the form of truancy or desertion; in the normal school, students simply abstained from participating in class. By refusing to offer opinions or respond to questions, they limited their labors to a bare minimum, maintaining a demeanor of docility while holding themselves aloof from officially sanctioned activity and any show of enthusiasm for it.[4] McNeil (1986:160–61) views such reticence as a reaction to apathetic or controlling teaching styles; students "sense when the teachers take the work seriously," and respond to minimal teaching with minimal effort of their own. In the normal school, however, most students used this tactic more or less indiscriminately. Some teachers were more skilled than others at drawing out resistant students, but the resistance itself did not appear to be linked to a particular teacher or teaching style.

Walsh (1991:141), in contrast, views such resistance rather as a symptom of students' position within classroom power relations: "The condition of silence does not necessarily imply a lack of voice, identity, or an inability to express. People who are subordinated because of who they are within particular power arrangements sometimes choose not to speak, not to open themselves up or reveal their perspectives and thoughts to those who are differentially positioned." While this view better accounts for students' behavior, to read students' silence as a "choice"—"an active, momentary (and safe) response to oppressive conditions" (141)—seems overly optimistic with regard to its empowering potential.[5] Most of those who took this route seemed motivated less by indignation over classroom oppression than by paralyzing fear. More accurate is Walsh's description of students' silence as "a conscious and/or unconscious decision not to risk self-disclosure" (114). Class participation entails not only labor, but risk; and while this risk may derive from the alienating productive relations of the classroom, it is self-disclosure, rather than expenditure of effort, that is foremost in the minds of students who refuse to speak.

Silence was a distinctively female strategy, typical of rural girls from remote communities. Their refusal to respond to teachers' questions puzzled me at first, since they clearly often knew the answer. Occasionally, I would hear a hapless student whisper the answer to a friend after the teacher had given up and directed his attention elsewhere. It was hard to believe that giving a response, *any* response, could be more nerve-wracking than having the whole class's attention focused upon oneself, waiting, for what seemed like excruciatingly long periods. The rural girls' silence was usually ascribed to their difficulty in speaking correct Spanish and their fear of being laughed at by their classmates or corrected by the teacher.[6] Hill (1987:121) notes that women seem to be more sensitive to elite norms and to the stigmatization of vernacular speech than men, and this seemed to hold true in the normal school. Mention of students' shyness in class inevitably provoked references to their difficulties in speaking Spanish, and several girls described to me the fear of becoming the object of (to borrow a phrase from Oliart [1991]), *"la burla represiva":*[7]

Clara: If a girl participates, she might not say something right, and then the others laugh. Or she think she's going to say something wrong . . . Mostly that happens with the girls from the provinces, those who are more introverted. They don't participate, they're always afraid because they think they're going to talk wrong . . . even when they have the answer . . . It makes them afraid someone will say something, or laugh, and then the others get afraid.

Students, and many professors as well, spoke a dialect of Spanish that displayed noticeable influence from Aymara. Among rural students, this influence was often quite marked, especially in the confusion of Spanish vowels i/e and o/u and the lack of number and gender agreement. For some, addressing the class was equivalent to running a linguistic gauntlet, in which the inevitable stumble would bring down the ridicule of their classmates, or so they feared.[8] Lack of Spanish fluency was not students' only cause of difficulty; some whose speech was close to standard were also hesitant to speak before the class, due to uncertainty, disinterest, or simple stage fright. But with the urban girls and the boys, a teacher willing to wait, scold, or cajole could usually get some response, however minimal. With the rural girls, such efforts were often fruitless; faced with their chagrined yet stubborn silence, the teacher could only give up and move on to someone else.

In an investigative "Catch-22," those students who had the most difficulty speaking in class were, predictably, the least willing to be interviewed. Diana was an exception; generally quiet in class (making her outburst to the Agriculture teacher all the more surprising), she was affectionate and outgoing outside of it, though she harbored a bitter resentment against what she perceived as discrimination by some of the city girls. When she consented to be interviewed on tape, she began with a characteristically demure disclaimer:

Diana: I don't know how to talk at all. [soft laughter]
AL: Sure you do.
Diana: I don't know anything.
AL: I'll help you.
Diana: I won't make a peep.

Once begun, however, she spoke fluidly and earnestly of the frustration she and her peers felt in the classroom and the self-consciousness they suffered because of their nonstandard Spanish:

We always make mistakes, we're always lacking something; when we go up front to speak, we don't know how to express ourselves. Some words we don't understand. For the city girls it's easy—in the city there's television, there's radio, there's everything, right? They go to the movies and all, and in the country all that doesn't exist. We only have the radio; sometimes there isn't even electricity. They know how to talk perfectly, and so because of that, they can say about us, "Those girls don't know anything."

Students' silence came up often in my talks with teachers, provoking dispirited speculations as to its cause. Several blamed the rural family for providing an inadequate communicative environment for the child. This explanation was supported by many rural students themselves, some of whom felt their upbringing to be a cause of later difficulties. Rather than to cultural or linguistic deficiencies in the home, rural students' shyness might be ascribed to the relative isolation in which many of them grow up; occupied with field and household chores from an early age, they spend much more time alone than their urban peers. While Andean child-rearing has rarely been studied, popular opinion and anecdotal evidence point to a more authoritarian parental relationship than is the norm in the city; "baby talk" and nonessential conversation with children are less frequent than in urban homes, and children are expected to act independently from quite a young age.

Mateo: In high school I was real shy. My mother gave me that complex. Because, I was the only son and my mother, she kept a few sheep, and she'd tell me, "Go take the sheep out to pasture." She didn't let me go out with my friends. I was always doing chores . . . I never learned to open up, with other kids at my level.

Nicolás: That comes from the family itself. They're introverted, they don't have that direct communication with their parents or their siblings. We're a bit reserved . . . There isn't that interrelation that should exist, in the communication between parent and child; to talk with more confidence, about things that are a bit more intimate . . . So of course, when they come here they're thrown together with lots of people from other places, it's a little difficult.

Many saw their early school experiences as another source of verbal hesitancy. Some students and teachers recalled the regimented pedagogical techniques of primary school and viewed student passivity as a holdover from these earlier patterns. Others, however, saw students' reticence not simply as the result of earlier conditioning, but as a logical response to their current environment. Remedios had a broader range of educational experience than most students and tended to be highly critical of the institution and its staff. Having studied under more dialogic conditions elsewhere, her standards of what a classroom should be were considerably higher than those of students whose experience was limited to the Bolivian public schools:

Remedios: Most of the girls come from the country; they've never known that total instruction, since high school. They've always been treated with a certain indifference, and here, they're shown the same thing. The teachers treat them differently from the boys. That way, they're killing them; they'll never give their opinion, they'll never say what they think or feel . . . The teacher has to make the class active, with questions, no? Asking randomly, "You, you," and I know they would talk. But we don't have that in class. Instead, they stuff us with theory, theory, and more theory . . . lots of dictation. How are we going to learn to express ourselves with the method by which they teach us?

Another factor was the girls' self-consciousness in front of their male classmates, exacerbated by the boys' mockery of the embarrassed fidgeting and giggling that some girls displayed when called upon to speak. This self-consciousness has been noted in other educational settings as well, causing researchers to observe that co-education has its price as well as its advantages and that the advantages are often unevenly distributed by gender.[9] In her study of the academic and social outcomes of co-ed schooling in Peru, Violeta Sara-Lafosse (1992:92) observed: "Boys who study with girls participate to a greater extent than those who attend schools for boys only. The presence of female schoolmates encourages them to participate to a greater extent. In the case of women, coeducation has a polarizing effect, producing both high levels and low levels of participation—the presence of men stimulates the participation of some girls, but discourages the participation of others."

Sara-Lafosse also mentions the importance of "family conditioning" to female participation. Notably, the few girls who *were* assertive in class had mostly grown up in mining communities (renowned in Bolivia for their rhetorical fortitude and academic seriousness). They were also likely to be older (in their early to mid-twenties), and a few were already wives and mothers. While some of the city girls were similarly outspoken, many of them shared their rural classmates' timidity (though usually to a milder degree). Along with "family conditioning," it would seem that cultural and community conditioning also contribute to students' relative reticence or expressiveness.

Work experience was another important factor, especially in students' learning to overcome their shyness. Several boys confessed that they too had suffered from such self-consciousness, but had conquered their fear through exposure to the world of work or military service.

Faustino: Last year when I was in high school, I used to be afraid. Now when I don't know something, I say so . . . but when I used to go to the front of the class—Shit, everyone's looking at me [intake of breath, mock shivers], yow! Even knowing the answer, you lose the thread. But I learned, from being in the city, in the *cuartel*; now it's just normal . . . I got over that . . . sharing with my friends, talking, discussing things, there's that advantage in the dorm also.

Mateo: I overcame it thanks to work . . . leaving home, getting over my shyness, relating to other people, exchanging ideas, like I do with you . . . That way, bit by bit, I lost it.

Two of the more outspoken female students also cited organizational and work experience as factors contributing to their assertiveness:

Juana: I've always gotten involved in things, serving as recording secretary, or getting involved in the leadership. For example, in the countryside there was a mothers' club. I was the leader . . . I'd go to the federations, to meetings and such. And there I'd listen and think, speak, express myself. Whether well or poorly, but I'd talk . . . I see people, and I say to myself, "They're human, too, like me. I can talk, too, maybe better than them."

Antonia: I used to be like that, fearful. In high school when I was [interim] teaching, I used to be afraid, it gave me the shivers something awful! . . . I didn't know what to do . . . I had to beg another teacher to make the students line up for me. I'd say, "Please Professor, make them line up." And he wouldn't want to. Well, I had to make them line up myself. From that I learned, but it really cost me.

Most rural girls do not have access to such experiences, nor to the formative influence of military service, which also hones boys' verbal skills. The *cuartel* is far from a dialogic teaching environment, but recruits do gain a measure of maturity and self-confidence, learning to tolerate situations and fulfill demands not to their liking. When a recruit is questioned by a superior, hanging his head in bashful silence is not acceptable, and he learns this forcefully if necessary. While this may be comparable to learning to swim by being thrown into deep water, such training carries advantages that extend beyond the military environment. It is hard to imagine a graduate of the *cuartel* suffering the kind of timidity that Remedios describes:

Remedios: It comes from the yelling, from the treatment by the professors . . . The yelling makes one frightened. The girls think that if they comment in class, they'll be yelled at, and that will be hard on them, no? Supposedly, they're training us to be teachers, to have a profession, but for me they're doing something bad more than anything, some professors, with their way of treating us. They're creating a fearfulness inside us. They're killing us psychologically, by treating us badly. That's why the girls don't say much, for fear they'll get yelled at, or that their opinion will be rejected. That's why they don't talk. I know that those girls could get a good grade on a written exam, better grades than me. Because, inside themselves, they have thoughts, who knows, better than mine. They just can't express them outwardly, for fear of being rejected, of being yelled at . . . The boys, whether they speak well or poorly, are always going to come out ahead. If the teacher yells at them, it just rolls off their backs. While if he yells at the girls, we feel bad. We're like, crestfallen, maybe humiliated, you know? It's the *machismo*.

As Remedios's reference to *machismo* suggests, sexism in many forms contributes to girls being less outspoken than boys. As small children, Aymara girls are apt to spend their nonschool hours inside the home, occupied with domestic chores, rather than forming large play groups with a wealth of challenging social situations, as boys do. In grade school, girls have few opportunities to speak; many become retiring and passive, their early exuberance receding ever further into the past. Boys, on the other hand, go through school acquiring new verbal skills, until by high school they dominate classroom activity almost entirely. Aymara women tend to have less contact with the *mestizo* world than do men and are more likely to speak with an accent, making them self-conscious in situations where standard Spanish is called for. Even in situations where Aymara is used, it is rare for women to address a gathering or publicly call attention to their own speech (Luykx 1989b). Male and female students thus enter the normal school under different conditions. Boys have had their linguistic trial by fire, so to speak, before arriving, whereas the verbal participation demanded of the girls is, for them, unprecedented. For the boys, class participation is simply one more step in a process that has developed over years; for the girls, it is a social and linguistic challenge for which many are almost totally unprepared.

Also telling is Remedios's mention of boys' ability to win teacher approval whether they spoke well or poorly. Almost always, boys *would speak*, coherently or not, when called upon, whereas girls were more likely to freeze when they did not know the answer (and often even if they did). Some boys were especially adept in a certain speech style that involved talking *around* a topic, using key words and phrases, and creating an illusion of mastery while having only a vague idea of what one was talking about. While such performances were often woefully transparent, most teachers seemed, not dismayed by this, but satisfied that the student had fulfilled his discursive obligations. Sergio casually elucidated this strategy and noted the girls' lack of proficiency at it:

Sergio: When you don't know something really basic, you discuss it with phrases, as long as you talk a lot about it, right? You saw it when I was talking [in class]; for almost eight minutes, with no content really, I'm simply going round and round, and just at the end I'll focus on the central point . . . You could count on one hand the guys that really participate, who talk, knowing what they're talking about. There are a lot who stand out, simply by talking loud, but really they don't have that knowledge in their head, to defend something, to explain the plan of why, how, the specific forms, all that . . . The girls mostly just isolate themselves. They don't have the knowledge, and so with a few words they try to finish, and the professor doesn't correct them.

Such performances, if not always convincing, came closer to meeting teachers' expectations than did the girls' retreat into silence.[10] Much of formal schooling consists of achieving competency in a particular set of speech styles; students are praised for successful display of the required style, often regardless of actual content. Cazden (1988:184) refers to these "special forms of student language" as "not how students do talk, but how some teachers seem to want them to talk," and notes that "to the extent that a special register is expected but not explicitly taught, it forms part of the hidden curriculum of the entire school day."

Within the social distribution of speech styles in the *altiplano*,[11] prestigious styles such as academic speech are viewed as more "natural" to males than to females. Putting boys and girls in the same classroom does not seem to amend this discrepancy, and may even exacerbate it. If co-education is to have real impact, it must be all-encompassing, without sex-segregated activities or courses of study (Sara-Lafosse 1992:95). In order to be truly egalitarian, this would also have to include school living conditions, social norms, and teacher expectations; co-ed classrooms are clearly insufficient when boys and girls are subject to different standards of control and socialized to sharply contrasting social roles. The strategies employed by male and female students and their different degrees of engagement with school discourse indicate that co-education in Bolivia still has far to go. Still, both of the strategies described above can be read as evidence of students' alienation: in their adept use of an empty phraseology, boys demonstrate their skill at "working" the system that commodifies their linguistic production; girls forego the greater academic rewards such exposure might bring, instead conceding only the minimum effort necessary to get by.

We have seen that rural girls' shame over their imperfect Spanish is a major reason for their silence. Fiske (1989:64) claims that embarrassment is a key form of popular pleasure; still, embarrassment among peers is one thing, mortification in front of one's social superiors and rivals another. While it may provoke playful or silly behavior—like that of two girls who, after a group presentation in which they did not talk at all, went back to their seats and started slapping at each other—this is less evident of pleasure than of tension after a failed performance. One student's embarrassment may be pleasurable for his or her classmates, however. Students regularly laughed at their classmates' more serendipitous verbal errors, and the boys often amused themselves by trying to make presenters laugh or falter with comic grimaces and gestures out of the teacher's range of vision. Such behavior, like Foley's "making out games" and other classroom shenanigans, subverts the official purposes of the lesson; student presentations become occasions for entertainment and escape from the academic regimen, without ever leaving the confines of the classroom. Like the "factory games and status play" characteristic of wage workers (Berger 1968:206), such "goofing off" is an index of students' alienation from the official purposes and expressive modes of the classroom; the class, like the shop floor, is momentarily transformed from a site of coerced labor to one of vernacular cultural pleasures (cf. Willis 1981a:53–56).

While the burlesqueing of classroom activity may have a solidary function, the silence of the girls was less an expression of solidarity than a defensive reaction to the threat of ridicule. Even if students' reticence is linked to the alienation of school discourse, they themselves may not see this as their primary reason for abstaining, or consider their silence a form of resistance against the school. Claims that such behavior points to a nascent student-class consciousness, or that students resist teachers' efforts to make them participate because this "would be tantamount to admitting that the reified knowledge of the school was legitimate—that they could accept selling their labor power and produce products that had primarily an exchange-value" (Everhart 1983:115) substitute the researcher's reasoning for students' own. As Piven and Cloward note, "People experience deprivation and oppression within a concrete setting, not as the end product of large and abstract processes . . . Workers experience the factory, the speeding rhythm of the assembly line, the foremen, the spies, the guards, the owner, and the pay check. They do not experience monopoly capitalism."[12]

Students experience not the hegemony of reified knowledge or the commodification of their linguistic production, but rather the frustration of incomprehension, the shame of a disparaged accent, and the fear of their classmates' ridicule. As a product of these experiences, their silence—resistant though it may be— is a resistance born not of solidarity but of isolation. The threat of ridicule may be more perceived than real, but that perception arises from a long history of very real discrimination. Even if linguistic lapses do not produce instant derision in the classroom, their repercussions may be felt later in the girls' dormitory, where the barbs of prejudice fly more freely. This may be partly what students mean when they express the fear that others will "laugh at them"; girls who are already self-conscious about projecting a provincial image do not want to reinforce that image, or give their potential tormentors any more ammunition. The boys, having eliminated or suppressed such conflicts in their dormitory, have less reason to fear speaking out in class.

Though lack of Spanish fluency was a key factor in students' silence, it would be a mistake to explain their reticence solely in terms of "linguistic competence." Issues of power and prestige also affect speakers' verbal production, though the results may mimic the effects of technical deficiency. Walsh (1991:38) criticizes the Chomskyan notion that competence determines performance, as ignoring the impact of speakers' sociocultural reality on speech behavior. She argues for a more Bakhtinian view, claiming that distinctions of competence/performance or *langue/parole* are illusory and "negate the inherently social reality of language as communication" (40).[13] Bourdieu (1984:40) claims that "technical competence is to social competence what the capacity to speak is to the right to speak, simultaneously a precondition and an effect," and notes that "women differ from men not so much in strict technical competence as in their manner of affirming it."

The forms of competence expected of and allowed women are quite different from those expected of and allowed men. Students' classroom strategies indicate that the gender gap in social competence is at least as significant as the difference in technical competence. The difference stems in part from each group's perception of their speaking rights. Teachers would likely assert that all students have an equal right to speak in class; but the distance between theory and practice may be considerable. Indeed, egalitarian "norms" may be less a reflection of actual usage, than of the official denial of power relations in discourse.[14] We must examine not only the dominant definition of speaking rights, but also how these are perceived by those who do not exercise them.

Part of institutional life is learning one's speaking rights and restrictions. Transmission of these rights and restrictions accompanies the teaching of virtually all academic material; they are suffused throughout the entire school day. The discrepancy in how male and female students exercise their speaking rights indicates that each is socialized to a different set of rules regarding the appropriateness and value of their speech; this is also evident from the normal school's restriction of most public speaking roles to males. School research has focused more on literacy skills and verbal fluency, neglecting students' perceptions of their speaking rights and the ways in which they learn the various sanctions on women's speech (Kramarae 1981:83). Without claiming that girls experience such sanctions for the first time upon entering school,[15] the school is undoubtedly a key site for refining, expanding, and reinforcing them. Even within the school, staff are not the only transmitters of sanctions on the speech of certain groups; one's peers often play this role as well, as interactions between male and female, urban and rural students have shown.

Aside from the silencing effect of classmates' real or potential ridicule, the lack of authority of the female voice is an important factor. In school ceremonies, speaking roles intended to evoke respect or solemnity were given to boys. On the rare occasion that a girl led the morning assembly, she usually had difficulty maintaining order. Many girls seemed to concede the lack of authority of their own voices, and were typically inaudible when a teacher managed to coax them into responding. Occasionally, a girl's volunteered answer would be ignored by the teacher, only to be acknowledged when offered later by a boy. Teachers often told their classes that "the *señoritas* need to work on developing a good speaking voice." It would seem that, in a variety of situations, the voices of female students were ignored or denigrated even when they did choose to speak.[16]

National Reality Class, November 29, 1991. The professor discusses grades; many students are missing their makeup exams. Paco suggests that, instead of a written test, each student give an oral expositon in front of the class. It will help them gain experience and lose their fear of speaking, he argues, while showing their knowledge of the material as well as a written exam would. Pía mutters, "Shut up" under her breath as José and another boy express support for the idea. The teacher asks if there are any other opinions; the girls stare blankly or look down at their desks. The motion passes.

Silence, School Knowledge, and Classroom Praxis

Despite the predominance of nondialogic classroom techniques, the lack of class participation was a matter of concern to several professors. While a few resorted to sarcasm or ridicule when faced with students' refusal to speak, others made frequent entreaties for discussion, at times practically pleading with students to participate. Several utilized the technique known as "Philips-66," in which students formed groups of six, took six minutes to discuss a given topic, and then presented their conclusions. The aim was to foster small group discussion and then general participation, but the results were predictable and consistent: one or two boys per group dominated both the group work and the presentation of conclusions, so that class discussion usually consisted mostly, if not solely, of six or seven boys. Students were well aware that this technique did little to include the rest of the class:

Remedios: It has a positive and a negative side. Positive, because there's participation by the students. Negative, because there's participation, but not by everybody. They always choose a leader of the group, and it's him who talks most. And so it ends up the same.

Faustino: The teacher tells a group to present a topic, and just the one who knows talks; he gets up and speaks for the whole group, but the others don't speak at all. I'd say that each one should do his own work, and from his own work defend what he's done, individually.

Ironically, one reason for the dearth of female participation stemmed from teachers' attempts to make the process more egalitarian. When told to form groups of six, the girls often formed single-sex groups, but the teachers invariably broke these up and made students work in mixed groups, feeling that this was more in line with the progressive ideals of co-education. As a result, every group had at least one boy, and girls who otherwise would have had to participate deferred to his leadership and became passive pseudo-participants. Despite lackluster results, Philips-66 was the principal technique teachers used to increase student participation. It did create some semblance of class discussion, but it did not effectively increase most students' engagement with the material, nor did it address the overwhelming predominance of males in classroom discourse. In a system built upon the assumption that students are consumers rather than producers of knowledge, teachers cannot expect to reverse this principle instantaneously simply by making students work in groups.

Another technique for fostering discussion was the "round table," in which students moved their desks into a circle and individual comments were solicited; but this was not very conducive to female participation either. A breakdown of male and female speech in one such class revealed that the former surpassed the latter by a 3:1 ratio, both in number of speaking turns and total speaking time; boys' average turn length was also greater than that of girls. Furthermore, the bulk of female participation was due to a single student: Verna, a slightly older mother of two, who hailed from a mining community and was an exceptionally serious, intelligent, and articulate student. She alone accounted for half of female students' speaking turns and over two-thirds of their speaking time. If her participation is factored out, that of the other female students appears even more dismal.

With regard to Sara-Lafosse's (1992:91) four indicators of student participation—asking questions in class, expressing ideas in class, speaking in public meetings, and protesting against injustices—male students ovewhelmingly dominated the first three categories. Female students were somewhat more likely to register protests (such as complaints about deadlines or amount of work) than to speak in meetings or class discussions, perhaps because such protests did not require the formal academic speech used in other contexts. Contexts in which girls actively participated tended to be those in which (1) "school knowledge" did not predominate, (2) they had both a direct interest and relevant knowledge, and (3) "correct" Spanish was not required. For example, girls sat passively during one student meeting until the topic of levying a fee for a class project came up; they then became suddenly animated, eager to have a say in how much money they would pay and how it would be spent. Similarly, when class time was set aside to decide what dances would be performed in upcoming school programs, girls were active participants (though seldom leaders) in the discussion. Clearly, they were capable of expressing their opinions under certain circumstances.

Native Languages class was another "special case" with regard to students' verbal expression. Though participation was limited here as well, students did derive a semisubversive pleasure from speaking Aymara in the classroom and having their own linguistic knowledge raised to the level of academic knowledge (though it was also often criticized as "incorrect"). Like Hogar, which also drew on students' knowledge, Native Languages class had a higher degree of participation, by female as well as male students, than almost any other. Professor Ramírez did not have an exceptional rapport with students, but there was more laughter in his class than most—not the derisive laughter that pitted students against each other, but the solidary humor of shared meaning. His Aymara examples often provoked a ripple of student chatter, also in Aymara. When he told students they would be using more Aymara in class, one boy joked, "Morning assembly in Aymara!" Students who responded in Spanish when questioned were teased good-naturedly and told to speak Aymara. After a long school career of being told to do the opposite, many students found Native Languages class an empowering experience, despite its significant limitations.

What the above situations share is a temporary blurring of the enforced dichotomy between students' own knowledge and "school knowledge." José described this dichotomy—and students' attempts to bridge it—in the realm of language:

José: If we don't learn many new terms, scientific terms, we won't be able to express ourselves. One has to know lots of terms in Spanish that are sometimes hard to interpret ... What we speak is common speech for common folk, but others, professionals, use strange words, and one is taken aback. If you don't know what they mean, you're lost. But one who has more or less of an idea, in what moment to use that word—he interprets it: "Aah, that's what it means. It's used in this place so it means that, let's see." But if he's not interested, he just goes on the same. It's the same when someone's talking. In books too, there are words that are so unfamiliar, and one doesn't know, one can't interpret.

Most of the students who had more confidence and skill at navigating unfamiliar linguistic territory were those with a broader range of life experience. Several male students had worked or traveled for a few years before entering the normal school. Female student leaders were almost all married (some with children) or had worked outside the home. Clearly, students' behavior and attitudes were mediated, not only by the texts and discourses offered them by the school, but also by their previous life experiences and opportunities for social participation in different contexts.

Viewing students as the raw materials in a productive process intended to transform them into citizens, we might say that much of schooling is devoted to replacing those cultural adherences that stand in the way of "nationalization" with others more conducive to the consolidation of nationalist ideology. However, while the stripping away of previous loyalties targets all students more or less equally, the process of constructing new ones targets mainly males. Certainly this is so with regard to developing socially valued linguistic skills and constructing an "academic" voice to replace the Aymara one, considered unfit for both academic and nationalist purposes. As a result, rural female students, muted in their capacity as indigenous subjects and marginalized as academic subjects, take refuge in that most elemental form of resistance: silence.

Cheating

Cheating reflects the centrality of copying and memorization to Bolivian schooling. It was common practice in the normal school, mainly via the use of crib notes and covert collaboration between students. This was defined as illicit only during tests; on other assignments, verbatim copying from books or notes and collaboration between students was allowed, even encouraged. But at exam time, copying left off and memorization took over—or was supposed to. Often copying remained an important resource, depending on the student's level of resourcefulness.

Cheating seemed more common among the girls, but it may simply be that they more readily admitted it, or that the forms they practiced were more visible. While students of both sexes practiced solitary cheating (use of crib notes), whispering answers from friend to friend was a highly valued social activity among the girls. The illicit collusion and the excitement of evading detection forged bonds among students; helping another cheat was a hallmark of friendship and trust. As they got to know me better, students would half-jokingly whisper entreaties for my help during tests, and eventually cheated in front of me without fear of disclosure, reinforcing my stance as one aligned with students rather than with faculty. Crib notes did not fulfill the social functions that collaboration on tests did, but were a significant part of students' material culture. The skill and effort with which they fashioned their illicit aids were often comparable to that which might have enabled them to pass tests honestly. Professor Torres described their techniques with grudging admiration:

Professor Torres: There are many strategies . . . They put the test on top of their notebooks and in between they put the cheat sheet . . . There are also crib notes in miniature, folded up like an accordion, in one hand. They go along moving it with their fingers, that's one technique. Another would be, the girls leave their purses or baskets at their side, and inside the basket, they open their notebooks. The teacher can't go look inside; he's controlling things from afar, so they open the notebook inside the bag and cheat from there too. The teacher has to be very keen to detect those cases . . . Here they use a pen. They take the cartridge out, and inside they put a little piece of paper . . . [laughing] They're very ingenious really, very ingenious.

While the main goal of solitary cheating was improving one's grade, with collaborative cheating the social benefits rivaled the academic ones. Mutual cheating was less likely to "pay off" academically, since those who practiced it were usually partners in ignorance rather than serious schemers. It often served as a sort of private "making out game," making exams easier and more enjoyable. For students as for factory workers, illicit alliances and shortcuts not only minimize the amount of labor expended, but also relieve boredom and subvert the work situation to other ends. Ultimately, they may generate more nonmaterial than material gains (Foley 1990:112), in terms of personal satisfaction, group solidarity, and the preservation of a space for oppositional practice.

Cheating was seldom addressed openly by teachers, but one (who was new to the school) did bring up the topic with his class. Declaring himself "an enemy of those who cheat," he complained that students judged professors by the degree to which they "collaborated" with students in fixing grades, and looked down on the few truly demanding teachers. Alluding to rumors of students buying tests from teachers and selling them to their classmates, he exhorted those who observed such "anomalies" to investigate and report them. His statements provoked an unusually active response from the class, who alternately disputed them, mentioned those cases they knew of, and speculated on the causes (mostly blaming the previous year's teacher). Such openness about school practices was rare, but it is doubtful whether it had much effect on the level of cheating, or whether the teacher's efforts to enlist student aid in rooting out perpetrators were successful.

Berger (1968:206) mentions two common responses to alienation in work: the invention of "factory games and status play," and the withdrawal of emotion. In cheating, both factors are present. While some forms are more akin to boredom-relieving "games" or the acting out of social bonds, others manifest students' withdrawal from the official goals of the class. This was partly due to students' feeling that teachers' demands were unfair; if academic requirements are not seen as legitimate, neither do the means of fulfilling them have to be. Much cheating arose from the frustration and despair of being unable to understand (or at least memorize) the material. For a student in the throes of a test, the immediate goal is to pass, and cheating may be the easiest and surest way.

Norman Keill (1964:828), in a wide-ranging, cross-cultural survey of adolescence, notes that the most common reason for cheating is that "the pressure to succeed, reinforced by the fear of failure, overwhelms considerations of honor." Philip E. Jacobs[17] found the principal causes of cheating among U.S. college students to be overemphasis on grade-examination procedures and a widespread tradition of student tolerance toward the practice. These were important factors in the normal school as well, but a deeper motive is hinted at in Keill's observation that educational skills should enable students to deal with "the realities of life" (828). Part of schoolwork's alienation is, precisely, its estrangement from what students consider "real life." If school knowledge is seen as devoid of practical value, existing mainly for the purpose of being reproduced on tests, students have little incentive not to pass by any means they can. José saw this lack of personal investment in one's work, combined with factors such as the lack of texts, as contributing to an epidemic of copying:

José: One doesn't want to go beyond what's necessary. There isn't that individual sacrifice ... One gets an assignment, something to be researched; he'll have photocopies from last year, his uncles or brothers are teachers, so he takes it, and redoes it, and lends it. It makes the rounds here, there, all over the school! . . . There aren't books, either; where are we going to research it? . . . If someone finds one book, it gets passed all around the school.

While many students who did not habitually cheat found the practice offensive, Juana offered another interpretation, interesting for its relevance to the relation between school practices and ethnic identity. Juana was a forceful defender of the rural girls and of her own Aymara identity, and viewed cheating as merely the natural result of comradeship and indigenous logic:

Juana: It's cooperativism; that is, there's a certain comradeship among students. Like before, there were the original ways, the *ayni, aynuqa, mink'a* [traditional Aymara forms of collective labor], all those things. So now, of course they haven't been totally forgotten . . . Because of friendship, they help each other. The girls, boys too, they work as a unit, they collaborate.

José, on the other hand, whose background was even more firmly rooted in rural Aymara culture than was Juana's (who was from a mining area), reacted scornfully to such reasoning:

José: No, I think she's wrong in that. That's with regard to the economy, to agricultural production—there you do have that; there it's practiced. But in an academic institution, one is there to excel, to better oneself, there can't be that stuff. On exams, you're testing your own capacity, individually. There it can't be cooperative! Sure, you can say, "How nice," certainly we have to valorize the cooperation among *campesinos*, like among brothers, with mutual help, in farm production, in work, yes. But here, studying, I think not. On a test, it can't be; you can't have that mutual help [laughing], it's absurd!

One might read Juana's explanation as a kind of making-out game itself, using the discourse of cultural revitalization to rationalize a practice that even other rural students considered simply an everyday vice. Either way, the degree to which cheating can be read as a form of resistance, either against the repression of traditional cultural practices or against the commodification of students' linguistic labor, is questionable. In one sense, cheating not only evades official control of the labor process, but also constitutes a refusal to surrender oneself to the academic exchange. Everhart (1983:217) reads it as an act of defiance that recognizes school knowledge as reified and divorced from students' own cultural system. Students' typical complaints about schoolwork—"It's just words" or "What does that stuff have to do with me?"—constitute a vernacular critique of precisely this type. In another sense, however, cheating constitutes a surrender to the process of commodification, in that it takes the meaninglessness of the academic exchange to even greater extremes. While highlighting the reification of school knowledge, as a strategy it furthers that reification rather than challenging it. It is both an implicit critique and a passive acceptance of the commodification of linguistic expression, similar to the other illicit exchanges that form part of the school's linguistic economy.

The Linguistic Black Market: Illicit Exchange in the Academic Economy

Corruption in the Normal School

One broad and murky area of school practice highlights the difficulty of determining what constitutes "resistance." Collectively referred to as "corruption," these practices evade institutional control and circumvent the legal limits of the institutional economy, but simultaneously fortify the principles on which that economy is based. They include the exchange of money or goods for grades (or the artificial lowering of grades to compel students to enter such exchanges); extortion and mishandling of student monies; and, after graduation, the frequent bribery and political favoritism that enter into job assignment and promotion. Some corrupt practices were initiated by students, some by teachers, and some by both in collusion. Together, they contributed to a general atmosphere of dissolution that deeply affected students' feelings about their chosen profession and contrasted sharply with the idealistic expectations with which they had arrived.

Alienation leads to the withdrawal of motivation from work and a subsequent "disengagement of self" from the occupational role (Berger 1968).[18] This disengagement, linked perhaps to teachers' feelings of disillusionment and powerlessness within their jobs, seemed to be a key factor in their participation in corrupt practices. If "teachers constitute the most finished products of the system of production which it is . . . their task to reproduce" (Bourdieu and Passeron 1977:97), corruption might be read as the ultimate commodification of linguistic labor. At the same time, such practices can be construed as teachers' own resistance against the system in which they work. Either way, corruption is an index of alienation, a measure of the degree to which teachers have abandoned the search for virtue and meaning within their occupational role.

It is not my intention here to indict individual teachers, nor to indulge in what McLaren (1986:209) refers to as some radical educators' tendency to use them for "intellectual target practice." There are many dedicated Bolivian teachers whose strivings toward a pedagogical ideal are regularly thwarted by institutional roadblocks. Their occupational culture is a contradictory mix of adherence to arbitrary bureaucratic norms and evasion of those norms when possible.[19] My aim is rather to recognize the constraints and pressures placed on teachers by the alienating regime in which they labor and to examine the distortions resulting from the relations that govern their daily practice.

In the normal school, some corrupt practices centered on grades, while others did not. The former, examined in the following section, bear more directly on the alienation of students' labor. The latter were more akin to the graft, extortion, and financial irregularities that can arise in any institution marked by an extreme imbalance of power. Students were subject to certain legitimate charges: for tuition, the electricity in the dorms, registration for athletic contests, examination fees, fines for individual infractions of school rules, dance costumes for student programs, the elaborate meals prepared for high-ranking visitors, and "projects" to improve the school infrastructure. The lack of explicit norms for collecting these fees, coupled with students' lack of recourse within the school bureaucracy, made them subject to abuse. Complaints arose especially with regard to the "projects," which sometimes did not materialize after moneys had been collected, and the electricity fees, which seemed excessive (though this was hard to prove since students had no access to the electric bills). A particular point of contention during my stay was the collection of tuition, which, according to many students, was beset with irregularities (specifically, students claimed that the tuition charged was more than the official sum they had heard announced on the radio).[20]

In addition to the various school fees, students were sometimes fined for infractions of the rules: chronic lateness, absenteeism, or drinking. This last was more open to abuse, both because it was considered a more serious transgression and because perpetrators were usually apprehended in view of few, if any, witnesses. The clandestine nature of their dilemma made the unlucky inebriates easy targets for the extortion of "hush money" by their discoverer.

José: The corruption begins at the top here. The inspectors do the same . . . for every violation of the school rules. And that guy [the inspector] finds any number of violations, for example for drinking. Often the rector doesn't know. Lots of guys have told me how, for every violation, they've paid up to a hundred pesos. Once he made four couples pay a hundred pesos each [to avoid being expelled] . . . Now, that eight hundred pesos, where does it go? I'd think that every weekend there are such violations . . . The inspectors must not sleep at night; it's said they go out in the middle of the night [to catch people]. So, one gets used to it; those things happen. People who have paid him once, they know him; they commit another transgression, they give him money, that's it. Kind of like paying admission.

Such strong-arm practices, while sharply criticized by students, were related less to the student condition *per se* than to their general subordination. As institutional subjects, they were vulnerable to arbitrary demands of money more or less when staff members saw fit. While this contributed to a generally authoritarian atmosphere and highlighted the power relations within the institution, it was not a direct result of the commodification of students' academic production—unlike those illicit and semilicit exchanges that centered on grades.

The Illicit Trade in Academic Commodities

Parallel to the official exchange of schoolwork for grades, there existed an illicit trade in both grades and academic commodities. Most teachers based their grades on academic performance, but there were enough willing to "cut deals" that such exchanges formed a decisive part of several students' academic careers. Some such deals were sought by students themselves; others were imposed by individual teachers, in which case students had little power to resist. These private arrangements confirmed students' suspicions that grades were simply a commodity exchangeable for other commodities, rather than a reflection of what they actually learned in class. Mateo described a typical procedure by which students might improve their grades "under the table":

Mateo: Say a student has bad grades—he doesn't know what to do, the professor is being a little, inflexible, I'll say. He doesn't want to help the student out, especially if the student is not well-liked by him. Because they always look for that; they even notice how you greet them. If you don't greet them, they get you for that. So, the student has no choice but to go talk to him. My friend did that. He'd done poorly in one class. He said to me, "What should I do?" And I said, "Well, we'll go talk to him" . . . "Professor, please, help us out, he's in bad shape." "Yes," he says, "but this guy won't study, what's his problem?" "Aah, come on, Teach, what the hell. We're all human, and we can work it out among ourselves. How about a soda?" I tell him. "Yeah, yeah, yeah, go get it," he says. So we brought him a bottle of soda. "Well, give me five pesos in addition, and we're okay," he says.

AL: And just like that, for five pesos and a soft drink? That's awfully cheap!

Mateo: Yes, now he has his grade [laughter]. It wasn't much either. He only needed two or three points. Lots of guys were running around like that, saying, "I'm in trouble." But in the end they show up with good grades; I think they must have done that.

The question of students' economic exploitation is complicated by their complicity in the exchange. Teachers were not the only ones to initiate such arrangements; students and even parents sometimes sought them out themselves. Given the frequency of such exchanges, parents may feel that their children will be at a disadvantage relative to others if they rely solely on academic skills to get good grades.[21] When kin networks are activated to improve a student's grades, questions of exchange and commodification become less distinct, but not irrelevant. Bourdieu (1977) analyzed how kin ties can serve as cultural capital, resulting in benefits that are manifested primarily in the realm of prestige but have an undeniable, if indirect, economic significance. The influence of kin ties on grades thus can be considered part of the normal school economy. Several students had kin or fictive kin among the faculty, a fact that caused a certain amount of ill feeling between local and nonlocal students, since the latter perceived themselves as unfairly disadvantaged with regard to grades (see chapter 3). Students' impression that grades were not commensurate with effort, but rather were determined by forces outside their control, fostered an attitude of cynical resignation among some:

José: This school functioned really badly last year; it's said there were certain incidents of corruption, by the professors themselves . . . This year I didn't make any effort to get good grades. Because the one who sacrifices more sometimes ends up with a lower grade . . . The teachers are from right here—they help out the local students. We can't do anything. If we try to say something to their face, who knows, they'll flunk us even worse. So we watch ourselves in that regard. The corruption is in the grades, sometimes one is failed unfairly. And others, who can't do anything in class, they don't have even one failing grade, imagine . . . Right now in my class for example, there are two who can't read . . . How can they have passed? What does one know about their grades, their notes? If one doesn't read, on the exam, how does he answer? How can he read it? You see? So, I think this year I'll see what kind of teacher comes out of here. That same one is going to go spread knowledge in the schools? He's not going to teach a thing.

A common complaint among teachers in general is that students do not take their work seriously, that they care only about grades. In the normal school, however, similar complaints often came from students, frustrated over *professors'* failure to take their work more seriously and dismayed by the handling of grades as commodities to be bought and sold. The contrast between the exalted ideology surrounding education as the pure pursuit of knowledge and the mercantile reality of the school's informal economy was profoundly disillusioning to some; Diana lamented that "they say that before, grades were written in blood. But it's not like that anymore . . . "

One practice that straddled the borderline of legitimacy was teachers' habit of selling photocopied outlines or summaries to students. These usually sold at about twice the normal rate for photocopies in the city—somewhat expensive, but perhaps justifiable given the professor's time and trouble in preparing them. Students alleged, however, that some teachers made the purchase of such summaries mandatory, regardless of whether students considered them necessary:

Mateo: They sell photocopies, maybe to save time, but I think it's absurd. Because one gets the photocopy and, sometimes, as you know, we Bolivians are not used to reading, right? We prefer to just have someone explain it; we're used to doing it that way. So we just file it away, and it's no good for anything.

AL: But the students buy them just the same, even if they don't intend to read them?

Mateo: Sure. Because it's worth grades too. He who doesn't buy it loses, could be ten, five points they're worth . . . Five points is five points, and for two points, for one point, people have had to repeat a year . . . Some teachers say, "Well, he who wants to can buy it or not, but don't be complaining later, because this is worth five points. Like a research paper this is going to count." So the student is forced to buy it, to gain a few more points.

Such "borderline" practices allowed teachers to use their power over students to their economic advantage without entering into overt bribery. Still, the purest example of the commodification of linguistic products was undoubtedly the illicit sale of monographs. Before graduating, each student had to research, write, and defend a monograph on an assigned topic. That some students bought their monographs instead of writing them might not qualify as an outstanding example of cynicism—students the world over have been known to buy term papers and pass them off as their own—except for the fact that some were procured from teachers themselves. Others were obtained from teachers at other schools or from the spouse of a staff member who reportedly sold them for a hundred pesos (about thirty dollars). The fact that students were willing to spend what was, for them, quite a large sum, testifies to their consternation before the task of producing an original text based on individual research.[22] The monographs students wrote themselves consisted mostly of verbatim passages culled from the relevant sources; synthesis, analysis, and interpretation were apparently not required. For those unable or unwilling to do even this much, there were other means at hand:

Mateo: It's not easy to get them out of the library. But the professors have them ... The student goes and says, "Look Professor, I have to present a monograph on this topic. Please, can't you help me out?" "Ah, I think, no, let's see, come back tomorrow." If the student makes a good impression, he gives it to him right then ... If he doesn't like him, he says, "Come back tomorrow." So, if he's made a good impression, everything's fine. "Yes, I have it," he says ... "Here it is, but it isn't free." "Yes, well, how much would you charge me for this, Professor?" says the other. "Let's see, it would be around eighty, a hundred pesos. I'll give it to you for eighty," he says. "Okay?" "Fine." It's a lot, no? It depends on the topic too ... Done, he prints it out for him, charges his hundred, his eighty pesos. Sure.

It was somewhat gratifying to discover that the administration reacted strongly when the traffic in monographs was brought to light. After graduation, two professors were dismissed for this offense, and the staff member whose spouse students had pointed out to me as another source did not return after vacation. But selling monographs was not the only variation on this theme; deprived of one resource, students and professors were able to work out alternative arrangements:

> Mateo: [Professor X] charged me twenty pesos for a book . . . The teacher, according to the subject, has the obligation to help the student. But not to charge. To help, or even to lend books—but no, you have to go ask, because those guys, they grab you, they say, "Ah, this one hasn't come to me for help," and then maybe on the panel you have the bad luck to get him, and, "He didn't come to me," bam. You see? It's the luck of the draw, on the panel. In whichever of the panels he can ruin you. It seemed better to say, "Okay, teacher," accept what he said, so that's what I did. He said, "I have this book, ooh, everything is right here! You have to get this book . . . Here you have it already served, boy! With this you just have to copy it!" "Okay, fine," I told him, "How much, professor?" He told me thirty at first, and he gave it to me for twenty . . . He didn't want to lend it, he didn't want to give me the bibliography. He didn't want to do anything. So, I had to pay him twenty pesos, so he'd give me that book. And I wanted to take it back—"Ah no, go on and take it!" he told me.

Such tactics were used more often against third-year students, who faced increasing pressure to pass as they approached graduation. They were also more adept at setting up such transactions, due to their knowledge of the school's informal workings and the greater familiarity they enjoyed with teachers. Goffman (1961:53–54) noted that, over time, inmates acquire inside "lore" about the institution that they can use to their advantage. Learning the "secondary adjustments" of institutional life allows inmates to skirt the system—"to obtain forbidden satisfactions or to obtain permitted ones by forbidden means"—without challenging staff. These secondary adjustments may also be functional for the institution, relieving the pressures generated by the system's own internal contradictions. Deprived of their recourse to cheating, bribery, and plagiarism, more students would no doubt fail to graduate than presently do. The number might even be so high as to reveal the degree to which the institution fails to provide students with a meaningful education.

Sexual Favors and Harassment

If it was hard to collect first-hand accounts of corruption in general, sexual relations between students and teachers was an infinitely more difficult subject. Several students attested that such incidents did occur, as part of the illicit economy by which money, goods, and other favors were exchanged for grades. Though unsupported by direct evidence, these second-hand accounts were common enough to warrant mention, with the qualification that they are, in the final analysis, hearsay. Even if one chooses not to believe them—and to assert them as facts would be unjustifiable without further investigation—they are significant for their role within the lore of the institution and in students' perceptions of the relations governing it (and them).[23] Furthermore, from a purely pragmatic perspective, one might ask whether there is greater motivation for students to invent such stories, or for staff to deny them.

Sergio: The professors themselves treat some of the girls with, always with certain intentions, give her low grades, so that she'll come talk about it. That is, that's what I have knowledge of . . . Then they manipulate [the situation]. They go along saying that, one way or another, the grade can be improved. "Come to my room," right, that's how it starts.
Remedios: The professors take advantage. I think they already have picked out who they're going to make fall to them . . . It happened there [in another normal school] too; one professor called the girls for a meeting and told them to their faces to come that night, if they wanted to fix their grade . . . Often the girls go along, simply in order to pass the course, and what's she going to say to her father? That's why we need a counselor here, to talk about these situations. But there isn't one . . . The girls don't know who to complain to. Because in the end everyone is going to treat them badly or want to expel them. Right now there isn't really anyone to confide in. It's as if we were alone here, without any recourse.

Sexual harassment of female students might be expected, given what we know of sexual harassment in other cultures and the deep-rooted sexism of Bolivian society. The principle of male dominance is a prominent thread in the tapestry of Bolivian nationalist ideology, inclined as it is toward military exploits and values, and also intersects in complex ways the discourses of race and ethnicity (cf. de la Cadena 1991). While sexual remarks and innuendo about female students and staff were extremely rare in public, in line with the outward sexual conservatism of *altiplano* society, students indicated that this was not the whole story. On the contrary, it appeared that sexual speculation about students was a significant part of some teachers' occupational culture.

Mateo: The girls don't talk, but the teachers themselves do . . . Especially on Teachers' Day [after drinking], in those circumstances . . . They say it real clearly, pleased with themselves [laughter] . . . Like, "This one, I've been with her." "That one, that's the one I'm checking out now . . . She thinks she's a little saint, she's a proud little thing; just the same she's going to fall into my arms!" They talk however they want! They're like that. That's the sad reality.

According to Mateo, sexual favors were one of several things (including money, consumer goods, and farm produce) that could be exchanged for grades. Aside from the implications for students themselves—for their vulnerability to exploitation and their opportunities for academic advancement—sexual harassment, extortion, and bribery reveal the interface between the linguistic economy of the school and other economic realms within and beyond its walls. The mechanisms of commodification in schools may differ from those of the marketplace, but the products of both realms share their basic nature as commodities. Indeed, "commodification" implies precisely this: the abstraction of a product's particular qualities and its exchangeability for any other commodity. Thus, only those students who truly had nothing to exchange—neither academic skills, nor money, nor sexual appeal, nor family connections—or, barring that, were unwilling to exchange it (out of reticence, poverty, or personal principle) were inevitably doomed to academic failure.

After Graduation: "Knowing the Ropes" to Getting a Job

The atmosphere of corruption permeating Bolivia's educational system is exacerbated by the common belief that many
teachers attain their positions through political connections
rather than merit. In interviews, teachers themselves admitted
that such was often the case. Students' feeling that the quality
of their education was determined by "politics" increased their
sense that matters strongly affecting them were outside their
control. Their growing awareness of the political currents that
steered the school bureacracy soon dispelled any notion of school
as a pristine realm where virtue and knowledge are shielded
from the insidious influences of the outside world. School administrators had to be adept politicians; avoiding undue obstacles and delays, whether for new desks or for a meeting with
the regional supervisor, depended upon staying in the good
graces of educational authorities. Students also were well aware
of these tacit considerations; they chose as sponsor of their
graduation the head of the regional development corporation,
an ADN party official who was well placed to bestow
infrastructural improvements upon the school.

The network of corruption does not end at the school gate;
the illicit economy students discovered in the normal school
was, in effect, part of their professional training, preparing
them for situations they would encounter after graduation. In
Bolivia's educational hierarchy, the amount of bureaucracy is
high and accountability is often low. Progress through the system depends on a series of gate-keeping encounters, each of
which holds the potential for graft. Learning to negotiate such
interactions is a critical part of new teachers' socialization.

The first official encounter the normal school graduate faces
is that of seeking a teaching position. While all teachers are
guaranteed a job, the question of where that job will be is open
to negotiation. Mateo described a hypothetical teacher's meeting with the supervisor who will decide his assignment.[24]

Mateo: There's like an interview. You ask if he has a vacant
post in his sector . . . He looks—"In such-and-such a place,
this teacher won't be returning, they're making a change . . . "
But it doesn't happen just like that! Go in, sit down, talk to
him, and he tells you, "Fine, go to work," with your memo-

randum, no? You have to make a series of, how would you say, soften him up, no? Be real friendly with him, talk about this and that, invite him for a meal . . . He acts like he's real busy, but really they're just sitting around scratching themselves. So, he says, "Wait a moment, I'll be right back. Can you wait just a bit?" Until finally you have to say, "Sir, please, I'll acknowledge [your help]." Then finally it's, "Yes, sure, what's up? Now we'll chat; let's go outside." After already waiting long hours . . . He takes you to one of those little cafés, and you have to pay, right? If it's midday, buy him lunch, oh man, for them that's living! . . . You talk, "Well, so you've graduated," "Yes, I graduated this year." You tell him all about it, no? "How's the normal school?"—and then he'll say, "Well, there's a post I could give you, but you'll have to acknowledge it." So you say, "How much of an acknowledgement?" "Come back tomorrow; we can talk then," he says. They always want you to come back . . . "Come on, we'll go have some drinks." That's where it starts—ching ching [of the glasses], "What do they have here? Let's have a meal . . . " Then the talk really starts. "How much would you say, let's see, where do you want to go? But, another professor wanted to go there; I'll talk to him, but you have to put down so much," he tells you, 200 or 250 pesos . . . You put the money down, and boom, he does your paperwork . . . He does it in secret, nobody has to see. Then it's, "Come tomorrow, or this afternoon," he says, and then he takes care of you in a hurry! . . .

AL: And those that can't pay so much, or want to pay less, what happens with them?

Mateo: They're sent far away, to the frontier regions, where one has to travel a week to get there, and not just travel, but two or three days on foot. And they're on the border, in the mountains. Where the schools are really far and you have to worry that something might happen to you out there. You know, the mountains are full of animals . . . You can't even just go peacefully; you have to go with that thought that something could happen to you . . .

Finding a post does not mean the teacher can then simply dedicate him or herself to the formidable task of teaching under what are often very challenging conditions. New teachers occupy the lowest rung of a hierarchy in which advancement is necessary in order to increase one's meager salary or get moved to a better post. Promotion is by categories, based on seniority and successful completion of an exam. In practice, however, other considerations often enter in:

Mateo: They ask for your documents in order for you to get promoted, see? So what happens?. . . You go and, "Ooh, it's been filed!" they tell you. "Now what do I do?" "You have to present a memorandum so they'll look for it." "Yeah, and what's a memorandum cost?" "Fifteen, ten pesos". . . So, you present it, and once again it's, "Okay, come back tomorrow." They stamp your copy, and you go back the next day. "Ah yes, which one was it? I'll look for it . . . Come back a little later," they tell you. Until finally you say, "Please, look, I don't have time. I'll acknowledge you." That's the word you always have to use. "I'll acknowledge you, please sir." "Yes but, mmm, then come back a little later," he tells you. "Just wait for me ten minutes," he says. "About how much would you say, give me ten pesos, I'll get it for you right away," he says. You see? But, what are you going to do?. . . Then tac tac, in that moment he finds it for you, "Here it is!"

Greasing the wheels of bureacracy is only part of being promoted; next comes the exam. Mateo claimed, however, that a well-placed bribe could substitute for passing (or even taking) the exam:

Mateo: There too, politics ruins everything. Who gets promoted? Those who have money. . . One who doesn't have money stays back, even if he did well on the exam, he stays in the fifth category. Why? Because he didn't pay anyone off. While one who did pay, even if he didn't take the exam or failed the exam, just the same he'll get promoted.

Many students enter teacher training with high ideals of serving their pupils and their country, determined to eschew the corruption that most are well aware of by high school. As they grow more familiar with the system, such ideals may be beaten down by harsh realities. Many conclude that fighting the system is futile and that their only choices are to become "just another crook" (un corrupto más), or to seek comfort from the frustration and poverty of professional stagnation in the knowledge that they have held fast to their integrity. While honesty was often trumpeted as the primary virtue of the teacher, it was commonly held to be incompatible with advancement.

Students are not alone in their frustrations; many teachers spend a lifetime "swimming against the current" in an effort to practice their profession in accordance with their ideals. After years of experience, many blame the system itself for its failings, rather than corrupt individuals. The teachers' union official and former university professor quoted below had long ago given up ideas of reform, and chose to work instead for a radical restructuring of the entire political system:

> All the efforts they make within the system collapse in failure because of that very system. I'll give you an example: one of the best tests to become a principal would be for the candidates to elaborate an operating plan for their school, and have competitions for that school, very concrete. So, the idea was well received, there was even participation from the union, parents, students, all very well structured. Within this system, this principal, what does he do, if he doesn't know how to draw up an operating plan? He *buys* an operating plan, and presents that. How the system distorts all the changes that could be made!

Organized Resistance: Student Responses to Corruption

Collective responses to corruption in the normal school were rare, and their prospects far from good. Students sometimes held meetings in which perceived injustices were hotly argued and possible solutions proposed. But this seldom resulted in action by the administration; most often, the proposals never went beyond the confines of the meetings themselves, largely because students felt too intimidated to confront the administration with their allegations. Aside from their subordinate position, students' transitory status also worked against them. Lacking the historical knowledge and social memory that would have given greater depth to their struggles (cf. Alonso 1988:140), students fought the same battles every few years. Teachers and administrators had experience in deflecting the complaints of generations of students, but students had little knowledge of either grievances or successes from before their time; their political power was short-circuited by the fact that, within the institution, they existed in a different time frame than did staff.

When such knowledge was available, students tried to use it in defense of their interests. José described a plan by the dorm students, fed up with what they perceived as regional favoritism, to hold their final practical exams in a neutral site, away from local students' family ties:

José: For the practicum, we're going to request that we leave here, go to other provinces. Not here, on their turf . . . One learns from experience. Because, in years past, the old students have told us about how certain things happen when they have the practicum here. Like I told you, the professors are corrupt . . . Maybe they've taken bribes; some students, who knows, have passed with money, with beer, you know? So we don't want that.

More often, students felt too intimidated to push their protests very far. They claimed that staff were quick to identify troublemakers, and were hesitant to demand reforms for fear of reprisals. As Remedios put it: "We don't have any right to protest. If we complain . . . we're on the blacklist." While there was an official grievance procedure, it was rarely if ever used to accuse staff members of improprieties. As for taking their complaints to a higher level, students felt that such action would also bring repercussions. In any case, given the personal relationships between school personnel and education officials, such action seemed unlikely to result in change.

AL: What can students do, if they notice some injustice in their treatment by the inspectors or the professors? Who can they complain to?
José: For example, if you get caught by the inspector, and there's no solution—according to the rules, if there's no solution here with the administration, you have higher authorities. Directly, one can go there, you can appeal to them.
AL: And does that really happen?
José: No . . . Up until now I haven't seen it. I think they go—but I don't know if they cover their faces or don't give their names . . . [laughter] With a hood, who knows, but they go to complain. Then the complaint is transmitted to the rector, and then here the rector says, "Some students are complaining to the authorities." So they know who has recently gone to complain. "Let them make their insinuations openly.

They should speak up . . . " No way; it's hard. That's no good. They're not going to speak up. That's what makes me maddest, as a Bolivian . . . Even if they expel me, I'd go, with my reasons, I'd go as far as was necessary. But they don't want to. They're just humble, quiet. There's no progress.

The fact that teachers were of their same class and ethnic background made such abuses of power all the more disillusioning for students. Unlike the rural teachers of decades past, who were usually *mestizo* outsiders expected to exploit rural people whenever possible, today's teachers are better positioned to show solidarity with the students and communities they serve. When this solidarity was violated, students saw teachers as betraying not only their future colleagues, but their own people as well. Day-to-day instances of petty exploitation undermined the revolutionary ideals evoked in classrooms and school assemblies. Lofty expressions of ethnic pride and professorial virtues began to ring false as students grew aware of other currents at play in their environment. Some saw both students' and teachers' illicit practices as specifically antipatriotic, a form of "cheating" one's country and one's people for the sake of individual gain.

José: [on students who cheat] . . . It's nothing more than graduating and making money. Not knowing, they just cheat and so go on not knowing anything. What does it matter to them, if they teach the children well or not . . . They're cheating their country, primarily. After that, their family. After that, their people, their class, the peasants. Those to whom they should give the most, give more good ideas, whom they should guide . . . We're cheating our own homeland, doing these things. Because, like I told you, Bolivia won't be able to progress like this. This way, we'll go on being backward, just go on the same. If everyone has that idea that Bolivia should move forward—well then, everyone should be trying to excel.

Diana: I don't like those things. If I don't know, then I flunk, totally, I'll stay back. If not, what kind of teacher will I be, how will I teach the children? Why should I be cheating the children, if they're of my own class? That can't be. I'd rather repeat a year, two, three, four years, that way I'll come out knowing more, learning more, and I'll be a good teacher.

Exchange Partners in the Academic Economy

Students' references to "who's cheating whom" and the circulation of commodities throughout the normal school bring to mind Willis's notion of teaching as an exchange. The educational exchange of respect for knowledge is the key to a chain of subsequent exchanges: knowledge for credentials, credentialed work for pay, and pay for goods and services (Willis 1981a:64). The school is also home to numerous other axes of exchange, activated by different exchange partners in more or less antagonistic relationships to each other. For students, the primary exchange partner is obviously the teacher, to whom they offer respect in exchange for knowledge, and linguistic products in exchange for grades. It is also the teacher whose control they try to evade, minimizing their labor via slacking off, cheating, and other forms of resistance. Students and teachers are not equal partners in exchange, however. Teachers hold the rarer commodity; students' need for qualifications and the power relations governing the institution make it a "seller's market" for school knowledge. A teacher who "shortchanges" students by failing to deliver the agreed-upon amount of knowledge is unlikely to suffer serious consequences, whereas a student who fails to deliver the agreed-upon amount of respect is likely to be expelled. In addition, the exclusion of students' own knowledge from school knowledge and cultural capital places them in a position similar to that of workers who "freely sell" their labor, in the absence of any alternative.

Further evidence of this partnership's inequality was the fact that students could be coerced into exchanges beyond those to which they agreed by entering the institution. Nevertheless, the illicit nature of these exchanges placed students and teachers in collusion with each other. Opposed within the exchange, students' and teachers' shared need for secrecy united them in opposition to the adminstration. The same occurred between students and administrators with respect to higher authorities. For example, students once wanted to leave school for several days to research an assignment. The rector agreed to permit it, on one condition: that the regional educational supervisor not find out.

When teachers and students mutually minimize their effort in the classroom, teachers also reduce their own outlay in another exchange: that of their labor for the wage paid them by the government. In one sense, the students involved are short-changing the government as well, in that the grades they receive are essentially a deferred wage. Thus the state is more than simply a regulator of the exchanges between teachers and students; it is a partner in exchange as well. Furthermore, since students' grades imply a level of training that some of them have not, in fact, received, one also could argue that these students are shortchanging their future pupils, whose parents pay taxes for schools under the assumption (or the hope) that teachers will possess a certain level of competence. Students' claims that corruption and cheating are equivalent to "cheating the country and the children" thus provided a fairly accurate description of the exchange relationships involved.

In contrast with other forms of student resistance, many of the practices described above are undertaken in collusion with teachers—a kind of "reciprocal manipulation" (Scott 1985:309) between opposed parties with complementary interests. If this can indeed be termed resistance, it is directed not against teachers *per se*, but against the administration or the institutional regime in which students live. Such practices also raise the question of teachers' motives; financial gain is obviously a factor, but it is not the only one. Bolivian teachers are likely candidates for resistant behavior; in a sense, they are also alienated workers, though not in precisely the same ways that students are. Notoriously underpaid, their work combines high responsibility with low authority. Teachers collectively resist the government that controls their labor via marches, strikes, and other "non-everyday" acts. But their alienation is also evident in their daily working lives, that is, in their interactions with students. McNeil (1986:69) claims that teachers' lack of power over policy leads them to seek other areas where they can exercise authority and control; the obvious choice is the classroom. Teachers may express resentment over low pay by "minimal" teaching (marked by chronic lateness and scant preparation) and petty economic exploitation of students. "Resistance is not necessarily directed at the immediate source of appropriation . . . Appropriation in one sphere may lead its victims to exploit small openings elsewhere that are perhaps more accessible and less dangerous" (Scott 1985:35). These openings may appear in the form of other human beings even more vulnerable to appropriation. Of course, whether this should be considered "resistance," or simply social pathology, is questionable. Scott asserts that "when a poor man survives by taking from others in the same situation, we can no longer speak of resistance" (35).

While I would tend to agree, such practices are certainly related phenomena that can illuminate, and be illuminated by, the study of truly resistant practices. Many of the tactics by which teachers take out their laboral frustrations on students are also found in the arsenal of everyday resistance inventoried by Scott; as he himself notes, "The peasantry has no monopoly on these weapons, as anyone can easily attest who has observed officials and landlords resisting and disrupting state policies that are to their disadvantage" (29–30). Furthermore, teachers share an occupational culture analogous, though not equivalent, to the "popular culture of resistance" evoked by Scott, Willis (1981a), Foley (1990), and other ethnographers of subaltern groups. Occasional graft and grade inflation are part and parcel of that culture, which is even more cohesive in rural schools where teachers live, work, play, eat, drink, and complain together twenty-four hours a day.

When the agreed-upon exchange between teachers and the government breaks down, there appears that most typical phenomenon of Bolivian schooling—the strike. Strikes show how different exchange relationships intertwine; by withholding their labor from the state, teachers inevitably withhold it from their students as well. This proves to be a double-edged sword for the relationship between teachers and parents. Though many working-class and peasant communities often support them, school strikes clearly run counter to their immediate interests. While striking teachers depend on the political solidarity of parents and communities, they also benefit from the difficulty that strikes cause their supposed allies, in that it increases public pressure on the government to resolve the conflict. The sheer frequency of strikes can be a major obstacle to students' academic progress, leaving teachers caught between their union and the communities they serve. Maintaining the pressure of the strike without alienating parents so much that broad-based support is damaged constitutes a difficult balancing act for unionized teachers.[25] Forging a unified position from the myriad and conflicting interests of differently positioned social groups is not easy. It is precisely the effort to make some interests, rather than others, the basis for group action and alignment that constitutes the political work of "articulating" a historical bloc (Hall 1986a, 1986b).

That such contradictory interests may exist within social groups, and even within individuals, is evidence of the various subject positions that every social being simultaneously or alternately occupies. The intersecting exchange relationships within the academic economy also display this multiplicity of being. Thus far, teachers have been cast as "managers" and students as "workers" with respect to the school's production of knowledge and ideology. But these are not static relationships between eternally opposed antagonists, so much as temporary (albeit habitual) role relationships in a shifting complex of exchange patterns, in which "resistance" is directed along different axes at different times. If students and teachers constitute different "classes" within the productive sphere of the school, it may be useful to think of class—from the point of view of the individual—as a momentary role relation defined by specific exchanges, rather than a fixed status.[26] While the habitual occupation of a particular class position by a group of individuals will tend to generate a set of material and symbolic practices associated with that role—a "class culture," if you will (Bourdieu 1984)—this does not preclude those individuals from occupying different roles with respect to different exchange relationships in which they may be simultaneously engaged.

Cynicism and Hypocrisy

The above analysis relies more on students' accounts of events than on first-hand observations, a risky methodology when dealing with sensitive topics. Still, actors' own accounts are essential to the ethnographer; "however partial or even mistaken the experienced reality of human agents, it is that experienced reality that provides the basis for their understanding and their action" (Scott 1985:46). Students felt corruption to be central to the exchange systems comprising the normal school economy, and this perception shaped their actions and their understanding of the institution.

Cynicism was a common reaction to the practices students observed around them, molding their views of their own training and of the educational system in general. In what may come as a surprise to those accustomed to a different student discourse, the words *justice* and *morality* appeared frequently in students' assessments of what their educational environment lacked:

Mateo: Sometimes it hurts . . . As teachers, they should be examples for us, because they're the reflection of us. They should enlighten us, with their culture and their education, with their *morality*. But it's just the opposite; here they practice despotism, immorality, corruption. So in what condition does that leave us, the students? We end up losing, so we follow the same road . . . That's why education in Bolivia is upside down and always will be. It begins at the top . . . with the Minister of Education, I'd say. And ending with the janitor of an elementary school.

With such attitudes as prevalent as they were, it is easy to see why students rejected teachers' authority over them as hypocritical. Those who refrained from cheating, drinking, and bribery did so out of fidelity to their own moral compasses, rather than to the professed standards of the institution. As Sergio declared, with a resigned shrug: "They say it's prohibited to drink, but there are the teachers themselves, saying, 'Here, have a drink.' And what can one say?" The sense of pervasive hypocrisy gave rise to the opinion that disciplinary sanctions were unfair—not because students were innocent, but because staff lacked the moral authority to punish them. José expressed this frustration in his account of being called in for an "orientation" by the *inspectora*:

José: Part of me wanted the orientation. I want to see how she orients people, because several girls have told me she does nothing but scold them. I could set her straight: "Teacher, where am I? In a jail cell, or in a Department of Orientation?" I'd say, if she scolded me. "Fine, I'll stay or I'll go; you orient me. Because if I've done something wrong, maybe for the first time, then I need some orientation." That's what I'd tell her. What could she say?

Such scenarios were, of course, doomed to remain fantasies; the adoption of such a morally superior tone by a transgressing student would not be warmly received by school personnel, and students had few illusions in that regard. At the same time, the most thoroughly disillusioned students were perhaps *least* likely to challenge the hypocrisies they perceived. As Reisman notes:

> Many observant young people . . . are actually overpersuaded to the point of believing that every occupation is a racket and that at best some of the racketeers are less pious about it than others. And this, I suspect, is one of the reasons they tend to withdraw emotional allegiance from their work—with the impression that they have no control over it anyway, that it is all in the hands of the mysterious men upstairs who run the show. If there is greater wisdom in their belief that all occupations, like all forms of power, are corrupting in some degree, there is also greater resignation, greater passivity and fatalism. (Reisman 1968:58)

A case in point is Mateo's summing up of the corruption issue, which disturbed him deeply but left him feeling powerless to effect change. Worn out by his vacillation between submission to conditions beyond his control and determination to do his individual best as an honest teacher, he foresaw a day when he would either have to leave teaching altogether or succumb to the prevailing tide:

Mateo: Yeah, there are conscientious teachers, but—sometimes, we let others take away our conscience. For a few miserable pesos maybe, like I was telling you, everyone seeks their own interest . . . Perhaps even I would, if they told me, "Here, take this." Or maybe like the bigshot politicians, they give you a car, you know, or a house maybe. What do I do? Lose out on a house? So, I'd have no choice but to become just another crook.

Though a good student academically, Mateo was the most openly critical of all those I met at the normal school—the most "alienated" (in the popular sense of the term) from the official ideology of the institution.[27] Kaufman points out that while the nonconformist is alienated from society, those who conform may be alienated from themselves (in Schacht 1970:xl). But in a challenge to more traditional ideas about hegemony, Scott argues that those subjects who believe most deeply in the promises of the dominant social order are less likely to accept the inevitable gap between those promises and reality. Paradoxically, subjects' acceptance of a hegemony's professed principles may serve them as a resource for the construction of critique. "The very process of attempting to legitimate a social order by idealizing it always provides its subjects with the means, the symbolic tools, the very ideas for a critique that operates entirely within the hegemony. For most purposes then, it is not at all necessary for subordinate classes to set foot outside the confines of the ruling ideals in order to formulate a critique of power" (Scott 1985:338).

Those students who were most critical of the educational system were often those with the most ambitious notions of schooling's potential, the most given to fervent expressions of the principles that echoed so hollowly around them every day. Although literal, direct challenges such as José's imagined confrontation with the *inspectora* were destined to remain in the realm of fantasy, other challenges did arise, half-concealed by the rhetoric of ceremonial patriotism or the swirling kaleidoscope of folkloric practices. The following section examines the indirect yet pointed critiques embedded in students' popular culture and how students used these forms to give voice to their own interpretations of national, ethnic, gender, and professional identity.

Student Resistance through Expressive Practices

Popular Parodies: The Satirical Performance of Ethnic Conflict

Many forms of student resistance are related to linguistic production and its commodification by the school. Some, like silence, impede the productive process by withdrawing the participation of the producer. Others, like cheating and corruption, are more ambiguous; rather than challenging the process of linguistic commodification, they carry it to its logical extreme. While these practices run counter to institutional norms, they do not signify *alternatives* to those norms so much as *responses*; they are more reactive than creative. In contrast, the following pages describe a fundamentally different type of resistance, arising from students' own expressive culture.

If domination can be subtle and largely unconscious, so can the challenges raised against it. The ways subjects rework the ideological framework of institutional life may not be perceived as "political" by actors themselves, but rather as "cultural" or simply "recreational." The richest forms of student resistance are often found in these indirect challenges to the dominant order.[28] National, class, gender, and ethnic ideologies are transmitted (and contested) not only in classrooms, but in ceremonial contexts, both official and student-controlled. Indeed, the organization of verbal and visual expression in such contexts may be more amenable to semiotic challenges than is the discourse of the classroom. Students' expressive practices exhibit a life-affirming creativity that contrasts sharply with the pessimistic tactics of withdrawal and escape. They comprise a true alternative to linguistic commodification: a nonalienated popular culture based in students' own experiences, tastes, and values, filled with subtle and not-so-subtle commentaries on the ethnic, nationalist, class and gender discourses of the school—commentaries that, in the classroom, are regularly stifled or frozen into rigid slogans precluding critique.

These popular practices relied heavily on the language of parody.[29] Their images were drawn from the disruptive interface where indigenous culture meets the dominant institutions of Bolivian society. A regular context for these performances was the *hora cívica* program presented by students every Monday morning. The central number was usually a traditional folkloric dance, performed earnestly with great attention to details of costume. Occasionally, however, students performed a dance favored by urban youth, and this was always an opportunity for gleeful farce. Urban fashions and dance movements were exaggerated to the point of absurdity, in a wordless but pointed rejoinder to upper- and middle-class notions of style.

Another dance, known as *doctorcitos*,[30] featured young men in black trousers and waistcoat, fedora, spectacles, and a cane, often with a pink paper nose (suggesting drunkenness) and an imposing moustache of paper or ink. The students' version included bespectacled young women as well, each in severe white blouse and black skirt, city shoes and nylons, with her hair pulled back into a bun and carrying a clipboard in the manner of an executive secretary. The dance itself consists of short, trotting steps punctuated every few seconds by an exaggerated bow and tipping of the fedora as pairs of dancers face one another. The effect is one of bumbling, drone-like bureaucrats whose identical mannerisms and pompous gestures suggest the upper-class products of over-education.[31] The dance is essentially a denaturalization of bourgeois norms; when such norms are made into a comic spectacle, their assumed superiority is shattered, along with their ideological power to define a social ideal. In Fiske's (1989:94) terms, their credibility is weakened to the extent that their discursivity is foregrounded.

Students' favorite target for parody was not the upper class itself, but the upwardly mobile[32]—especially the Aymara migrants who define much of urban La Paz's cultural flavor and whose cultural practices provided students with a bottomless trunk of humorous resource material. One highly successful performance featured "The Imperial Brass Band of Oruro," a dozen male students in improvised silly versions of middle-class dress (complete with the ubiquitous fedora and dark glasses), soundlessly flailing away at their instruments while dancing to a recorded *morenada* (a rhythm common to urban celebrations such as Oruro's *carnaval* and La Paz's *Gran Poder*) in an unmistakable parody of immigrant style. As in much of Bolivia's popular literature (as well as the girls' dorm), those seeking to cross class and ethnic boundaries were targets of even sharper ridicule than those firmly ensconced in society's upper echelons.

Class and ethnicity were often conflated in students' performances, as they are in Bolivian society itself. Foley notes how class and ethnic signifiers can meld together, making ethnicity a class stigma and provoking conflict over social identities. Ethnically marginalized working-class youth express this conflict in "counter-cultural practices that appropriate and invert mainstream, bourgeois expressive practices" (Foley 1990:185). Still, the above examples belie the claim that such ethnic/class conflicts "represent a new dynamic in late or advanced capitalist societies" (185). Even in Bolivia, which has barely completed the transition from feudalism to capitalism, class and ethnicity are simultaneously invoked in multilayered criticisms of dominant social practices.

The burlesquing of urban styles was given a gender twist in the *fonomímicas*, in which a pair of students acted out the theme of a popular song playing in the background. The theme was always the same: boy woos girl while girl adamantly rejects boy. As in the dances described above, costumes provided a meta-communicative frame of interpretation, letting the audience know who was to be the target of parody before the music had even begun. The girl wore a silky blouse with narrow skirt and high heels or sleek pants and boots, hair long and loose or sophisticatedly swept up, as opposed to the full skirts and braids worn by rural girls. The boy's costume consisted of sport shirt, dress shoes, dress pants or jeans, dark glasses, and (most important) a leather or denim jacket—never worn, but instead draped off one shoulder and shifted from side to side as the boy paced in despair over the girl's rejection of him. As the couple lip-synched the words of the song, the boy would beseechingly approach the girl, who responded with increasing forcefulness—first turning away, then slapping his face, and by the last verse violently shoving him away (perhaps even knocking him down if he were a particularly enthusiastic actor). All students thoroughly enjoyed this type of performance, but the girls, whose position in the school (as in society at large) was one of relative powerlessness, and whose romantic woes were often compounded by what they perceived as male indifference in such matters, took special delight in watching the girl physically and emotionally dominate the boy and exercise over him the power of refusal. The righteousness of her actions was reinforced by the words of the song, which revealed her previous abandonment by the same suitor who now futilely begged her forgiveness.

Another *fonomímica* was a duet in Aymara and Spanish (with both characters dressed in traditional peasant clothes, though the male character wore dark glasses) between a haughty, fussy female and a grinning, mischievous male who pursued and pestered her, pinching, tickling, and grabbing at her skirts in a suggestive manner. The male character was played by a girl—Sara, who was in fact something of a tomboy (and virtually the only female student who ever wore pants outside of gym class). Some of the boys reacted skeptically when she first appeared on stage (remarking, "What's the matter, aren't there any guys in that class?"), but Sara's gleefully lascivious performance and her partner's scandalized disdain soon had the entire assembly in stitches. One might wonder why a girl was chosen to play the male role, given that *fonomímicas* were rare opportunities for students to publicly act out romantic or sexual themes without fear of official censure. The answer, it seems to me, is twofold. First, this *fonomímica* was more explicitly sexual than most; such aggressive behavior by an actual male might have created a more threatening scenario, robbing the scene of its humor value. Second, the masquerade permitted the girls to control both sides of the portrayal, so that the male figure was not only rejected by the female, but shown to be a buffoon as well.

The *fonomímicas* shared a deliberately paradoxical portrayal of gender relations. On the one hand, dominant gender ideology was reinforced: man as pursuer (either lecherous or lovestruck), woman as prey (rejecting or teasing, never caught). On the other hand, the performances' content either mocked men's obsession with sex or emphasized the emotional payback brought on by their faithlessness. Though locating women's power solely in the granting or withholding of sex, these performances were clearly empowering for the girls, judging by their enjoyment of them. Fiske (1989:45) claims that "popular readings are always contradictory; they must encompass both that which is to be resisted and the immediate resistances to it"; their progressive potential lies in the combination of "both the forces of domination and the opportunities to speak against them . . . to oppose or evade them from subordinated, but not totally disempowered, positions (25)." Expressive practices that do not set up a problematic cannot comment on it. In contrast, another Aymara duet (acted out but not lip-synched) showed a peasant couple engaged in traditional activities. The girl at first rejects the boy's tentative advances, but she eventually turns to him and they dance together. The mood was haunting rather than humorous, as there were no urban elements to be satirized (in contrast to Sara's character, whose dark glasses served as a marker of urban influence as well as masking her femininity). Unlike the urbanized male, portrayed as either emotionally or physically threatening, the *campesino* swain was hesitant and respectful—and as a result got the girl.[33]

While student performances expressing alternative views on gender were relatively few, there were many expressing outrage over both past Spanish colonialism and current institutionalized racism. Civic programs often featured poems with revolutionary or *indigenista* themes, recited either in Spanish or in impassioned Aymara with the speaker in full traditional dress. *Hora cívica*'s "open mike" periods sometimes showcased (male) students decrying racism, poverty, or the shortcomings of their own education, or eulogizing an indigenous martyr on the relevant historical anniversary. Poems and speeches were one more arena for contesting dominant ethnic and class images but seldom provoked the enthusiastic response and full audience engagement that more humorous forms did. Serious performances usually dealt with historical themes, while satirical ones addressed current conflicts well within students' own experience. More important, the former did not allow spectators the pleasure of producing their own meanings; they were, in Fiske's terms, "readerly texts," providing ready-made meanings for audience members to passively consume. In contrast, students' parodies were "producerly texts," inviting the audience to participate in the construction of meaning (Fiske 1989:103–4). By showing rather than telling, such performances were accessible to the multiple social relevances that audience members brought to them (122–27).

Student humor reached its highest pitch in the *veladas*: variety shows featuring musical acts, dances, skits, contests, and a play. The *veladas* presented for graduation and Mothers' Day were veritable banquets of ethnic and political satire; the mood of these nighttime events was playful and rowdy, in contrast to the (mostly) solemn programs presented on patriotic holidays. One skit lampooned candidates in the upcoming presidential election, gathered for a press conference. The boys playing the candidates strutted and pontificated in their best *caudillo* style, insulting each other, making outrageous campaign promises, pandering shamelessly to various groups, and elbowing each other for the best view of the television camera until they were in a collective brawl on the floor. Another was a takeoff on "*La Tribuna Libre del Pueblo*,"[34] a TV program hosted by media personality and CONDEPA politician Carlos Palenque. The student portraying Palenque gave a convincing rendition of his soothing, beneficent manner, but the real laughs were generated by his "guests," who ranted and rambled about trivial, absurd problems in a parody of Palenque's followers and their televised complaints of bureaucratic snarls, unpaid debts, medical dilemmas, and vicious landlords. Student players imitated with keen accuracy the vocal style of Palenque's Aymara constituency, whose speech reveals both their rural origins and their urban connections. Their dead-on impressions drew gales of laughter from the audience, who knew this vocal style well—no doubt several students' parents were themselves CONDEPistas.

The centerpiece of the program was the play, a comedy about an Aymara family who send their oldest son abroad.

Some of its funniest moments involved the negotiation of ethnic and linguistic boundaries; one scene featured the parents showing off their son's new passport, which classified its dark-skinned, obviously indigenous owner as "not even *mestizo*, but white!"—as his mother (played by Juana) exclaimed in an outburst of maternal pride. In another scene, the younger son (played by Sergio) attempts to write a letter to his brother, as dictated by his mother. The pair displayed remarkable wit and comic timing in their struggle to render orthographically the illiterate mother's vernacular terms of endearment for her son. The play drew an enthusiastic response from the audience, who knew all too well the problems entailed in negotiating two cultures. It spoke to their experience in a way that National Reality class never could.[35]

While the existence of an official space for nonalienated student expression is encouraging, that space was quite limited. Plays were rehearsed during students' free time, under the direction of the language teacher; they were not integrated into the regular curriculum, nor were their social and political themes made the subject of class discussion. Fragments of Aymara gave the plays a vernacular tone and contributed greatly to the humor of the characters, but there were no plays performed in Aymara. One girl nominated for a major role was hesitant to accept because she was not a fluent Aymara speaker; but her classmates assured her that it didn't matter, she just had to say *choy* (analogous to a Mexican character only having to say *caramba*). Despite the obvious pleasure students took in producing the plays, they were neither written nor chosen by students.

More autonomous expressions of student culture were found in those skits that students composed themselves. In addition to those described above, I observed one (part of an *hora cívica* program) that explicitly addressed the teacher/student conflict. In the skit, a teacher tried frantically to control four oversized pupils, who were entirely engrossed by the model cars and toys they had brought to school with them. After several minutes of ineffective railing, the teacher finally managed to settle them down for a lesson. The lesson itself portrayed what is perhaps the quintessential classroom experience of the Aymara schoolchild: in a litany every Bolivian student knows well, the teacher tried to teach his obstreperous pupils the five Spanish vowels.[36] However, he could not pronounce them correctly himself; loudly and deliberately, he intoned "Aah—oo—ee—oo—ee" and when the students repeated after him, shouted, "No, no! Aah—oo—ee—oo—ee!" The students finally gave up and went back to their play, eventually knocking over chairs and destroying any semblance of order in the "classroom." Understandably, students drew far more amusement from this portrayal of official linguistic hypocrisy and triumphant student intransigence than did faculty members.

Bauman and Briggs (1990:63) note that "play frames not only alter the performative force of utterances but provide settings in which speech and society can be questioned and transformed." Authoritative texts are, by definition, maximally protected from compromising transformations (77); those texts whose protection is shattered by subversive satire are therefore vulnerable to the loss of their authority. In the skit described above, the "text" of the lesson is challenged both by students' refusal to acknowledge its authority and by the implication that the teacher himself is guilty of the same errors that it is his job to correct (a point several students mentioned to me as being true of teachers they had known). Authoritative utterances are vulnerable to ironic reinterpretation precisely because their authority depends on others' acceptance of it. For students to challenge this authority explicitly, or within the confines of the classroom, was beyond the pale; they could do so only outside of class, in interviews (framed as confidential, private expression) or in satirical performances (framed as play). Still, these isolated, seemingly frivolous moments accumulate to form a subversive public discourse spanning many speech events; as links in an intertextual chain of oppositional meaning, they hold open a counter-hegemonic space over time (Bakhtin 1986). Notably, many of the concerns students expressed in interviews—teacher incompetence, ethnic rivalries, linguistic difficulties, political corruption—were the very ones burlesqued in their skits.

Of course, not all popular forms are "progressive." Some elements of student culture may reinforce the dominant ideology. Still, any discourse that playfully inverts authoritative meanings, recontextualizing them within a carnivalesque frame, strikes a blow against the hegemonic tendency to make the sign "uniaccentual," to reduce it to a single possible reading (Volosinov 1976:23). From this perspective, even a skit whose satire consisted of little more than vulgar sexual puns could be considered significant, in its use of the sign's multivocality to suggest forbidden meanings and express resistance to adult authority.

Paradoxically, subversive themes were manifested most creatively during those events meant to reinforce institutional unity. Since overt censorship would have threatened the image of unity by highlighting institutional power relations, staff were more tolerant of suggestive or subversive humor than at other times, making such events unique opportunities for symbolic resistance. Goffman (1961:94) examined the part such events play in the functioning of total institutions, temporarily bridging the staff-inmate divide in expressions of "unity, solidarity, and joint commitment to the institution," often characterized by role releases (or reversals) and suspension of the usual formalities, tasks, and constraints.[37] On special occasions in the normal school, teachers danced with students, sometimes even inviting a few to drink with them, and on Students' Day prepared and served them an elaborate meal.[38] Goffman's analysis of these displays is not limited to their institutional functionality, however:

> A society dangerously split into inmates and staff can through these ceremonies hold itself together... [but] there is often a hint or a splash of rebellion in the role that inmates take in these ceremonies. Whether through a sly article, a satirical sketch, or overfamiliarity during a dance, the subordinate in some way profanes the superordinate... A total institution perhaps needs collective ceremonies because it is something more than a formal organization; but its ceremonies are often pious and flat, perhaps because it is something less than a community. (Goffman 1961:109–110)

Significantly, those ceremonies that generated a real feeling of *communitas* among students were those providing the greatest space for resistant behavior and subversive satire, whereas more serious ones did often appear "pious and flat." At times, the attempt to paper over internal conflicts with public affirmations of unity only made them more conspicuous.

Everhart claims that cultural forms based on humor contrast with reified classroom knowledge in that they are controlled by students themselves. In deciding "what is funny and what is not, what can be taken to be irreverent and what is sacred," students appropriate an area of school practice to their own purposes—unlike those domains in which their speech and movements are externally controlled and their own judgement counts for little (Everhart 1983:162). He celebrates these forms with little regard to their content, even claiming that "resistance occurs in part . . . from [students'] lack of understanding about the very 'value' of the commodity that they had produced" (162). I prefer to view such forms as evidence, not of students' ideological blindness, but of their cognizance of the power relations governing their lives. The content of their popular expressions reflects the schisms running through the institution and the larger society; even a casual practice like cheating is in some sense a commentary on the reification and commodification of knowledge and linguistic expression. There is more than indiscriminate defiance of authority at work here.

The Public Celebration of Indigenous Culture:
A Male Sphere of Resistance

Aside from the ironic play of ethnic meanings, students engaged in expressions of indigenous culture that were decidedly nonironic—whose earnestness would in fact have been disastrously deflated by any suggestion of irony. These consisted mainly of indigenous dances, songs, and poems performed in *hora cívica* and holiday programs. Such forms, arising from students' own cultural tradition, were not seen as appropriate targets for satire. Unlike the urban songs and dances whose burlesqued reworkings provided such amusement, these had, for students, the naturalness of lifelong familiarity, and were always performed sincerely, even reverently. This was especially true of the poems; these ranged from the romantic to the patriotic to the philosophical, but of special interest were those recited in Aymara, usually in traditional peasant costume. These usually addressed the Aymaras' long history of oppression, often invoking long-dead martyrs in passionate laments whose sheer emotional pitch far surpassed other types of recitations, usually reaching a crescendo of shouting and breaking of the voice whose dramatic effect was quite singular. While these overwrought performances might have seemed vulnerable to parody by virtue of their very intensity, the seriousness of the subject matter, and the accepted legitimacy of the indigenous aesthetic associated with it, precluded any such break in the performative frame.

Although these performances were an institutionalized part of school culture and did not challenge school practices *per se*, they obviously challenged the dominant social order of urban *criollo* tastes and values. Despite its residual nature, such poetry constituted an unequivocally oppositional commentary on the present. Williams (1977:122) notes the capacity of traditional cultural forms to operate in present cultural processes, but also warns: "It is crucial to distinguish this aspect of the residual, which may have an alternative or even oppositional relation to the dominant culture, from that . . . which has been wholly or largely incorporated into the dominant culture."

It is possible to read institutional expressions of indigenous culture—poetry, dance, Native Languages class—as hegemonic incorporations of autocthonous strains too prevalent to eradicate or ignore. They have become an integral part of the official construction of ethnic and national identity in schools (as well as in tourism and other areas of cultural production). As such, they shield the school (somewhat) from charges of racism and cultural imperialism, while the principles orienting school practice continue to be those of the dominant *criollo* society. Still, in providing a space for the expression and maintenance of indigenous cultural forms, such practices represent significant gains achieved through popular pressure. Such "alternative political and cultural emphases," even when ostensibly incorporated, are indicators of what the hegemony has had to work to control (Williams 1977:113). While specific forms of oppression differ in the degree to which they allow subordinates to construct an autonomous culture, a social space "in which the definitions and performances imposed by domination do not prevail" is essential for the development of symbolic resistance (Scott 1985:328). So often, that cultural refuge is limited to the "offstage" areas of social life; the emergence of explicitly resistant forms onto the public stage of legitimized expression constitutes a significant penetration of the dominant order.

Coincident with that penetration, however, is an equally significant limitation: namely, the exclusion of females from the most forceful expressions of indigenous culture. In the familiar pattern, female participation varied in inverse proportion to the use of prestigious speech styles. In dances, male and female students participated to an equal degree; musical performance was heavily dominated by boys, though occasionally a girl would sing to male instrumental accompaniment. Girls as well as boys recited poetry, but less frequently and usually on romantic or historical themes; political or Aymara poetry was an exclusively male domain. Given that rural girls' lack of Spanish fluency was often cited as their reason for abstaining from public speaking, Aymara poetry would have seemed the ideal solution. This possibility was precluded, however, by girls' exclusion from all highly prestigious verbal genres, including Aymara ones. Clearly, resistant forms that challenge one sort of repression may strengthen or fail to address others; penetration of the dominant ideology on one front does not signify penetration on all fronts.[39]

Folk Culture vs. Popular Culture

While the foregoing arguments focus on the practices of indigenous rural subjects, they draw heavily upon theoretical studies of urban popular culture. John Fiske's insightful analyses have done much to define the area of pop culture studies and to suggest its possible articulation with other areas of social theory (reproduction and resistance theory, social and psychoanalytic theories of subjectivity, etc.). Nevertheless, his oversimplified view of folk culture—indeed, his virtual dismissal of it—is clearly unsuitable to the analysis of a cultural scene like the one at hand. Fiske (1989:169–70) conceives of folk culture as limited to isolated tribal societies, whose interaction with industrial capitalism is negligible and whose cultural traditions exert no significant influence at the national level. Due to its indigenous majority and high rural-urban migration, Bolivia's folk culture exercises a powerful influence on urban popular culture, and vice versa. While middle- and upper-class *criollos* have not been studied as intensely as their indigenous compatriots, even a surface familiarity with *paceño* popular culture reveals that indigenous influence extends far beyond indigenous communities. The assertion that "cases such as that of the conquered Greeks culturally influencing the Roman dominator are not encountered in Bolivia" (Albó 1979:312) is contradicted by ample evidence of such influence in a number of areas.

In Bolivia, the category of "the folk" rivals that of the nation itself; the folk collectivity that many refer to as "the Aymara nation" includes over three million people, spread across three countries. In a challenge to traditional notions of folklore, Rowe and Schelling (1991:4) assert that "in some regions (such as the Andean) the cultures referred to as folkloric have upheld their own alternative ideas of nationhood and have been capable of challenging the official state. In these circumstances, the idea of folklore breaks down, since the phenomena it refers to challenge the legitimacy of the society voicing the idea itself." In Bolivia, the degree to which the idea of folklore "breaks down" is debatable, since that idea is perhaps most powerful precisely among those sectors generating folkloric forms; at the same time, "folklore" has a stronger political connotation in Bolivia than in Europe or North America. On the one hand a repository for traditional cultural forms, it is also "a way of referring to contemporary cultures which articulate alternatives to existing power structures" (4). In contrast, Fiske spells out what he sees as the differences between folk and popular culture:

> Folk culture, unlike popular culture, is the product of a comparatively stable, traditional social order, in which social differences are not conflictual . . . Popular culture, unlike folk culture, is produced by elaborated industrialized societies that are experienced in complex and often contradictory ways . . . Folk cultures are much more homogeneous and do not have to encompass the variety of social allegiances formed by members of elaborated societies. (Fiske 1989:169–70)

What Fiske fails to account for is the possibility (or rather, the frequent reality) of traditional folk cultures existing *within* a heterogenous national culture. Bolivian society is experienced as complex, contradictory, and conflictive precisely because it is *not* a fully elaborated industrialized society, but rather one in which different modes of production (material and symbolic) lurch along together in uneasy coexistence. If "popular culture is made at the interface between the cultural resources provided by capitalism and everyday life" (129), it must be recognized that the "everyday life" of many Bolivians derives largely from folk culture, and that its location in a rural milieu does not prevent it from interfacing with the cultural resources provided by capitalism.

Has Bolivia's folk culture then been transformed into popular culture? Not if we accept Fiske's assertion that "popular culture, unlike folk culture, is made out of cultural resources that are not produced by the social formation that is using them" (170). A key feature of popular culture is that it draws upon the materials of the dominant ideology to create its own oppositional meanings. But the expressive practices examined above, while resisting, inverting, and satirizing the dominant culture in ways characteristic of "the popular," do so by drawing upon an indigenous cultural tradition (though not exclusively). In part, this is a result of Bolivia's colonial history. Many of the dances commonly thought of as most representative of Bolivia's folkloric tradition (*awki-awki, diablada, saya,* etc.) themselves arose as social commentaries on colonialism. An interesting feature of this tradition is the way historical conflicts are evoked to comment on current conflicts. When Bolivians speak of colonialism, they do not conceive of it as a closed chapter in history; rather, they draw an explicit connection between the Spanish conquest and the continuing domination of Indians by whites (and of Bolivia by the "developed" nations), and this is connection is evident in their expressive practices as well.

A historically situated interpretation of folk practices not only permits an exploration of how they are employed in modern struggles against modern forms of domination; it also provides a clearer picture of the processes of cultural transmission, one less vulnerable to the pitfalls of a theoretically static "Andeanism" (Starn 1991).

> This idea of invented, emergent cultural practices and forms contrasts with the anthropological notion of a historical cultural tradition that is passively inherited. An ethnic culture's cultural practices and forms are, therefore, whatever the group invent from their present struggle *and* from their past . . . If "ethnic cultural forms" are produced or created in a historical class context rather than passively inherited, "cultural distinctiveness" becomes problematic and impossible to study without references to ongoing class struggles. (Foley 1990:166)[40]

Bolivian folk culture maintains a strong continuity with precapitalist traditions, but it is hardly isolated from the conflicts of contemporary society. To further complicate the picture, a principal source of material for Bolivia's urban popular culture is, precisely, rural folk culture (though considerably reworked by the forces of national and global capitalism). In a double-edged process of cultural revitalization and hegemonic incorporation, indigenous folklore and ethnicity have emerged as defining features of Bolivian nationalism. While partly due to the external mobilization of ethnic resources in the service of capitalism (i.e., tourism), this is also a response to popular pressure.

When Fiske speaks of popular culture as reworking the cultural resources produced by others, he is referring to "the people's" appropriation of the products of the dominant ideology (for example, alternative readings of television shows or the individual meanings imposed on mass-produced fashions). Bolivian popular culture does employ cultural resources produced by others, but these resources are just as often drawn up from below as pulled down from above. Many folk elements are incorporated into popular culture by urbanites who are themselves a far cry from "the folk."[41] Bolivia's popular culture springs not from the lowest sector of society (i.e., inhabitants of remote rural areas where folklorists seek out the purest expressions of "authentic" folk culture), but from those whose location in the city (and within reach of the mass media) signifies a step up in the social hierarchy. Conversely, in a city made up largely of rural migrants, popular culture achieves its resonance as much through its evocation of the folk aesthetic as from its relevance to life under urban capitalism (cf. Archondo 1991). As Rowe and Schelling (1991:2) affirm, "Traditional and modern worlds are no longer separate . . . many people in Latin America live in both at once."

There is, therefore, a mutual feedback of considerable historical depth between Bolivian folk culture and popular culture. The distinction between the two is blurred in forms such as the *doctorcitos* dance, which comments on the pretensions of modern capitalism by recasting the objects of derision into a traditional form of parody. While urban popular culture draws upon rural folkloric forms, rural folk culture incorporates images from urban popular culture in order to burlesque it.

Bolivia belies Fiske's (1989:171) assertion that "folk culture outside the social conditions of its production is always *theirs*; popular culture is *ours*, despite its alienated origins." The dominant construction of Bolivian national identity is such that even nonindigenous, urban Bolivians have a strong sense of "ours-ness" toward rural folk culture. Official culture, popular culture, and folk culture are tied up in an uneasy relationship, giving rise to differing allegiances within and across social groups. Urban aficionados of rural folklore may eulogize indigenous musical traditions while openly scorning the popularized strains that draw upon them; conversely, indigenous musical traditions are maintained in part by government-sponsored festivals and popularization via the mass media.[42]

Today, any large folk culture is likely to find itself in a conflictive relationship with the virtually inescapable influence of post-industrial mass culture. Therefore, Fiske's (1989:171) assertion that "popular culture is a culture of conflict in a way that folk culture is not" is far too simplistic. The folk culture of a subordinated group automatically becomes a "culture of conflict" by virtue of its contact with the surrounding dominant/industrialized culture. This contact inevitably leads to battles not only for the survival of the folk culture, but for control over its meanings and images.

> In Peru, Bolivia, Guatemala and Paraguay, the strength of native and *mestizo* cultures makes the term folklore and the approach associated with it (the preservation of rural performances and artefacts by members of the other, modern culture) incapable of containing the phenomena they are supposed to frame . . . The academic study of folklore focuses on local communities and ethnic groups in a manner that isolates them from the broader structural constraints of a society which, with the expansion of capitalism and the culture industry, has altered the characteristics and function of practices traditionally carried out by and for the peasantry. (Rowe and Schelling 1991:5–6).

Of course, the alteration of the function and characteristics of peasant practices is not always a bad thing; in the normal school, the discontextualization of folkloric forms from the peasant community and their recontextualization in conjunction with urban cultural forms allowed them to serve as critiques of the latter; it is in folklore's uses as a challenge to dominant practices, rather than simply a refuge from them, that it leaves off being merely alternative and becomes oppositional.

A final difficulty with the traditional conception of folk culture relates directly to the educational system and its construction of ethnic and national identities. Fiske includes among folklore's essential characteristics its operation outside of established social institutions such as the church, the school, and the mass media. So what shall we make of the existence of an official division of folklore within Bolivia's Ministry of Education, or the performance of folkloric dances as an indispensible part of school life, from the early grades to the normal school? A primary function of public education is to foster in students a strong identification with the nation, transcending class or ethnic loyalties. But in the normal school, these loyalties were also strongly reinforced, though more through students' own popular practices than by teachers or the official curriculum.

Fiske (1989:170) argues that "conceiving popular culture as a form of folk culture denies its conflictual elements . . . The idea of the people as an industrial equivalent of the folk is all too easily assimilated into a depoliticized liberal pluralism." A more productive approach might be to conceive of "the folk" as a rural equivalent of "the people," and of folk culture as just as conflictive, contradictory, and potentially progressive as popular culture.[43] A sharp distinction between folk culture and popular culture is hardly useful once "the folk" begin to participate in wider circles of signification, influencing and being influenced by them. Foley (1990:199) suggests we let go of such rigid dichotomies and talk instead about "the cultural politics surrounding shifting cultural forms and identities in a highly fluid cultural tradition." This gives us a more active picture of students' socialization as well; rather than simply being inculcated with a prefabricated ideology, students bring their own meanings and practices to the pedagogic situation. The outcome is a combination, often conflictive, of what they bring and what they encounter there. Thus, the productive system of schooling is not composed solely of the school and its formal organization; nonformalized aspects of student culture, outside the direct control of school officials, play a productive role as well.

What Counts as Resistance?

Which of the practices described here fulfill a counterhegemonic function, and which fail to address the structures of power, or even reinforce them? We have seen that practices and postures that challenge one form of oppression may reinforce others—or perhaps even the very structures they challenge, as the antischool ethos of Willis's "lads" ultimately reproduced them as workers within the class hierarchy. Nevertheless, the lads' antagonistic stance fostered within the school an alternative set of values that otherwise would have been absent. In effect, by placing collective interests over individual ones, the lads sacrificed their individual futures to maintain a cultural space apart from the school's mainstream values. Although their resistance ultimately bound them even more tightly to the structures they rejected, imagining the school without their defiant presence gives an even bleaker picture. Furthermore, though their oppositional behavior may ensure them a future of tedious manual labor, that does not erase the freedom and *communitas* they enjoyed during their school years. It is in school that students first struggle to maintain the autonomy of identity that institutionalized labor works to erode. We might even turn Willis's model of working-class cultural reproduction around and argue that the solidary pleasures of shop-floor culture draw as much upon the creative camaraderie of high school resistance, as vice versa.

Still, it cannot be denied that many forms of student resistance yield dubious results in terms of students' power to control their own labor or conditions of existence, or to expand critical debate in the public sphere. In the normal school, most of students' resistant behavior emphasized escape, rather than challenge.[44] Instead of protesting school policies prohibiting wooing couples from even holding hands or talking together too frequently, students sneaked into town or the *bosquecillo* for stolen moments of unobserved intimacy. Instead of challenging irregularities in the collection of tuition, they pleaded lack of money to avoid paying a few *pesos* more; when some pressed for a collective solution to the problem, their heated meetings ultimately came to naught. While José's imagined confontation with the *inspectora* and Mateo's "hidden transcript" of official corruption and incompetence seem to display a more conscious oppositionality, they did not directly challenge the conditions they denounced. "No matter how elaborate the hidden transcript may become, it always remains a substitute for an act of assertion directly in the face of power" (Scott 1990:115).

Cheating and other academic improprieties, while "resistant" on a surface level, can also be read as conforming to the commodification of linguistic expression. This sort of resistance "skirted around and teased the predominance of reified knowledge but did not reject or transcend it" (Everhart 1983:162). Still, such pessimism seems less justified with regard to other strategies. Everhart celebrates the more creative forms of student resistance, but ultimately consigns them to the role of cultural pressure valves, allowing repressive structures to continue by providing momentary outlets for the inevitable resistant impulse. The limited capability of subaltern meanings to seize the floor merely "gives the impression of power while ignoring the conditions under which relative powerlessness exists" (250.). In his view, such resistance is more a reaction to oppressive social relations than a conscious opposition of them; it "does not oppose as much as it forms a separate reality." He claims that this is because students lack a collective self-consciousness of how reified knowledge ultimately leads to estranged labor. "Students know something is 'wrong' but they cannot easily articulate what is to be done" (229).

But do students really lack a collective awareness of the estranged nature of their labor? While they do not express their complaints in the language of the social theorist, many are quite articulate in their assessment of what is wrong with the system. Perhaps practices such as cheating do constitute mere reactions, rather than challenges, to the reification of school knowledge. Perhaps attempts to reappropriate class time by "goofing off" cannot be considered successful, given that "the relationship of the student to the forms of reified knowledge remains the same—estranged" (194). Yet such forms do preserve an area of practice that is not surrendered to external control; students' communicative action does escape reification, if only momentarily.

Furthermore, the public performances in which students interrogate the ethnic, class, and gender hierarchies governing their society are clearly not mere "reactions" to the reification of school knowledge. Everhart (1983:256) remains pessimistic, citing students' proclivity to use communicative action "for its own sake" rather than as a forum for political opposition. But the significance of such forms may not depend solely on their underlying motivations. Willis (in Foley 1990:x) notes that expressive practices give rise to critiques and penetrations of dominant ideology "almost as the byproduct of the application of sensuous human capacities to immediate ends." Similarly, Bourdieu (1984:4) sees them as representing a popular aesthetic "in itself," rather than "for itself." Still, the former is certainly a prerequisite to the latter. If our goal is to expand the domain of unalienated practice, expanding opportunities for popular expression, even "for its own sake," would seem to embody at least some progressive potential. The motivation behind such practices may be recreational pleasure or a sense of solidarity, rather than social critique; but their effects are pleasurable for a reason.[45] The feelings generated by these "minor liberations" from hegemony may be linked to underlying notions of what a just society would make possible; often it is these momentary glimpses of *communitas* that keep alive the vision of what might be. While this may not qualify as "cognition" or revolutionary consciousness, neither can it be dismissed as irrelevant (cf. Willis 1981b; Willis and Corrigan 1983).

Nor should all potentially political expression be judged by our own cultural standards. The blustering machismo of Willis's lads is central to their cultural identity. While it is logical that their resistance should be expressed in that way, that sort of masculine identity is not central to Aymara culture, and certainly not in relation to school. Given such cultural and historical factors as the Aymaras' high regard for schooling in general, the residue of centuries of colonialism, and the absence of a vibrant, autonomous youth subculture (at least in the countryside), one would expect Aymara students' resistance to emerge via other, less confrontational means.

Of course, resistance must move beyond the symbolic if it is to produce real change. In their analysis of the eventual failure of British youth subcultures, Clarke and colleagues conclude that "the problematic of a subordinate class experience can be 'lived through,' negotiated or resisted [at the symbolic level]; but it cannot be *resolved* at that level or by those means" (1981:64; original emphasis). Still, a symbolic space for alternative or oppositional meanings is essential in order for direct action to take root and develop. *Hora cívica,* despite its limitations, did provide a forum for students to express their political ideas.[46] José's desire for a public debate on ethnic discrimination may have been quashed, Mateo may have felt compelled to guard his criticisms of the system in a hidden manuscript, but that did not prevent each of them from undertaking his own analysis of the problem and sharing it with others when possible. Giroux (in McLaren 1986:xii) sees student resistance as deriving not only from the need to counter external domination, but also from "the need to dignify and affirm those experiences that make up their lives outside of school . . . Resistance is as much a matter of self-confirmation as it is a reaction to repressive ideologies and practices." Practices that resist the commodification of expression may not be explicitly revolutionary, but they are life- and self-affirming and in that sense empowering, both individually and collectively.

Scott (1985) warns against limiting our analysis of resistance to its behavioral manifestations; to do so "reduces the explanation of human action to the level one might use to explain how the water buffalo resists its driver or why the dog steals scraps from the table" (38). Behavior is never self-explanatory; analysis must also include the domain of ideology and meaning. Furthermore, it is in their behavior that dominated groups are most constrained, whereas the realm of belief and interpretation is much harder to control (322). This view expands the possibilities for counter-hegemonic action among subaltern groups. Though intangible, ideological resistance reveals itself in language—in the offstage comments, conversations, jokes, and folksongs deriving from actors' own collective experience. In his inventory of "weapons of the weak," Scott includes "disbelief in elite homilies" (350); internal skepticism remains a bastion of resistance even when resistant action is impossible. One day in Native Languages class, my eye happened to fall upon the graffiti carved into the chair in front of me. Many chairs were donations from Kennedy's Alliance for Progress, and prominently displayed the program's logo. On this one, the logo had been altered with the aid of a pocketknife and pen; instead of *"Alianza para el progreso,"* it now read *"Alianza para si mismo"* ("alliance for themselves"). I had heard other Bolivians assert that foreign aid benefits the donors more than the recipients, but none so succinctly as the anonymous student who had literally reworked a sign of elite origin into his or her own subversive message.

Another indicator of resistant ideology is the use of derisive nicknames for those in power, or slang terms revealing alternative values or interpretations. Students had secret nicknames for those staff members who were perceived as most arbitrary in their treatment of students, and some of their most common slang terms addressed the student-teacher relation itself—for example, the epithet *corcho* ("teacher's pet") and the corresponding verb *corchear* ("to suck up to"). The former was sometimes teasingly called out when a student pursued a teacher after class to ask a question. While the teasing was good-natured, the underlying message was unmistakable: attempts at private communication with teachers crossed a social boundary and threatened student solidarity. Persistent violation of this boundary brought more serious censure from one's classmates. Several students, particularly those who had found themselves at odds with the *inspectora* at one time or another, had harsh words for Antonia, who was quite friendly with her and considered by some to be her "spy." Remedios expressed a common sentiment about such transgressive familiarity:

Remedios: There are students who are squealers. Gossips, you might say. Mostly to gain the professors' preference or affection . . . One day they'll be professors themselves, and with that sort of gossiping, people are going to start to hate them, so they're just hurting themselves. And when they realize it, it'll be too late.

Such antagonisms may belie the cohesiveness of student solidarity against external authority, but they also reveal a *standard* of solidarity that is no less real for being broken at times. Even in total institutions, where real group loyalty is rare, "the expectation that group loyalty should prevail forms part of the inmate culture and underlies the hostility accorded those who break inmate solidarity" (Goffman 1961:61). Furthermore, such sentiments reveal a strong ideological current that is unmistakably inimical to official values. Ostracism of those members who try to curry favor with elites is evidence of an autonomous subaltern culture with sanctioning power (Scott 1985:41). Even when behavioral compliance is near complete, the undercurrent of muttered insults, subversive slang, and aloofness from staff interests indicates that "the elite's libretto for the hierarchy . . . is, at the very least, not sung word for word by its subjects" (42).

Getting "inside subjects' heads" is the ethnographer's most elusive goal. Methodologically, it is where the interview takes over from participant observation. Still, those opinions that subjects are willing and able to communicate to a cultural outsider are never the final word on what social phenomena "mean." If they were, interpretation and analysis would be superfluous. It is the combination of contradictory motives and meanings—conscious and unconscious, collective and individual, spoken and unspoken—that calls forth both the ethnographer's interpretations and the politician's manipulations. Without such contradictions and intertwinings of meaning, the notion of "ideology" would be meaningless.

Recognition of the contradictory nature of ideology and practice leads us to yet another dilemma: where, within the tangle of actions and interpretations, does the truth of the situation lie? In one sense, of course, the question is meaningless; to privilege one strand over all the others erases (or at least glosses over) the very contradictions one wishes to study. Still, many theorists imply the existence of an ideological "bottom line" hidden within subjects' practices by adopting an ultimately optimistic or pessimistic stance. The search for this bottom line underlies much of the theoretical soul-searching over the category of resistance. What precisely constitutes resistance, and beyond this, what constitutes *significant* resistance? Take, for example, Turton's broad view: "Any, even barely conscious, acts which tend to negate or counter deeply engrained bureaucratic mentalities and forms of discipline may be highly significant . . . From a theoretical or methodological point of view the form of resistance as such is of less interest than an analysis of a particular social relation and its context" (1986:41).

From a pragmatic point of view, however, the form of resistance and its impact on social relations may be of almost exclusive interest. For the political activist, the significance of "barely conscious" acts pales in comparison to those that signify an emerging class, ethnic, or gender consciousness. Individual acts that do not accumulate into a collective force have scarce political potential; a fleeting thought of utopia or rebellion means little if it does not erupt into an act of will. Social theorists trying to combine objective analysis with transformative politics often vacillate between these two points of view. Scott (1985), for example, in one breath warns against romanticizing the weapons of the weak, claiming that "they are unlikely to do more than marginally affect the various forms of exploitation" (29–30), and in the next declares them "equally massive and often far more effective" than more conspicuous or confrontational forms of defiance (32).

Compliance does not signify consent, nor does acquiescence to an unpleasant fact of life constitute ideological support of that fact; but the one may mimic the effects of the other. If the effects are the same, one might argue, what difference does it make whether subjects assent in their heart of hearts to the ideals of the dominant order? Does "resistance" that ultimately reinforces oppressive social structures—like the antischool values of Willis's "lads"—merit the name? The answer lies partly in viewing the situation diachronically. Actors may exclude from their discourse those options that seem out of reach, but consciously prefer them. Since conditions may change, it is conceivable that presently latent options might enter the realm of active discourse and even practice, at such time as they become real possibilities. If, on the other hand, there is alignment between elite and subordinate values, the new conditions' potential for the fracturing of hegemony is reduced. The maintenance of symbolic resistance—even if it is "only" symbolic—holds open an ideological space, in anticipation of the day when it may become something more.

A case in point is the domain of official school rituals, such as the normal school's *hora cívica* programs. Though student-produced, these followed a fairly rigid format of traditional music and dance, patriotic hymns, recited proverbs and poetry, and political or historical speeches. There was little doubt that, for many, *hora cívica* was devoid of any real patriotic fervor; whatever nationalist sentiments students possessed at other times were overshadowed by the ritual's enforced nature. While students did not go so far as to mock the national symbols, a fair number displayed their detachment via rowdy behavior or early morning yawns. When rituals intended to evoke an elevated emotion become empty and routinized, the associated emotion may itself be regarded with suspicion. "Sanctity can become eroded by an inordinate exercise of power . . . When acceptance of a ritual is coerced, it is transformed into a lie" (McLaren 1986:185). Implicitly defined by this element of coercion, school rituals failed to arouse the intended solidarity or enthusiasm, and in fact "served to dismember whatever minimal communitas already existed" (185). In fact, student *communitas* was generated by precisely the opposite circumstances: those in which unplanned or incongruous behavior caused a "frame break"

(Goffman 1974) that disrupted the ritual's integrity. The discipline of morning assembly was usually strong enough to discourage such breaks, but such was not always the case in class; and it was classroom disruptions that tended to produce the strongest sense of community and bonding among students (cf. McLaren 1986:221).

Nevertheless, routinized hypocrisy can become a way of life. Describing students' participation in rituals in which they no longer believe, McLaren cites Rappaport's claim that "acceptance may be more profound than belief, for in his participation the performer may transcend his own doubts by accepting in defiance of them."[47] Compliance may not signify *belief* in official school values, but it does constitute *conformance* with them. Moreover, the mental dissonance of skeptical compliance may be dulled by repetition; students who faithfully carry out tasks they view as meaningless may become teachers who do the same, or who require their students to do so.

This chapter has focused on the ways in which students resist; equally significant are the ways in which they express support for dominant values. Even in private interviews, many students expressed satisfaction with the school curriculum, with the displacement of the Aymara language by Spanish, even with the strict control that the institution exercised over them. Hegemonic influences penetrate the actions even of those who decry the dominant system; a student who laments the fact that fewer children are learning to speak Aymara may, in another context, scornfully deride her rural classmate's lack of sophistication. Rather than declaring hegemony to be "present" or "absent" in a given subject or situation, we must recognize its contradictory nature as an eternally incomplete project. By characterizing subjects' alignment with some elements of hegemony as "false consciousness" (or some equivalent term), we not only fail to recognize the multiplicity of subject positions from which individuals respond, but also close off discussion at the very point where it ought to begin: examining the contradictory makeup of subaltern ideology, tracing its various strands, and discovering how they are mobilized in social practice.

Thus, the issue of incorporation is also important to the question of "what counts" as resistance. Some have argued that, for ethnically subordinated students, academic success means not only exchanging their labor for a title, but exchanging the meanings, values, and practices of their home culture for those of the middle class; that, in essence, they must give up their ethnic identity for one more thoroughly permeated by hegemony. Bourdieu and Passeron (1977:119) claimed that "children from rural areas, confronted with the simultaneous experience of forced acculturation and insidious counter-acculturation, can only choose between duplication and acceptance of exclusion." Even the later Bourdieu (1984:384) saw only two options for the dominated: "loyalty to self and the group (always liable to relapse into shame), or the individual effort to assimilate the dominant ideal" and abandon the goal of collectively regaining control over social identity.

Are these really minority or working-class students' only choices? Is it impossible to maintain control over one's social identity while succeeding within the system? Some would answer yes, maintaining that securing access to cultural capital (and subsequent class mobility) means foregoing the chance to challenge that standard via a more combative ethnic or class position. However, this view neglects the possibility that subaltern students may transform the middle class by entering it, as much as they transform themselves in order to get in. Foley notes that "middle-class Mexicano [students] who were 'making it' did not necessarily abandon their historical ethnically expressive cultural practices. Instead, they simply added competencies in deceptive communication to the general expressive repertory that they learned growing up in a vibrant regional and ethnic speech community" (Foley 1990:197). His subjects not only retained the expressive practices of their home culture, but viewed their success in the Anglo world as a form of ethnic resistance (201). While their success led away from the valorization of Mexicano culture, their "resistance" was rooted in class and racial oppression and contained creative and progressive elements. In the normal school, there were students such as José, who worked hard to succeed within the dominant culture, but on his own terms. A good student academically, he had well-formulated criticisms of how the school was run, and definite ideas about maintaining control of his own social identity:

José: There's a certain antipathy between me and the *inspectora*... She's treated me like an *indio*, a peasant—I am! I am, but a remodeled peasant, no longer like before—a totally different kind of peasant. I think things over very well before acting. Not like her. But she thinks maybe that I'm an idiot, that I don't know anything. She can say to me, "You're just a peasant," but maybe someday we might run into each other in the university, who knows? . . . I've had to instruct Diana on how to act, "You can't let her [dominate you]. You have to talk this way . . . " With good reason the *inspectora* says "Ah, the *india* thinks she's something. She didn't used to be like that!" And it's true, maybe; that's how we have to be, no? We don't have to be humiliated, with our heads bowed—no way. They're not going to humiliate me unjustly—nobody nowhere. I stand up for myself, wherever I am . . . If I make a mistake, let them punish me, yell at me, whatever. But without any justification, no way.

While the presence of indigenous elements in official constructions of national identity can be read as the incorporation of a potentially threatening strain, it also represents the successful forcing of at least part of the indigenous agenda onto the public stage. When even the president makes a point of publicly ingesting *coca* and lauding its medicinal and cultural values, thus complicating his relations with the United States and its imposed drug policies, can this be interpreted as simply the hegemonic incorporation of indigenous symbols? A more credible (and politically empowering) interpretation is Fiske's (1989:193) claim that "what is called 'incorporation' is better understood as a defensive strategy forced upon the powerful by the guerrilla raids of the weak." Even where the co-optation of subaltern meanings and practices is more successful, Fiske points out that "there would be no need for capitalism (or patriarchy) to promote its value so assiduously if there were not ample popular experience of its inadequacies and inequalities" (160).

Incorporation happens, but invoking it in reference to a particular cultural form should not foreclose the question of that form's significance (any more than the term "false consciousness" should with regard to expressions of ideology). The notion that popular resistance serves merely as a safety valve, permitted by the dominant society in order to maintain a more flexible containment of opposition, is not only a political dead end, but also denies popular culture's validity and potential; furthermore, such a stance is more likely to alienate the popular sectors than to mobilize them. A more realistic view recognizes that "the forms of opposition are as numerous as the forms of subordination, but running through them all, sometimes acute, sometimes muted, is this central thread of antagonism" (169).

Ethnographers focusing on cultural reproduction and resistance consistently reaffirm the value of resistant activities and everyday cultural practices in strengthening the bonds of collective identity and creating dignity and meaning in subjects' lives. The concept of resistance is a watershed in the interpretation of educational processes, breaking with traditional explanations of school failure and deviant behavior and recasting these phenomena in a framework that "has little to do with the logic of deviance, individual pathology, [and] learned helplessness, and a great deal to do, although not exhaustively, with the logic of moral and political indignation."[48] This indignation is evident in students' own analyses; and even where it is absent, that does not imply a neat division between forms of resistance that are politically significant and those that are simply pathological, asocial, or even invisible. "The existence of those who seem not to rebel is a warren of minute, individual, autonomous tactics and strategies which counter and inflect the visible facts of overall domination, and whose purposes and calculations, desires and choices resist any simple division into the political and the apolitical" (Colin Gordon, in Foucault 1980:251).

For such individual acts to enlarge the space of popular practice, rather than simply maintain a bulwark against hegemony's further encroachment, they must become not only collective, but also informed by a collective awareness of their significance. The "truth" of such acts lies in their potential—a term suggesting both possibility and the as-yet-unrealized nature of that possibility. Only a perspective that recognizes and accepts both the penetrations and the limitations of popular practice and subordinate ideology can theorize how that potential might be realized.

Fiske (1989:177) focuses on "those moments where hegemony fails, where ideology is weaker than resistance, where social control is met by indiscipline" as "the theoretically crucial ones in popular culture, for they are the articulation of the interests of the people." While defining hegemony's failures rather than its successes as the "theoretically crucial moments" may seem arbitrarily optimistic, it is also strategic. Part of a transformational politics is identifying the progressive potential in popular practices, and then working toward conditions that will allow that potential to be realized; in essence, *deciding* which moments will be the "theoretically crucial" ones and then working to make them so. In his advocacy of a "progressive skepticism," Fiske approximates Henry Giroux's (1988:xxxii) manifesto that radical pedagogy, in order to become a viable political project, must combine the language of critique with the language of possibility. Not all popular practices are inherently progressive; but the contradictory nature of subaltern culture is itself a political resource. It makes the work of purposeful articulation between the theoretical and the popular—that is, politics—not only necessary, but possible.

7

An Alternative Vision: Notes toward a Transformative Bolivian Pedagogy

If theory accompanies anger it will lead to effective solutions to the problems at hand.

—Julia Lesage, "Women's Rage" (1988:428)

Día del Indio, Los Pozos (August 1, 1993)

Word around the normal school had it that the peasants were gathering in the town plaza to celebrate Bolivia's Día del Indio (Day of the Indian), with a rally by the *kataristas*, though whether this referred to the *indigenista* political party (Movimiento Revolucionario Tupac Katari) or the nascent terrorist group (Ejército Guerrillero Tupac Katari) was unclear.[1] A few professors were heading over to watch, and I asked if I could tag along. They became noticeably uncomfortable; two of them murmured something about going over later and beat a hasty retreat, but two others politely agreed to accompany me. We started off toward town, but as we approached the plaza, my companions decided to take a short detour, telling me to go on, they would catch up with me later.

In the plaza I found around three hundred *campesinos*, carrying *wiphalas* (Aymara flags) and *pututus* (ram's horns, traditionally blown to summon the community or mark moments of high ceremony and worn as a symbol of Aymara leadership). After half an hour of marching solemnly around the plaza, calling out slogans apropos to the occasion, the crowd stopped to listen to speeches (in Aymara) about racial oppression and injustice. No one approached me to make small talk, but neither did I feel any particular hostility. Afterward, some remained in the plaza to chat, while others headed back to their homes in the surrounding hills. I walked back to the school and, at a discreet distance from the plaza, was joined on the road by the professors.

The next day was the official celebration. The opening speech by a local politician lauded the peasants and their victories: the agrarian reform, the educational reform, and the nationalization of the mines (he did not mention current plans to re-privatize them). The main speech was by the head of the local development agency, a prominent ADN party member who would later sponsor the normal school's graduating class. He spoke optimistically of how Bolivia was "becoming integrated without ill will . . . We celebrate this day with great joy, because in time the country will belong to the Indians. The government will be in their hands . . . Before Elizardo Pérez, education was denied to our peasant brothers;[2] that's why our Aymara and Quechua nations remain backward; we don't have worthy representatives, leaders at the national level." (The leader of the Peasant Federation Tupac Katari sat at his side, expressionless, throughout). He heralded the coming liberation of the Indians, noting, "They are human beings, equal to the *mistis*" (*mestizos*). After lauding "the father of the revolution," Victor Paz Estenssoro, he ceded the stage to a program of traditional music and dance, followed by a marching band from the school *Hacia el Mar* ("Toward the Sea"), who carried a paper-maché ship symbolizing Bolivia's claim to its lost coastline. He then led the children in cheers for Bolivia and El Día del Indio, telling them, "Very good, children, you've answered well. Bolivians have to shout loud. That's why the Indians are oppressed—they don't know how to shout; they don't know how to express themselves." He extolled the virtues of the "simple but hardworking" Aymaras and past martyrs for independence, Bolívar and Sucre as well as Tupac Amaru, Tupac Katari, and Bartolina Sisa. There were several nationalist hymns, more speeches about national humiliation and oppression, and a poem about the virtues and trials of the Aymara nation, all in Spanish. At the end, one of the normal school students recited an impassioned poem in Aymara, dressed in traditional peasant costume.

Walking back to the normal school afterward, one professor remarked to another, "What won't the peasants do, huh? If Goni [presidential candidate Sánchez de Lozada] comes to pass out food, they'll all be for Goni."

Socialization and the Multiple Subject

Scholars from throughout the political spectrum agree that schools are key sites of socialization. The traditional notion of socialization has a generally positive connotation, as the minimum necessary for the continuation of society; in these pages, however, "socialization" has been examined under a more critical lens. In schools, it involves learning to labor under specific relations of production and shaping one's products to the commodity forms the school demands. Schools socialize students by casting them as particular kinds of subjects, in relation to teachers, knowledge, their own productive activity, and various social groups within and beyond the nation. Though the practices and relations imposed by the school are selective, they (and the subject positions they generate) are naturalized, so that the hegemonic conditions of schooling are perceived (if at all) simply as the normal requirements of group learning.

Chapter 4 explored how the school positions students as national, class, ethnic, and gendered subjects. These subject positions are constructed largely (though not exclusively) through language—through "discourses predicating identities" (Mato 1992). Situating students within such discourses disarticulates them from certain social identities and rearticulates them to others, with the aim of producing "citizens"—weakening those bonds that challenge or compete with the claims of the nation-state, and creating in their place subjective bonds of self-identification as *bolivianos.* This process, and its naturalization, are manifestations of ideology, understood as a practice of representation aimed at producing a specific articulation—"that is, producing specific meanings and necessitating certain subjects as their supports" (Coward and Ellis 1977:67).

If that were all there was to it, social reproduction would function easily and smoothly. But subjectivity is more than simply "an effect of language" (Giroux, in Walsh 1991:xxii). Students are social agents as well as social subjects; they bring their own meanings and practices to the school and generate new ones from their contact with it. While absorbing to some degree the nationalist and ethnic meanings that permeate school ceremonies and curricula, students also challenge and rework these meanings in the spaces allowed them, advancing alternative conceptions of nationalism that refuse to surrender their class and ethnic content. While holding fast to class solidarities, students also draw upon the meanings and practices of their home culture, valorizing Aymara ethnicity and subverting the urban orientation of the "national culture," trying to forge a coherent identity from subject positions that recent social changes have brought into unprecedented conjunction. Their use of tradition, rather than being isolationist or anachronistic, explicitly engages that tradition's interface with the urban belief systems that threaten it. Tradition is employed, not simply as a cultural refuge from the assault of modern forces, but as "the imaginative reconstruction of the past in the service of current interests" (Scott 1985:146).[3] Parody is a crucial resource in this enterprise, a means of deflating the supposed superiority of urban cultural practices and uncovering the traces of their selective naturalization.

Students' attempts to construct new subjectivities and challenge old ones are hindered by a school discourse in which subject positions are assumed, rather than questioned. As Bakhtin observed, "language is not a neutral medium that passes freely and easily into the private property of the speaker's intentions; it is populated—overpopulated—with the intentions of others."[4] Shaping this discourse to one's own intentions is even harder in a second language, one that carries the weight of colonialism and stigmatizes speakers of nonstandard varieties. In such circumstances, even apparently trivial linguistic interactions bear the traces of social history, at once reflecting and reproducing structures of domination (Thompson, in Bourdieu 1991:2). Still, language is complex and contradictory; its "cultural work" is not limited to reproducing the dominant ideology (Fiske 1989:180).

While social reproduction involves subjects' interpellation into particular subject positions, these are not constructed solely within the dominant ideology and then simply imposed on subaltern groups. Rather, they are created in the space beween the two, and their fixation within chains of signification is a never-ending struggle over meaning. Such discursive struggles occur not only in people's attempts to rupture, contest, or supplant particular ideologies, but also when they "interrupt the ideological field" by transforming or rearticulating the meaning of existing terms (Hall 1985:112–13)—as in the reworkings that the terms *indio* and *campesino* have undergone and continue to undergo, both from above and from below. As social movements develop around the contestation of existing ideologies, "meanings which appear to have been fixed in place forever begin to lose their moorings." If the challenge to old meanings becomes strong enough, society may even cease to reproduce itself functionally in quite the same way that it did before, and "social reproduction itself becomes a contested process" (112–13).

Classic theories of subjectivity stressed the resolution of contradictory forces in a unified social subject. In contrast, recent approaches emphasize the struggle rather than its resolution, positing a "disunited, contradictory subject, in which the social struggle is still ongoing, in which contradictory subject positions sit sometimes uncomfortably, sometimes relatively comfortably, together" (Fiske 1989:180–81). The multiple nature of subjectivity has important implications for the articulation of social groups to particular ideologies. Most importantly, it destroys the notion of a necessary correspondence between class position and ideology (cf. Mouffe 1981; Hall 1985; Laclau and Mouffe 1985; Bhabha 1994:19–39). Once we recognize that different social contradictions have different origins, interacting with class divisions but not reducible to them, the category of "false consciousness" ceases to be useful, if indeed it ever was. Social actors can no longer be viewed as irrational subjects who "do not grasp their own interests," or are "so broken by circumstances [that they] cannot be expected to think straight" (Ollman 1976:245). Hegemony is durable precisely because it appeals to certain interests of those whom it subordinates (Hall 1986b); for example, students' submission to an alienating regime of knowledge allows them a degree of social mobility that would otherwise be out of reach. Challenging that regime's legitimacy entails greater risk than simply working to rise within it.

Hegemony functions by favoring certain subject positions over others; it articulates groups and individuals around oppressive ideologies by foregrounding selected interests that are real, if not always "progressive." Aymara people's ideologies about school have been articulated to perpetuate a certain type of education responding to certain of their interests (i.e., achieving social mobility within the extant class/race structure). A student who downplays her indigenous origins and adopts an urban style does so because she has chosen an identity that is empowering for her in ways that another is not. Labeling this choice "false consciousness" dismisses out of hand the factors leading to it, when it is precisely these that must be examined. The term itself is "a clear admission that culture, values, and ideology cannot be read directly off objective, material conditions" (Scott 1985:317). While the "non-necessary correspondence" that makes hegemonic articulation possible precludes the notion of an inevitable, unilinear progress toward liberation, it also implies a certain freedom. It means that the result of subjects' efforts at embracing, rejecting, appropriating or challenging official ideologies is never a foregone conclusion.

Political Practice and Popular Culture

The dethroning of class as the sole determinant of ideology has implications for political practice as well. In the constellation of factors vying for subjects' allegiances,

> class may be applicable to some situations but not to others; it may be reinforced or crosscut by other ties; it may be far more important for the experience of some than of others. Those who are tempted to dismiss all principles of human action that contend with class identity as "false-consciousness" and to wait for Althusser's "determination in the last instance" are likely to wait in vain. In the meantime, the messy reality of multiple identities will continue to be the experience out of which social relations are conducted. (Scott 1985:43)

A transformational politics that does not take these multiple identities into account risks isolation and obsolescence. Certainly the class-reductionist perspective of Bolivia's radical left has hindered its ability to win over the indigenous majority (in contrast, Carlos Palenque's skillful blend of ethnic, class, gender, nationalist, and religious symbolism raised him practically to the status of a "popular religion"). Popular culture has often been dismissed by radical activists as distractionary at best, reactionary at worst. It is this attitude, in part, that has prevented oppositional ideologies from becoming popular. Traditional theories of incorporation have tended to dismiss those tactics of popular resistance that aim at survival rather than the overthrow of dominant structures; but this position is ultimately self-defeating, in terms of articulating a progressive historical bloc.

> Instead of being valued for these everyday resistances, the people are demeaned as cultural dupes for finding pleasure or satisfaction in them . . . It is hardly surprising that the people, in their variety of social allegiances, are reluctant to align themselves with political and cultural theories that demean them, that fail to recognize their pleasures or their power, and whose emphasis on structures and strategy can seem disconnected from the practices they have evolved by which to live their everyday lives within and against the system. (Fiske 1989:163)

In a country such as Bolivia, where ethnicity is such a pervasive force and popular culture provides one of the few arenas for resistant pleasure in an arduous and oppressive existence, the left ignores such forces at its peril. While cultural forms of resistance may not constitute "always-already forms of socialist politics" (Willis and Corrigan 1983:102), no such politics can afford to ignore them; direct social action is only "the tip of the iceberg" of political life, broadly defined. A broadbased politics must be constructed in the space between progressivism and radicalism, macro and micro, building upon the already-existing connections between them and seeking "the conditions under which the submerged 90 percent of the political iceberg can be made to rear up and distort the social surface" (Fiske 1989:162). Popular meanings—shifting, multivalent, and generated from everyday experience—"do not take easily to central control, however benevolent" (187). Popular culture aims to expand the space for producing alternative meanings *within* dominant structures, not to overthrow them. But these meanings' failure to transcend the "progressive" and become "radical" is also their strength; a complete break with dominant structures of meaning would also break their relevances to life within those structures.

The popular practices of the normal school students (and of La Paz's urban Aymaras) are rich in social commentary about the class, gender, ethnic, and international hierarchies in which their practitioners are positioned. Yet most of Bolivia's ostensibly liberatory political movements have failed to harness this tide of popular discontent, in part because they define the basis of their resistance too narrowly. Traditional leftist parties find scant acceptance among those for whom ethnic identity is more salient than class, and their rigid dogmatism excludes such sectors from participating equally in producing their own resistant meanings. A movement that pretends to interpret the subjugated's experience of subjugation for them can never become truly popular (though it may find a following when its interpretation coincides with popular ones). Too often, the left (in Bolivia as elsewhere) has viewed ethnic and racial loyalties as competing with class solidarities and has downplayed them rather than building upon them (cf. Montoya 1991).

Conversely, ethnic-based political movements have often suffered from a view of indigenous identity rooted in the past, that excludes urban or syncretized forms from the bounds of "authentic" indigenous culture. Indigenous subjects who have incorporated many elements of urban *mestizo* culture are unlikely to embrace a movement that defines their identity for them, more narrowly than they would themselves. Such movements, like those they claim to represent, are caught between changing conceptions of indigenous identity, as social categories shift, disengage, and overlap in historically unprecedented ways. It is thus not surprising that the most popular political movements are those mixing urban and rural, *criollo* and indigenous elements. Palenque's mass media advocacy of Aymara culture resonates forcefully among the thousands of urban immigrants who had lacked a modern voice with which to speak indigenous meanings. And it is certainly no accident that the current government is headed by a U.S.-educated millionaire/ political insider, commanding all the cultural capital that elite credentials can bring, and a grass-roots (but also well-educated) advocate of indigenous rights. While neither of these movements may bring about radical change, those with such aspirations would be well advised to study their methods. Broad-based support comes through building bridges between radical and progressive sectors, not by burning them and then exhorting the masses to join the vanguard on the other side.

Articulation of a historical bloc is achieved via micro-level practices and meanings, as much as through macro-level forces. Fiske predicts that radical political theories that disdain engagement with the popular are doomed to fail, while "progressive" currents that fail to connect with radical movements at times of crisis will be similarly ineffective. "The micropolitics that maintains resistances in the minutiae of everyday life maintains a fertile soil for the seeds of macropolitics, without which they will inevitably fail to flourish" (Fiske 1989:93). Only a politics that recognizes the potential of various bases of identity—one that speaks to class *and* ethnic, rural *and* urban loyalties—can become truly popular in this sense.

Rehabilitating Marx: Hegemonic Subject Positions as Alienated Use Values

As should be clear from the preceding discussion, the present work rejects many of the tenets of traditional Marxism while retaining a basically Marxist framework. Those strains of contemporary social thought that have been most productive in terms of theory-building and explanatory power are those that go beyond Marxist axioms such as the reduction of all social conflicts to class, the inevitability of socialist revolution, and the relegation of ideology and signification to a posited "superstructural" realm, unidirectionally determined by the economic "base." A major weakness of traditional Marxism was its failure to account for the role of culture, language, and ideology in social reproduction. In 1977, Williams (1977:136) declared that "large-scale capitalist economic activity and cultural production are now inseparable," to the degree that the latter could no longer be considered merely "a superstructure" (if indeed it ever could). Rather than merely reflecting economic structures, culture, language, and ideology are central to the reproduction of the social formation[5]—"and, futhermore, are related to a much wider area of reality than the abstractions of 'social' and 'economic' experience" (111). That same year, Coward and Ellis (1977) called for a materialist theory of language that would address the relation between signification and identity—that is, the subject's positioning in language and ideology. Recognizing materialism's failure to show how the subject is constructed in ideological practice, they identified its most pressing task as that of theorizing the articulation of language and ideology, but declared that this challenge could only be met by the study of psychoanalysis (7). Without denying the importance of psychoanalysis to developing a theory of subjectivity, clearly no single field is sufficient to this task. Having expanded the notion of social reproduction beyond the economic realm, it is hardly useful to narrow it once again to the psychological. Social phenomena are much more than the sum of their individually lived components, and are forged in interactions across a number of arenas.

What, then, can be salvaged from Marxist theory? As a theory of economic determinism it is clearly inadequate, but it does shed light on processes of labor and production, cultural as well as strictly material. The theoretical model outlined in chapter 5 is an attempt to apply Marx's labor theory of value to the realm of linguistic production. There are two complementary movements at work here: the expansion of symbolic practices into the economic realm, where they take on a determining (not just determined) role; and the expansion of the notion of production to include the symbolic. The first proposition is addressed in the discussion of social reproduction as the reproduction of subject positions, via language and other cultural practices. The second proposition is based on the hypothesis that the model of capitalist production described by Marx is applicable to symbolic production.

The absence of a clear boundary between symbolic and material production, and the subsequent definition of symbolic activity as "labor," was outlined in chapter 5. To assert that symbolic labor enters into the capitalist processes described by Marx (alienation, commodification, appropriation), it was necessary to demonstrate that it is governed by capitalist relations of production. Without claiming that such relations govern *all* linguistic or symbolic activity (not all speech is "alienated," any more than all forms of of productive activity are), observations of linguistic production in the normal school and discussions with students and teachers led me to the conclusion that this was an accurate portrayal of what occurred there.

This was mainly a result of my attempts to discover the actual nature of what students produced and the relations governing their academic activity. It seemed clear that the "value" of students' production lay in (1) the use of their products as a basis for evaluating and positioning students in an academic and social hierarchy, and (2) the transformations that productive activity worked upon the producers themselves. In the exchange of schoolwork for grades, which were in turn exchanged for a title and its guarantee of a wage, schoolwork served as a transferable token of the work students had done on themselves through the completion of assignments. "Learning"—in the sense of critical engagement with course content—was not a required part of the process. More important was students' manipulation of a selected range of linguistic forms and their positioning as subjects in relation to these forms and to their own productive activity. A key feature of this relation is students' lack of control over what they produce and the conditions under which they work; their labor is, in this sense, alienated.

This led to the realization that what the students exchanged for grades were essentially linguistic commodities (defining "commodity" as something whose use value is transferred to another in exchange). It was clear that schoolwork had use value, and that these use values were not determined or realized by students themselves, but by the institution. Students were obliged to exchange their labor power, via the production of externally determined use values, because they were defined as capital-poor within the school economy. Their own knowledge was excluded from the institution's definition of knowledge and thus rendered valueless within the context of symbolic exchange. Students' position was similar to that of the wage worker, who has nothing to exchange but his or her labor power in the production of use values for someone else.

This formulation is linked to issues of identity via the specific use values produced by students' linguistic labor. As was shown in chapter 4, classroom discourse generates a series of subject positions around gender, class, ethnicity, nationality, and occupation. Since students' labor is alienated from their own purposes, they are engaged in the production of—and their own interpellation into—subject positions that they do not control. Nor could they freely and critically engage these subject positions within the restrictive parameters of classroom discourse. The relations governing symbolic production and exchange within the school were naturalized as the "givens" of formal education. This is the foundation of the hegemonic as it operates through schooling: students create use values for the nation-state by producing themselves as hegemonic subjects—

hegemonic because the subject positions being created are not under students' control and are also ideologically naturalized rather than being made vulnerable to critique. Students' alienated labor—the production of commodified use values under externally imposed conditions—is appropriated toward the production of themselves as hegemonic national subjects.

Numerous authors have pinpointed language as a central (though not the only) site for the construction of social identity. By legitimating certain language practices and stigmatizing others, the school creates/encourages certain cultural identities and represses others.[6] It also contributes to the creation of citizens and the consolidation of the nation-state, by disseminating nationalist ideology and delegitimating competing bases of identity. Within an academic regime that devalues indigenous culture, students are defined as capital-poor; lacking cultural capital, they are dependent upon the academic capital supplied by the school, and must exchange their labor to attain it, surrendering to the institution the use values produced by that labor.

B. F. Williams (1989:422) maintains that individuals with little power to define those aspects of their social role that they find problematic are likely to be more alienated that those whose sense of identity is aligned with role expectations. Though she refers to alienation in the psychological sense, by now it should be clear that such "subjective" alienation is rooted in individuals' lack of control over the subject positions into which they are interpellated—a lack of control brought about, in students' case, by the "objective" alienation of their symbolic labor. It is this linking-up of two large pieces of the theoretical puzzle—Marx's labor theory of value and a theory of subjectivity as constructed in discourse—that constitutes the core argument of the present work.[7]

Students try to reclaim their symbolic labor where possible, challenging or subverting old subjectivities and advancing new ones. Often this resistance posits a new kind of Aymara subject: one that is both consciously modern and proudly indigenous, that engages symbolic representations of the dominant urban culture and triumphs over them. Symbolic battles are also waged on the fronts of gender, class, and teacher-student relations, as seen in students' skits and other expressive practices. Within the realm of indigenous culture, students control their own meanings, and their knowledge is not defined as valueless. B. F. Williams (1989:422) cites Ronald Cohen[8] to the effect that "if alienation is a malfunction of modern society, ethnicity is an antidote," but also notes that this remedy "forces certain groups into positions of aliens in their own land—to be labeled an ongoing threat to the unity-through-homogeneity of the nation." As long as nationalism depends on the ideological elision of ethnic and class differences, the purposeful highlighting of ethnic identity will be considered a threat to the integrity of the nation.

Building a Democratic Pedagogy

What would a nonalienating mode of production in schools imply? Walsh (1991:97) hints at an answer in her own phrasing of the question: "What would it mean for schools and [teachers] to see children as experts?" Apple (in Everhart 1983:xiii) accuses schools of mystifying the production of knowledge by defining students as "consumers" rather than as participants in "the struggle to build and rebuild our educational, political, and economic relations . . . We don't create. Someone else does that. This is disturbing enough in general, but in education it is truly disabling." Portraying students as mere consumers devalues their own skills and experience, by constructing "knowledge" as something possessed and transmitted solely by the school.

Throughout his writings, Paulo Freire held that a central purpose of education should be to enable students to see themselves as sources of knowledge. McNeil (1986:16), lamenting the abstract and remote character of school knowledge and its subordination to bureaucratic ends, contends that "there is no necessity that school knowledge be significantly different in content or texture or credibility from the experimental knowledge of our lived culture." But if there were no such "necessity" (i.e., no benefit to structures of power as they currently exist), there would not be such a gulf between "school knowledge" and "real world knowledge" and students' academic labor would not be commodified and alienated as it has been shown to be. Recognizing students' own knowledge and cultural practices as legitimate means breaking the school's monopoly on academic capital, and this has implications that go far beyond the school itself.

Traditional pedagogy is clearly not the most effective at developing students' abilities to critically analyze the world around them and solve problems independently. Bourdieu and Passeron (1977:183–84) interpret this institutionalized "inefficiency" as the result of a trade-off between students' intellectual development and the maintenance of social hierarchy; "low technical efficiency may be the price paid for the educational system's high efficiency in . . . legitimating the 'social order.'" Similarly, Hall (1985:98) maintains that the purpose of ideology (constructed and transmitted via ideological apparatuses such as the school) is to reproduce social relations of production, recalling Althusser's maxim that "a technically competent but politically insubordinate labor force is no labor force at all for capital." If the school's main function were to produce competent, critical students, would it be based upon a model that rewards mimicry over competence and conformity over critique?

Some teachers attempt to transcend the ritualized exchange of linguistic commodities and to introduce more dialogic methods. But students, after years of schooling based on memorization and repitition, are often at a loss to respond to other methods; the preponderance of nondialogic teaching has a cumulative and dulling effect, overwhelming those isolated instances when teachers attempt to step outside of the official program (Everhart 1983:151). Such attempts, operating at cross-purposes with the institutional and ideological context in which they are embedded, are usually doomed to failure, reinforcing the feeling that real change in educational practice is impossible. Paradigm shifts are not made overnight, nor by the well-intentioned actions of a few individuals; this has led many radical educators, including those of the Bolivian teachers' union, to disdain what they call "reformism," as a partial, bourgeois solution. But while it takes more than individual gestures to change an entrenched system, individual gestures (and small collective ones) reveal how subjects view themselves within the matrix of structural relations. Even when unable to form explicit critiques of the dominant mode of schooling, students' forms of resistance serve as eloquent indicators of how they interpret their own alienation and where they perceive weak points in the structures of hegemony.

If the problems with Bolivian schooling are rooted in the relations of production under which it is organized, piecemeal pedagogical reforms will be of limited use. The effectiveness of reforms will depend upon changing the way that school knowledge and activity are conceived. Building a democratic pedagogy must begin by rejecting the notion of knowledge as accumulated capital—not only at the level of the classroom, but throughout the system as a whole (cf. Giroux 1992:98). Numerous authors have made valuable suggestions for reorganizing schooling as a truly dialogic, critical activity;[9] in the present context, it is worth synthesizing the central points made by some of these authors and seeing how they apply to issues of schooling in Bolivia.

McNeil (1986:6) claims that what is constructed as a "crisis" in educational quality is often actually a crisis in the legitimacy of school practices. In Bolivia, at issue is not only the legitimacy of school practices, but the legitimacy of the cultural practices of a subordinated social group. The conflict is essentially between different knowledge systems and the social groups generating them. While any institution whose prime function is socialization may become a battleground for competing knowledge systems (Everhart 1983:239), this is especially true of those that aim to socialize the children of one social group into the cultural practices of another.[10]

Despite schooling's hegemonic function, most would agree that the empowering *potential* of schooling (and its role as the principal avenue to social and political power) makes it a desirable thing for subordinated populations. The very fact that there is a crisis of legitimacy in schools points to an ideal of education still extant among students and communities (McNeil 1986:7). This ideal, and the recognition that it is not being met, is perhaps stronger among teachers than any other group. In Bolivia, demands for *"una educación liberadora"* and the formation of teachers and students as "factors for change" come out of one educational congress after another. Still, an analysis of educational documents and materials apart from the real conditions of their implementation "would be as misleading as a study of religious behavior which presumed to infer the believers' real practice from the canonical texts" (Bourdieu and Passeron 1977:211).

First and foremost in the reorganization of schooling must be the incorporation of students' language, culture, and experience into the curriculum—not simply as a way of "filling the gaps" in the traditional curriculum, but as a starting point for analyzing how those gaps arose in the first place (cf. Giroux 1992:118). Bilingual or mother-tongue education is necessary, but not sufficient (especially if it defines students' own speech as deficient relative to some linguistic ideal); students' own speech must be recognized as a source of knowledge and creativity. Similarly, the valorization of student's home culture is not effectively served by transmitting a reified version of that culture in some ghettoized corner of the curriculum. The vitality of cultural traditions depends less on the fanatical preservation of their "purity" than on their insertion into a variety of contexts and the versatility of their reinterpretations (Garcia Canclini 1989:12–13). Indigenous culture must be present in the curriculum, not just as an object of study, but as a means of engaging contemporary questions of cultural identity and conflict.

> What is suggested is a pedagogy in which there is a critical questioning of the omissions and tensions that exist between the master narratives and hegemonic discourses that make up the official curriculum . . . and the self-representations of subordinated groups . . . This requires forms of pedagogy that both confirm and critically engage the knowledge and experience through which students author their own voices and construct social identities . . . using what they know about their own lives as a basis for criticizing the dominant culture. (Giroux 1992:104)

We have seen that students are capable of coherent critiques of schooling, as well as creative commentaries on the social questions that schooling is supposed to address but more often suppresses. The attempt to bring these critiques into the classroom leads us to the question of how schools treat conflict. Apple (1990:58) argues that school knowledge is dominated by a consensus ideology, in which "conflict, either intellectual or normative, is seen as a negative attribute." In the normal school, teachers tended to shut down students' engagement of conflict, either by denying that conflict existed or by imposing artificial solutions. Teachers lamented the lack of scientific preparation in schools, but continued to rely primarily on the verbatim transmission of reified "facts," despite the fact that conflict, not consensus or the accumulation of facts within a shared paradigm, is the principal source of scientific advancement (119). The same can be said of issues of ethnic and national identity. By preventing students from critically engaging the conflicts shaping their society, teachers contribute to students' interpellation into subject positions not of their making. A critical pedagogy should provide students and teachers with the resources to make such contradictions productive, using them to interrogate social categories and the socialization process itself. Encouraging students to engage conflict is probably the single most productive activity that can happen in the classroom; not only does it foster a critical perspective among students, but it makes this perspective the foundation of a "school knowledge" that is both collectively constructed and directly relevant to students' experience.

This implies quite a different role for teachers than the one they presently fulfill. Basically, it entails teachers' learning to function as facilitators and (together with students) knowledge producers, rather than mere knowledge transmitters. Teachers have a responsibility to take students' grievances seriously, to make schooling a critical, dialogic enterprise, and to help students develop their private critiques within a framework of public debate.

> Interior, privatized resistance may have its progressive potential increased if it is given a social dimension—if, through formal or informal relationships, the social agent can connect with others, and can articulate his or her interior resistances with those of others. One function of the critic-theorist may be to assist in this socialization of the interior... through the provision of a vocabulary and a theoretical framework that will help the personal to be generalized outward. (Fiske 1989:190)

We can easily substitute "teacher" for "critic-theorist," to arrive at something like Freire's (1970) vision of the teacher's potential. Where pedagogical materials are scarce or outdated, teachers' role is even more critical. Until texts and school practices are redesigned to reflect students' sociocultural realities, "teachers should encourage students to critically view the realities portrayed in texts and perpetuated in practices as well as to interrogate their own realities in a critical manner" (Walsh 1991:91). Still, the assumed sacredness of the written word can be challenged only if students are recognized as sources of knowledge, rather than as mere receptacles to be filled with the knowledge of others.

Viewing teachers as transformative intellectuals also entails reevaluating the school's role in public life and situating it as the center of a public sphere that potentially includes the entire community. Everhart (1983:275) proposes that schools work with labor unions, activist groups, welfare agencies, and minority organizations, "to develop a critical awareness of the assumptions behind social relations." In Bolivia, this would involve not only incorporating students and parents into union debates, but also incorporating pedagogical issues (rather than simply salary disputes) into unions' agendas. Furthermore, plans for reform must contain policy structures for their implementation (such as coordination with curriculum planners, changes in teacher training, etc.), or they will continue to serve primarily rhetorical rather than pedagogical purposes.

The reformulation of the school's relationship to the community also implies a reformulation of the relationship between students and teachers and of students with each other. McLaren (1986:183) notes that school practices tend to work against the development of intense peer bonds among students. This was also the case in the normal school—especially, but not exclusively, with regard to male-female bonds. In addition, the social barriers that schools so diligently erect between teachers and students are inimical to the fostering of dialogic relations; since they are largely a result of relations of production that define teachers as transmitters and students as receivers of knowledge, such barriers would be anachronistic in a setting in which students and teachers were jointly engaged in the construction of knowledge.

On a pragmatic note, paying teachers a dignified wage would be an undeniable improvement. Not only would it increase job satisfaction, cut down on corruption, and allow them to dedicate more energy to teaching, it would also allow collective debate to be redirected toward issues of curriculum, methodology, and working conditions, rather than the constant struggle over salaries. The current system of guaranteeing every teacher a job, while justifiable from a certain perspective (and stubbornly defended by the union), draws many into the profession who have no particular aptitude or even liking for teaching. Of course, the normal school's function as an avenue of social mobility is a result of factors extending far beyond the institution itself. The embeddedness of educational problems in larger structures of poverty and discrimination is a testament to the fact that a democratic pedagogy and a democratic society go hand in hand.

Schooling as Cultural Critique

The alienated nature of schoolwork is especially significant because of the school's role in the construction of ethnic, class, gender, and national subjectivities. Since students do not control the use values they produce—since school discourse is not available for students' own ends—these subjectivities are sealed off from critique in the very place where they are produced. Transforming the relations of production in schools would mean that questions of identity could be openly and critically discussed, students' own knowledge could be brought to bear on the processes of identity formation, and students could weigh dialogically the consequences of "what they must become in order to get what they want" (Ollman 1976:146).

Conversely, it should be noted that most pedagogical methods are not inherently good or bad. "There is nothing wrong with rote memorization, as long as students are critically aware of what is being memorized, and for what purposes" (Everhart 1983:269). It is the relations in which such methods are embedded that determine their fundamentally democratic or alienating character (Bourdieu and Passeron 1977:106). Everhart (1983) sees the conflict as one between sets of interests that may in fact be incompatible: "Is a synthesis possible between the legitimate purpose of education—the presentation of basic factual knowledge—and claims by human actors that their labor power is to be controlled by them?" (252). The problem is defining "the presentation of basic factual knowledge" as education's only legitimate purpose. As Everhart himself notes, the issue is not the value of technical knowledge *per se*, but whether "this is the *only* type of legitimate knowledge students need, or if it is indeed the relevant standard against which all other knowledge is measured . . . Apparently, students think otherwise" (242–43).

Critical and factual perspectives can work together in the classroom—but only if students are encouraged to view even "factual" information critically. As we saw in chapters 4 and 5, course content ranging from straightforward scientific information, to value judgements about students' language, to speculations on racial and national character, were all presented as "facts" to be copied down and regurgitated on tests in the same undifferentiated manner. Adopting a critical perspective means not just including students' knowledge in the curriculum, but changing their relation to *all* school knowledge. Critical knowledge interrogates its own origins and functions, penetrating the ideological naturalization of social "facts." For students to gain a critical perspective on schooling, they must "learn to see educational practice as partly determinant of cultural reproduction, and question that which is being reproduced" (Everhart 1983:274)—essentially bringing the productive process in schools under students' and teachers' collective control.

García Canclini (1989:13) defines the task of the social sciences as "deconstructing the authoritarian base of our culture and revealing the way in which the habitual organization of our environment and our daily relations 'naturalize' antidemocratic conceptions of power." Aside from reclaiming the content of what is produced in school, studens must be able to interrogate the conditions of its production. Once classroom dynamics are denaturalized, the available range of pedagogical practice becomes potentially visible.[11] This may lead to its diversification, as part of the general expansion of an "oppositional public sphere" within the school (Giroux 1988). Students in the normal school were quick to suggest ways of expanding their opportunities for critique, from Paco's suggestion of oral exams to José's desire for a public debate on ethnic discrimination. The fact that the school suppressed such initiatives rather than building upon them attests to its essentially conformist and anticritical nature.

Crucial to the question of power relations in schools is women's role in the curriculum, in educational hierarchies, and in educational debates. Among the "structured silences" of school practice, gender issues are suppressed even more thoroughly than ethnic issues. Imagining an expanded public sphere of the type hinted at above, it is hard not to envision it dominated by males, like most areas of school life. While ethnic and class liberation are at least popularly viewed as ideals to be pursued, these discourses can also serve a hegemonic function by obscuring and trivializing women's oppression. The normal school students conceded the existence of sexism, but tended to scapegoat the rural family rather than tracing female students' mutedness to structures of power within the school itself. Women's educational subordination must be contested on many fronts; but allowing female students a legitimate voice in the classroom and in the symbolic life of the school must be among the first.[12]

Related to legitimizing students' own knowledge, speech, and cultural practices—and especially apropos to female students' subordination—is the question of self-esteem. Not only have many studies shown a link between self-esteem and academic success (Walsh 1991:114), it is also a fundamental prerequisite to the awakening of political consciousness, the affirmation of cultural dignity, and the formulation of strategic resistance (cf. Bourdieu 1984:395–96; Fiske 1989:69). A key measure of hegemony is the degree to which it leads the subordinated "to see [themselves] only through the eyes of the dominant class" (Bourdieu 1984:384). This is a central function of school socialization. In the normal school as in the North American middle school studied by McLaren, "ritualized classroom lessons tacitly created dispositions toward certain student needs while simultaneously offering to fulfill those needs. For instance, students were made to feel inadequate due to their class and ethnic status and hence the school offered to help socialize them into the 'appropriate' values and behaviors" (1986:215).

This debilitating construction of subaltern groups foments both social stratification and social control (Oliart 1991); students who internalize a definition of themselves as inadequate are unlikely to achieve a critical perspective on the institutions that so define them. Taking students' self-esteem seriously is an essential part of constructing a pedagogy in which "the self [is] seen as a primary site of politicization" (Giroux 1992:80). Just as no one field can meet all the challenges involved in developing a theory of subjectivity, so must the struggle to create a critical subject be fought on various fronts: cultural, linguistic, sociopolitical, and psychological. Seeking merely pedagogical solutions to students' failure and discontent is equivalent to "limiting the study of linguistic alienation to its phenomenology" (Rossi-Landi 1983:157); it is a symptomatic approach to a generalized social pathology.

The discussion thus far suggests that many of students' problems are closely interrelated. The underlying unity between "objective" and "subjective" alienation is reflected in the links between the exclusion of students' knowledge from official notions of what is worth knowing, the appropriation of students' linguistic labor toward the creation of subjectivities they do not control, and the construction of students as ethnically stigmatized, "capital-poor" consumers of information, with no legitimate claim to self-esteem. Meaningful pedagogical reform must address not only the stultifying methods typical of so many schools, but the epistemological assumptions that give rise to such methods. If knowledge is defined as the property of a few, to be unilaterally transmitted to the many in exchange for control over the meanings that shape their lives, reforms that fail to challenge this principle will not in themselves transform the system.

This is not to suggest that total solutions are the only ones worth pursuing. As is evident from the empowering function of students' popular practices, control over some area of expression is essential as a base from which to expand alternative meanings and formulate critique. In the constant war of position over social meanings, signs are never captured once and for all. The fact that students continue to question, challenge, and subvert entrenched structures of power attests to the irrepressible nature of human creativity and meaning-making. It also confirms that change can come only from below, for the simple reason that the interests of those above are already served by the status quo (Fiske 1989:19). Well-intentioned reforms imposed without input from students and communities allow school discourses to remain as "readerly texts" with ready-made meanings, rather than as joint constructions by students and teachers.

Fiske makes another point relevant to all attempts at political change, whether targeting a single school or the formation of a historical bloc: shared antagonism and a sense of oppositionality are more important to counter-hegemonic action than class similarity. In a country where class and ethnic divisions are so sharply felt, it is tempting to seek meaning and collective power in a narrowly defined identity politics. But where no one group constitutes a majority, there is strength in diversity. First we must reclaim the means of symbolic production for those whose labor sustains them and open a political space for the construction of alternative meanings; it is unproductive to define too narrowly what will fill that space, until it is won.

Directions for Future Research

Theoretical explorations of ethnicity have reached a watershed of sorts. The global interpenetration of systems of meaning has produced a situation much more fluid and complex than the conception of ethnic groups as bounded, isolated units can fruitfully address. In Bolivia as elsewhere, ethnic conflicts have as much to do with the flow of individuals and cultural forms across boundaries than with the maintenance of the boundaries themselves. Rather than fading away quietly, ethnic boundaries have become increasingly salient as they have grown more permeable. As identities become less clearly defined, the struggle to fix them in familiar patterns becomes more intense.

In Bolivia, the normal school is one channel for a rising current of class and ethnic mobility. But the tendency to redefine one's ethnic identity as one moves up the class ladder should not be read as evidence of a generalized "de-ethnicization" or the collapse of ethnicity into class identities. As indigenous people move into subject positions previously closed to them, ethnicity is reworked, but seldom abandoned. Not only are dominant conceptions of the national subject expanding to include indigenous symbols and practices (although often in tamed or touristic forms), but the denial of one's ethnic roots may be even more sharply stigmatized than subaltern ethnicities themselves. As ethnic boundaries become increasingly fuzzy and situational, those exemplifying this trend (los "cholos," los "en proceso") become ethnically defined by their status as boundary breakers. While this suggests a need to re-evaluate the theoretical framework based on the notion of discrete boundaries between ethnic groups (cf. Eriksen 1993), the continuing ideological importance of such boundaries implies that the relevance of that framework has not altogether disappeared. Raymond Williams (1977:11) suggests a starting point for such a reevaluation: "When the most basic concepts—the concepts, as it is said, from which we begin—are suddenly seen to be not concepts but problems, not analytic problems either, but historical movements that are still unresolved, there is no sense in listening to their sonorous summons or their resounding clashes. We have only, if we can, to recover the substance from which their forms were cast." Though Williams does not refer to ethnicity or nationality per se, these are certainly among the "basic concepts" coming to be viewed as problems rather than categories. There are few summons more sonorous, or clashes more resounding, than those inspired by ethnic and nationalist ideologies. When ethnic and national subjectivities combine in new ways, the substance of each is likely to undergo fundamental changes.

Williams suggests the emergence of a new class as a likely source of new practices and meanings. I would expand this to include the emergence of a new intersection between class, ethnic, and/or gender subjectivities. The social conflicts accompanying the emergence of Bolivia's indigenous professionals (and of an urban Aymara political constituency) are those of a group struggling to define itself, as other groups also try to define it. Schools are important sites for this process of definition; thus we would expect the schisms and solidarities shaping the ideological environment of the normal school to reflect those of Bolivian society. Since the normal school is where the teachers of future generations are formed, it may be that the limits of future debate are set there as well, though these limits surely will be contested by future students.

While previous studies have explored the reification of school knowledge, this approach has as yet made few inroads in the study of schooling in Latin America, where cultural and linguistic differences are education's primary challenges. Technical-pedagogical approaches or transitional bilingual education programs will not be sufficient to pull schools out of their "crisis." Such approaches isolate language as a manipulable factor in the educational process, failing to recognize that "as a social phenomenon, language cannot be abstracted from the forces and conflicts of social history" (Giroux, in Walsh 1991:xvii). This is especially true where those forces and conflicts center on the colonial and postcolonial domination of indigenous peoples. As issues of ethnicity and nationalism become increasingly important to the study of social conflict, the reification of knowledge and the alienation of symbolic labor in school contexts are fruitful areas for examining how ethnic and other subjectivities are prepared, not only for the capitalist labor market, but for the ideological requirements of the nation-state as well.

Much of nationalist ideology-in-practice occurs at the level of what Williams (1977:131–33) called "structures of feeling"—the evocation of a certain cultural style, a "quality of experience" that may be difficult to describe in concrete terms, but is instantly recognizable to subjects seeking confirmation of the ineffable uniqueness of their own national character. In defining the tensions generated by the clash between nationalist and other group loyalties, "we are also defining a social experience which is still *in process*, often indeed not yet recognized as social but taken to be private, idiosyncratic, and even isolating" (132). Students' fear of speaking out in class, their inner torments at finding themselves the targets of ethnic ridicule, and their conflicts with school personnel all may appear private and isolating to those who suffer them, but are revealed through analysis to be social (as well as psychological) in nature. Part of subjects' coming to a collective critical awareness is their learning to recognize these as social phenomena, to situate them historically in relations of power and processes of identity formation. Students at times approach such an awareness, both in private interviews and in collective expressions of resistance to ethnic, class, and gender subjugation. The fostering and expansion of arenas for such expression is thus crucial to students' achievement of this critical awareness and to their reclaiming control over the processes that shape their concepts of themselves.

Structural Pessimism vs. Strategic Optimism

Various authors have noted reproduction theory's tendency toward "structural pessimism"—the view that no change in education is possible without prior transformation of the political and socioeconomic structures in which schools are embedded (Bonder 1992:234). The viewpoints most prone to this tendency are those that fail to recognize students as protagonists in their own education; in contrast, those taking a more active view of students can hardly miss the persistent creativity with which they challenge and reshape the meanings and conditions imposed on them. Not only does structural pessimism do a disservice to students, it also ignores a promising area of counter-hegemonic practice. Though pessimism often presents itself as realism, it is as ideological a position as any other. No hegemony can encompass all of human practice; there will always be, at certain times and in certain areas of life, "practices and meanings which are not reached for" (Williams 1980a:43), or which, if reached for, escape hegemonic incorporation. In other cases, the same popular resonances that permit a resistant strain's incorporation may themselves maintain a link to its oppositional content. Nationalist ideology depends upon the articulation of popular meanings and pleasures, but these are neither predictable nor easily controlled; the meanings generated by any popular discourse "exceed its own power to discipline them" (Fiske 1989:104).

This is not to minimize the challenges that resistance to entrenched structures entails. But strategic optimism is essential in the face of such challenges:

> Certainly, we must be honest about the ways power, knowledge, and interest are interrelated and made manifest, about how hegemony is economically and culturally maintained. But, we must also remember, that the very sense of personal and collective futility that may come from such honesty is itself an aspect of an effective dominant culture. As an ideological form, it can lead us away from concrete action on the conditions which deny us "the values we most prize." (Apple 1990:161)

In other words, we must work collectively to make "despair unconvincing and hope practical" (Giroux 1992:105). A liberating, transformative pedagogy should infuse resistance with a critical consciousness, building a purposeful, forward-looking, even utopian counter-hegemony out of the submerged "good sense" (Gramsci 1971) that is the underpinning of resistant impulses, rituals, and attitudes. It is, in part, the limitations that hegemony imposes upon collective discourse (especially in schools) that keep most resistance within the realm of fractured, half-hearted, badly aimed gestures. The logic of despair orienting so much of the debate around education, while in one sense a recognition of hegemony's pervasiveness, also functions to constrain our notions of what is possible. While our aspirations need not be limited to a traditional Marxist framework, Ollman's (1976:238) words in defense of Marx are instructive: "With the development and/or discovery of each new social form our view of what is humanly possible has had to be extended. Consequently, those critics who declare Marx an impossible visionary strike me as vainly dogmatic as those of his followers who promise that this vision will come true."

Crises mark the beginning of a hegemony's disintegration. The crisis in Bolivian education is not merely economic or pedagogical, but rather a crisis of legitimation (Habermas 1976), a failure of the dominant ideology to meet the standards it has set for itself. The coming changes in Bolivian schooling may show that those who take most seriously the claims of the dominant ideology are best positioned to recognize and act upon its internal contradictions. If so, Aymara students' idealism regarding education may stand them in good stead. Pressure from indigenous groups already has resulted in far-reaching changes in school practice. With any luck, the question for the future may not be the one so often asked by teachers—Is real change possible?—but rather the one posed by Michael Apple (1990:59): "Can we deal with the political and economic realities of creating institutions which enhance meaning and lessen control?" There's only one way to find out.

Appendix: Interviewed Students

José was among the most articulate and best liked of the male students. Confident, handsome, good-natured, a talented student and athlete, he got along well with most other students, though he saw his relationship with some faculty members as antagonistic, due to his readiness to stand up for what he saw as his rights. José grew up in a peasant family of meagre means; as for so many Bolivian children, his primary school years consisted mainly of confusion, being lectured at in a language he did not understand. At the age of twelve or thirteen, José decided that he had to learn Spanish if he hoped to get anywhere in life, and proceeded to teach himself via the radio, the dictionary, and whatever means were at hand. By the time I met him, José's Spanish, though still marking him as a rural Aymara speaker, was quite fluent—certainly up to expressing the fervent intellectual curiosity that made interviews with him so lively. He was half of one of the more stable romantic unions in the school, with Diana, a childhood sweetheart from his home community.

Like several of the more academically talented students, José aspired to enter the university, but felt that his economic situation made this impossible, and thus chose the normal school instead. He felt disillusioned upon finding the level of instruction much less challenging than he had hoped. Nevertheless, while studying to become a teacher he also attended university classes on the weekends, and continued to nurture hopes of progressing even further in his education.

Diana was an earnest but not outstanding student from a small rural community, a sincere and affectionate girl who suffered from what she felt to be discrimination on the part of some of the other girls and the *inspectora*. She ascribed this partly to prejudice against rural students and partly to her adversaries' jealous desires to frustrate her relationship with José. She was more vocal and outgoing than most of the rural girls, and her cheerful assertiveness led us to become close friends within a few weeks of my arrival. She tended to be quiet and shy in class, but could be articulate when prodded by the professor, and even indignant when provoked. Nevertheless, her modesty and gentle self-deprecatory manner were such that I was surprised to learn that she was the first girl from her community to leave it in search of postsecondary education. Though she enjoyed children and the idea of becoming a schoolteacher, Diana hoped to use her future earnings to continue studying and perhaps pursue a career as an Aymara-language radio announcer.

Arturo was a big, handsome, good-natured young man whose athletic skill and easygoing manner made him a favorite among many. He could often be found at the center of a group that sang or shouted an accompaniment to the strains of his guitar. The son of a rural teacher, Arturo spent his early years in the countryside, moving to the city to finish high school. Upon completion of his military service, he entered a program that would have trained him to be a physical education teacher, but was forced to drop out because of the expense. An average student, Arturo seemed content with the program offered by the normal school. After the midyear vacation, however, he failed to return to school, and I heard through the grapevine that he had gotten one of the local girls pregnant and had to leave. Nevertheless, a few weeks later he returned to classes, without public comment; the girl in question was not seen in town again during the duration of my stay.

Soledad was a study in contrasts. She was stocky, with a sharp nose, round cheeks, and long black hair that was bobbed in front and worn loose or in a single braid (rather than the two braids characteristic of rural girls). Though she was a cheerful companion, our growing rapport eventually revealed that she had entered the normal school mainly to distance herself from a broken romance in the city, which was still the source of some pain to her.

Soledad was one of the more urbanized students, as was evident from her speech and dress. Despite this, she seemed to lack the self-confidence with which many of the urban girls carried themselves. She was uncomfortable with conflict, worried about others' opinions of her, and was often distressed at being caught in the middle of tensions between urban and rural girls in the dorm. She suffered a good deal from what she considered to be the slings and arrows of her classmates, and felt that despite her efforts to get along equally well with all, she was fated to remain the victim of malicious gossip and ill will. Her bouts of unhappiness contrasted sharply with her otherwise sunny nature and jolly, conspiratorial manner when gently teasing or sharing confidences. Both her outgoing personality and her tendency to seek solace from me when gripped by personal conflict made my friendship with her one of the closer ones I had among the students.

Roberto (Arturo's older brother), whose father and several siblings were schoolteachers as well, arrived during the second half of the research period, having transferred from another normal school due to difficulties there (the precise nature of which he did not reveal). He was intelligent, athletic, and possessed of an immense self-confidence that, in the opinion of some students, bordered on arrogance. Within a few weeks of his arrival he was elected class president and had established himself as a firm favorite among the girls. Some of the male students, however, took a rather dim view of his whirlwind style, perhaps feeling threatened by the ease and rapidity with which he inserted himself into the upper level of the student hierarchy. Roberto was every inch the politician: gregarious, ambitious, studiedly vague about his personal affairs, and generally at the center of action, whether it be an athletic contest or a class dispute with a professor. In an interview, he claimed that his history of transfers among several normal schools (under somewhat dubious circumstances) had been intentional. He said that one day he hoped to hold a leadership position in the teachers' union and to that end wished to become widely known among his future constituency. Of all the students I interviewed, Roberto was the only one who indicated an interest in becoming seriously involved in union politics after graduation.

Remedios was from La Paz, where both her parents were merchants; her father had served as director of an Adventist primary school. Prior to entering the normal school, Remedios studied nursing at a university in Lima, Perú, but economic circumstances forced her to abandon her studies. Nevertheless, she said that her dream had always been to become a teacher, and she was happy to take up study toward that end. At first, finding a niche in the student social scene had been hard for her, accustomed as she was to urban life and to the more vigorous intellectual atmosphere of the university. Confident and resourceful, she soon found friends and seemed reasonably comfortable within the more restrained social environment of the normal school. She was a quick, no-nonsense type of student who frequently spoke up in class and seldom backed off from a debate, whether with other students or the professor himself. She was one of the very few girls who regularly participated in class discussions. Though this distinguished her from the rural girls, she was admired for her firm ideals and strong personality and had friends both among rural students and those who shared her urban background.

Faustino was the son of laborers. Though born in "the provinces," his family moved to La Paz after he graduated from high school, and he considered himself to be "from the city." As a child, and between graduation and entering the normal school, he had the opportunity to travel a bit. As a result, he knew various parts of the country and seemed slightly more knowledgable than many of the other students. He also had something of a reputation for being constantly "on the make" with the girls, and was certainly more assertive in that regard than most of his fellows. Though his casual manner seemed to indicate that he took little in life too seriously, Faustino professed to having a lifelong ambition to become a teacher and in our interview waxed uncharacteristically philosophical about the nobility of the profession. Though he was one of the few who seemed sincerely enthusiastic about teaching, he also expressed a desire to carry his education even further and hopefully set foot in the university one day, perhaps to study computers.

Antonia was from a rural community distant enough that she spent many weekends at the school instead of making the long trip home. Her father was a rural schoolteacher, and she had often helped him in the classroom, as well as working for a few months as an interim teacher before entering the normal school. She knew well the joys, trials, and routines of a schoolteacher's life, and saw that life as the one she wanted for herself. She was the type of student for whom entering the normal school was so natural as to seem the only logical choice.

Antonia had definite ideas about what constituted a good teacher, and she deplored the tendency of so many students to withdraw from class participation, wondering aloud how they hoped to become teachers if they were afraid to speak in public. Though her own Spanish displayed marked interference from Aymara, she was less timid about public speaking than many of her classmates. She had an outgoing and friendly personality, and yet several students expressed an active dislike for her, largely because of her friendship with the *inspectora*. She spent a fair amount of her spare time in the *inspectora*'s living quarters and was suspected of acting as her spy among the students. Ironically, it seemed to be her very desire for approval that led to Antonia's becoming the focus of antagonism.

Carlos differed from the other students in a number of ways. At twenty-six, he was somewhat older than most. More importantly, he was from a different region. He grew up in a mining community where the social norms and political culture differed significantly from those of the Lake Titicaca area, and considered the latter's inhabitants to be overly reserved and puritanical by comparison. After a few years working in Argentina as a waiter, Carlos settled on the normal school as a safer and more secure alternative to mining work. Though he felt great nostalgia for the mining life and its singular culture, the arduousness and danger of the work led him to choose teaching instead, despite an avowed distaste for working with children. To make matters worse, he had transferred from another normal school that did not exercise such rigid control over its students (from which he was nevertheless expelled for alleged drunkenness), and the restrictive conditions of dorm life at Kollasuyo chafed at his bohemian nature.

Carlos experienced some difficulty at fitting into the social life of the normal school, primarily because he was one of the few students who did not speak Aymara (he was a Quechua speaker). Nevertheless, his extrovert qualities and the very novelty of his background attracted the attention of several other students, with the result that Carlos did not seem to lack friends. He was an enthusiastic participant in school activities and even took it upon himself to provide on-stage translation of one student production into Quechua (a task that was apparently symbolically and personally significant for him, though not really necessary in the practical sense). Near the end of the research period, he had some difficulties with the administration, which seemed to threaten his possibilites of graduating, but managed to clear them up just in time. As he had no family in the area, he asked me to serve as his *madrina de promoción*, and I was happy to comply.

Juana was also from a mining community, as one could almost guess from her assertive manner and her outspokenness in class. At twenty-three, she was older than most of the other first-year students, already married and mother of three small children (left to the care of family members while she pursued her studies). She seemed to possess a stability and wisdom beyond her years, which, combined with her maternal disposition, earned her the nickname "Mamá" among her dormmates, by whom she was well loved. Because of her trustworthiness and leadership abilities, she also sometimes served as a sort of deputy to the *inspectora*, but managed to carry out this role without being perceived as a teacher's pet. Rather, the girls preferred being under Juana's watchful eye rather than that of the *inspectora*, who was not particularly well liked.

Juana cast her lot definitively with the rural girls and was quick to speak out against prejudice wherever she perceived it. She considered herself a staunch defender of those too timid to defend themselves and had little love lost for those girls whom she felt put on airs and discriminated against the others. Her opinions were strong and well-developed, and she was knowledgeable about the larger history of such issues. In line with her no-nonsense nature, she chose teaching because it was the career that required the shortest and least expensive course of study. Despite this pragmatic reasoning, she seemed to possess many qualities—empathy, insight, and intelligence foremost among them—that would lead her to become a talented and dedicated teacher.

Clara was also originally from a mining center, but had lived almost all of her life in the city of La Paz. Her mother was a merchant and her father a city employee, though at the time I knew her, Clara was living not with them but with an aunt and uncle. She claimed to have aspired to become a teacher since childhood. Clara's style of dress, her short curly hair, and her general manner marked her as unmistakably urban, and she socialized mostly with girls of similar background. When asked about discrimination in the girl's dorm, she affirmed that all should be treated equally and that she did not discriminate or consider herself better than anyone else, but claimed that the rural girls kept to themselves and did not want to socialize with the city girls.

Clara was a cheerful and often comic companion; though she could be quite serious when the occasion warranted it, she did not give much thought to larger issues, such as politics or Bolivia's educational controversies. Athough she missed the freedom of urban life, she expressed overall contentment with the normal school program.

Nicolás, who graduated halfway through the research period, was probably the top student in the school, academically speaking. Intelligent, thoughtful, and athletic, he was liked and respected by the others, despite a generally reserved and serious demeanor. Nicolás was already married and, like Carlos and Juana, was from a mining center, facts which set him apart somewhat from the general student body. Though he understood Aymara reasonably well, his background was Quechua, though he did not advertise this fact as conspicuously as Carlos did.

Nicolás grew up in a family where discipline was at a premium, and placed much importance on giving conscious attention to one's personal formation. Though a model student, he was by no means quiescent and had definite opinions about the shortcomings of the training he was receiving. Nevertheless, even before graduation he had a line on a promising teaching position and seemed destined for success at whatever he put his mind to.

Sergio was, for me, one of the more intriguing cases among the student body. Handsome, graceful, and well-spoken, his eloquence in class and cool reserve out of it made him one of the highest-status students in the school. Though perceived as arrogant by some of the boys, he was admired from afar by several of the girls. He was romantically linked to one of the prettier third-year girls, unusual for a first-year student, but quite in keeping with his reputation as "big man on campus" and general sophisticate.

Sergio was also something of a brooder; though he participated more than most in the school's civic programs and student productions, his manner was often somewhat aloof, as if he were just passing through, obviously destined for better things. Indeed, I often wondered myself what he was doing there, since his urban background and intellectual gifts seemingly would have pegged him for the university. Unlike most of the students, he initially exhibited little interest in my presence; his attitude seemed to be one of "too cool to care." Eventually, though, by virtue of my participation in a couple of discussions in his anthropology class, he came to see me as a potential sounding board for his intellectual frustrations. When he finally agreed to grant me an interview, I was taken aback by his frankness and the sadness of the personal history he revealed.

Mateo was one of the oldest members of the student body, already thirty-two when he graduated halfway through the research period. A self-proclaimed jack-of-all-trades, he worked for several years before entering the normal school, mainly in construction, but also as an interim schoolteacher in a remote rural community. Mateo had a cheerful, easygoing manner that made him an enjoyable companion and an accomodating informant; he was well-liked by his fellows and known for some rather inspired comic performances in school programs. Nevertheless, he was also one of the most alienated students that I met during my stay. In interviews and informal conversations he regaled me with tales of incompetence, corruption, and exploitation of students by professors and educational authorities, and he expressed deep frustration with what he considered the prevalence of such tendencies, not only within the school, but throughout Bolivia in general. He was a good student academically, but felt that teachers were out to get him because of his insistence on "speaking the truth." It was through Mateo (and later, Sergio) that I realized that student alienation and poor school performance do not necessarily go hand-in-hand. I had the opportunity to observe Mateo in his practicum, teaching a class of second-graders under the evaluating eye of the professor. He struck me as a talented teacher, good with children and exhibiting a positive, dynamic classroom style; this made it all the more surprising to discover that he had entered the normal school solely under pressure from his mother, with no desire for teaching whatsoever (though by his third year he was beginning to view the idea with slightly more enthusiasm).

Notes

Preface

1. "Popular" both in the sense of "widely read" and in the more Latin American meaning of "identified with a subaltern or revolutionary perspective."

2. This is not to imply that the "ethnography" sections are straight presentations of fact, with all the analysis reserved for the "theoretical" sections. Rather, it is a distinction between levels of analysis, intended to make the book more user-friendly to various audiences.

3. A Spanish version is also in preparation, for publication in the Andean region.

4. On one occasion a student did object to my taking pictures in class; I discussed his objections with him and backed off considerably (though not completely) from this activity. I suspect that others also felt uncomfortable with the taking of more "candid" shots, but were too shy to say so. I later spoke to several students about the necessity of the pictures for my work, venturing that it was only fair that I take a few for my own purposes, considering the amount of time and trouble I put into taking pictures requested by them. At no other time did students indicate that they felt my presence to be intrusive or undesirable.

5. Positioning myself as a pseudo-student no doubt contributed to the critical stance this work takes toward teachers; McLaren notes that he felt more sympathetic toward teachers when he took on their role (1986:118). Everhart maintains that fieldworkers must be partly socialized by their subjects in order to understand their lives, and claims that subjecting himself to the same restrictions as the junior high school students he studied led them to treat him as a peer, regardless of his age (1983:287). I had a chance to feel even more solidly aligned with students when I was called into the Department of Orientation for a "disciplinary talk" on account of behavior that one faculty member considered unfitting and a poor example for students

(walking arm-in-arm with a male friend who came to visit and drinking a beer with him just outside the school gates). The rector and academic director later apologized for the incident, saying that the faculty member had acted on his own without authority from them.

6. Balancing these interests is harder with research subjects taken from the ranks of the elite. Marcus (1986) notes the tendency of anthropologists to limit observation to society's "victims," and Willis maintains that the role of ethnography is "to show the cultural viewpoint of the oppressed" (1981a:202). Certainly, the oppressed are more often studied than are elites, largely because elites have much more leeway in refusing. Despite rare attempts to expand ethnographic inquiry beyond subaltern populations (such as Cohen's [1974] study of London stockbrokers), the dilemma of elite subjects seems unlikely to present itself with great frequency in the near future.

Introduction

1. Levinson and Holland (1996) give an incisive overview of recent currents in educational theory.

2. But see Masemann 1974; Hornberger 1988; and Levinson, Foley, and Holland (eds.) 1996.

3. This is changing; while translations of critical works in education often take years to appear in Spanish (if they do at all), in the mid-1990s there began to appear in Bolivia pirated photocopies of works by authors such as Michael Apple and Henry Giroux, translated unofficially in Argentina and circulated hand to hand among interested scholars and students. The participation of foreign and foreign-educated scholars in the elaboration of educational policies has also been significant. Bolivia's current educational reform, for example, takes an explicit view of the school as an institution of past cultural domination and future cultural revitalization.

Chapter 1. *Ethnicity and the Construction of Nationhood*

1. Throughout the Andes, Quechua speakers outnumber Aymara speakers by approximately 8 million to 3 million. However, since most Quechuas live in Peru, while most Aymaras are Bolivian, their numbers within Bolivia are more nearly equal. The department of La Paz, where this study was conducted, is in the heart of the Aymara culture area; Quechua speakers are relatively few in number, mostly migrants from other parts of the country. While the Aymara and the Quechua speak different languages and consider themselves distinct peoples, they share many cultural traits; some scholars (Libermann, Godínez,

and Albó 1989, and Urban 1991, among others) suggest that the two groups have melded to form a single cultural complex (though certainly not without internal variations). For a tracing of the historical relation between Aymaras and Quechuas before the Spanish conquest, see Hardman (1985).

2. Bolivian politics is notoriously unstable, constituting a complex tangle of personalities and acronyms. Those interested in delving into the history of shifting coalitions, rapid-fire military coups, and short-lived military-civilian *juntas* are referred to James Dunkerly's excellent *Rebellion in the Veins: Political Struggle in Bolivia, 1952–1982*.

3. In 1997 Banzer assumed the presidency once again; his 23 percent of the popular vote was the highest received by any candidate, giving him the decisive advantage in the postelection interparty negotiations for the presidency.

4. Albó (1993b) analyzes the process leading to Cárdenas's selection, and the corresponding integration of a more "multiculturalist" orientation into the MNR's official ideology.

5. Though only in their fifties, both Palenque and Fernández suffered sudden and untimely deaths before the 1997 elections—Fernández in a plane crash and Palenque of a heart attack—effectively slowing the impetus of *"cholo"* political movements in Bolivia for the time being (see note 26). For a fascinating and detailed account of Palenque's rise, see Archondo (1991). An analysis of how the *Palenquismo* phenomenon reflects other features of Bolivian ethnic conflict, political life, and popular culture can be found in Luykx (1993).

6. COB leader Oscar Iturralde, cited in Davila (1991:11).

7. The name is taken from the *nom de guerre* of eighteenth-century Indian rebel leader Julián Apasa.

8. While information provided by the capture of two EGTK leaders in May 1992 indicated that the group perhaps extended further than originally suspected, activity eventually died down, and the group has been little heard from of late. Though it proved unable to generate much revolutionary momentum, the EGTK is significant as a manifestation of indigenous discontent and rejection of the political process; it is also noteworthy for the fact that the area in which the present research was carried out happened to fall within the EGTK's limited radius of operations.

9. In essence, as economist Humberto Compodonico put it, "the Bolivian state and the banking system legalized dollars from drug trafficking" (Andreas 1991:15). Many U.S. bank deregulation policies of the Reagan era had similar effects, facilitating the laundering of cocaine profits in Miami.

10. From Jeroen Strengers: "La Pesada Carga de la Deuda," CEDOIN, La Paz, 1985. Cited in Nash (1992:276).

11. I heard one Bolivian punster ironically refer to this as the *yuqallazación*. *Yuqalla* is the Aymara word for "boy," and carries a derogatory connotation similiar to the use of that word to refer to African-American men in the United States. The use of puns to suggest subversive meanings "more true" than official ones is discussed in Fiske (1989:106–12).

12. Despite this, countless white and *mestizo* Bolivians adamantly assured me that there is no racism in Bolivia, that discrimination is due solely to *classism*. This view may be linked to the postrevolutionary project to de-emphasize ethnicity and highlight class identity. Ironically, Bolivians tend to have an extreme notion of U.S. racism, corresponding more to the pre-civil rights era than to the present, and were invariably incredulous when I remarked that racism in Bolivia struck me as even sharper (in terms of the acceptability of racist talk and images, segregation of certain occupations and public spaces, etc.) than in the United States.

13. All selections from works in Spanish have been translated by the author.

14. Not that urban linkages are a crucial part of life for *all* Aymara communities. Given their low population density, geographical remoteness, and the scarcity of modern forms of transportation in many rural areas, many *altiplano* communities still have very little contact with larger population centers. In such cases, the school is usually the primary agent of outside influence. This study focuses on an area of Aymara culture which, while remaining fundamentally rural, is nonetheless heavily influenced by contact with the urban center.

15. Albó and Preiswerk (1986) provide an analysis of Gran Poder, its history and participants.

16. Aymara and Quechua are also offered at the university level, though the quality of instruction is inconsistent and seldom informed by recent linguistic research.

17. In one of the more transparent examples of this derogatory attitude toward "Indianness," Aymara surnames such as Mamani or Quispe are sometimes used as general epithets for persons thought to be of low social status.

18. During the 1992 municipal elections, Carlos Palenque was frequently and unfavorably compared with political rival Ronald MacLean, who was considered refined, well-educated (in the United States), and well-spoken (i.e., displaying an eloquent command of the prestige variety of Spanish). Palenque, in contrast, identified himself with La Paz's indigenous migrants, found fame playing folkloric music and later as a radio and tv host, and sprinkled his speeches with Aymara phrases. His wife was a prominent member of his political team, which was seen as even more vulgar.

19. "MENTISAN—soothes everything: for colds, for burns, for falls . . . " In Spanish, the construction *para caídas,* "for falls," forms a pun with the word *paracaídas,* "parachute."

20. Cf. Marx's definition of the State as "an illusory community" (*The German Ideology,* 1846), in which the interests of the dominant class are falsely represented as the interests of all. Still, there are other significant interests at work besides class interests; for that reason I refer to "dominant sectors" rather than "the dominant class." Zinn (1980:9) likewise critiques "the pretense that there is really such as thing as 'the [nation],' subject to occasional conflicts and quarrels, but fundamentally a community of people with common interests . . . as if there really [were] a 'national interest.' "

21. I am discounting for the moment those daily rituals such as one finds in schools (the singing of the national anthem, etc.) to focus here on those integrative ceremonies explicitly set apart from normal daily practice.

22. A strong argument could be made that the most powerful force for Bolivian unity is *futbol* (soccer); Bolivia's participation in the 1994 World Cup provoked an outpouring of nationalist sentiment rarely seen outside of such contests. While this patriotic solidarity transcended class and ethnic divisions, it did not always cross the gender gap (and in fact tended to exacerbate it).

23. While such features are of course not really "given" so much as socially constructed, their supposed naturalness is part of their construction. The fact that such attachments are perceived by those who share them as "primordial" is more crucial to their effectiveness than is the question of their actual primordiality.

24. These terms (especially *indio*) often have a derogatory connotation; I use them here because they are the ones most commonly used in Bolivia. Also, "people of indigenous, mixed, and European descent" is inadequate, since ethnicity is more a question of social identity than of geneology *per se.* While the conventional hierarchy of *indio, mestizo,* and *blanco* "no longer adequately describes the complexities of increasingly typical social entanglements" (Albro 1995:8), ethnicity continues to be described in such terms by the actors involved. Discrepancies between the ethnic "map" and the "territory" tend to lead, not to the abandonment of such terms, but to their redefinition, as well as to the emergence of other, competing terminologies. The ideological conflation of the terms *indio* and *campesino* (peasant) is discussed below.

25. The term *mestizo* varies in meaning from country to country; in Bolivia, it refers to people of mixed descent who wear western dress, speak Spanish, and may or may not speak an indigenous language as well. In the *altiplano, mestizos* are generally city or town dwellers; the peasantry is almost entirely Aymara or Quechua.

26. *Cholo* originally referred to *indios* who abandoned the traditional markers of indigenous identity to adopt a more *mestizo* image. As urban migration rapidly swells its ranks, this category has shifted to include urban dwellers of indigenous background who actively pursue economic or political power, but retain strong ties to their culture and language of origin (Max Fernández and Carlos Palenque, mentioned above, were archetypal *cholo* politicians). Changes in *cholo* identity and social position are explored in Bouysse-Cassagne and Saignes (1992) and Albro (1995).

27. Similarly, Albó (1993a:28) notes that "the percentage of the population for whom this consciousness [of nation and citizenship] is the most fundamental group identity is growing more and more, especially in the vast urban areas and in the intermediate sectors that no longer recognize their ancient roots."

28. As numerous authors have noted, the notion of "race," as a supposedly empirical biological classification, is so problematic that the temptation is to reject it outright. Still, "race" as a social and ideological construct is extremely powerful; racial divisions, as discursive constructions constitutive of social reality, are very real, and it is in that sense that the term is used here. Since "race" is frequently conflated with "ethnicity" in Bolivian popular discourse, the parsing of too fine a distinction would hardly be useful in the present context.

29. Today, *indio* is used in informal contexts, often by indigenous people themselves, to refer to one whose habits mark him as ignorant, brutish, or generally "uncivilized." Many upper-class Bolivians still also use it in casual reference to a group with which they have little social contact and thus need not worry about offending.

30. In *Semana de Última Hora,* June 4, 1976, cited in Albó 1988:33 (original emphasis). For other personal testimonies on the subject of Aymara identity, see Montoya and Lopez (eds.) 1988.

31. Albó's later work (1988, among others) moves away from this position, claiming that, despite the transformations, deteriorations, and disarticulations they have suffered, the Aymara remain "a people not ready to die out," and that proletarianization has given rise to an urban variant of Aymara culture that continues to develop according to its own logic.

32. Stuart Hall (1986c:16) notes that "in national and ethnic struggles in the modern world, the actual field of struggle is often actually polarized in [a] more complex and differentiated way. The difficulty is that it often continues to be described, theoretically, in terms which reduce the complexity of its actual social composition to the more simple, descriptive terms of a struggle between two, apparently, simple and homogenous class blocs."

33. Sharon Welch, *Communities of Resistance,* 83. Cited in Giroux (1988:218).

34. This generalization is drawn from the expressive behavior of the most politicized members of each group, whose visibility is often out of proportion to their actual numbers, creating an impression of unanimity where such may not actually exist. In reality, the correspondence between class position (or ethnicity) and ideology is seldom so neat. See Mouffe (1979) and Hall (1986b) for discussions of such "non-necessary correspondences."

35. Anderson (1983) explores how the state itself sometimes produces revolutionary nationalisms as a strategy for consolidating its hegemony. I refer to "the state," not as an external agent organically distinct from civil society, but as the collection of public and private apparatuses, institutions, and practices through which the balance of dominant interests (class and otherwise) is exercised. This conception, originating in the writings of Antonio Gramsci, is elaborated in Althusser (1971), Bourdieu (1977), Mouffe (1979), Bennet et al. (1981), Laclau and Mouffe (1985), Hall (1985, 1986c), and Alonso (1988), among others.

36. The mines did show lower profits under state control; but this was partly due to the decrease in mineral actually present and to the fact that the miners' new political power led to a much higher standard of living than they had previously enjoyed. Predictably, increased worker control led to smaller profits; but by casting this in terms of "efficiency," the state can portray the conflict as a merely technical-managerial problem, unrelated to class dynamics.

37. An account of Katari's rebellion and related campaigns can be found in Cárdenas (1988).

38. This archetypal image is depicted both in a gruesome diorama in the Casa Murillo on Calle Jaén and in a mural at the normal school that served as the site of the present study. The latter includes a heroic caption of Katari's last words (roughly, "I will return as millions"); the former is presented without commentary.

39. As well as an ethnic classification, *chullpa* is the name given to the mummified remains of ancient Andeans.

40. *Los Taquipayas,* Discolandia, Dueri & Cia. Lmtda., La Paz, 1991.

41. "Because Bolivians are like that. We're backward." The word *atrasados* is a pun, simultaneously invoking the meaning of "backward" in the cultural sense and the more everyday meaning of "late."

42. "Idiot! Instead of learning English, why didn't you learn how to swim?"

43. In this regard, it is worth noting that Third World denunciations of First World imperialism, while valid, are also often a means to avoid confronting the reality of internal colonialism.

44. See note 35, above.

Chapter 2. *Rural Schooling in Bolivia*

1. For accounts of Bolivia's indigenous education movement, see Choque et al. (1992) and Luykx (1993).

2. One finds frequent references to "hygiene" in descriptions of Bolivian rural education. While there is little specific information about this part of the prerevolutionary curriculum, one suspects that it was (at least in part) a euphemism for the inculcation of urban cultural practices and attitudes targeting the body, sexuality, etc.

3. Census figures for 1992 show 24.7 percent of women and 8.5 percent of men, or 16.9 percent of Bolivia's adult population, to be illiterate. Illiteracy among rural dwellers (44.5 percent for women and 17.6 percent for men; 31.2 percent overall) is over three times that of urban dwellers (14.5 percent for women and 3.5 percent for men; 9.2 percent overall). The definition of "literacy" was not made explicit; hopefully it indicates more than the ability to write one's name, but this cannot be assumed. The census also indicates that 85 percent of Bolivian children ages 6–14 attend school. Not only is the figure lower in rural than in urban areas (78.5 percent as opposed to 90.9 percent), but the gap between male and female enrollment is also greater in rural areas (82.2 percent/74.6 percent, as opposed to 92.3 percent/89.5 percent in urban areas) (INE 1992).

4. The practical importance of this aim is demonstrated by the fact that two-thirds of Bolivia's food supply is produced by peasants, mostly Aymaras and Quechuas (Rance 1991:31). Left to their own devices, "unintegrated" peasants may have concerns outweighing that of feeding the cities. After the 1953 Agrarian Reform, which gave peasants control over their land, agricultural produce available for sale in the cities diminished, while the average weight of indigenous army draftees increased considerably (Alexander 1982:22).

5. Among the Huaorani of Ecuador, the relation between schooling and national integration is even more direct; upon receiving a school, a Huaorani community (now a "village") appears on the national map, and the newly constituted "villagers," now formally recognized as Ecuadorian citizens, must vote, get birth and marriage certificates, and own identity cards (Rival 1996).

6. Along with increased access to education, land pressure in the countryside is a major factor, so that "rural push" and "urban pull" together encourage the tide of migration.

7. In many rural areas, schooling is available only through the primary level, so that children either stop at the fifth grade or are sent to the provincial or departmental capital to continue their education. Many of the subjects of this study spent their early years in the countryside, only to relocate to the city for this purpose during adolescence.

8. A more cynical analysis of the current educational reform might suggest that the new emphasis on valorizing indigenous cultures and rural lifeways (in contrast to the previously generalized assumption of the superiority of all things urban and occidental) springs less from a newly acquired cultural sensitivity on the part of government planners than from a desire to stem the flow of urban migration by convincing rural dwellers to stay where they are.

9. This contradiction is reflected in a hotly debated aspect of the reform: secondary schooling's division into two tracks, leading to the *bachillerato humanístico* and the *bachillerato técnico*, respectively. It is not hard to see how this might map onto existing social divisions, perhaps replacing the rural/urban split as the principal means of class-based stratification of students.

10. This division is to be phased out under the reform.

11. Although I was told on numerous occasions that promotions depended more on applicants' party affiliations or willingness to pay bribes than on their exam performance.

12. See Luykx (1989b) for a detailed comparison of urban and rural, primary and secondary teachers with regard to their social position and relations within Bolivian rural communities.

13. Despite its apparent cynicism, this sentiment was echoed (somewhat less harshly) by the USAID Mission to Bolivia (1975:1–8), in reference to the system of normal schools in general.

14. A common critique of the government's proposal has been that it strayed considerably from the one generated by the 1992 conference, especially as regards the proposed administrative changes and (predictably) the role of the teachers' union. Critics argue that the plan, which ostensibly calls for a more democratic pedagogy, was arrived at by non-democratic means and is a Trojan horse for covert aims such as the weakening of teachers' bargaining power and the withdrawal of government responsibility for secondary education.

15. Although what some view as a wasteful and inefficient bureaucracy may be functional in terms of providing employment, cultivating political support, and insulating decision makers from the demands of their constituency.

16. Strictly speaking, the Reform Law does not mention privatization; the consternation arises from the fact that it guarantees all Bolivian children access to *primary* education, without explicitly affirming government support for secondary education. The ambiguous wording is interpreted by many as evidence of the government's tacit withdrawal from secondary education. Given that currently barely one-half of urban children and only 1 percent of rural children ever reach the secondary level at all (MDH/SNE 1994:9), it might be argued that ensuring access at least through the primary grades would be a significant improvement over actual educational levels.

17. This is not to imply that all or even most teachers are opposed to the reform. While many are skeptical or opposed to certain points, many others strongly support the plan, especially its pedagogical aspects. The impression of near-unanimous opposition derives more from the heavy-handed discipline that the union leadership imposes on its members (such as obligatory participation in marches and strikes) than from any real consensus on the issue.

18. Formally, private school teachers have their own union and are not represented by the FDTEULP. But there is some overlap, since many public school teachers moonlight in private schools (as well as other jobs). La Paz's rural teachers have their own departmental federation, but it lacks the political clout of the FDTEULP.

19. This, and the fact that the union carries out many functions ostensibly pertaining to the Ministry of Education, has drawn harsh criticism from the Ministry itself (MEC 1989:75–76).

20. Throughout its 60-year history, the POR has had considerable influence on the development of Bolivia's labor movement. For a more detailed account of this history see G. Lora (1977). (Guillermo Lora is the intellectual head of the POR, while his younger brother, Miguel Lora, is an influential leader and chief rhetorician of the FDTEULP.)

21. The generally low quality of public schools coupled with frequent and lengthy strikes have led to a proliferation of private schools in recent years; practically all parents who can afford private school for their children do so, and many public schools charge small monthly "quotas," in return for which teachers continue to work during strikes.

Chapter 3. Student Life at the Normal School

1. Names of places, persons, and institutions have been changed to protect the anonymity of the subjects.

2. Statistical data on students are from a survey conducted during the second half of the research period, with 165 of 220 students responding. While percentages are not exact, they coincide with my own and the faculty's impressions and can be assumed to roughly reflect the student body as a whole. In 1972, a nationwide study indicated that, of 4210 rural normal school students, 20 percent were of urban background, 40 percent "semi-urban," and 40 percent of peasant origin (Albó 1981:18).

3. The term *ama de casa* (housewife) is often a catch-all category for women not employed outside the home. Of course, in many peasant families, neither parent is employed outside the home. Many "housewives" clearly could be considered "farmers" as well.

4. Argentina's high wages draw many young Bolivians to seek temporary jobs there.

5. By "clearly defined" I do not mean that such groups are static entities. They are often quite flexible, constituting "situational identity groups" rather than fixed cliques. But while group membership may be flexible, the groups as symbolic categories are quite persistent and extremely salient for students (cf. Foley 1990:77–78).

6. Descriptions of those students who appear frequently in the text are included in the Appendix.

7. MacLeod (1987) reports a similar leveling of aspirations among inner city youth in the United States.

8. Peruvian teachers (Motte 1995) and university students in Teacher Education (Portocarrero and Oliart 1989:117) have expressed reasons virtually identical to those mentioned by the normal school students. Also notable is a 1970 Bolivian survey in which 19 percent of 1,100 finishing high school students indicated that they planned to enter teacher training, although only 15.9 percent of those surveyed indicated an *interest* in teaching as a career (Albó 1981:19).

9. In 1992, citing an overabundance of teachers, the government announced that no new normal school students would be admitted. Public pressure (including a hunger strike by several applicants) resulted in an agreement to open one school in the department of La Paz. The community of Los Pozos then mobilized around the argument that, if the other normal school were allowed to admit new students, Kollasuyo should be also. Applicants' parents turned out in large numbers to meet with the departmental supervisor, adamantly defending their position. Interestingly, their arguments hinged not on the general desirability of training more teachers, but on the question of where their children would go if not admitted. They eventually were admitted, two months after the school year had begun.

10. Several individuals were present as irregular or marginal members of the school community. One of these was, of course, myself; in addition, several children of female personnel either lived on the grounds or were frequent visitors. A few Aymara women and their children ran small stores just outside the school gates, providing dry goods and occasional meals to students and faculty. Finally, two old and destitute Aymara men entered the school grounds every day or two in search of kitchen leftovers or meals provided to them by female staff members.

11. The school had a cafeteria where perhaps half of the students and faculty regularly ate. The others ate at one of the small stores *(kioskos)* mentioned above or in their homes in town.

12. "Ideology" refers here, not to subjects' explicitly expressed opinions about education, but rather to their implicit assumptions about what schooling should and does entail. It is in this sense somewhat misleading to speak of ideology and practice as two separate phenomena, given that school ideology is built up from the minutiae

of daily practice. Many institutional practices appear so natural, even trivial, that the ideological framework they compose—and impose— persists without comment or critique. It is this naturalization of practices expressing arbitrary and entrenched relations of power that defines those practices as ideological; they are the material components of an unspoken ideology about the exigencies of living and learning in groups.

13. Arturo claimed that several years before students had requested, and somehow managed to obtain, the privilege of "auto-control." According to his (unconfirmed) account, that year saw an unprecedented number of student pregnancies, and the experiment was subsequently abandoned.

14. One of the *inspectora*'s duties was keeping track of female students' menstrual cycles. While the ostensible reason was to allow the girls to be excused from gym class on those days, it also served to keep the administration apprised of students' reproductive status. While not in itself preventive of sexual activity, the regulation of such a personal function added to the sense that students' intimate activities were the legitimate object of institutional surveillance.

15. Girls had an advantage in this regard, since many of them carried their knitting with them for just such moments.

16. My relative autonomy in this regard was a source of envy among students; unlike them, I could arrive late for assembly without fear of reprimand, attend only those classes which I chose, and even spend days away from the school without asking permission. In an environment marked by rather spartan living conditions and few indulgences, the freedom to work according to my own schedule became a treasured luxury. It was the desire to maintain my "personal economy of action," more than anything else, that led me to give up eating in the cafeteria with the students; by taking my meals outside (as most of the professors also did), I could work until I reached my own "stopping point," rather than having to drop everything at the sound of the bell.

17. While students' academic labor is examined in later chapters, the appropriation of their nonacademic labor (especially the use of manual labor as a form of punishment) has important implications for the formation of an ideology of education. The extension of institutional control into areas unrelated to academic performance increases students' sense that they "belong" to the institution, i.e., that it has a legitimate claim on any and every aspect of their existence. This is quite in line with the nature of normal school training, not as the mere imparting of a set of skills, but rather as a process of socialization/identity formation whose object is the entire person.

18. McLaren (1986:195) has observed that those areas "off-limits" to students are usually much more physically comfortable than those areas not "off limits." Students never entered the rector's quarters and

only entered his office if summoned there for the most serious of disciplinary talks. The rarity of entering staff members' rooms was apparent in the students' initial hesitance (and subsequent pleased curiosity) upon entering mine; later, several girls used it as a refuge of sorts when the noise or controversy of the dorm became overwhelming.

19. It is true that the bulky *pollera* is not really convenient for desk-sitting; but this practical consideration in no way obviates the significance of its absence from student's symbolic repertory. Notably, when new students were admitted near the end of the research period, many girls arrived wearing the *pollera*, a clear indicator of their novice status.

20. In the area of personal expression, girls appeared to have an advantage, since virtually all of them could knit and crochet (all students were required to do so for home economics class, but the girls were the most accomplished). Still, the theme of suppressed creativity inevitably calls to mind one shy urban girl who, upon discovering my collection of colored chalk (the room in which I was housed contained a large blackboard), immediately set herself to writing on the board her name, astrological sign, and other personal data, including "ability: composing verses."

21. During the entire exchange, Diana addressed the teacher with the informal *tú*. While it was unusual for students to address staff in such a casual manner, this teacher tolerated it (and thereby received it) more than most. His occasional feigned offense at such informalities usually did more to encourage than to halt them.

22. In retrospect, this incident is confusing, since many students later came to me with similar complaints, though at the time many seemed prepared to defend the *inspectora*. This may have been because, when the incident occured, the first year students (the majority of the dorm population) had been at the school for only a few months. Also, the accusing student was in fact perceived by many as a demagogue who made accusations to bolster his chances in the election, more than out of any real concern for justice. In the end, he became president anyway, and later fell into further disfavor when financial discrepancies in his administration's accounts were discovered.

23. This should perhaps come as no surprise, since Foucault (1977) seemed generally unconcerned with the analysis of oppression as part of a transformative politics, instead adopting an almost blithely celebratory stance toward power (by virtue of its creativity) that elides the question of its unequal distribution and application.

24. This critique applies to Foucault 1977; but see his discussion of power and resistance in *The History of Sexuality, Volume 1: An Introduction* (1980, Vintage Books, New York), ch. 4.2.

25. I would exclude from this charge his more recent work (1984, 1991).

26. A derogatory derivation of *mama*, the Aymara female term of address.

27. Such conflicts affirm Weis's (1996:x) call for anthropologists to pay more attention to the relational component of identity; clearly, one's self-concept has as much to do with what one feels one is *not*, as with what one *is*.

28. For a more detailed examination of Aymara attitudes toward the military, the complexities of this relationship, and the toll it takes on family and community relations, see Luykx (1989b).

29. The timing of this announcement, less than a week after the town's patron saint festival, suggests that it was motivated by the unregulated celebratory activities of some students.

30. The degree to which these disputes were "merely personal" is open to question. The collapse of the *interno* slate was reportedly sparked by Sergio's voting for himself to lead the ticket, a move that José considered arrogant and in bad taste. This difference in concep-tions of acceptable behavior may be linked to the discrepancy between the assertive personal style characteristic of urban students and the greater reserve typical of rural dwellers.

Chapter 4. Curriculum and Identity

1. A challenge to such study is the need to theoretically connect collective phenomena such as nationalism, class conflict, sexism, and ethnic rivalries to the individual, often unconscious psychological fac-tors that also enter into identity formation. While the present work focuses on explicitly *social* processes, fuller comprehension of the formation and articulation of ideologies in individuals, communities, and nations ultimately will mean integrating sociopolitical, historical, anthropological, and psychological approaches. Bold efforts in this direction include Stahr and Vega (1988) and Oliart (1991).

2. Walsh (1987:197) similarly notes: "The child's construction of a meaning (semantic) system and of a social system thus take place side by side as two aspects of a single unitary process."

3. Significantly, a key feature of structural racism, sexism, and other forms of oppression is the severe restriction of the range of subject positions available to a given group of individuals.

4. The degree to which children are expected to surpass the class position of their parents, rather than follow in their footsteps, might be considered one of the benchmarks of modernity.

5. Not that class stratification is absent from the first years of school; children are socialized as class subjects from an early age, but this process intensifies as they advance toward the entrance into working life. In many countries, stratification occurs at the individual

level (via tracking, etc.), while in others it occurs at the institutional level; schools themselves are segregated by class or race, so that the composition of the student body within each school is fairly homogenous. Bolivian schools are mostly of the latter type, though this is less true in urban areas.

6. Nestor García Canclini: "Materiales para el seminario Cultura Popular en América Latina." (ILAS, University of Texas at Austin, 1989.) Cited in Oliart (1991:204).

7. This is not always so; as we saw in chapter 1, ethnic, class, and national subjectivities may be redrawn in periods of national crisis. Recent debates over identity indicate that Bolivia is entering another such period of collective redefinition. Still, the rhetorical naturalization of subject positions—i.e., the use of terms denoting social categories without interrogating said terms or categories—remains a common means of limiting debate, in schools as elsewhere.

8. Class discussions and comments are presented in English translation, except for cases where the translation is problematic or the original language highlights some feature to be examined.

9. Monje was the regional ADNista development official who sponsored the normal school's graduating class that year.

10. Black nationalist Leroi Jones (1968:359) defined nationalism as "the militant espousal of the doctrine of serving one's own people's interests before those of a foreign country, e.g., the United States."

11. The comment about the impossibility of comparing cultures, for example, was immediately followed by a discussion of the importance of writing to a culture's "level of development," and Bolivia's high level of illiteracy.

12. Bourne (1988:96) notes that "at different times, different sites are seen as productive of ability, of power to rule. The entry of less powerful groups into these sites (as we have seen happen in education generally) may only cause prestige to shift to another area."

13. Of course, there is always ideological space for teachers to accept the mantle of the organic intellectual rather than the burden of the laborer, without sacrificing proletarian solidarity. Given that links to universities and the middle class have been crucial to many revolutionary movements, teachers' class ambiguity need not be viewed as blunting their revolutionary potential—but it does chafe against the rigidly dogmatic socialism of the POR and the FDTEULP.

14. This distinction is often expressed as *"educación en la vida"* (education as a part of life) vs. *"educación para la vida"* (education as preparation for life), with the former viewed as an expression of the Marxist unity of theory and practice.

15. Exceptions included Agriculture class, where students worked in the school's fields as part of their classwork, and Handicrafts, where they did projects in pottery, knitting, leatherwork, and other crafts.

16. Previous research (Luykx 1989b) revealed such demands to be a common source of complaints about teachers.

17. The Aymara word for "thief."

18. One example of the tenor of the times is the silent film *La Profesía del Lago* (The Prophecy of the Lake), by Bolivian film pioneer José María Velasco Maidana, which centers on a young woman of "high society" who falls in love with one of the *pongos* on her family's *hacienda*. The theme of interracial/inter-class romance was so shocking to "respectable" Bolivians—"as if one might fall in love with an animal"—that the film not only was banned after two days, but was ordered to be burned as well (Iturri 1988:4).

19. Nor is it retroactive; illiteracy is disproportionately high among older people, which has been a factor in the disruption of traditional rural status hierachies.

20. Although the present work focuses on representations of *altiplano* dwellers, racist stereotypes of other indigenous groups were also present, though less frequently. For example, during a class discussion on evolution, one student asked if mankind continues to evolve today. The teacher replied that Amazon tribes of "animal-humans" are still adapting to their environment, but that "we" have reached the peak of our physical evolution and continue progressing through such intellectual means as science and technology.

21. Such regional stereotypes are deeply rooted in Bolivia, reinforced regularly in everyday discourse and popular culture; for a more detailed listing of the traits ascribed to inhabitants of various regions, see Pike (1977:77–78).

22. As an example of the opportunism of the *mistis*, one professor recounted how Andres de Santa Cruz (one of Bolivia's "founding fathers") switched from the royalist to the *independentista* cause just before the end of the war in 1825. The use of this potentially subversive bit of history for a dubious rhetorical purpose demonstrates the importance of the *articulation* of ideological elements (rather than just content) in the maintenance of hegemony.

23. During a sociology class, one student asked about land taxes for common pasture; the teacher replied that it is important to register land in the names of individuals, or else there is no official owner. There was no mention of how this law contributed to the dispossession of indigenous lands and the dissolution of rural communities.

24. Ideological assumptions were frequently embedded in parts of lessons that were "given" in order to highlight another (often relatively trivial) point. For example, in a lesson on reading comprehension of a newspaper article on Peruvian president Alberto Fujimori's "auto-coup," the teacher asked, "Who supports the constitutional president of Peru? The international—?" (eliciting "community" from the class). The question was intended to test students' comprehension of the article, not

to provoke discussion of the international reponse to Fujimori's dissolution of Parliament. Political content was habitually enfolded in pedagogical objectives that precluded the problematization of that content.
Chapter 5 examines in detail how the structuring of schoolwork and
classroom interactions served as a check on the critical examination
of official meanings.

25. Grammatical realizations encode differences, not only among
a variety of possible social groupings, but among flexible ways of
discursively positioning oneself within or in opposition to these social
groups; "[speakers] producing these forms seem then not only to be
reflecting social structure and self-identity in their speech, but actually to be producing the social structures and identities within the
classroom" (Bourne n.d.:11). Words—especially such ideologically
charged terms as ethnic labels—are not neutral symbols, but rather
"the means through which we absorb and rework the histories of our
ancestors, the sociocultural design of our surroundings, and the political and economic moments in which we (and our antecedents) reside" (Walsh 1991:65).

26. Interestingly, Lagos (forthcoming) notes that the current government displays the opposite tendency, legitimizing ethnic and gender differences within a generally "multiculturalist" discourse, while
simultaneously overlooking (or playing down) class differences.

27. Though the boundary is a very fuzzy one, complicated by
centuries of *mestizaje* and also by the growing numbers of rural-urban
migrants. It is the *ideological* reality of the division that is really at
issue here, however.

28. This view was not unanimous. Some students who spoke
Aymara fluently considered its inclusion in the curriculum a waste of
time; its strongest supporters tended to be those whose command of
Aymara was more precarious. Escobar (1972) notes a correspondence
between negative language attitudes and indigenous language fluency,
since those who use the indigenous language in daily communication
are more likely to have suffered for it.

29. Several other teachers also complained of students' habit of
speaking "Aymarañol." Hill (1987:130) notes the tendency to express
solidarity around the indigenous language through an attitude of "lexical purism" that views hispanicized speech as spoiled and polluted;
she points out that "lexical purism is largely a losing battle, as precisely those speakers who are most concerned with it are also the
most exposed to Spanish influence."

30. Many were also centuries old, such as *nayax janiw puirkti* ("I
can't"), which incorporates the (phonologically adapted) Spanish verb
poder. This is similar to rejecting as "improper English" expressions
incorporating French roots no longer recognized as such by native
English speakers.

31. This teacher spent most of one day's lesson trying to get students to distinguish between /s/ and the Castilian /z/ ([ø]), which does not occur in Andean Spanish. Later, when Professor Ramírez used this as an example of orthographic distinctions that do *not* reflect phonological difference, he was surprised to hear students' tongue-twisting attempts to produce two different fricative sounds, and remarked, "Who talks that way?"

32. School staff invariably viewed students' "mixing" of Spanish and Aymara as a linguistic vice revealing lack of control over either language. This attitude is described by Flores, Attinasi, and Pedraza ("La Carreta Made a U-Turn: Puerto Rican Language and Culture in the United States," *Daedalus* 110 [Spring 1981]:199):

> Codeswitching is viewed as the tragic convergence of two nonstandard vernaculars, and is thus assumed to epitomize the collapse of the integrity of both. It is in this context, where practical bilingualism occurs most spontaneously and expressively, that the charge of alinguality has gained its widest currency. For many observers . . . codeswitching amounts to contamination and interference, an easy recourse to compensate for incomplete resources in either idiom. (Cited in Walsh 1991:105)

In her study of Mexicano/Spanish bilinguals, Hill (1987:128) noted a similar attitude: "Speakers consider their usage in both languages . . . to lie in a zone of imperfection somewhere between the ideal versions of them . . . Thus, all speech is considered to be dominated by mixing and error." Claims that bilingual students (and their parents) suffer from "semilingualism" (the inability to speak any language well) persist, despite an abundance of linguistic and educational research to the contrary (Walsh 1991:62).

33. Paraphrased from a class lecture.

34. Some argue that this is simply a result of obligatory gender marking in Spanish and that the masculine forms are actually "generic." This argument fails, since the conflation of generic and specific masculine forms infuses even "generic" usages with an implied masculinity. Furthermore, English contains many of the same structural regularities to which such an argument has been applied, and yet speakers and writers (academic and otherwise) have found it not only desirable but quite possible to substitute other, truly generic forms.

35. R. Connell distinguishes between "distributive justice," or equality of educational access, and "curricular justice," or equality in the realm of curricular knowledge and representation (*Schools and Social Justice*. [Philadelphia: Temple University Press, 1993], 19. Cited in Levinson and Holland 1996:4).

36. Juan Carlos Gorlier, "Notas sobre producción de consenso" (Buenos Aires, 1989). Cited in Bonder (1992:235).

37. The relegation of female teachers to the "domestic arts" and the primary grades is the norm in Bolivia.

38. Oddly enough, this did not provoke mention of Bolivia's only female president, Lidia Gueiler Tejada, who served briefly during 1979 and 1980. A discussion of whether her election (by Parliament, not the citizenry) affected the status of Bolivian women in general would have been interesting, but like so many potentially interesting class discussions, died before it even got started.

39. Abortion was mentioned occasionally, but never as a question of women's rights, nor in conjunction with any discussion of contraception or family planning. During a presentation on infant and maternal mortality, one student mentioned that 80 percent of hospitalizations of Bolivian women are due to complications from illegal abortions, mostly in Santa Cruz, where people are "more liberal." On another occasion, the agriculture professor digressed from his discussion of spontaneous abortion in guinea pigs to mention those induced in human beings by "criminals."

40. Skinner and Holland (1996:283–84) note that, among Nepalese students, disavowal of caste differences has become a mark of the "educated person"; in other countries, the same seems to occur with regard to gender differences.

41. The demarcation of drinking as a male sphere also limited female participation in the faculty's informal social networks. On occasions when male faculty drank, female staff members drank much more moderately and retired from the festivities early, since "men get unpleasant when they drink so much." Women's *de facto* exclusion from such events, and from the related camaraderie among male professors, administrators, and education officials, had effects similar to the exclusion of North American professional women from informal "good old boy" networks.

42. Some may be tempted to read this as a manifestation of the "gender complementarity" that has become such a common theme in academic explorations of Andean culture. However, the different values assigned to different types of labor means that "complementarity" may have little to do with "egalitarianism" (de la Cadena 1991).

43. This is precisely opposite the scheme described by Willis (1981a), whose "lads" valorized manual labor for its masculine symbolic value, while mental labor (such as schoolwork) was rejected as effeminate. However, it corresponds to a previous study (Luykx 1989b) that found Aymara men predominating in public performative roles involved in community decision making, while women participated in a collective or behind-the-scenes capacity. Cortina (1992) has also observed that, even when women's presence in labor or educational organizations is increased, they are often relegated to carrying out the "domestic" chores of the organization, while high-profile positions involving prestigious forms of speech are filled by men.

44. "The Outer Word and Inner Speech: Bakhtin, Vygotsky, and the Internalization of Language," in *Bakhtin: Essays and Dialogues on His Work*, G. S. Morson, ed., (Chicago: University of Chicago Press, 1986), 31. Cited in Walsh (1991:90).

45. Of course, this is more true for some students than for others; for those for whom teaching is already something of a family tradition, their professional socialization may constitute continuity with their origins rather than rupture.

Chapter 5. Commodified Language and Alienated Exchange in the Normal School

1. The emphasis on verbatim copying of lessons is partly due to the scarcity of textbooks; when students' notes are their only study material, there is an understandable desire that they be exact and uniform. During previous research (Luykx 1989b), Bolivian primary teachers also justified these methods by explaining that students needed practice in reading and writing Spanish and that parents liked to see written evidence of their work at the end of the day.

2. The studies cited were of public primary schools, which account for the bulk of data on Bolivian schooling. Though one might assume that high school instruction would fall somewhere between the primary school and the normal school in terms of opportunities for student participation, it has yet to be studied in any depth.

3. Luykx (1992) describes the distinctive speech style associated with this type of speech event.

4. As part of a national curriculum overhaul in the late 1980s, teachers were instructed to stress "objectives" (specific skills that students should acquire via the completion of each unit) rather than simply "contents." In practice, the objectives are often presented as simply one more list for students to copy down.

5. Such mistakes reveal both the degree to which students ignored content when copying lessons, and the low comprehension with which they handled academic discourse. One boy, speaking on "The Economic Crisis," began: "*Nos vamos a hablar de la inflamación . . . *" (inflammation), rather than "*inflación*" (inflation). Though his error prompted a collective guffaw from the class, it brings to mind Bourdieu and Passeron's (1977:133) warning that "when teachers joke about such gems, they forget that these misfirings of the system contain the truth of the system."

6. Since most students had relatives and neighbors with *minifundios* of their own, the question seemed either ingenuous—one more indication of the lack of connection students drew between their own

knowledge and what they learned in school—or simply intended to score points for "participation" (more likely in Faustino's case).

7. The pedagogical processes by which school knowledge is produced are effectively blind to the particular subject matter. Comparing the normal school with McNeil's description of a U.S. high school, we can note the similar way in which two opposing political philosophies are treated in two different institutions on two different continents:

> Capitalism, the importance of political parties, free enterprise, and progress are all aspects of our system that were mentioned with an aura of respect or reverence, then left as slogans. The intent seemed to be to have students internalize the affective component of the terms so that their trust of the system would be enhanced . . . Students did, for the most part, internalize some of the emotional quality of the term, while remaining unable to explain it. (McNeil 1986:170)

The substitution of emotional affect for detailed understanding is also hinted at in Bourdieu and Passeron's (1977) discussion of "affiliative language" and Williams' (1977) "structures of feeling." In his study of a North American Catholic school, McLaren (1986:228) also observed the contradiction between the generally critical attitude toward the existing social order and the ritualized structural relations through which lessons were transmitted.

8. This was evident from their comments; some argued that humans had evolved independently on each continent or that the different human races had evolved from different species of monkeys; one boy claimed that the divine origin of the Bible was proven by the fact that it predated the development of writing.

9. This was largely due to the phonological, lexical, and grammatical influence of Aymara on *altiplano* Spanish, described in detail in Mendoza (1988) and Stratford (1989).

10. This was startlingly demonstrated in a language lesson on "How to Read a Book"; after cautioning students to read only in the correct light, setting, mental state, and posture, the teacher instructed them to "examine and reflect upon" the title, author's name, editorial information, and each chapter, in order without skipping around randomly. He went over the parts of the book—spine, cover, table of contents—as one would the anatomy of some exotic animal. Students copied the information diligently, with no sign that they considered it irrelevant or common knowledge. The concept of the "native reader" is presented here in condensed form; a more detailed exposition of the cognitive and sociocultural factors involved can be found in Luykx (1992).

11. Bourdieu and Passeron (1977:120) note that "the primacy of oral transmission [in schools] must not conceal the fact that communication is conducted through a spoken word dominated by the written word."

12. Different responses of male and female students to this situation are treated in Chapter 6.

13. Similarly, McNeil (1986:158) found that "teachers who teach defensively do not fit any one ideological or demographic category, and they use these techniques of classroom control with students of all ability levels."

14. Payne and Balderrama argue that "without a clear idea of one's own culture, it is logical to seek refuge and the solution to problems in foreign models" ("Contenido y método de la enseñanza en Bolivia," Comisión Episcopal de Educación, La Paz, 1972. Cited in Albó 1981:25). And not only in schooling; much of Bolivian cultural production is disparaged for being "copied from outside" (especially from the United States). Amid intense pressure to locate the standard of excellence outside itself, "imitativeness" appears as yet another blot on the national character.

15. Lesage uses the phrase in a somewhat different (though related) sense, to refer to ostensibly leftist scholars who use commodified knowledge of critical theory as a pathway to elitist professional advancement.

16. This also makes it not immediately recognizable as "ideology," perhaps because the term itself calls to mind an intangible "something" floating above the world of daily material practice.

17. Williams (1980:39) notes that the transmission of an effective dominant culture via educational institutions "is now a major economic as well as a cultural activity; indeed it is both in the same moment." While I do not examine schooling as an economic activity at the national level, its importance in this regard (as a source of employment, as a response to the rural land crisis, as a factor determining consumption patterns, etc.) should not be overlooked.

18. Giroux (1992:121) claims that "how subjects are constituted in language is no less important than how they are constructed as subjects within relations of production"; I would argue that the first is, in fact, an example of the second.

19. For a more detailed critique of Rossi-Landi's "semiotic homology" between language and economics, as well as other theoretical models of "alienated language" (specifically Everhart 1983 and Foley 1990), see Luykx (1993).

20. The focus here is on students as linguistic workers, but the model is really two-fold: in one sense, students are workers and teachers are managers, enforcing the conditions to which low-level workers are subject. From another angle, teachers are the workers and students the raw materials upon which they exert their efforts; the discursive skills inculcated during students' educational "processing" are the "value added" by virtue of teachers' linguistic work. Teachers' labor is alienated in ways similar (though not identical) to that of

students; teachers transmit cultural capital but are not its ultimate owners (at least not in Bolivia, where teaching is not a high-prestige job). Despite a temptation to view them as such, due to their structurally antagonistic relationship to students, teachers do not control the conditions (or the means) of linguistic production, nor the cultural capital that it is their job to transmit.

21. Aside from relegating most cultural or ideological phenomena to the realm of superstructure, Marx's elision of the question of symbolic value is manifested in his theoretical reduction of all labor to abstract, homogenous labor power, quantifiable in terms of time. While the higher wage earned by skilled workers is partly attributable to the greater amount of labor required to reproduce them, this does not account for the different wages earned by different *social* categories of workers doing the same work (men and women being the most obvious example).

22. Citations of Marx are from Tucker (1978), with corresponding page numbers, unless otherwise indicated. Specific works are abbreviated as follows: EPM—*Economic and Philosophical Manuscripts* (1844); GI—*The German Ideology* (1846); WLC—*Wage Labor and Capital* (1847); Gr.—*The Grundrisse* (1858); Cap1—*Capital*, Volume 1 (1867).

23. For a detailed account of the history of the term *alienation*, see Alonso Olea (1988).

24. I would include in this trend the rather incredible statement by even so noted a scholar as Walter Kaufmann, to the effect that "even if one associates the condition Marx indicts with alienation, it is far from clear what it has to do with capitalism" (in Schacht 1970:xlii).

25. For example, the register in which students were taught to phrase official correspondence, though relatively incomprehensible to them, was vital to the fulfillment of their future professional duties (many no doubt used their copied examples as verbatim models during their first year of actual teaching).

26. "Pre-Capitalist Economic Formations," pp. 80–81. Cited in Ollman (1976:182) (Marx's emphasis).

27. The school's ideological hegemony is pervasive even in a country such as Bolivia, where many people still have little or no direct experience with schooling. Those sectors marginalized from the educational system come to be defined by their very exclusion, at worst as "savages" and at best as "illiterates." As Rival (1996:153) notes, "Once the school institution has transformed local social relations, pre-school identities can no longer exist."

28. Although the cultural capital acquired solely through schooling is seldom granted the same legitimacy as that inherited from one's family background (Bourdieu and Passeron 1977).

29. Foley (1990) reports a similar tendency of teachers and administrators to stifle student debate on issues of ethnic conflict—

despite some students' desires to deal openly with such issues in class—ostensibly for fear that such debate would "get out of hand" or further inflame hostilities.

Chapter 6. Student Resistance to Commodification and Alienation: Silence, Satire, and the Academic Black Market

1. This may be due to the importance of modern and postmodern urban influences on the formation of First World youth countercultures; while indigenous rural youth are by no means totally isolated from such influences, their engagement with them is much less intense, and they are not a central factor in group identity.

2. Their interviews with me served a similar function, providing a sounding board (and implied validation) for grievances, frustrations, and hopes that they could not express publicly.

3. False deference is an unmistakable sign of social power; in general, elites control the public stage, while subordinates have only the "offstage areas" from which to mock and negate the dominant order (Scott 1985:25). This makes the rare public breach of deference, such as Diana's backtalk to the agriculture professor and the group reaction it provoked (see chapter 3) all the more exceptional (and all the more thrilling for students).

4. This distancing of one's identity from one's work is a key index of alienation. Eggan (1974:316) describes a similar process among Hopi children, who responded to "enforced education" by adopting "a surface accomodation to the situation until such time as they were able to return to their own meaningful world." She cites an elegant passage by Robert Ezra Park, to the effect that one can "make his manners a cloak and his face a mask, behind which he is able to preserve . . . inner freedom . . . and independence of thought, even when unable to maintain independence of action." *Race and Culture*, (New York: The Free Press, 1950).

5. Shor (1996:14) refers to such self-marginalizing tactics as "self-protective negative agency."

6. Philips (1983) found that Native American students' refusal to speak in class stemmed not from fear of the teachers but from the threat of ridicule by their (non-Indian) classmates; cf. Foley (1996) for a different interpretation of Indian students' silence and its relation to both students' self-esteem and the cultural stereotype of the "silent Indian."

7. "Repressive ridicule." Oliart uses the term to refer to Peruvian women's fear of dressing in a manner that might suggest pretensions of urban sophistication and thus provoke derision from others.

8. An Aymara accent also can be cause for negative evaluation by teachers. One teacher explained to me why he had recommended

against passing a student on his final practical exams (in which students are observed while practice teaching), mentioning, among other factors, the boy's accent: "He had lots of mistakes in his language, and if the teacher talks that way, the students will do the same. For example, '*sais*,' [*seis*, 'six'] he said, no? [laughter]. He was constantly saying '*sais*,' he at least should have changed to another number if he can't pronounce that one."

9. Remedios mentioned that when she studied in an all-girl school, the level of class participation was much higher.

10. Still, while the boys' strategy is more successful in terms of impression management, one might consider the girls' strategy more successful in terms of not surrendering one's linguistic labor to an alienated enterprise.

11. See Luykx (1989b) for a more detailed examination of this distribution.

12. *Poor People's Movements: Why They Succeed, How They Fail* (New York: Vintage 1977). Cited in Scott (1985:43).

13. Susan Stewart (1986) provides a related argument in her discussion of Bakhtin's "antilinguistics."

14. Sherzer (1987:102) cautions against the failure to distinguish between ideal and real speech patterns; in a survey of men's and women's speech, he noted that the formalized ritual speech genres that define leadership roles among the Kuna, while theoretically available to both sexes, were in practice restricted only to men.

15. The Aymara family and community place their own restrictions on women's speech, which children learn even before they reach school age (Luykx 1989b). It may be that female students would participate more if classroom situations were more like those in which women participate in Aymara communities (e.g., informal exchanges in small all-female groups, rather than individual speeches to a large mixed audience). But while attention to the types of participant structures in which women feel more comfortable speaking is important, it should not lead us toward the sort of "cultural difference" explanation that elides questions of power and prestige.

16. A handful of assertive female students were exceptions to this rule, and were all the more appreciated by their professors for that reason. However, the fact that they were seen as so exceptional, rather than as examples of what other female students might also achieve if encouraged, reveals the common belief in Bolivia (noted also by Miracle [1973]) that girls are not expected to excel academically.

17. *Changing Values in College* (New York: Harper & Bros., 1957), 2. Cited in Keill (1964:828).

18. This does not always mean one is unhappy in one's job; in some circles "it is fashionable, almost de riguer, to be cynical about one's work . . . The sophistication and subtlety of one's cynicism can be quite highly rewarding, thus creating a situation in which one can

be quite alienated from work but quite satisfied with one's job" (Berger 1968:206). This was evident among many Bolivian teachers with whom I spoke, and seems to be common in academia generally.

19. The normal school teachers of course had their own occupational culture, distinct from that of students. While the dubious practices described here were an integral part of that culture, it also included, for example, collective drinking, playing music, and grousing about students and the government. While the present work focuses mainly on students, teachers' efforts to carve out a space for nonalienated practice in their professional lives are worth mentioning. One example was the musical group formed by four or five teachers, who performed on festive occasions to an enthusiastic student audience. Another was Professor Torres's decoration of his room with portraits of Beethoven, Einstein, Darwin, and Charlie Chaplin, in striking contrast to the pin-up girls adorning some teachers' walls. While both types of images represent attempts to create a personalized space in an environment of institutional conformity, the former exhibit a deliberate inclination toward more prestigious and intellectual cultural forms. "If the professionals do not always have the taste to match their means, the teachers hardly ever have the means to match their tastes, and this disparity between cultural and economic capital condemns them to an ascetic aestheticism (a more austere variant of the 'artist' lifestyle) which 'makes the most' of what it has" (Bourdieu 1984:287).

20. Students who had studied at other normal schools claimed that such grievances were not universal and that elsewhere students actively organized to prevent such problems or rectify them when they did occur.

21. Some professors expressed resentment and frustration over parental pressure to pass their children regardless of academic performance; they also mentioned (with relief) that this normal school was better than others in that regard.

22. The tacitly accepted schism between real world knowledge and school knowledge is threatened when students are required to defend their written work orally. This was brought home to me early one morning in the girls' dorm, by a student who woke me with entreaties to explain the content of a monograph that she desperately thrust into my hands. Half-asleep, I skimmed the document and explained it to her as best I could, only later realizing that it was the monograph that she herself had supposedly written and had to defend in front of a panel of professors that afternoon.

23. The issue of students' sexual exploitation is also presented for reasons of solidarity; when forced to choose between students' interests and faculty or institutional interests, I generally chose the former, positioning myself on the side of those who were the subjects rather than the wielders of institutional power. While seldom accessible via

traditional investigative methods, sexual relations across institutional boundaries so often constitute one of the "structured silences" in educational contexts that the risks inherent in treating the subject seemed to me a lesser evil than that of reproducing that silence in the present work. I once asked a staff member if any such problems had occurred within the institution, and was told with an air of sincerity that they had not. I was inclined to distrust this answer, since a student had recounted to me a specific incident from the year before, in which a faculty member was dismissed and the student in question expelled. I assumed that my relationship with the staff member, while good, was not intimate enough to override his concern for the reputation of the institution, and did not press him further.

24. While I was unable to interview any female graduates about this process, this is clearly another situation in which the camaraderie around drinking provides an advantage to male students, whereas female students are again vulnerable to sexual pressure or coercion.

25. Furthermore, Bolivian parents seem less and less willing to sacrifice their children's immediate educational interests for the sake of class solidarity, as is shown by the growing shift toward private schooling. The last major teacher's strike (in 1996) was widely considered a failure, largely due to lack of public support.

26. Of course, classes as collective social entities endure despite individuals' passage in and out of them. Still, this does not mean that classes (or other social groupings) operate as monolithic entities mutually opposed in a static, *a priori* relation. "The various formations of the people move . . . across social categories, and are capable of adopting apparently contradictory positions either alternately or simultaneously . . . Popular allegiances . . . are context- and time-based, not structurally produced: they are a matter of practice, not of structure" (Fiske 1989:24–25).

27. While most treatments of student alienation center on academic failure, the link between the two is far from direct. In her study of a North American public school, McNeil found that "questions about the credibility of school knowledge *cut across achievement levels, across the social class distinctions* perceived by teachers, *across gender lines* and other categories education researchers use to categorize student differences" (McNeil 1986:87; original emphasis).

28. Bhabha (1994:20) claims that "forms of popular rebellion and mobilization are often most subversive and transgressive when they are created through oppositional *cultural* practices." Cf. also Apple (preface to Everhart 1983).

29. Basso (1979) and Limón (1982, 1989) have also noted of the use of play frames to put an ironic and critical twist on the dominant discourse. Within these performative frames, members of subordinated groups employ their shared knowledge of ethnic and class conflict

to challenge the legitimacy of dominant norms and deflate the prestige of the dominant group. The concept of 'framing' is taken from Goffman (1974).

30. A diminutive of "doctor," referring not to medical doctors but to lawyers, or to the learned and urbane in general.

31. *Doctorcitos* provides a modern parallel to the older *awki-awki* dance, in which boys dress as hunched old men of European appearance, with long white beards and canes, hobbling about in a parody of colonial-era elites. While the accouterments of upper-class identity have changed, they are still mocked in ways similar to those of centuries ago.

32. This same target for popular humor is found in Perú; Oliart (1991:207) cites Vásquez and Vergara's description of carnival representations of *"la pakina,"* a young peasant woman just back from a stay in Lima, wearing too-tight, too-bright clothes, putting on airs and belittling her native (Quechua) culture ("¡Chayraq! Carnaval ayacuchano," Lima, CEDAP/Tarea, 1988:248).

33. Significantly, the female character in this performance was absorbed in activities of her own, rather than simply ignoring or taunting the male, and finally joined him as an equal partner in the dance, rather than being "caught."

34. Roughly, "The Voice of the People"; the show offers airtime to viewers seeking redress for official abuses or aid for more personal difficulties (often extended by the station itself).

35. As the research came to an end, students were preparing another play, entitled *Miss Ch'ijini.* While I did not have a chance to find out much about the piece, the title (combining the prestigious English term of feminine address with an Aymara word meaning "planted field") suggests another variation on the theme of social and ethnic mobility.

36. Aymara has only three vowel phonemes; thus confusion of the Spanish vowels e/i and o/u is the shibboleth of the native Aymara speaker. Rural elementary school teachers typically spend much time and effort trying to eradicate this and other features of their pupils' Aymara accents.

37. This "temporary liberation from the prevailing truth of the established order" and "suspension of all hierarchical rank, privileges, norms, and prohibitions" is also central to Bakhtin's concept of the 'carnivalesque.' *Rabelais and His World* (Cambridge: MIT Press, 1986), 10. Cited in Fiske 1989:82.

38. Some students expressed discomfort over these releases, due to the fact that they were only temporary and more symbolic than real. Girls complained of pressure from teachers to drink, in a situation they seemed to perceive as sexually dangerous. Boys, on the other hand, complained that teachers' gusto in such events was not matched

by a similar enthusiasm in the classroom, nor the holiday camaraderie by a more abiding concern for students' interests.

39. The findings of Willis (1981a), Fiske (1989), and Foley (1990) lead one to similar conclusions.

40. This also serves as a critique of "cultural difference" explanations of minority school failure.

41. See, for example, Albo and Preiswerk's (1986) analysis of La Paz's *Gran Poder* festival and the shift in participation from predominantly rural migrants to the urban middle class.

42. Rowe and Schelling (1991:4) note that "in Latin America the idea of folklore has been bound up with the idea of national identity, and has been used by the state . . . to bring about national unity." They also claim that the disconnection of folkloric forms from their traditional contexts "involves gain as well as loss, since the new spaces of representation (provincial and departmental capitals and sometimes the national capital) can challenge the national political order and its versions of national identity" (59). On a more ominous note, Gilka Wara Céspedes (1993:79) mentions the appropriation, after the violent coup of 1980, of a popular anthem by folkloric group Los Kjarkas for mass-media use as the musical signature of the military regime.

43. Scott (1985:319) argues that the reinterpretation and blending of those beliefs emanating "from above" and pre-existing beliefs extant in agrarian societies make it possible to speak of folk socialism, folk nationalism, and folk communism just as one speaks of "folk religion."

44. Fiske (1989:57) distinguishes two types of popular pleasures: those of evasion, centering on the body, and those of producing meanings, centering on social relations and identity. Correspondingly, the normal school students tried to evade institutional control over their physical life, but responded to dominant definitions of social relations and identity with creative (and public) semiotic challenges.

45. Fiske (1989:47) defines popular pleasure as "the pleasure of producing one's own meanings of social experience and the pleasure of avoiding the social discipline of the power-bloc."

46. Of course, students were less willing to risk public expression of ideas sharply opposed to those of faculty. The possible privatization of schooling was the subject of several student speeches, whereas corruption in the educational system was seldom if ever publicly addressed (though it came up frequently in students' private interviews).

47. Roy A. Rappaport, "Adaptation and the Structure of Ritual," in *Human Behavior and Adaptation*, N. Blurton Jones and V. Reynolds, eds. (Society for the Study of Human Biology, 1978), 85. Cited in McLaren (1986:130).

48. Henry A. Giroux, *Theory and Resistance in Education: A Pedagogy for the Opposition.* (South Hadly, Massachusetts: Bergin and Garvey, 1983), 107. Cited in Walsh (1991:129).

Chapter 7. An Alternative Vision: Notes toward a Transformative Bolivian Pedagogy

1. The research site was within the EGTK's radius of activity; several walls throughout town displayed the group's graffiti, calling for the extermination of whites and the return of land and power to Bolivia's indigenous inhabitants.

2. August 1 was declared Day of the Indian in 1931, partly in honor of the founding of Warisata. The Educational Reform of 1953 was also promulgated on that date, making it a holiday of special significance for rural education.

3. This may be common to many subaltern expressive practices; Bhabha (1994:7) notes that hybrid Chicano art "does not merely recall the past as a social cause or aesthetic precedent; it renews the past, refiguring it as a contingent 'in-between' space, that innovates and interrupts the performance of the present. The 'past-present' becomes part of the necessity, not the nostalgia, of living."

4. *The Dialogic Imagination*, ed. M. Holquist, trans. C. Emerson and M. Holquist (Austin: University of Texas Press, 1981), 249. Cited in Walsh (1991:32).

5. Ollman sees the contemporary flourishing of the "consciousness industry" as the result of waning belief in the market and in people's place in the social hierarchy as natural phenomena. "The conscious production of ideology becomes, as a consequence, all the more essential for the survival of capitalism" (Ollman 1976:230–31).

6. Henry Giroux, *Theory and Resistance in Education: A Pedagogy for the Opposition* (South Hadley, Massachussetts: Bergin and Garvey, 1983), 214. Cited in Walsh (1991:4).

7. If I were to choose the next piece of the puzzle to "link up," it would be the integration of a psychoanalytic perspective into these formulations about symbolic labor and the production of subjectivities. Provocative efforts in this direction with regard to ethnicity, class, and gender include de la Cadena (1991) and Oliart (1991).

8. "Ethnicity: Problem and Focus in Anthropology," *Annual Review of Anthropology* 7, 1978.

9. Cf. Postman and Weingartner (1969), Freire (1971), Everhart (1983), McNeil (1986), McLaren (1986), Giroux (1988), Walsh (1991). Shor (1996), written in a style accessible to teachers, students, and theory buffs alike, is the best guide I know for creating a democratic, critical "speech community" in the classroom; I cannot recommend it highly enough.

10. Similarly, Geertz (1973b: 274–75) notes: "If the general strike is the classical political expression of class warfare, and the coup d'état of the struggle between militarism and parliamentarianism, then

the school crisis is perhaps becoming the classical political—or parapolitical—expression of the clash of primordial loyalties."

11. This orientation also allows for the location of academic difficulties in academic structures, rather than in students' inherent "deficiencies" (Walsh 1991:110).

12. Gender equity is an explicit part of Bolivia's educational reform, but often lacks a matching commitment among educators themselves, or is perceived (with some justification) as a condition imposed by foreign funding agencies (see Luykx [forthcoming]).

BIBLIOGRAPHY

Abercrombie, Thomas. 1991. "To Be Indian, To Be Bolivian: 'Ethnic' and 'National' Discourses of Identity." In *Nation-States and Indians in Latin America.* Greg Urban and Joel Sherzer, eds. Austin: University of Texas Press.

Albó, Xavier. 1979. "The Future of the Oppressed Languages in the Andes." CIPCA, La Paz.

———. 1981. "Idiomas, Escuelas y Radios en Bolivia." Sucre: UNITAS-ACLO.

———. 1988. "Introducción." In *Raíces de América: El Mundo Aymara.* Xavier Albó, ed. Madrid: UNESCO/Alianza Editorial.

———. 1990. "La Paz/Chukiyawu: Las Dos Caras de una Ciudad." La Paz: CIPCA.

———. 1991. "El retorno del indio." Revista Andina 9(2), December.

———. 1993a. "Our Identity Starting from Pluralism in the Bases." In *The Postmodern Debate in Latin America.* John Beverley and José Oviedo, eds. Durham, NC: Duke University Press.

———. 1993b. "¿... Y de Kataristas a MNRistas? La Sorprendente y Audaz Alianza entre Aymaras y Neoliberales en Bolivia." La Paz: CEDOIN-UNITAS.

———. and Matias Preiswerk. 1986. *Los Señores de Gran Poder.* La Paz, Bolivia: Centro de Teología Popular: Taller de Observaciones Culturales.

Albro, Robert. 1995. "Realpolitik and Reciprocity: Ritual Transformation and Electoral Stumping in Provincial Bolivia." Paper presented at the 94th Annual Meeting of the American Anthropological Association, Washington DC, Nov. 15–19.

Alexander, Robert J. 1982. *Bolivia: Past, Present, and Future of Its Politics.* New York: Praeger Publishers.

Alonso, Ana Maria. 1988. "The Effects of Truth: Re-presentations of the Past and the Imagining of Community." *Journal of Historical Sociology* 1(1).

Alonso Olea, Manuel. 1988. *Alienación: Historia de una Palabra*. México, DF: Universidad Nacional Autónoma de México/Instituto de Investigaciones Jurídicas.

Althusser, Louis. 1971. "Ideology and Ideological State Apparatuses." In *Lenin and Philosophy and Other Essays*. Translated by B. Brewster. London: New Left.

Amadio, Massimo, and Madeleine Zúñiga. 1989. *La Educación Intercultural y Bilingüe en Bolivia: Experiencias y Propuestas*. La Paz: UNESCO/MEC/UNICEF.

Anderson, Benedict. 1983. *Imagined Communities: Reflections of the Origin and Spread of Nationalism*. London: Verso.

Andreas, Peter. 1991. "Coca Denial." NACLA Report on the Americas, 25 (1), July, pp. 14–15.

Appadurai, Arjun, and Carol Breckenridge. 1988. "Why Public Culture?" *Public Culture* 1(1), pp. 5–10.

Apple, Michael. 1986. *Teachers and Texts: A Political Economy of Class and Gender Relations in Education*. New York: Routledge, Chapman & Hall, Inc.

———. 1990 (1979). *Ideology and Curriculum* (2nd edition). New York: Routledge, Chapman & Hall, Inc.

Archondo, Rafael. 1991. *Compadres al Micrófono: La Resurrección Metropolitana del Ayllu*. La Paz: HISBOL.

Arguedas, José María. 1986. *Nosotros Los Maestros*. Collected and edited by Wilfredo Kapsoli. Lima: Editorial Horizontes.

Arze Aguirre, René Danilo. 1987. *Guerra y Conflictos Sociales: El Caso Rural Boliviano Durante la Campaña del Chaco*. La Paz: Centro de Estudios de la Realidad Económica y Social (CERES).

Atahuichi Salvatierra, Ricardo Tito. 1990. *La Política Educativa y la Escuela en Bolivia*. La Paz: HISBOL.

Avineri, Shlomo. 1968. "Alienation and Property." In *Social and Political Thought of Karl Marx*. New York: Cambridge University Press.

Bakhtin, M. M. 1986. *Speech Genres and Other Late Essays*. Translated by Vern W. McGee, edited by Caryl Emerson and Michael Holquist. Austin: University of Texas Press.

Baptista Gumucio, Mariano. 1974. *Analfabetos en Dos Culturas*. La Paz/Cochabamba: Los Amigos del Libro.

Barth, Fredrik, ed. 1969. *Ethnic Groups and Boundaries: The Social Organization of Culture Difference.* Boston: Little, Brown & Co.

Barton, Robert. 1968. *A Short History of Bolivia.* La Paz: Los Amigos del Libro.

Basso, Keith. 1979. *Portraits of "The Whiteman:" Linguistic Play and Cultural Symbols among the Western Apache.* New York: Cambridge University Press.

Bauman, Richard, and Charles Briggs. 1990. "Poetics and Performance as Critical Perspectives on Language and Social Life." *Annual Review of Anthropology,* 19.

Bennet, Tony, Graham Martin, Colin Mercer, and Janet Woollacott. 1981. "Antonio Gramsci." In *Culture, Ideology and Social Process: A Reader.* Tony Bennet, Graham Martin, Colin Mercer, and Janet Woollacott, eds. London: Batsford Academic & Educational Ltd., in association with The Open University Press.

Berger, Bennet M. 1968 (1962). "The Sociology of Leisure: Some Suggestions." In *America, Changing . . . : Essays Contributing to an Understanding of Contemporary Life.* Patrick Gleeson, ed. Columbus, OH: Charles E. Merrill Publishing Company.

Bettelheim, Bruno. 1968 (1961). "The Problem of Generations." In Gleeson.

Bhabha, Homi K. 1994. *The Location of Culture.* New York: Routledge.

Bonder, Gloria. 1992. "Altering Sexual Stereotypes through Teacher Training." In Stromquist 1992a.

Bourdieu, Pierre. 1977. *Outline of a Theory of Practice.* Cambridge, UK: Cambridge University Press.

———. 1984. *Distinction: A Social Critique of the Judgement of Taste.* Cambridge, MA: Harvard University Press.

———. 1991. *Language and Symbolic Power.* Introduction by John Thompson. Cambridge, UK: Polity Press.

———, and Jean-Claude Passeron. 1977. *Reproduction in Education, Society, and Culture.* Translated by Richard Nice. London: Sage Publications.

Bourne, Jill. 1988. "'Natural Adquisition' and a 'Masked Pedagogy.'" *Applied Linguistics* 9(1), March.

———. n.d. "Towards an Alternative Model of 'Second Language' Learning." Unpublished ms., University of Southampton.

Bouysse-Cassagne, Thérèse, and Thierry Saignes. 1992. "El Cholo: Actor Olvidado de la Historia." Revista UNITAS 5, pp. 21–29. March.

Bowles, Samuel, and Herbert Gintis. 1976. *Schooling in Capitalist America: Educational Reform and the Contradictions of Economic Life*. New York: Basic Books.

Briggs, Lucy Therina. 1985. "Bilingual Education in Bolivia and Peru." In *Language of Inequality*. Nessa Wolfson and Joan Manes, eds. New York: Mouton Publishers.

Buechler, Hans C., and Judith María Buechler. 1971. *The Bolivian Aymara*. New York: Holt, Rinehart & Winston.

Burke, Melvin. 1971. "Land Reform in the Lake Titicaca Region." In *Beyond the Revolution: Bolivia Since 1952*. James M. Malloy and Richard S. Thorn, eds. Pittsburgh, PA: University of Pittsburgh Press.

Calderón G., Fernando. 1977. "The Quechua and Aymará Peoples in the Formation and Development of Bolivian Society." In *Race and Class in Post-Colonial Society*. Beccles, Suffolk: UNESCO/William Clowes & Sons Ltd.

Cárdenas, Victor Hugo. 1988. "La Lucha de un Pueblo." In *Raíces de América: El Mundo Aymara*, Xavier Albó, ed. Madrid: UNESCO/Alianza Editorial.

Carnoy, Martin. 1974. *Education as Cultural Imperialism*. New York: D. McKay & Co.

Carter, William E. 1965. *Aymara Communities and the Bolivian Agrarian Reform*. Gainesville: University of Florida Press.

———. 1971. *Bolivia: A Profile*. New York: Praeger Publishers.

———. 1977. "Trial Marriage in the Andes?" In *Andean Kinship and Marriage*. Ralph Bolton and Enrique Mayer, eds. American Anthropological Association special publication no. 7, Washington, DC.

Cazden, Courtney. 1988. *Classroom Discourse: The Languages of Teaching and Learning*. Portsmouth, NH: Heinemann.

———, and Dell Hymes, eds. 1972. *Functions of Language in the Classroom*. New York: Teachers College Press.

Choque, Roberto, Vitaliano Soria, Humberto Mamani, Esteban Ticona, and Ramón Conde. 1992. *Educación Indígena: ¿Ciudadanía o Colonización?* La Paz: Ediciones Aruwiri, Taller de Historia Oral Andina.

Clark, John, with Stuart Hall, Tony Jefferson, and Brian Roberts. 1981. "Subcultures, Cultures and Class." In Bennet, Martin, Mercer, and Woollacott.

Clifford, James, and George E. Marcus, eds. 1986. *Writing Culture: The Poetics and Politics of Ethnography.* Berkeley/Los Angeles: University of California Press.

Cohen, A. 1974. *Two Dimensional Man: An Essay on the Anthropology of Power and Symbolism in Complex Society.* Berkeley/Los Angeles: University of California Press.

Comaroff, John L., and Jean. 1987. "The Madman and the Migrant: Work and Labor in the Histocial Consciousness of a South African People." *American Ethnologist* 14(2).

Conde Mamani, Ramón. 1992. "Lucas Miranda Mamani: Maestro Indio Uru-Murato." In Choque et al.

Copana Yapita, Pedro. 1981. "Linguistics and Education in Rural Schools Among the Aymara." In *The Aymara Language in Its Social and Cultural Context.* M.J. Hardman, ed. Gainesville: University Presses of Florida.

Corrigan, Philip, and Derek Sayer. 1985. *The Great Arch: English State Formation as Cultural Revolution.* New York: Basil Blackwell.

Cortina, Regina. 1992. "Gender and Power in the Teachers' Union of Mexico." In Stromquist 1992a.

Coward, Rosalind, and John Ellis. 1977. *Language and Materialism: Development in Semiology and the Theory of the Subject.* New York: Routledge & Kegan Paul.

Davila, Soñia. 1991. "In Another Vein." NACLA Report on the Americas, 25 (1), July, pp. 10–16.

de la Cadena, Marisol. 1991. "'Las Mujeres Son Más Indias:' Etnicidad y Género en una Comunidad del Cusco." *Revista Andina* 9(1). Cusco: Centro Bartolomé de las Casas.

D'Emilio, Anna Lucia. 1991. "Bolivia: La Conquista de la Escuela. El Proyecto Educativo de los Guaraní-chiriguanos." In *Etnias, Educación y Cultura: Defendiendo lo Nuestro.* La Paz/Caracas: ILDIS-Bolivia/Editorial Nueva Sociedad.

Diez Astete, Alvaro. 1995. *Antropología de Bolivia.* La Paz: Secretaría Nacional de Educación/Ministerio de Desarrollo Humano.

Dirks, N. B., G. Eley, and S. B. Ortner. 1994. Introduction to *Culture/Power/History: A Reader in Contemporary Social Theory.* N. B. Dirks, G. Eley, and S. B. Ortner, eds. Princeton, NJ: Princeton University Press.

Dunkerly, James. 1984. *Rebellion in the Veins: Political Struggle in Bolivia, 1952–1982.* London: Verso.

Eggan, Dorothy. 1974. "Instruction and Affect in Hopi Cultural Continuity." In *Education and Cultural Process: Toward an Anthropology of Education.* George D. Spindler, ed. New York: Holt, Rinehart & Winston, Inc.

Eriksen, Thomas Hylland. 1993. *Ethnicity and Nationalism: Anthropological Perspectives.* Boulder, CO: Pluto Press.

Escobar, Alberto. 1972. "Lingüística y Política." In *El Reto del Multilingüismo en el Perú.* Lima: Instituto de Estudios Peruanos.

Everhart, Robert B. 1983. *Reading, Writing and Resistance: Adolescence and Labor in a Junior High School.* Preface by Michael Apple. Boston: Routledge & Kegan Paul.

Farthing, Linda. 1991. "The New Underground." NACLA Report on the Americas, 25 (1), July, pp. 17–23.

Feld, Steven. 1987. "Dialogic Editing: Interpreting How Kaluli Read *Sound and Sentiment.*" *Cultural Anthropology* 2(2) May:190–210.

Fiske, John. 1989. *Understanding Popular Culture.* Boston: Unwin Hyman.

Foley, Douglas. 1990. *Learning Capitalist Culture: Deep in the Heart of Tejas.* Foreword by Paul Willis. Philadelphia: University of Pennsylvania Press.

———. 1996. "The Silent Indian as a Cultural Production." In Levinson, Foley, and Holland.

Foucault, Michel. 1977. *Discipline and Punish: The Birth of the Prison.* New York: Pantheon Books.

———. 1980. *Power/Knowledge: Selected Interviews and Other Writings, 1972-1977.* Edited by Colin Gordon. New York: Pantheon Books.

Freire, Paulo. 1970. *Pedagogy of the Oppressed.* New York: Seabury Press.

Gailbraith, John Kenneth. 1968. "Labor, Leisure, and the New Class." In Gleeson.

García Canclini, Nestor. 1989. "La Política Cultural en Países en Vías de Subdesarrollo." *Antropología y Políticas Culturales: Patrimonio e Identidad.* In Rita Ceballos, ed. Buenos Aires.

———. 1990. *Culturas Híbridas: Estrategias para Entrar y Salir de la Modernidad.* México: Grijalbo.

Geertz, Clifford. 1973a. "After the Revolution: The Fate of Nationalism in the New States." In *The Interpretation of Cultures.* New York: Basic Books, Inc.

————. 1973b. "The Integrative Revolution: Primoridal Sentiments and Civil Politics in the New States." In *The Interpretation of Cultures.* New York: Basic Books, Inc.

Gill, Lesley. 1988. "Señoras and Sirvientas: Women and Domestic Services in La Paz, Bolivia." Paper presented at the XIV International Congress of the Latin American Studies Association, New Orleans, March 17-19, 1988.

Giroux, Henry A. 1988. *Teachers as Intellectuals: Toward a Critical Pedagogy of Learning.* Bergin & Garvey, Granby, Mass.

————. 1992. *Border Crossings: Cultural Workers and the Politics of Education.* New York: Routledge.

Goffman, Erving. 1961. *Asylums: Essays on the Social Situation of Mental Patients and Other Inmates.* Garden City, NJ: Anchor Books.

————. 1974. *Frame Analysis.* New York: Harper & Row.

Gramsci, Antonio. 1971. *Selections from the Prison Notebooks of Antonio Gramsci.* Edited and translated by Quintin Hoare and Geoffrey Nowell Smith. New York: International Publishers.

Greaves, Thomas. 1972. "Pursuing Cultural Pluralism in the Andes." Plural Societies, Summer.

Gupta, Akhil, and James Ferguson. 1992. "Beyond 'Culture': Space, Identity, and the Politics of Difference." *Cultural Anthropology,* 7(1), February.

Habermas, Jürgen. 1968. *Knowledge and Human Interests.* Beacon Press, Boston.

————. 1976. *Legitimation Crisis.* Boston: Beacon Press.

Hall, Stuart. 1985. "Signification, Representation, Ideology: Althusser and the Post-Structuralist Debates." *Critical Studies in Mass Communication* 2(2) June.

————. 1986a. "On Postmodernism and Articulation." *Journal of Communication Inquiry* 10(2).

————. 1986b. "The Problem of Ideology—Marxism without Guarantees." *Journal of Communication Inquiry* 10(2).

————. 1986c. "Gramsci's Relevance for the Study of Race and Ethnicity." *Journal of Communication Inquiry* 10(2).

Hamel, Rainer Enrique. 1983. "El Contexto Sociolingüístico de la Enseñanza y Adquisición del Español en Escuelas Indígenas Bilingües en el Valle del Mezquital." *Estudios de Lingüística Aplicada* (July) México: CELE/UNAM.

Hannerz, Ulf. 1987. "The World in Creolisation." *Africa* 57(4), 546–59.

Hardman, M. J. 1985. "The Imperial Languages of the Andes." In *Language of Inequality*. Nessa Wolfson and Joan Manes, eds. New York: Mouton Publishers.

Heath, Shirley Brice. 1983. *Ways with Words: Language, Life and Work in Communities and Classrooms*. New York: Cambridge University Press.

———, and Richard Laprade. 1982. Castilian Colonization and Indigenous Languages: The Cases of Aymara and Quechua. In *Language Spread: Studies in Diffusion and Social Change*. Robert L. Cooper, ed. Bloomington: Indiana University Press.

Hill, Jane H. 1987. "Women's Speech in Modern Mexicano." In *Language, Gender, and Sex in Comparative Perspective*. Susan Philips, Susan Steele, and Christine Tanz, eds. New York: Cambridge University Press.

Hill, Jonathan, ed. 1988. *Rethinking History and Myth: Indigenous South American Perspectives on the Past*. Urbana: University of Illinois Press.

Hobsbawm, Eric. 1983. "Mass-Producing Traditions: Europe 1870-1914." In *The Invention of Tradition*. Eric Hobsbawm and Terence Ranger, eds. New York: Cambridge University Press.

Hornberger, Nancy. 1988. "Iman Chay? Quechua Children in Peru's Schools." In *School and Society: Learning Content through Culture*. Henry Trueba and Conchita Delgado-Gaitan, eds. New York: Praeger Publishers.

Instituto Nacional de Estadística (INE). 1992. *Censo Nacional de Población y Vivienda, 1992: Resultados Preliminares*. La Paz.

Isbell, Billie Jean. 1977. *To Defend Ourselves: Ecology and Ritual in an Andean Village*. University of Texas at Austin: Institute of Latin American Studies.

Iturri Salmon, Jaime. 1988. "El Cine Boliviano: Entre la Censura y la Denuncia." La Paz: URUS Comunicación Social, Cuadernos de Comunicación no. 4 (marzo 1988).

Jackson, Philip. 1968. *Life in Classrooms*. Holt, Rinehart & Winston, New York.

Jones, Leroi. 1968. "Black Is a Country." In Gleeson.

Keill, Norman. 1964. *The Universal Experience of Adolescence*. Boston: Beacon Press.

Klein, Herbert. 1982. *Bolivia: The Evolution of a Multi-Ethnic Society.* New York: Oxford University Press.

Kramarae, Cheris. 1981. *Women and Men Speaking: Frameworks for Analysis.* Rowley, MA: Newbury House Publishers.

Laclau, Ernst, and Chantal Mouffe. 1985. *Hegemony and Socialist Strategy: Towards a Radical Democratic Politics.* Translated by Winston Moore and Paul Cammack. London: Verso.

Lagos, María L. (forthcoming). "Bolivia La Nueva: Constructing New Citizens." *Journal of Latin American Anthropology.*

Lesage, Julia. 1988. "Women's Rage." In *Marxism and the Interpretation of Culture.* Cary Nelson and Lawrence Grossberg, eds. Urbana: University of Illinois Press.

Levinson, Bradley A., and Dorothy Holland. 1996. Introduction to Levinson, Foley, and Holland.

Levinson, Bradley A., Douglas E. Foley, and Dorothy Holland, eds. 1996. *The Cultural Production of the Educated Person: Critical Ethnographies of Schooling and Local Practice.* Albany: State University of New York Press.

Libermann, Kitula, Armando Godínez, and Xavier Albó. 1989. "Mundo Rural Andino." In *Para Comprender las Culturas Rurales en Bolivia.* Xavier Albó, Kitula Libermann, Armando Godínez, and Francisco Pifarre, eds. La Paz: MEC/CIPCA/UNICEF.

Limón, José. 1982. "History, Chicano Joking, and the Varieties of Higher Education: Tradition and Performance as Critical Symbolic Action." *Journal of the Folklore Institute* 19(2).

———. 1989. "Carne, Carnales, and the Carnivalesque: Bakhtinian Batos, Disorder, and Narrative Discourse." *American Ethnologist* 16(3).

Lofgren, Orvar. 1989. "The Nationalization of Culture." *Europaea* 19.

López, Luís Enrique, and Ingrid Jung. 1989. "El Castellano del Maestro y el Castellano del Libro." In *Temas de Linguistica Aplicada.* L. E. López, Inés Pozzi-Escot, and Madeleine Zúñiga, eds. Puno, Perú: CONCYTEC/PEB-Puno.

Lora, Guillermo. 1977. *A History of the Bolivian Labour Movement 1848-1971.* Edited and abridged by Laurence Whitehead and translated by Christine Whitehead. New York: Cambridge University Press.

Luttrel, Wendy. 1996. "Becoming Somebody in and against School: Toward a Psychocultural Theory of Gender and Self Making." In Levinson, Foley, and Holland.

Luykx, Aurolyn. 1989a. "Foundations of Ethnic Taxonomies in the Andes." *Florida Journal of Anthropology* (14).

————. 1989b. "Language, Gender, and Education in a Bolivian Aymara Community." Unpublished master's thesis. University of Florida at Gainesville.

————. 1992. "Hablantes Nativos, Lectores Nativos: Algunos Aspectos de la Relación entre el Lenguaje Oral y Escrito, y sus Implicaciones para el Sistema Educativo Boliviano." Proceedings of the Encuentro Anuo de Etnología, MUSEF, La Paz.

————. 1993. *The Citizen Factory: Language, Labor and Identity in Bolivian Rural Teacher Education.* Unpublished Ph.D. dissertation, University of Texas at Austin.

————. (forthcoming). "Gender Equality and Cultural Relativism: The Bolivian Dilemma in Intercultural Education." *Journal of Latin American Anthropology.*

MacLeod, Jay. 1987. *Ain't No Makin' It: Leveled Aspirations in a Low-Income Neighborhood.* Boulder, CO: Westview Press.

Mamani Caprichi, Humberto. 1992. "La Educación India en la Visión de la Sociedad Criolla: 1920-1943." In Choque et al.

Mannheim, Bruce. 1984. "*Una Nación Accoralada:* Southern Peruvian Quechua Language Planning and Politics in Historical Perspective." *Language in Society* 13: 291-309.

Marcus, George E. 1986. "Contemporary Problems of Ethnography in the Modern World System." In Clifford and Marcus.

————, and Michael M. J. Fischer. 1986. *Anthropology as Cultural Critique: An Experimental Moment in the Human Sciences.* Chicago: University of Chicago Press.

Masemann, Vandra. 1974. "The 'Hidden Curriculum' of a West African Girls' Boarding School." *Canadian Journal of African Studies* 8(3).

Mato, Daniel. 1992. "A Provisional Map of Competing Discourses Predicating Pannational and Transnational Identities in 'Latin America,' in Times of Globalization." Paper presented at the 1992 Annual Meeting of the American Anthropological Association, San Francisco, December 2-6.

McLaren, Peter. 1986. *Schooling as a Ritual Performance: Towards a Political Economy of Educational Symbols and Gestures.* Introduction by Henry Giroux. London: Routledge & Kegan Paul.

McNeil, Linda M. 1986. *Contradictions of Control: School Structure and School Knowledge.* London: Routledge & Kegan Paul.

MDH/SNE (Ministerio de Desarrollo Humano/Secretaría Nacional de Educación). 1994. *Reforma Educativa: Propuesta.* La Paz

MEC (Ministerio de Educación y Cultura). 1989. *Plan de Emergencia Hacia una Reforma Educativa (Propuesta del Ministerio de Educación y Cultura al Gobierno de Unidad Nacional y a la Comunidad Boliviana.* La Paz.

Mendoza, José. 1988. "Algunos Rasgos del Castellano Paceño." Unpublished monograph. Universidad Mayor de San Andres (UMSA), La Paz.

Michenot, Elizabeth. 1985. "Bilingüismo y Educación." *Revista Faces* 1, UMSS, Cochabamba, Bolivia.

Miracle, Andrew. 1973. *Educational Congruency in a Stratified Society: A Bolivian Case Study.* Unpublished master's thesis, University of Florida, Gainesville.

————. 1976. *The Effects of Cultural Perception on Aymara Schooling.* Unpublished Ph.D. dissertation, University of Florida, Gainesville.

Montoya, Rodrigo. 1991. "Etnia y Clase en el Perú." *Márgenes: Encuentro y Debate* (Lima) 4(7).

————, and Luis Enrique López, eds. 1988. *¿Quienes Somos? El Tema de la Identidad en el Altiplano.* Lima: Mosca Azul/Universidad del Altiplano.

Motte, Dominique. 1995. *Enseñar en el Perú: ¿Un Pacto Cultural o un Trueque Mercantil?* Cusco: Centro de Estudios Regionales Andinos "Bartolomé de Las Casas."

Mouffe, Chantal. 1981 (1979). "Hegemony and Ideology in Gramsci." In Bennet, Martin, Mercer, and Woollacott.

Muñoz, Hector. Forthcoming. "Experiencias Sociales y Comunicativas como Factores de la Enseñanza/Aprendizaje del Lenguaje en Contextos Indoamericanos." In *Sobre las Huellas de la Voz.* Ingrid Jung and L. E. López, eds. Editorial Morata, Madrid.

Murra, John. 1972. "El 'control vertical' de un máximo de pisos ecológicos en la economía de las sociedades andinas. In *Visita de la Provincia de Leon de Huánuco en 1562.* John Murra, ed. Huánuco: Universidad Nacional Hermilio Valdizan.

Murray, Thomas R. 1983. "The Symbiotic Linking of Politics and Education." In *Politics and Education: Cases from Eleven Nations.* Oxford: Peramon Press.

Nash, June. 1979. *We Eat the Mines and the Mines Eat Us: Dependency and Exploitation in Bolivian Tin Mines.* New York: Columbia University Press.

———. 1992. "Interpreting Social Movements: Bolivian Resistance to Economic Conditions Imposed by the International Monetary Fund." *American Ethnologist* 19 (2), May, 275-293.

Nuevo Miami Herald (NMH). November 25, 1992. "Oposicón da nueva sorpresa." Reuter.

Norton, Robert. 1984. "Ethnicity and Class: A Conceptual Note with Reference to the Politics of Post-Colonial Societies." *Ethnic and Racial Studies* 7(3), July.

Oliart, Patricia. 1991. "'Candadito de oro, llavecita filigrana . . .': Dominación Social y Autoestima Femenina en las Clases Populares." *Márgenes: Encuentro y Debate* (Lima) 4(7).

Ollman, Bertell. 1976 (1971). *Alienation: Marx's Conception of Man in Capitalist Society* (2nd edition). New York: Cambridge University Press.

Pérez, Elizardo. 1962. *Warisata: La Escuela-ayllu.* La Paz: Burillo.

Philips, Susan U. 1983. *The Invisible Culture: Communication in Classroom and Community on the Warm Springs Indian Reservation.* New York: Longman.

Pike, Frederick. 1977. *The United States and the Andean Republics: Peru, Bolivia, and Ecuador.* Cambridge, MA: Harvard University Press.

Popular Memory Group (PMG). 1982. "Popular Memory: Theory, Politics, Method." In *Making Histories: Studies in History-Writing and Politics.* Richard Johnson, Gregor McLennan, Bill Schwartz, and David Sutton, eds. University of Birmingham, UK: Center for Contemporary Cultural Studies.

Postman, Neil. 1988. "Social Science as Moral Theology." In *Conscientious Objections: Stirring Up Trouble about Language, Technology and Education.* New York: Knopf.

———, and Charles Weingartner. 1969. *Teaching as a Subversive Activity.* New York: Dell Publishing Co.

Primov, George. 1980. "The Political Role of Mestizo Schoolteachers in Indian Communities." In *Land and Power in Latin America.* Benjamin Orlove, ed. New York: Holmes & Meier, Inc.

Ramos, Pablo Sánchez. 1988. *Decentralización Educativa y Disgregación de la Consciencia Nacional.* La Paz: Universidad Mayor de San Andres.

Rance, Susanna. 1991. "The Hand That Feeds Us." NACLA Report on the Americas, 25 (1), July 1991, pp. 30-36.

Reisman, David. 1968. "Where Is the College Generation Headed?" In Gleeson.

Rival, Laura. 1996. "Formal Schooling and the Production of Modern Citizens in the Ecuadorian Amazon." In Levinson, Foley, and Holland.

Rosaldo, Renato. 1989. *Culture and Truth: The Remaking of Social Analysis.* Boston: Beacon Press.

Rosenberg, Fulvia. 1992. "Education, Democratization, and Inequality in Brazil." In Stromquist 1992a.

Rossi-Landi, Ferrucio. 1983. *Language as Work and Trade: A Semiotic Homology for Linguistics and Economics.* South Hadley, MA: Bergin & Garvey Publishers, Inc.

Rowe, William, and Vivian Schelling. 1991. *Memory and Modernity: Popular Culture in Latin America.* New York: Verso.

Salazar Mostajo, Carlos. 1984 (1943). *¡Warisata Mía! y otros Artículos Polémicos* (2nda edición). La Paz: Editorial e Imprenta "Amerindia."

Sara-Lafosse, Violeta. 1992. "Coeducational Settings and Educational and Social Outcomes in Peru." In Stromquist 1992a.

Schacht, Richard. 1970. *Alienation.* Introductory essay by Walter Kaufmann. Garden City, NJ: Anchor/Doubleday.

Schaff, Adam. 1980. *Alienation as a Social Phenomenon.* New York: Pergamon Press.

Scott, James. 1985. *Weapons of the Weak: Everyday Forms of Peasant Resistance.* New Haven, CT: Yale University Press.

———. 1990. *Domination and the Arts of Resistance: Hidden Trascripts.* New Haven, CT: Yale University Press.

Seeman, Melvin. 1975. "Alienation Studies." *Annual Review of Sociology* 1:91-123.

Sherzer, Joel. 1987. "A Diversity of Voices: Men's and Women's Speech in Ethnographic Perspective." In *Language, Gender, and Sex in Comparative Perspective.* Susan Philips, Susan Steele, and Christine Tanz, eds. New York: Cambridge University Press.

Shor, Ira. 1996. *When Students Have Power: Negotiating Authority in a Critical Pedagogy.* Chicago: University of Chicago Press.

Skinner, Debra, and Dorothy Holland. 1996. "Schools and the Cultural Production of the Educated Person in a Nepalese Hill Community." In Levinson, Foley, and Holland.

Soria Choque, Vitaliano. 1992. "Los Caciques-Apoderados y la Lucha por la Escuela (1900-1952)." In Choque et al.

Stahr, Marga, and Marisol Vega. 1988. "El Conflicto Tradición-Modernidad en Mujeres de Sectores Populares." *Márgenes: Encuentro y Debate* (Lima) 4(3).

Starn, Orin. 1991. "Missing the Revolution: Anthropologists and the War in Peru." *Cultural Anthropology* 6(1).

Stewart, Susan. 1986. "Shouts on the Street: Bakhtin's Anti-Linguistics." In *Bakhtin: Essays and Dialogues on His Work.* Gary Saul Morson, ed. Chicago: University of Chicago Press.

Stratford, Billie Dale. 1989. *Structure and Use of Altiplano Spanish.* Unpublished Ph.D. dissertation. University of Florida, Gainesville.

Stromquist, Nelly P. ed. 1992a. *Women and Education in Latin America: Knowledge, Power and Change.* Boulder, CO: Lynne Reinner Publishers, Inc.

———. 1992b. Introduction to Stromquist 1992a.

———. 1992c. "Feminist Reflections on the Politics of the Peruvian University." In Stromquist 1992a.

Swedenburg, Ted. 1990. "The Palestinian Peasant as National Signifier." *Anthropological Quarterly* 63(1).

Tamayo, Franz. 1975. *Creación de la Pedagogía Nacional* (third edition). La Paz: Ministerio de Educación.

Tambiah, Stanley. 1989. "Ethnic Conflict in the World Today." *American Ethnologist* 16(2).

Taussig, Michael T. 1980. *The Devil and Commodity Fetishism in South America.* Chapel Hill: University of North Carolina Press.

Trujillo, Armando. 1996. "In Search of Aztlán: Movimiento Ideology and the Creation of a Chicano Worldview Through Schooling." In Levinson, Foley, and Holland.

Tucker, Robert C. 1978. *The Marx-Engels Reader* (2nd edition). New York: W. W. Norton & Company, Inc.

Turton, Andrew. 1986. "Patrolling the Middle Ground: Methodological Perspectives on 'Everyday Peasant Resistance.'" *Journal of Peasant Studies* 13(2), January.

Urban, Greg. 1991. "The Semiotics of State-Indian Linguistic Relationships: Peru, Paraguay, and Brazil." In *Nation-States and Indians in Latin America.* Greg Urban and Joel Sherzer, eds. Austin: University of Texas Press.

———, and Joel Sherzer. 1991. "Introduction: Indians, Nation-States, and Culture." In Urban & Sherzer.

USAID Mission to Bolivia. 1975. *Education in Bolivia: A Preliminary Sector Assessment.* La Paz: USAID.

Volosinov. V. N. 1976. *Marxism and the Philosophy of Language.* Translated by Ladislav Matejka and I. R. Titunik. Cambridge, MA: Harvard University Press.

Walsh, Catherine E. 1987. "Language, Meaning and Voice: Puerto Rican Students' Struggle for a Speaking Consciousness." *Language Arts* 64(2), February.

———. 1991. *Pedagogy and the Struggle for Voice: Issues of Language, Power, and Schooling for Puerto Ricans.* Series introduction by Henry Giroux. New York: Bergin & Garvey.

Wara Céspedes, Gilka. 1993. "Huayño, Saya, and Chuntunqui: Bolivian Identity in the Music of 'Los Kjarkas.'" *Latin American Music Review* 14(1), Spring.

Weber, Max. 1978. *Economy and Society: An Outline of Interpretive Sociology.* Guenther Roth and Claus Wittich, eds. Berkeley: University of California Press.

Weis, Lois. 1996. Foreword to Levinson, Foley and Holland.

Williams, Brackette F. 1989. "A Class Act: Anthropology and the Race to Nation Across Ethnic Terrain." *Annual Review of Anthropology* 18.

———. 1991. *Stains on My Name, War in My Veins: Guyana and the Politics of Cultural Struggle.* Durham, NC: Duke University Press.

Williams, Raymond. 1977. *Marxism and Literature.* Oxford: Oxford University Press.

———. 1980a. "Base and Superstructure in Marxist Cultural Theory." In *Problems in Materialism and Culture: Selected Essays.* London: Verso/NLB.

———. 1980b. "Means of Communication as Means of Production." In *Problems in Materialism and Culture: Selected Essays.* London: Verso.

Willis, Paul. 1981a. *Learning to Labor: How Working-Class Kids Get Working-Class Jobs.* New York: Columbia University Press.

———. 1981b. "Cultural Production Is Different from Cultural Reproduction Is Different from Social Reproduction Is Different from Reproduction." *Interchange* 12(2-3), 48-67.

————, and Philip Corrigan. 1983. "Orders of Experience: The Differences of Working Class Cultural Forms." *Social Text* 7 Spring/Summer.

Witte, John F. 1980. *Democracy, Authority, and Alienation in Work: Workers' Participation in an American Corporation.* Chicago: University of Chicago Press.

Woolcott, Harry F. 1974. "The Teacher as an Enemy." In Spindler.

Wright, Patrick. 1985. *On Living in an Old Country: The National Past in Contemporary Britain.* London: Verso.

Yapita Moya, Juan de Dios. 1981. "The Aymara Alphabet: Linguistics for Indigenous Communities." In Hardman.

Zinn, Howard. 1980. *A People's History of the United States.* New York: HarperCollins.

INDEX

Abortion, 163
Academic capital, 59, 305. *See also* Cultural capital
Academic performance: and alienation, 328, 357n.27; role of culture in, xxxiii–xxxiv
Acculturation, 288. *See also* Ethnic mobility
Acuerdo Patriótico, 4
ADN (Acción Democrática Nacionalista). *See* Banzer Suárez, Hugo
Afro-Bolivians, 20
Agency, xxxiv–xxxv, 105–6. *See also* Social reproduction
Agrarian reform. *See* Land reform
Agriculture class, 96, 221, 345n.15
Alienated language, other models of, 352n.19
Alienation, 172, 200–201, 262, 353nn.23, 24, 354n.4; and cheating, 240; and class participation, 231; and commodification, 208; and ethnicity, 305; and pedagogy, 191–92; and school failure, 328, 357n.27; of students' labor, 194, 198, 199–205, 281, 311, 316; of students' speech, 211; subjective and objective, 200–201, 212, 304, 313; of symbolic labor, 302; teachers',

242, 258, 356n.18; from work, 193, 239, 335–36n.18. *See also* Labor Theory of Value
Althusser, Louis, 195, 200, 306
Andeanism, xxxviii–xxxix, 276
Anthropologists, public image of, xxiii–xxiv, 38. *See also* Ethnography: practice of
Anthropology, xxvi–xxvii, xxxvii. *See also* Ethnography
Apple, Michael: diffusion of works in Latin America, 332n.3; "neutrality" in social analysis, xxvi–xxvii; origins of mass schooling, 42; schools' treatment of conflict, xxxvi, 308; strategic optimism, xxix, 318
Appropriation of students' labor, 209, 211, 212–13, 302, 313
Archipelago model, 11–12
Articulation: of historical bloc, 259–60, 290–91, 301, 314; of ideology, 127–28, 210, 297–98, 317–18, 344n.1, 346n.22; of student identities, 168–69, 296. *See also* Hegemony
Aymara (language): influence on Andean Spanish, 108, 223–24, 268, 269–70; in La Paz, 13–14; displacement by Spanish, 287; excluded from academic

379